Back to Black

As Latin America's flagship "racial democracy," Brazil is famous for its history of race mixture and fluid racial boundaries. Traditionally, scholars have emphasized that this fluidity has often led to whitening, where individuals seek classification in white, or lighter, racial categories. Yet, *Back to Black* documents a sudden reversal in this trend, showing instead that individuals are increasingly opting to identify with darker, and especially black, racial categories. Drawing on a wealth of quantitative and qualitative data, David De Micheli attributes this sudden reversal to the state's efforts at expanding access to education for the lower classes. By unleashing waves of upward mobility, greater education increased individuals' personal exposure to racial hierarchies and inequalities and led many to develop racial consciousness, further encouraging black identification. This book highlights how social citizenship institutions and social structures can work together to affect processes of identity politicization and the contestation of inequalities.

David De Micheli is Assistant Professor of Political Science and Ethnic Studies at the University of Utah. He was previously Post-Doctoral Fellow at the Center for Inter-American Policy and Research at Tulane University. De Micheli's research has appeared in *World Politics*, *Government and Opposition*, and *Latin American Politics and Society*.

Back to Black

*Racial Reclassification and Political
Identity Formation in Brazil*

DAVID DE MICHELI
University of Utah

CAMBRIDGE
UNIVERSITY PRESS

Shaftesbury Road, Cambridge CB2 8EA, United Kingdom

One Liberty Plaza, 20th Floor, New York, NY 10006, USA

477 Williamstown Road, Port Melbourne, VIC 3207, Australia

314–321, 3rd Floor, Plot 3, Splendor Forum, Jasola District Centre,
New Delhi – 110025, India

103 Penang Road, #05–06/07, Visioncrest Commercial, Singapore 238467

Cambridge University Press is part of Cambridge University Press & Assessment,
a department of the University of Cambridge.

We share the University's mission to contribute to society through the pursuit of
education, learning and research at the highest international levels of excellence.

www.cambridge.org
Information on this title: www.cambridge.org/9781009472395

DOI: 10.1017/9781009472401

© David De Micheli 2024

This publication is in copyright. Subject to statutory exception and to the provisions
of relevant collective licensing agreements, no reproduction of any part may take
place without the written permission of Cambridge University Press & Assessment.

When citing this work, please include a reference to the DOI
10.1017/9781009472401

First published 2024

A catalogue record for this publication is available from the British Library

Library of Congress Cataloging-in-Publication Data
NAMES: De Micheli, David, 1989– author.
TITLE: Back to Black : racial reclassification and political identity
formation in Brazil / David De Micheli.
DESCRIPTION: Cambridge, United Kingdom ; New York, NY : Cambridge
University Press, 2024. | Includes bibliographical references and index.
IDENTIFIERS: LCCN 2024000003 | ISBN 9781009472395 (hardback) |
ISBN 9781009472401 (ebook)
SUBJECTS: LCSH: Black people – Brazil – Politics and government. | Black
people – Race identity – Brazil. | Identity politics – Brazil. |
Brazil – Race relations – Political aspects. | Brazil – Politics and
government – 2003–
CLASSIFICATION: LCC F2659.N4 D388 2024 | DDC 305.896/081–dc23/eng/20240229
LC record available at https://lccn.loc.gov/2024000003

ISBN 978-1-009-47239-5 Hardback
ISBN 978-1-009-47235-7 Paperback

Additional resources for this publication at www.cambridge.org/ 9781009472395

Cambridge University Press & Assessment has no responsibility for the persistence
or accuracy of URLs for external or third-party internet websites referred to in this
publication and does not guarantee that any content on such websites is, or will
remain, accurate or appropriate.

Merely by describing yourself as black you have started on a road towards emancipation, you have committed yourself to a fight against all forces that seek to use your blackness as a stamp that marks you out as a subservient being.
—Steve Biko, "The Definition of Black Consciousness"

A casa grande surta quando a senzala aprende a ler.
The masters lose their minds when the slaves learn to read.
—Totonho

Contents

List of Figures		*page* ix
List of Tables		xiii
Acknowledgments		xv
1	Introduction	1
2	The Puzzle of Racial Reclassification	27
3	Theory: Racial Reclassification as Political Identity Formation	56
4	Education as a Mechanism of Exposure	95
5	Education and Reclassification: Testing the Hypothesis	132
6	Affirmative Action and Reclassification	171
7	Implications for National Politics	209
8	Conclusion	248
References		265
Index		291

An online appendix for this publication is available at
www.cambridge.org/ 9781009472395

Figures

1.1	Racial composition of Brazil, 1992–2019	*page* 2
2.1	Racial composition of Brazil, 1992–2019	29
2.2	Percentage change in racial category between 2000 and 2010 by birth cohort	33
2.3	Inter-census difference in white population, 2000–2010	35
3.1	Education completion rates for Brazilians aged 22–26 by race, 1960–2010	70
3.2	Population aged 15–18 with primary school completed by income quintile, 1992–2014	72
3.3	Public spending on university education, 2000–2015	73
3.4	All government spending on education, 1995–2015	74
3.5	Population aged 18–24 with high school completed by income quintile, 1992–2014	76
3.6	Population aged 18–24 with some university education by income quintile, 1992–2014	76
4.1	Average partial effects of education on Pr(racial ID), 1986–2008	125
4.2	Predicted probabilities of racial consciousness by education and racial ascriptions, 2008	127
4.3	Probabilities of racial ID by level of racial consciousness, 2008	128
4.4	Marginal effects of education and racial consciousness by racial ascription, 2008	130
5.1	Pr(nonwhite ID) relative to 1993 by education and subsample, 1998–2015	141

List of Figures

5.2	Change in Pr(nonwhite ID) between 1993 and 2015 by education	142
5.3	Change in Pr(racial ID) relative to 1993 by education, 1998–2015	143
5.4	Change in Pr(nonwhite ID) between 1993 and 2015 by education and cohort	145
5.5	Educational access by income quintile, 1981–1990	146
5.6	Change in Pr(nonwhite ID) between 1982 and 1990 by education and income	147
5.7	Change in Pr(nonwhite ID) between 1993 and 2015 by education and gender	150
5.8	Change in Pr(nonwhite ID) between 1993 and 2015 by education and region	153
5.9	Inter-census difference in white population, 2000–2010	155
5.10	Municipal-level high school attendance rates among Brazilians aged 15–17, 2000 and 2010	157
5.11	Municipal-level university attendance rates among Brazilians aged 18–24, 2000 and 2010	158
5.12	Histograms of change in relative racial group size, 2000–2010	164
5.13	Average partial effect of change in education attendance rate on relative racial group size by affirmative action status, 2000–2010	169
6.1	Regression-adjusted estimates of treatment effects on Pr(racial ID)	185
6.2	Treatment effects conditional on education and skin tone	186
6.3	Predicted probabilities of racial ID by experimental condition	189
6.4	Comparison of means of item counts by treatment group	193
6.5	Estimated proportions of respondents responding affirmatively to sensitive item	194
6.6	Parallel trends violations based on difference-in-differences estimates of affirmative action prior to implementation (1991–2000)	198
6.7	Difference-in-differences estimates of state-level affirmative action on relative group size, 2000–2010	199
6.8	SDID estimates of racial affirmative action on relative population size in census, 2000–2010	200

List of Figures

7.1	Average partial effect of racial ID on electoral support, 2002–2018	215
7.2	Predicted probabilities of PT support by racial ID and education, 2002	219
7.3	Round 1 PT electoral support by level of education, 1994–2006	220
7.4	Regression-adjusted estimates of PT support by racial ID and education, 2006	221
7.5	Mean first-round PT support by racial ID and education, 2002–2006	222
7.6	First-round vote choice of university-educated voters by racial ID, 2006	222
7.7	Left self-placement by education and racial ID, 2014	224
7.8	First-round PT support by racial ID and education, 2006 and 2010	225
7.9	Marginal effect of university education (vs. less than primary) on first-round electoral support, 2010	227
7.10	Racial and educational profile of June 2013 protesters, Sao Paulo	229
7.11	Preferred 2014 presidential candidate of June 2013 protesters, São Paulo	230
7.12	Electoral support for Rousseff by education and racial ID, 2010 versus 2014	232
7.13	Socioeconomic profile of pro-impeachment protesters, Sao Paulo 2015–2016	235
7.14	Socioeconomic profile of impeachment counterprotesters, Sao Paulo 2015	236
7.15	First-round Bolsonaro support by education and racial ID, 2018	240
7.16	First-round vote choice of university-educated by racial ID, 2018	241
7.17	Average marginal effect of university education on first-round electoral support by racial ID, 2018	242
7.18	First-round support for leftist candidate (Haddad or Gomes), by education and racial ID, 2018	243
7.19	Second-round Bolsonaro support by education and racial ID, 2018	244

Tables

1.1	Relative proportion of black (or Afro-national) and indigenous populations in Latin America	page 21
2.1	Estimates of inter-census racial reclassification, 2000–2010	34
2.2	Comparing self-identification with racial ascription by interviewer	53
3.1	Federal education reforms, 1988–2012	92
4.1	Basic characteristics of interviewees	99
4.2	Estimated effects of group consciousness on racial ID	129
5.1	Birth cohorts in PNAD sample	138
5.2	Affirmative action policies by state and year of passage	160
5.3	Pearson's correlation coefficient of change in high school attendance and change in relative proportion of racial group in municipality, 2000–2010	162
5.4	Fixed-effects estimates of change in relative racial group size, 2000–2010	167
6.1	Survey primes	189
6.2	List experiment design	192
6.3	Difference-in-differences estimates of effects of affirmative action usage on racial identification	205
7.1	Surveys for analysis of general elections	217

Acknowledgments

This book grew out of the doctoral dissertation I completed at Cornell University in 2019. Though research can be an uncertain and lonely process, I am happy to report that I look back on my time in graduate school with only fondness and nostalgia. I feel grateful to have been surrounded by generous, supportive, and brilliant friends and colleagues, without whom I could not have produced the book you read today.

First and foremost, I must thank my dissertation committee, Ken Roberts, Michael Jones-Correa, Gustavo Flores-Macías, and Jamila Michener. Each one provided healthy doses of skepticism and pushed me to sharpen my arguments in ways that greatly improved the project. In particular, Ken Roberts was – and remains – an invariably attentive, generous, and supportive mentor from the day I arrived to Cornell. I am grateful to him for making my experience in grad school so rewarding and sane. I also could not have maintained my sanity without the many friends I made in graduate school and in the field. Chief among them are Whitney Taylor, Michael Allen, and Liz Acorn, who shaped a time in my life when I considered friends my family. I am also grateful to have crossed paths with Natalie Letsa, Martha Wilfahrt, and Robert Braun, whose friendship I value to this day. Many others also helped me survive Ithaca's unending winters along the way, including Cait Mastroe, Julius Lagodny, Jimena Valdez, Jake Swanson, and Aditi Sahasrabuddhe.

I also incurred many intellectual debts while a post-doctoral researcher at the Center for Inter-American Policy and Research (CIPR) at Tulane University. Rachel Schwartz, in particular, was a generous friend, colleague, and drinking buddy. I also had the good fortune to share my time there with Stefanie Israel de Souza, Caitlin Andrews, Moisés Arce, and Ann Mische, all of whom contributed their interdisciplinary insights to this book. And last but certainly not least, the support and generosity of Sefira Fialkoff and Ludovico Feoli made my time at Tulane not only possible but also fruitful and rewarding – even amidst the onset of the COVID-19 pandemic.

CIPR also generously funded a book workshop in January 2020, where participants Jana Morgan, Raúl Madrid, and Taeku Lee provided detailed and critical comments on the entire manuscript. Their focused feedback guided many of my revisions and resulted in a significantly improved manuscript. I'm also grateful to Deborah Yashar, who provided insightful feedback on portions of the manuscript and whose own work on ethnic politics in Latin America inspired my interest in this topic. At an earlier stage, my dissertation also benefitted tremendously from generous feedback at the Mark Claster Mamolen workshop sponsored by the Afro-Latin America Research Institute at Harvard's Hutchins Center. Comments from Reid Andrews, Alejandro de la Fuente, Sidney Chalhoub, and other workshop participants helped me to better situate these patterns historically. And their continued support for the development of Afro-Latin American Studies has been an inspiration.

This book was also made possible by the support of my friends and colleagues at the University of Utah. In Political Science, I must thank Claudio Holzner, Laura Gamboa, Michael Dichio, and Jim Curry. In Ethnic Studies and Transform, I also thank Edmund Fong, Darius Bost, Wanda Pillow, Annie Fukushima, and Kathryn Stockton. All of these folks have offered advice, support, and friendship that not only helped me complete this manuscript but also made my transition to the tenure track and life in Utah smooth and enjoyable.

In Brazil, I benefitted invaluably from the generous and warm support of friends and colleagues along the way. First, I must call out César Zucco, who is responsible for first introducing me to the empirical puzzle I analyze in this book during a meeting at the Fundação Getúlio Vargas in Rio de Janeiro in the summer of 2015. Though he may not remember it, it's possible this book would not have been written without that informal meeting. Antonio Guimarães at the University of São Paulo and Liana Lewis at the Federal University of Pernambuco helped me secure research affiliations that made this field research possible. In São Paulo, I owe a huge debt to Thiago Silva, who helped me really get my fieldwork rolling by providing access to important research sites, insight and information, space to conduct interviews, and many fruitful contacts. I also thank Frei David Santos, Cássio Nascimento, and Gilmar Camará, Priscila Rodrigues, and Milena Lopes, for providing contacts and/or facilitating access to hard-to-reach populations.

In Recife, I also benefitted from excellent research assistance from students at UFPE, who transcribed interviews, helped pilot a survey instrument, and helped me navigate Recife. In particular, I thank Cláudia Brito, Jadson Freire, and Rutt Keles. Also in Recife, I am glad to have met Ben Junge, who has become a great friend and endless source of insight on Brazil.

In Brasília, Marco Pereira provided much-needed assistance at Inep, *Instituto Nacional de Estudos e Pesquisas Nacionais*, and without the insights and expertise of Adriano Senkevics, my analysis of the post-hoc panel data in Chapter 6 would not have been possible. With this work, I also owe a debt of gratitude to Rodrigo Arruda, whose long-distance research assistance was also critical to completing the analysis. For helpful discussions along the way in Brasília, I thank Maria Tannuri-Pianto, Mathieu Turgeon, Sergei Soares, and Rafael Osório. My friend Carlos Oliveira also came through for me on multiple occasions, helping me to smoothly navigate Brasília's web of agencies. Above all, I am most indebted to the many Brazilians who agreed to be interviewed by me during my field research – and the countless others not mentioned here but who helped shape this project – for generously donating their time and for tolerating my *sotaque*.

None of this research would have been possible without the generous support of the organizations that provided funding for this research. The bulk of this fieldwork and original data collection was made possible by a Doctoral Dissertation Research Abroad Fellowship from the Fulbright-Hays Foundations, as well as a Doctoral Dissertation Research Improvement Grant (award number 1647203) from the National Science Foundation. This project has also counted on internal grants at Cornell from the Department of Government, the Graduate School, the Mario Einaudi Center for International Studies, the Latin American Studies Program, and the Center for the Study of Inequality. At the University of Utah, additional research was funded by the Department of Political Science, the Center for Latin American Studies, the School for Social and Cultural Transformation, and the College of Social and Behavior Sciences. I am very grateful for all of their support.

Finally, on a personal note, my sister, Ceresa, has provided unending love and support from my earliest days, and especially during grad school. Through ups and downs, I have always been able to count on

Donna and Billy Schroeder for love, support, and life advice. I must also thank Shannan Mattiace, my adviser at Allegheny College and friend, without whose encouragement and affirmation I never would have considered pursuing graduate school in the first place, and who first introduced me to the topic of ethnoracial politics in Latin America. And last but not least, I thank my partner, Jonathan, who inspires me every day with his brilliance, curiosity, and sense of humor. His love and support not only helped me complete this book but even got me to think that maybe "this is the place."

I

Introduction

"That's when I was like, 'I'm black,' you know?" These are the words of Jorge, a university student living in Recife, a coastal city in northeastern Brazil. Like many others I met, Jorge tells me that he is classified as white on his birth certificate but that today he self-identifies as black. Recounting the details of his personal transformation, Jorge reports that while growing up he didn't often think about himself in racial terms, per se, but over time he came to understand his past experiences as profoundly racialized. In Jorge's words, he came to "discover [him]self" as black.

Tiago, also a university student in Recife, tells a similar story. Like Jorge, Tiago reports that he is classified as white on his birth certificate but today identifies himself as black. He explains that his racial transformation began when his friends from university inadvertently led him to a black movement event. There, Tiago heard the personal anecdotes of racism and discrimination shared by activists. He reports that he was surprised by how much their stories resonated with him because at the time he had not yet considered himself black. But identifying with these stories led Tiago to ask himself "how had I not realized this before?" He said, "I looked back said 'jeez, that all happened to me because I was black. Because I *am* black.' It was really just like that. It was a discovery."

In many ways, there is nothing remarkable about the racial trajectories of these two young men in Brazil, a so-called "racial democracy" that often serves as a point of contrast to the rigid and institutionalized racial boundaries of the United States or South Africa. This context of fluid and ambiguous racial boundaries has long enabled individuals to cross racial boundaries and change their racial self-identifications – that is, to

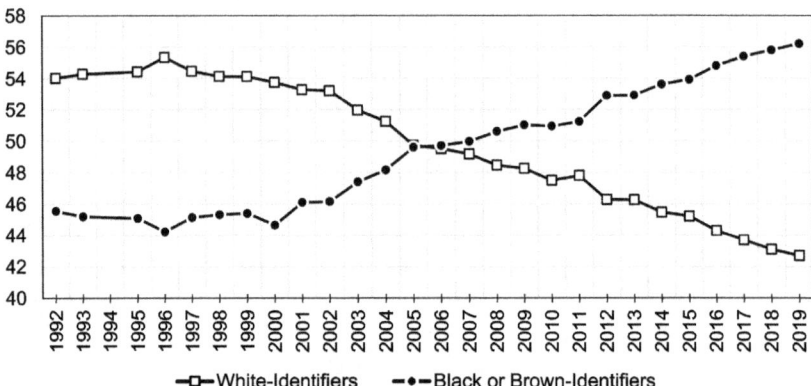

FIGURE 1.1 Racial composition of Brazil, 1992–2019
Sources: *Censo Demográfico*, IBGE; *Pesquisa nacional por amostra de domicílios* (PNAD), IBGE.

reclassify.[1] At the same time, however, this history of racial boundary crossing is also what makes these accounts significant. For although the Brazilian case is known for racial fluidity, it is also known for profound racial inequalities and veiled racism, which have long been said to incentivize reclassification *toward whiteness*, when possible.

Not so since the early 2000s. In more recent years, many Brazilians such as Jorge and Tiago have come to demonstrate a marked and growing tendency to reclassify instead *toward blackness*. Figure 1.1 shows the racial composition of Brazil from 1992 to 2019 as determined by the census bureau and illustrates this reversal of the status quo. Indeed, between the 2000 and 2010 censuses, the Brazilian population unexpectedly flipped from majority- to minority-white – a sudden structural shift that, as we will see, cannot be explained by intergroup differences in demographic trends or changes in census enumeration practices. What has instead become clear is that Brazilians are increasingly adopting the stigmatized labels of blackness.

This book analyzes this sudden reversal in patterns of racial reclassification, what I term the reclassification reversal, to shed new light on the processes of mass identity change and politicization. Empirically, its purpose is to explain why Brazilians are increasingly adopting nonwhite

---

[1] Throughout this book, I use the term "reclassification" to refer to *changes* in individuals' racial self-identification. I use the term "identification" to refer to one's subjective self-classification in a racial category at a given point in time. Though related, identification is static whereas reclassification is dynamic.

identities, why this tendency has increased so suddenly, and why they appear to be defying the conventional wisdom that expects reclassification toward whiteness. In seeking to provide satisfying answers to these questions, this book contributes to the broader theoretical agenda of understanding the "identity-to-politics link," that is, the processes that translate social categories into politicized identities and into bases of group or collective politics. I focus particular attention on understanding one element of these processes, the formation of a group consciousness that shapes one's perceptions and understandings of power – what I refer to as political identity. I leverage the puzzling variation evident in the reclassification reversal to distill empirically verifiable insights into the causes, mechanisms, and consequences of identity formation and politicization. The argument I develop directs attention toward the ways in which state-led efforts at educational expansion have reshaped individuals' subjective self-understandings, led individuals to cross social boundaries they previously recognized, and imbued newfound identities with political meaning.

THE ARGUMENT

I argue that the reclassification reversal is the consequence of expanded access to education, which has unintentionally led many Brazilians to develop racialized political identities. State-led efforts to better include lower-class sectors of the citizenry through social policy expansion have unleashed unprecedented waves of upward mobility for members of the lower classes, many of whom have options in their racial identifications and who are traditionally susceptible to practices known as whitening. Unprecedented access to secondary and university education, in particular, has increased the exposure of newly mobile citizens to information, social networks, and the labor market. In turn, this increased exposure has brought many face-to-face with racial hierarchies and inequalities in their pursuits of upward mobility, altering the personal experiences that inform their racial identifications and their political identities. The increasing adoption of nonwhite – and in particular black – identities can be understood as an articulation of newfound and racialized political identities.

From a macro perspective, the ostensibly sudden onset of the reclassification reversal can be explained by the timing of institutional reforms that expanded the nature and accessibility of social benefits allocated to citizens by state. Prior to redemocratization in the 1980s, literacy requirements for voting rights excluded large segments of the poor from the franchise, and social benefits were allocated on a corporatist basis, often accessible only to formal labor sectors and state-sponsored unions. The new and progressive 1988 constitution lifted literacy requirements for political citizenship and, moreover, codified universal social rights for all citizens, including the right to education. In the context of a newly expanded franchise, politicians and parties on the left and right faced pressure to compete for the votes of the poor masses, generating the political will and incentives to create, reform, and fund universal and targeted social policies. The federal government increased spending at all levels of education, restructured incentives for administrators, and altered pathways of resource delivery to circumvent political manipulation by subnational governments. Specifically at the university level, state and federal governments vastly increased enrollments at new and preexisting public universities, ensured greater inclusion through means and race-targeted affirmative action policies, and created financial programs to support students wishing to attend private universities.

The net result has been remarkable improvements in quality and access to education, even at the lowest levels of Brazil's income structure. Household survey data indicate that among those in the bottom income decile, primary school completion rates increased from 10 percent in 1992 to over 65 percent by 2014; over this same period, high school completion increased tenfold in this decile, from 3 to 30 percent; and between 2000 and 2010 alone, overall university completion rates increased more than 65 percent among the adult population (25 years or older), from less than 7 to 11 percent. By 2010, university access more generally reached historically unprecedented levels, with an additional 25 percent of the adult population completing at least some university education.[2] Alongside these trends in educational expansion also came the stunning shift in patterns of racial reclassification. Analysis of reclassification between the 2000 and 2010 censuses estimates that the brown and black categories were, respectively, 10 and 30 percent larger than anticipated, and that these discrepancies were indeed due to mass reclassification (Miranda 2015).[3] It is no coincidence that these developments played out in tandem.

For decades, the Brazilian case has served as the perennial paradox in the comparative study of racial politics. Despite structural conditions of deep and durable racialized inequalities and the persistence of

---

[2] See Table 3547 of the 2010 census at https://sidra.ibge.gov.br/pesquisa/censo-demografico.
[3] See Table 2.1.

widespread discrimination, Brazil has often stood apart from similar cases for the absence of politicized racial differences or cleavages. From a strictly structural perspective, the politicization of racial differences in Brazil has long been overdetermined. But such expectations overlook the important role that citizenship institutions play in translating material conditions or group-based discrimination into political worldviews and action, into identity politics. Broadly construed, the argument I develop in this book highlights the ways in which citizenship institutions (the accessibility of education) and social structures (racial hierarchies and inequalities) interact to shape the microlevel processes of identity change and politicization.

CONTRIBUTIONS

A Policy Feedback Account of Identity Politicization

This book contributes to theoretical debates on when, why, and how ethnic and other identities become politicized. In recent years, scholarship in the comparative ethnic politics literature has coalesced around instrumental explanations for the politicization or political salience of social identities, with a central focus on institutional incentives as the primary determinants of the identities articulated in the political arena.[4] These arguments encompass electoral rules that incentivize particular "minimum-winning coalitions" (Huber 2017; Posner 2005), norms or traditions inherited from colonial states (Laitin 1986), or incentive structures that simply render identities a convenient political means to some material end (Bates 1974; Chandra 2004; Hoddie 2006; Laitin 1998; Nagel 1996). But as we will see in the case of Brazil, it is not always safe to assume that identities are given, ready-made, and available for mobilization from above or below, or for the pursuit of material interests. Without consideration for the informal social hierarchies that can stigmatize social categories, identities that appear electorally or politically strategic might not in fact be viable bases for mobilization. Just as Madrid (2012) argues regarding other contexts in Latin America, ethnoracial hierarchies and fluid boundaries have long deterred identification with devalued social categories, such as indigenous or black. In

---

[4] See Laitin (1986) for a less instrumental argument about the role of institutions in these processes. Similarly, Yashar (2005) allows for a rationalist understanding for the role of citizenship institutions in shaping collective action per Olson (1965) but offers a less materialist account of identity-based mobilization.

such a context, the willingness of individuals to adopt and articulate stigmatized identities in the political arena – whether these identities are at all available for mobilization – is also a function of the social disincentives perpetuated through institutional racism, disincentives that must be overcome.

My account highlights that social citizenship institutions can play a critical role in this regard. I build on the oft-cited tenet of policy feedback scholarship that "new policies generate new politics." In this case, the policies I emphasize are what Marshall (1950) classically termed social citizenship – the right to live as a full member of society according to prevailing standards, which encompass health, welfare, and not least of all education.[5] Specifically, I identify the ways in which educational policy reforms altered the quality and experiences of citizenship among Brazil's poor masses, encouraging and empowering them to contest social hierarchies and articulate stigmatized identities in the political arena. At first glance, it may seem that this argument comports with instrumental explanations for identity salience, which point to state institutions as causal factors. But close examination of longitudinal patterns in the Brazilian case makes clear that citizenship institutions matter not by generating new incentive structures for black identification, per se, but by altering the personal and subjective experiences of citizens. In this case, reforms to educational policies and priorities expanded access to primary, secondary, and university education, unleashed waves of upward mobility for lower-class sectors, and set these citizens on new personal and professional trajectories. In the process, citizens gained greater exposure to information, social networks and movements, and the labor market, all of which altered the logics, discourses, and subjectivities that impact individuals' self-understandings. In short, reforms to social citizenship institutions altered the personal and subjective experiences that inform citizens' racial identifications and identities. In turn, these identities have "fed back" into the political process by impacting their willingness to articulate racial identities in the political arena. So conceived, the politicization of stigmatized identities and the reclassification reversal itself can be understood as consequences of the punctuated extension of (social) citizenship rights and benefits to formerly excluded sectors of society.

---

[5] In his classic essay, Marshall theorizes a triumvirate of citizenship rights, also including civil and political citizenship: respectively, rights to individual freedom (i.e., speech, association, property) and to participate in the exercise of power (i.e., voting, officeholding).

An Empirical and Systematic Analysis of the Identity-to-Politics Link

Beyond the comparative ethnic politics literature, this book also contributes to the interdisciplinary study of identity and group politics by providing a systematic and rigorous empirical analysis of identity formation processes. In recent years, prominent critics have urged scholars to avoid the analytical pitfalls of groupism and to disaggregate the processes of identity formation and politicization. Most famously, Brubaker and Cooper (2000) criticize what they see as abuses of constructivism in the rapidly growing identity politics literature, citing scholars' tendency to conflate categories with groups, and categories of analysis with categories of practice (also see Lee 2008; Smith 2004). Instead, scholars ought to more thoroughly scrutinize whether social categories qualify as "identities," that is, categories of self-understanding "used by 'lay' actors ... to make sense of themselves, of their activities, of what they share with, and how they differ from, others" (Brubaker and Cooper 2000, 4).[6] And, scholars ought to focus attention on understanding "the ways in which self-understandings may harden, congeal, and crystallize" (Brubaker and Cooper 2000, 1), and problematize, rather than assume, that microlevel identities scale up into fully fledged "groups" (Brubaker 2004), or what Bartolini and Mair (1990) call "cleavages." Lee (2008) echoes these calls, urging scholars to focus on what he terms the "identity-to-politics link," the disaggregated sets of processes that lead from social categories to politicized identities, to group or collective politics.

Despite these prominent calls from scholars, we still possess relatively few empirical and systematic analyses of the microlevel processes of identity formation and politicization.[7] To be sure, this is a tall empirical order, as not just any context can offer empirical leverage in the way that Brazil's reclassification reversal can. Fewer still pair this kind of phenomenon with a wealth of data sources that can be mined to shed light on these processes. Thus, one simple, but no less important, contribution of this study is the close, empirical examination of these distinct identity processes. By integrating and analyzing a wealth of data from multiple sources – including original qualitative data and survey experiments, longitudinal analysis of microlevel and municipal census data, national public opinion surveys, and a panel dataset of university students – we gain a comprehensive and empirical account of the identity-to-politics link.

---

[6] This comports with Brubaker and Cooper's acceptance of categories of practice, as contrasted with categories of analysis.
[7] Recent exceptions include Laitin (1998), Masuoka (2017), and Davenport (2018).

A Reassessment of Racial Politics in Brazil

Finally, this book also contributes to the comparative racial politics literature, especially interdisciplinary debates on the significance and political relevance of race in the Brazilian and Latin American contexts. As Clealand (2022) argues, while the study of race in comparative politics remains woefully underdeveloped, Latin American contexts provide rich and ample opportunity to probe, theorize, and test new theoretical perspectives on racial politics, especially regarding the consequences of fluidity and identification. In this regard, one contribution of this book is the empirical documentation of the reclassification reversal, which runs counter to scholarly wisdom. A long line of research in anthropology and sociology, in particular, established the idea that racial fluidity and black stigmatization produce whitening, especially among the upwardly mobile (Cardoso and Ianni 1960; Degler 1971; Harris 1952; Silva 1994; Wagley 1965). This study is not the first to take notice of and scrutinize the reclassification reversal (Jesus and Hoffmann 2020; Miranda 2015; Soares 2008). But it is the first to document these patterns *and* provide a theoretical and empirically tested account of its causes, mechanisms, and consequences for Brazilian (racial) politics. More so than the studies that precede it, this book probes and triangulates multiple types and sources of data to make sense of this new era in Brazilian racial politics. The central finding in this regard is that upward mobility does not inevitably produce whitening and has instead come to produce darkening in recent decades. What's more, the coincidence of the reclassification reversal and unprecedented waves of upward mobility for lower-class Brazilians also suggests a parallel with cases like the United States, often discussed in juxtaposition to Brazil's racial politics. To be sure, black-identified Brazilians do not exhibit the level of group cohesion witnessed in the United States. But just as the experiences of upward mobility were shown to deepen blacks' racial consciousness in the wake of the Civil Rights Movement (Dawson 1995; Hochschild 1995), so also have Brazilians exhibited greater racial consciousness in Brazil's era of social inclusion.

This should not be taken to mean that Brazil's racial politics now resembles, or will resemble, the hyper-politicization of race evident in the United States or South Africa. But falling short of the extreme outcomes in these canonical cases also should not overshadow this period of flux in Brazilian racial politics. In particular, this book's findings regarding patterns of racial identification, the political content of racial identities, and the consequences for political behavior signal two important changes in this case. The first is growing heterogeneity *within* racial categories in racial subjectivities, that is, the logics and discourses individuals employ to rationalize their way into or out of racial categories. The traditional interpretation of Brazilian racial subjectivity emphasizes colorism, or racial classification based on fine, phenotypical distinctions made between individuals. But increasingly, and especially among black identifiers, colorist logic is being replaced (though not fully supplanted) by a political understanding of blackness based on shared experiences of racism and discrimination and the desire to contest racial hierarchies. Black movements in Brazil have long sought to promote this way of thinking to encourage race-based mobilization among the masses. But until recently, these efforts were met with resistance from the very communities they aimed to represent (Burdick 1998b; Hanchard 1994). Yet more now than ever before, Brazilians are exhibiting a willingness to claim and politicize blackness.

Second and relatedly, there are clear signs that these race-conscious Brazilians carry these identities into the political arena and incorporate them into their political calculations. Political scientists have long remarked on the absence of racial politics in Brazil's electoral arena, in particular. Despite profound structural inequalities, Brazil did not see the emergence of race-based political parties, nonwhite candidates struggled to win elections, and racial differences did not map onto partisan or electoral preferences (Mainwaring 1999; Mainwaring et al. 2000; Samuels and Zucco 2018). But as I show in this book, the reclassification reversal is not a purely sociological phenomenon. Alongside this sea change in racial subjectivity has emerged a new, if overlooked, electoral constituency of highly educated black identifiers who prove themselves committed leftist voters. This is a pattern that emerges after the electoral realignment that followed the 2005 *mensalão* corruption scandal and is one that holds through the polarization of the 2018 election of Jair Bolsonaro. Taken together, this growing leftist constituency and new understandings of blackness reveal cracks in Brazil's status as the perennial paradox in the comparative study of racial politics, a context decidedly lacking politicized racial differences. Simply put, it is no longer tenable to dismiss race as politically irrelevant in contemporary Brazil.

ALTERNATIVE EXPLANATIONS

The argument I advance in this book departs from dominant theories in the comparative ethnic politics literature to explain identity politicization. My focus is on social citizenship institutions, their impacts on micro-level subjectivities, and their consequences for identification and political behavior. This explanation is more compelling, I submit, because it better accounts for the timing of the reclassification reversal and the longevity of newly adopted racial identifications evident in the census. Though I dedicate significant attention to the effects of education on reclassification, let me also clarify that I do not intend to advance a monocausal theory of racial reclassification or identification. My argument is probabilistic and non-exhaustive; I do not argue that educational expansion explains reclassification in all cases nor that education supplants all other factors already known to impact racial identification. Indeed, a large interdisciplinary literature has well established that myriad factors beyond phenotype impact racial identification, including family socialization, social movements, and the media. I do not deny or dismiss the impact of these factors but argue instead that the effect of education matters separate and apart from such factors. Beyond these sociological arguments, my argument must also be situated against prevailing explanations from the literature, which face limitations in explaining this case of identity change and politicization.

Affirmative Action

Among those familiar with Brazil, the likely knee-jerk explanation for the reclassification reversal is the advent of affirmative action policies. Indeed, since the early 2000s, the federal and state governments in Brazil have begun to experiment with such race-targeted policies, predominantly in the form of quotas in university admissions. Scholars hypothesize two ways in which affirmative action can impact racial identification. The first comports with an axiom in the identity politics literature that institutions incentivize identification and identity salience (Chandra 2012). In this view, identification and salience are the simple product of means-ends calculations in contexts of resource scarcity. Affirmative action policies have featured explicitly in this literature. Nagel (1996), for example, argues that affirmative action incentivized Native American identification in the United States; Hoddie (2006) argues that preferential policies incentivized ethnic identities in China and Australia; and Chandra

(2005) argues that in India, these policies incentivized excluded groups to mobilize and demand inclusion as policy targets. In the Brazilian case, journalists and public intellectuals echo this logic, often crying foul of the incentives for blackness and so-called fraud these policies are said to generate (e.g., Fry 2007; Fry and Maggie 2004). But as we will see in Chapters 5 and 6, such crude instrumental motivations struggle to account for the long-term identity change in this context of racial fluidity and stigmatized blackness. In other words, such perspectives fail to fully consider the conditions and social forces that have long *dis*incentivized blackness in the first place. Considered in its full context, affirmative action offers only short-term and risky benefits to manipulating one's racial identification, and these simply cannot explain long-run behaviors that outlast short-term payoffs.

A second set of explanations based on affirmative action focuses on how states "make race" by naturalizing or making salient social boundaries and differences (Bourdieu 1985; Marx 1998). In one vein, scholars have focused on official censuses as sites where states institutionalize and actively shape boundaries and identities (Kertzer and Arel 2002; Lieberman and Singh 2017; Omi and Winant 1994). This line of argument finds a seemingly clear parallel in the Brazilian case, where scholars have pointed to the census as a major explanation for racial fluidity and weak racial consciousness (Loveman 2014; Nascimento 2016; Nobles 2000). However, the state's classification scheme and enumeration practices have remained unchanged in recent decades. Thus, these factors simply cannot account for the dramatic shifts evident over this period.

Yet another vein of state-centered arguments emphasizes the symbolic dimension of state policies and institutions and their impact on racial subjectivities. From this perspective, affirmative action policies are a prominent piece of a broader shift in symbolic state institutions and the state's posture toward the racial question, which lend legitimacy to alternative racial discourses or make salient altered racial boundaries and identities. There is merit to this argument. The state's racial stance has indeed shifted over the course of the twentieth century, from one of eugenic race science at the turn of the twentieth century, to the oft-touted colorblindness encapsulated in the idea of "racial democracy," to a recognition of racial difference and discrimination perhaps best exemplified by affirmative action. The reclassification reversal coincides with this color conscious era, which also included other symbolic changes such as establishing a national racial consciousness holiday, mandating the teaching of African and Afro-Brazilian teaching in public school curricula, and founding a new governmental agency tasked with promoting racial equality. These are meaningful changes to the state. But while they might have contributed to a greater acceptance of blackness broadly, the major shortcoming of this symbolic institutional explanation is that diffuse, national-level factors are analytically too blunt to account for individual-level variation in reclassification; they simply cannot explain microlevel variation in reclassification. Though we should not deny their symbolic significance, we also must acknowledge that symbolic institutional explanations leave more to be said about who reclassifies and why they do so.

Of the alternative explanations outlined in this introduction, I devote most attention to those related to affirmative action in the chapters that follow. In Chapter 5, I analyze the hypothesized effects of educational expansion prior to the passage of the 2012 federal affirmative action law, and show that these findings are not contingent on the presence of state-level affirmative action policies. In Chapter 6, I employ a variety of empirical strategies to directly test the effects of affirmative action, separate and apart from the effects of educational expansion. My analyses provide mixed support, at best. While there is evidence that affirmative action amplifies the effects of educational expansion, affirmative action policies are neither necessary nor sufficient conditions for the reclassification reversal.

Mobilization from Above

A prominent line of research in identity politics, and ethnic politics in particular, attributes the politicization of identities to political elites. Particularly in contexts where elites seek political office to gain access to patronage or state resources, scholars argue that politicians politicize or incentivize identification through top-down electoral mobilization. In this view, rent-seeking politicians mobilize social cleavages that are sizable enough to win elections and maximize distributive payoffs for voters and elites (Huber 2017; Posner 2005; also see Chandra 2004). In these instrumental accounts, political elites are the central agents, and voters comply in order to receive their own post-electoral payoffs. These theories assume stability in the size and boundaries of social groups that are problematically unstable in the Brazilian case. But the implication nonetheless is that elites may have incentivized nonwhite identification by promising group-targeted benefits in electoral campaigns.

These explanations, however, fall short in this context. As noted earlier, scholars of Brazilian electoral and party politics have traditionally argued that there are few social bases in Brazil's fragmented electoral system, let alone racial ones. In more recent years, scholars have identified class and region as salient electoral differences (Handlin 2013; Hunter and Power 2007). But mainstream studies conducted in the decade following redemocratization identified few sociodemographic correlates of electoral preferences, leading scholars to conclude that politicians have not courted votes along group lines (Mainwaring 1999; Mainwaring et al. 2000; Samuels 2006). Moreover, scholars argue that the persistence of traditional, clientelistic politics has disarticulated social differences (Hagopian 1996). As I discuss in Chapter 7, racial politics scholars doubt some of these claims from the party and electoral systems literatures and have identified salient racial differences in electoral behavior even at the height of state's embrace of colorblind racial democracy discourse (Castro 1993; Soares and Silva 1987; Souza 1971; Valente 1986). But even these scholars agree that, while race has been too quickly dismissed by political scientists, there is little evidence to suggest race forms the basis of top-down electoral strategy.[8] Indeed, non-white politicians are woefully underrepresented among officeholders in Brazil (Janusz 2018; Johnson III 1998, 2015), and those who win office do so by avoiding explicit racial appeals in their campaigns (Mitchell 2009; Oliveira 2007; Valente 1986). From the electorate's perspective, it remains unclear that voters prefer candidates of their race or color (Aguilar et al. 2015; Bueno and Dunning 2017), and evidence from Brazil and elsewhere in Latin America suggests all voters simply prefer lighter-skinned candidates (Contreras 2016; Janusz 2018).[9] Recent research by Janusz (2021, 2023) indicates that elites do respond strategically to racial considerations by changing their own racial identifications. But, Janusz argues, the causal direction is reversed: demographic structures impact candidates' racial identifications, not the other way around. But above all, there simply has been no significant or recent pattern of explicit, top-down electoral mobilization of blackness in Brazil. Electoral mobilization from above finds little traction on this question.

---

[8] One important exception is Johnson (2020a), who argues that darker-skinned voters are targeted disproportionately for vote buying. The purpose of race-targeted vote buying, however, is not to politicize racial differences.

[9] Black movement activists who bemoan racial underrepresentation also identify this as a culprit, encapsulated in the refrain *negro não vota em negro*, or blacks do not vote for blacks (Moura 1994, 222).

Mobilization from Below

Another alternative explanation attributes identity politicization to social movements and bottom-up mobilization. Of particular note is McAdam's (1982) seminal study of black organizing and political cohesion in the U.S. Civil Rights Movement. For McAdam, one important function movements provide is cognitive liberation, or the ability for aggrieved or oppressed populations to "define their situations as unjust and subject to change through group action" (McAdam 1982, 51). Thus, social movement organization entails the activation and cohering of identities for the purpose of pursuing political action. Other scholars agree, arguing that social movement participation itself can play a role in fomenting political consciousness and in leading individuals to develop and articulate interests and claims in the political arena (Klandermans 1992; Roberts 1998; Stokes 1995).[10] Other prominent social movement scholarship has promoted the view that collective and politicized identities are both causes (Friedman and McAdam 1992; Klandermans 2002) and consequences (Escobar and Alvarez 1992) of mobilization.[11] As I detail in Chapters 3 and 4, social movements and new social networks via the pursuit of education forms part of the exposure-via-education argument. And there is no denying that many racially conscious Brazilians seek out social movements as venues in which to articulate racialized political identities. But the role of social movements is, in and of itself, an unsatisfactory causal explanation for two primary reasons.

First, I argue that the educational services the black movement organizations provide to low-income households play an important role in

---

[10] Rueschemeyer, Stephens, and Stephens (1992, 54) write that class interests are often ill defined, heterogeneous and contradictory, and that part of the political project of class-based mobilization is engaging in a process of defining and articulating "class interests." This is similar to Thompson's (1963) notion of class identity formation via mobilization.

[11] The politicization of ethnic identities elsewhere in Latin America has been associated with bottom-up social mobilization, namely in Yashar's (2005) influential account of the sudden emergence of indigenous movements. The processes Yashar identifies do not translate well to the Brazilian case, however. There is a key distinction in the spatial distribution of indigenous communities in many Latin American countries and Afro-descendants in Brazil. Many indigenous communities were spatially concentrated and had carved out enclaves of autonomy far-removed from the reach of the state. As Yashar argues, increased contact of these enclaves with state authority through decentralizing neoliberal forms gave rise to ethnic grievances that inspired, in part, mobilization in the first place. While Brazil is home to spatially concentrated maroon communities of Afro-descendants in rural areas (known as *quilombos*), these communities represent a small minority of Brazil's Afro-descendant population. The large majority resides in urban areas, takes part in the modern/industrial/informal urban economy, and does not necessarily maintain a way of life distinct or separate from mainstream society.

these processes, and research discussed earlier has shown that social movements are certainly capable of fomenting consciousness and inspiring identity change. But it remains unclear that the Brazilian black movement could or would have had such a large effect on the mass public in the absence of broader educational reforms that expanded access to primary and secondary education and created demand for university access. As I detail in later chapters, several of my interviewees discussed their contact with the black movement, reporting that this raised questions and doubts about themselves, altered their ways of thinking about blackness, and fomented a racialized view of Brazilian society. But many interviewees also explained that their first contact with the movement came inadvertently, often through new social contacts from university or in pursuit of low-cost services, like preparatory courses for the university entrance exam. Without the prior reforms that increased enrollments in and completion of primary and secondary schooling, demand for higher education and the altering of social networks would certainly have been less, and consequently so also this inadvertent exposure to the black movement. Educational reforms were crucial to generating bottom-up demand for universities, and this – indirectly – increased exposure to social movements. This should not be read as a dismissal of the important role that black movements play in the reclassification reversal. But for the reason outlined here, I theorize social networks and movements as one pathway through which education exerts a causal effect rather than as an independent cause that operates distinctly from education, or that would have succeeded in bringing about the reversal absent broader educational reforms.

Second, the challenges that Brazil's black movement has historically faced in mobilizing the masses also raise doubts about the movement as an independent cause of sudden mass change. No doubt, social movements broadly have been key actors in Brazil's major political developments and institutional reforms, including democratization and the constitutional convention in the 1980s (Alvarez 1990; Garay 2016; Keck 1992). Specifically, the black movement has more recently exerted significant influence by shaping policy at the highest levels of the Brazilian government, pressuring the state to acknowledge racial discrimination and adopt affirmative action, and occupying key offices in federal government agencies since the 2000s (Htun 2004; Paschel 2016a). But while successful in influencing elites and policy at the national level, the black movement has historically struggled to mobilize the masses at the grassroots (Hanchard 1994; Marx 1998). Scholars disagree on why, but one compelling explanation advanced by Burdick (1998b, 1998a) is that the movement's leadership and rank-and-file tend to be populated by middle-class professionals, who face resistance from the masses to being mobilized along racial lines. This is in part, Burdick argues, because the movement's prerequisite that participants adopt politicized black identities is a hurdle too great for Brazil's darker-skinned masses, who prefer to distance themselves from blackness – a point echoed more recently by Alves (2018).[12] While race-based activism and mobilization occur in some interest arenas (Caldwell 2007; Perry 2013; Smith 2016), it remains unclear how widespread black movement participation has become among the mass public. It is thus important to draw a distinction between influencing elites and mobilizing the masses. Social movements have recently made great strides, but the black movement in particular has long struggled to mobilize and connect with the mass constituencies it aims to represent. What has changed in recent times, I argue, is the receptiveness of certain sectors of the public to the black movement's message *when they encounter it*, a change brought about by upward mobility and educational expansion. For this reason too, social movements are better conceived as one possible (but not exclusive) pathway of exposure-via-education, rather than an independent or competing cause of wide-scale reclassification.

Cleavage Structure

Finally, structural theories attribute identity salience to cleavage structure, or the degree to which multiple group memberships coincide with or cut across one another. Most prominently, Horowitz (1985) argues that conflict between groups is more likely when groups are organized vertically, in some form of hierarchy (also see Dunning and Harrison 2010; Rogowski 1990). Cederman et al. (2013) similarly argue that civil war onset is more likely when political and economic inequalities map onto group lines. The logic here is relatively simple: objective structural

---

[12] Indeed, in a reflection on the challenges facing urban activists combatting racialized violence in São Paulo, Alves (2018, 219) writes "if we are not able to make the oppressed recognized himself as black, how are we to organize to face the police on the streets?" Attention to class-based differences in black movement participation is a point that has also been echoed by Brazil-based scholars working on this issue. Legendary activist and scholar Clóvis Moura (1994, 221), for example, writes of "two black universes, one *lettered* and the other *plebeian*, [which] almost never cross in political practice, especially racial politics" (Author's translation. Emphasis in original.). Also see Moura (1994, 219–34).

conditions of group-based inequality produce identity politics.[13] Indeed, Brazil's income distribution is among the most unequal in the world (Hagopian 2018; Lustig 2015; Morley 2001), and class inequalities have historically mapped cleanly onto racial hierarchies (Andrews 1991; Hasenbalg 1979; Silva 1978; Telles 2004). Moreover, like the United States and South Africa, Brazil continues to contend with the legacies of colonialism and the practice of slavery. Again, the politicization of racial differences in Brazil has long been overdetermined.

Yet, prior to the 2000s, scholars remarked on the weak politicization of race in Brazil, despite these conditions (Hanchard 1994; Lieberman 2003, 2009; Marx 1998). The coincidence of race and class cleavages simply cannot account for the timing of the reclassification reversal in Brazil. What's more, the period of time that coincides with the reclassification reversal was one of *declining* inequality and a *narrowing* of the gap between white and nonwhite Brazilians (IPEA 2016; Klein et al. 2018; López-Calva and Lustig 2010; Neri 2011). If anything, the structural coincidence of race and class that are said to underpin identity politicization was becoming increasingly crosscutting just as racial identities have become more politicized in Brazil. As we'll see, Brazilians exhibiting a politicized racial consciousness often point to structural conditions to legitimate the view that race deserves greater attention in Brazilian politics, but the structure of racial and class cleavages in particular cannot account for the timing of the reclassification reversal. To boot, like symbolic national institutions, structure also cannot explain microlevel variation in who chooses to reclassify or assume a politicized black identity.

RESEARCH DESIGN AND METHODS

This book employs multiple methods and analyzes multiple sources of data to provide support for the educational expansion argument and assess alternative explanations. In particular, I build and test this argument by relying on qualitative and quantitative data collected during more than 18 months of in-depth fieldwork in São Paulo and Recife – two major urban centers located in culturally distinct and the most densely populated geographic regions of Brazil. The data I present in

---

[13] Outside of the conflict literature, scholars are more skeptical that structural conditions of inequality lead to identity politicization. See Gaventa (1982), Laitin (1986), Roberts (2002), and Yashar (2005).

this book is the product of sequential stages of data collection, beginning with inductive field research that included participant observation and in-depth interviews with reclassifiers. This initial field research generated the hypothesis that better-educated Brazilians were most likely to adopt nonwhite identities over time, and provided additional avenues of inquiry to situate these patterns in Brazil's historical and macro-level context. Having refined and developed the hypothesis, I then set out to test these insights rigorously and systematically with a wealth of additional data. In the end, the data analyzed in this book include:

- Ethnographic interview data with thirty-four Brazilians of various educational attainments, including both reclassifiers and non-reclassifiers;
- A synthetic panel dataset of birth cohorts, comprised of more than 137,000 observations, constructed from annual demographic surveys between 1992 and 2015, as well as additional surveys from 1976 to 1990;
- A multilevel panel dataset of 5,500 municipalities in Brazil between 1991 and 2010, as well as state-level affirmative action laws, decrees, and policies;
- A panel dataset of federal university students' racial identifications in high school and when registering for the university entrance exam, constructed post hoc from the Ministry of Education's embargoed surveys of public-school students;
- Survey experiments conducted face-to-face with randomly sampled Brazilians in 2002 and 2018; and
- Public opinion surveys, including sociological studies of racial identification collected between 1986 and 2008, surveys of protesters from 2013 to 2016, and national surveys for five presidential elections between 2002 and 2018, among others.

This book joins other recent books that leverage longitudinal and subnational variation in a single context to distill generalizable theoretical insights (see Pepinsky 2019). For these purposes, the Brazilian case is particularly well positioned to shed light on the processes of identity formation and politicization. Indeed, to the extent that Brazil has appeared in the literature on ethnic and racial politics, scholars have noted the weak politicization of racial differences (Bueno and Dunning 2017; Hanchard 1994; also see Yashar 2005). In comparative studies, Brazil is typically analyzed as a "negative" case lacking racial politics, one that demands explanation or offers crucial variation on variables of theoretical interest (e.g., Lieberman 2003, 2009; Marx 1998; Nobles 2000).[14] By and large, scholars have agreed that race has been politically relevant in this context only insofar as elites have *dis*articulated racial differences by constructing a racially inclusive nation that whitewashes Brazil's history as the single largest and longest-running participant in the slave trade, as well as the legacies of slavery in shaping present-day inequalities (Andrews 1991; Loveman 2014; Skidmore 1993; Telles 2004). Previous scholarship suggests, therefore, that this ought to be an *unlikely* case for the formation of political identities rooted in *racial* categories of social membership. Yet at the same time, the fluidity of racial boundaries renders the Brazilian case "exceptional" (Pepinsky 2017), one where such identity change is not only possible on such a wide scale, but possible to detect and analyze empirically and systematically.

The downside to mining a single domestic context for data and insights is that doing so potentially limits whether these findings generalize to other contexts. But there are two reasons to not so quickly dismiss this phenomenon or these findings as singularly Brazilian. The first pertains to the applicability of these findings elsewhere in Latin America, a region that has undergone a sea change in its ethnoracial politics. Over the past three decades, the region has witnessed the rise of indigenous social movements and political parties, the constitutional codification of ethnoracial rights, and the implementation of race-targeted affirmative action policies. Brazil has charted some of this new territory. But these significant changes have arrived to a wide array of countries, including Bolivia, Ecuador, Peru, Guatemala, Colombia, and Mexico. What's more, national census bureaus across the region have begun to more uniformly and consistently collect ethnoracial population data, rendering visible for the first time, in some cases, ethnoracialized populations previously obscured by national myths of racial unity. Mexico's census bureau has even gone so far as to include measures of skin tone in its national household surveys – an indication of the state's greater willingness to recognize and potentially redress racialized inequities.

More data ought to facilitate extensions of the longitudinal analysis I conduct of Brazil to other cases, as well as mapping of variation across cases. And while data collection efforts do not yet permit longitudinal comparisons in the same depth across the region as a whole, there are nonetheless indications of significant growth in black (Afro-descendant)

---

[14] See Seigel (2005, 2009) for a counterpoint on the typical analysis of the Brazilian case in comparative studies.

and indigenous identification in a number of cases. This is true even outside of Brazil and the Caribbean, where Afro-descendant identifiers already comprise large shares of national populations. Indeed, Table 1.1 shows that between countries' two most recent censuses, the relative size of self-identified indigenous populations grew at significantly high rates in Argentina, Colombia, Costa Rica, Guatemala, Paraguay, and Venezuela.[15] These proportions more than doubled in Brazil and Nicaragua and nearly tripled in Chile. Similarly, the number of self-identified black or Afro-descendant identifiers grew significantly in Guatemala, Puerto Rico,[16] and Mexico, more than doubled in Ecuador, and tripled in Uruguay – a country that once celebrated itself as "the white nation" (Andrews 2010). To be sure, variation in enumeration practices in these cases complicates inter-census and cross-case comparisons, so these statistics should be interpreted with caution. But nonetheless, these statistics seem to suggest that the patterns and trends that the Brazilian case has thrown into sharp relief are potentially representative of broader, region-wide change.

Latin America is also far from the only region where one encounters fluid ethnic or racial boundaries. Indeed, analyses of the United States – where boundaries are believed to be rigid – have documented racial reclassification following changes to racial measurement on the census (Davenport 2018, 2020; Masuoka 2017), as well as prior to these changes in enumeration practices (Waters 2002). Beyond the Western Hemisphere, the type of identity change manifest in reclassification also finds a parallel in the adoption of the national identities of titular nations in Laitin's (1998) post-Soviet republics of Eastern Europe. And similar forms of ethnic reclassification have also occurred with non-Han ethnic minorities in China, aboriginal populations of Australia, *bumiputeras* (sons-of-the-soil) in Malaysia, and Assamese linguistic identities in India

---

[15] By contrast, the relative size of Bolivia's indigenous population appeared to fall from 62 to 40 percent between 2001 and 2012 due to the classification scheme employed in the census. The number of self-identified indigenous Bolivians enumerated, however, actually grew by nearly 30 percent, from just over 3 to 4 million. But there are too many methodological inconsistencies to place weight on these fluctuations. See Morales (2019) for extended discussion of the Bolivian case.

[16] Like Brazil, Puerto Rico has been analyzed as case of whitening in in the past (e.g., Loveman and Muniz 2007), but has seen a precipitous decline in the white-identified population. Between 2000 and 2020, the relative size declined from 84 to 60 percent, based on the 2000 census and the American Community Survey in 2010 and 2020. While black identification is on the rise, the "other race" category has grown most as a consequence.

TABLE I.I *Relative proportion of black (or Afro-national) and indigenous populations in Latin America*

	Indigenous ID			Black or Afro-national ID		
	2000s Census	2010s Census	% Change	2000s Census	2010s Census	% Change
Argentina	1.55%	2.47%	59	---	0.39%	---
Bolivia	61.97	40.28	-35	---	0.23	---
Brazil	0.20	0.43	115	6.21	7.52	21
Chile	4.58	12.44	172	---	0.06	---
Colombia	3.35	4.31	28	10.40	6.75	-35
Costa Rica	1.68	2.42	44	1.91	1.05	-45
Ecuador	6.83	7.03	3	2.23	5.25	135
El Salvador	---	0.23	---	---	0.13	---
Guatemala	39.41	43.43	10	0.04	0.32	606
Honduras	---	7.25	---	---	1.39	---
Mexico	9.23	21.50	133	1.16	2.15	86
Nicaragua	1.84	4.43	141	---	---	---
Panama	---	11.91	---	---	8.94	---
Paraguay	1.19	1.73	45	---	0.06	---
Peru	---	25.80	---	---	3.57	---
Uruguay	---	4.90	---	2.00	7.84	292
Venezuela	2.22	2.66	20	---	3.60	---
Puerto Rico	0.17	0.17	1	7.57	11.30	49

Black categories exclude *mestizo/a*, *mulato/a*, and other mixed categories except in Colombia, where black and *mulato/a* categories are lumped in the census. Statistics come from national census bureaus in each country, and the decennial census in nearly all cases. Exceptions include Puerto Rico, for which statistics come from the 2010 and 2020 American Community Survey (identification as black or African American alone); Mexico, for which the 2000s figure comes from the census bureau's annual household survey; and Uruguay, the 2000s figure for which is also drawn from the annual household survey, as presented in Andrews (2010, table I.1). Guatemala's 2018 black population figure combines black and *Garifuna* identification. The Dominican Republic did not collect ethnoracial data in 2002 or 2010. See Supplementary Tables A5 and A6 for detailed information on sources.

(Hoddie 2006). Even Horowitz (1985), in his classic tome on intergroup conflict that spans much of the global south, acknowledges that "[i]t is not merely what is asked and how the [census] results are to be interpreted that counts. Individual answers are also manipulable, since there is an element of self-definition in ethnic affiliation" (195). In short, the instability in social boundaries and demographic structures as constituted by censuses is more widespread than is commonly acknowledged by political scientists. This study represents an effort to center and make sense of this variation in so-called "political demography" (Hoddie 2006; McNamee and Zhang 2019).

A second potential limitation to generalizability stems from the institutionalization of racial boundaries, which shapes not only how easily boundaries can be crossed in a given context, but the extent to which racial categories are top-of-mind among citizens, whether they "see" race at all (Brubaker et al. 2004). Where boundaries are less porous and racial membership rules are more strictly enforced, one is unlikely to find such wide-scale and uncontroversial reclassification as one does in Brazil. But even if such boundary crossing does not occur everywhere, there is good reason to expect the mechanisms and processes that underlie reclassification – the processes of identity formation and politicization – to generalize to other contexts or other categories of social membership, especially *stigmatized* categories. The transformations and processes that I detail in this book are fundamentally about how certain types of social differences become the basis of individuals' self-understandings (identities), how those self-understandings come to shape their beliefs about power (become politicized), and how these then shape political action and behavior (articulation). In this case, I argue that reclassification is an expression, or indicator, for these identity processes. But I do not argue that reclassification is a necessary ingredient or output of all identity processes pertaining to other kinds of social categories. What is more easily detected in the Brazilian case may be harder to detect in other contexts and with other social categories, and their empirical manifestations may well vary. Yet the mechanisms and processes of exposure could easily generalize to subordinate gender or sexual identities, for example. In the book's conclusion, I return to this discussion and discuss possibilities for generalizing the mechanisms and processes I identify to other stigmatized or subordinate social groups.

POSITIONALITY

As with any study, but particularly when the analyst is directly involved in data collection, we must carefully consider our positionality, that is, how one's presentation in racial, gender, class, and other terms can impact the methods and approaches one chooses, the data and information one can access, and one's interpretation of that information. There is no doubt that my presentation as a light-skinned, foreign researcher from the United States impacted avenues for data collection and the willingness of individual interlocutors to share their perspectives with me. This is especially pertinent to the one-on-one interviews that I personally conducted for this research. Though at times I relied on the help of Brazilian research assistants who aided this project in various ways (including conducting focus group interviews), the qualitative interview data I present throughout this book come from the in-depth interviews I conducted. Even under the best of circumstances, ensuring interviews come to fruition requires incredible persistence and logistical flexibility. But despite my best efforts, there were times where potential interviewees I pursued declined to be interviewed, often offering a polite explanation for why they could not participate. I cannot know for certain why these individuals did so. In one instance, I was made aware that a group of student activists with whom I had made contact discussed amongst themselves whether or not they would agree to speak with me about my research. In the end, many did, and these were among my most fruitful interviews. But in any case, the relevant point is simply that I cannot know what information I failed to get, or how my presence may have impacted the narratives told by my interviewees.

By the same token, however, it would be disingenuous to say that my positionality served solely as an obstacle to conducting this research. Indeed, the combination of my being read as white and introducing myself as American also served as an asset. Fulfilling the stereotypical image of the white American in the minds of Brazilians undoubtedly opened doors, greased wheels, and frankly generated some excitement on the part of my interlocutors. While some interviewees may have been turned off by my positionality, others expressed intrigue about the foreigner from the north who took an interest in their racial transformations. All this is not even to mention the countless other ways that my status as an American researcher aided my research, especially when contacting government agencies, politicians, and bureaucrats whose assistance and insights I also relied on.

Regardless of whether my positionality was an asset or an obstacle, the methodological concern is simply that this introduced bias into data collection and my analysis of that and other data. There is no denying or skirting this issue. Such bias is hard to measure or quantify, and as a counterfactual is impossible to observe. But the concern of bias is partly what motivates the triangulated and multi-method research design of this project. By relying on different methods employed sequentially, I am able to partially mitigate some of the effects of bias by verifying and cross-checking the information collected qualitatively with independent sources of data and analysis, including macro-level and microlevel census and survey data. As a result, the argument and findings I develop in this book do not hinge on any one particular method or piece of data, and instead piece together conclusions based on multiple independent data sources. While my analyses will no doubt raise questions that future analysts will further probe and interrogate, this research design offers some measure of insurance against the influence of my positionality on the findings.

PLAN OF THE BOOK

The chapters that follow define the puzzle at the heart of this book, develop the conceptual and theoretical argument, and provide empirical support for the causes, mechanisms, and consequences of the reclassification reversal. Chapters 2 and 3 elaborate the book's empirical, conceptual, and theoretical framework. Chapter 2 lays out the empirical and theoretical puzzle and lays to rest simple explanations for these patterns based on census enumeration practices and intergroup differences in demographic trends. I then situate these patterns historically, and emphasize that conventional wisdom in sociology and anthropology would not have predicted the reclassification reversal. With the puzzle established, Chapter 3 elaborates the educational expansion argument introduced here. I detail the macro-level institutional reforms responsible for setting off the reclassification reversal, and situate recent improvements in educational access against the backdrop of the twentieth century. I then transition to the microlevel, identifying and specifying the specific causal pathways through which educational expansion impacts individuals' racial subjectivities: by increasing their exposure to new information, social networks, and experiences in the labor market.

Chapters 4 through 7 present empirical analyses of the causes, mechanisms, and consequences of the reclassification reversal. Chapter 4 focuses on specifying and illustrating the causal pathways that link education to reclassification and racial consciousness at the individual level. I present qualitative evidence from in-depth interviews with reclassifiers. These data, which helped to generate the central hypothesis of this book, bring the theoretical mechanisms to life by illustrating what the processes of reclassification look like on the ground. In this chapter, I also present systematic tests of the mechanisms by analyzing public opinion surveys from 1986 to 2008. I show that greater education is indeed correlated with racial consciousness and black identification, but that this relationship only emerged as access to education became more inclusive in the 2000s. Chapter 5 focuses on testing the implications of the educational expansion hypothesis more rigorously. I conduct longitudinal analysis of a pseudo-panel of birth cohorts to show that better-educated Brazilians are those most likely to adopt nonwhite, and especially black, identities over time. I supplement this analysis with panel analysis of Brazilian municipalities, which lends further support to the argument.

Chapter 6 focuses on alternative arguments based on affirmative action. Drawing on original survey experiments and two panel datasets, I assess instrumental and symbolic arguments pertaining to these policies. My analyses include priming and list experiments, as well as difference-in-differences analyses of state-level affirmative action policies and the federal affirmative action law on university students. These analyses provide mixed support, at best, for these alternative arguments, but nonetheless show some added effect of these policies on reclassification. Overall, they suggest that affirmative action cannot be ruled out, but also is not central, to the reclassification reversal.

Chapter 7, the final empirical chapter of the book, draws out the implications of the reclassification reversal for political behavior in Brazil and situates these implications in the context of five presidential elections between 2002 and 2018. Contrary to the common view that race is irrelevant in Brazilian politics, my analyses reveal that highly educated black identifiers – those most likely to exhibit racial consciousness – have come to constitute a loyal leftist constituency in the Brazilian electorate. Finally, the concluding chapter, Chapter 8, situates my findings within and against prevailing theories in the comparative ethnoracial and identity politics literatures, and offers possibilities for extrapolation and generalization from this case. I conclude the book with reflections and speculation on what these findings may hold for the future of Brazilian politics.

NOTES ON RACIAL TERMINOLOGY AND OFFICIAL RACIAL CATEGORIES

Before proceeding, it is worth clarifying my analytical focus on official census categories and the racial terminology I employ throughout this book. First, the analytical and empirical focus of this book is on changes in how individuals choose to self-classify in the official racial categories determined by the state. This is motivated by the empirical puzzle centered in this study, and *should not* be interpreted to mean that identification with official census categories is the most appropriate, or singularly comprehensive, way to measure racial identity in this or any context. Indeed, a rich social science literature has analyzed the resonance of official categories with those employed colloquially (Bailey et al. 2018; Harris et al. 1993; Sheriff 2001; Telles 2004), and the group consciousness literature reminds us that identification is but one aspect of social identities, which vary in their strength of attachment as well as political content and attitudes. Where possible, my analyses go beyond census identification and include analysis of multidimensional measures of racial identity. But by and large, my analyses focus on census categories for the simple and practical reason that they provide the only consistent and longitudinal empirical data source for analyzing and testing claims about the reclassification reversal. A full accounting of the reversal's implications for colloquial racial terminology and discourses would surely be welcome, but this lies beyond the scope of the study at hand.

Second, those familiar with Brazil and other contexts in Latin America know that racial labels must be employed with care and precision. Because my focus is on patterns of census reclassification, I refer to official census categories when I use the words white, black, and brown (*branco, preto*, and *pardo*, respectively). Simply to avoid confusion, I steer clear of other racial labels despite their widespread usage in the Brazilian context. These include the notoriously ambiguous term *moreno* (roughly meaning dark) and *negro*, a label promoted by the black movement that is generally understood to encompass all Afro-descendants, but that can also stand in for black (*preto*) colloquially. When English translation is unclear or obscures some other meaning, I refer to the original Portuguese parenthetically. Additionally, I use the term "mixed-race" interchangeably with brown. And when I use the term "nonwhites," I refer to black and brown identifiers together. I do not include yellow or indigenous census categories among nonwhites, simply because these samples are too small to analyze with precision in my analyses. As a general rule, I refrain from referring to "whites" or "blacks" as self-evident categories or groups (Brubaker 2004), referencing instead white or black *identifiers*. I do this in recognition of the fact that racial categories are simply labels, not inherent or immutable characteristics. For the sake of readability, I at times refer to "black voters," for example. In these instances, such references indicate voters who identify with particular racial categories.

2

The Puzzle of Racial Reclassification

The patterns of racial reclassification introduced in this book only deepen the paradoxical nature of Brazil's racial politics. Indeed, scholars and observers have long invoked Brazil, the emblematic "racial democracy," as evidence of the claim that "race" is not a biological fact but a social construction. The history of miscegenation between Africans, indigenous populations, and Europeans paired with the absence of racial membership rules was said to produce a fluid system of classification rooted in phenotypical variation more than rigid rules of descent, such as in the United States. Fluid racial boundaries have enabled Brazilians to change their racial identifications with relative ease and without controversy. In fact, racial reclassification is not a new phenomenon in Brazilian society. But insofar as this occurred in the past, scholars have argued that rampant discrimination against the darker-skinned and the stigmatization of blackness traditionally led Brazilians to capitalize on racial fluidity in order to *whiten*, or at least lighten, when possible. The patterns that have emerged in recent decades, therefore, do not represent a renewal or intensification of past practices. They mark a sudden reversal of the status quo. Brazilians are increasingly defying the social forces that incentivize whiteness and claiming the devalued labels of blackness.

The purpose of this chapter is to motivate this study by establishing the empirical puzzle, defining the main dependent variable, and situating this "reclassification reversal" within Brazil's broader historical context of race-making and racial subjectivity. Specifically, I detail the contours of these patterns longitudinally and subnationally within Brazil, and I lay to rest simple explanations for the reversal based on census enumeration practices or intergroup differences in demographic trends. What has become abundantly clear instead is that Brazilians have been increasingly adopting darker, and especially black, identities since the 2000s. This does not mean that whitening, or lightening, has ceased to occur altogether; it simply means that, as a form of racial reclassification, whitening is no longer the net tendency among the mass public. Establishing the contours of this phenomenon will clarify the analytical focus of this study and bring into focus its contributions to literatures on racial subjectivity in Brazil and Latin America, as well as the broader identity politics literature in political science. By emphasizing that reclassification patterns have *reversed* in recent decades, this chapter presents trends that run counter to much sociological and anthropological research emphasizing whitening, or aspirations toward whiteness, as the dominant logic influencing racial identification in Brazil and elsewhere. Relatedly for political scientists, these patterns ought to serve as a reminder – and stark example of – the kind of instability that can result from the socially constructed and unstable nature of even racial boundaries, complicating theoretical or analytical reliance on stable demographic structures that are often presumed immutable.

I begin by detailing longitudinal and subnational variations in patterns of racial identification and reclassification in Brazil. I detail national and subnational patterns and consider the possibility that ostensible patterns of reclassification might be artifacts of intergroup differences in demographic trends or changes in census enumeration practices. Having established the puzzle empirically, I then motivate the puzzle theoretically by emphasizing that conventional wisdom from sociology and anthropology expects whitening, partly as an explanation for the apparent paradox of deeply entrenched racial hierarchies and inequalities alongside weakly politicized racial differences. I conclude the chapter with a partial explanation for the reclassification reversal, arguing that this change must be understood in relation to the state's shifting posture on the racial question and social inclusion – a posture that, spanning three centuries, has shifted from scientific racism, to racial democracy, to the contemporary period of racial recognition and social inclusion. What has remained alongside these important shifts in state posture is the influence of the state in shaping racial subjectivity.

THE RECLASSIFICATION REVERSAL

The dependent variable that I seek to explain throughout this book is racial reclassification, that is, *change* in the individual's racial self-identification

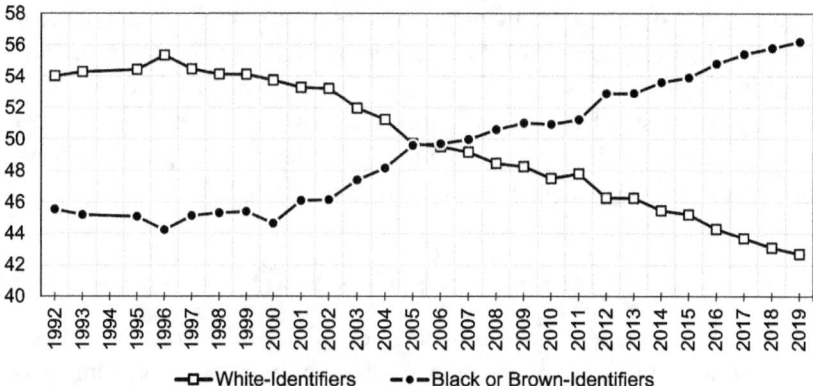

FIGURE 2.1 Racial composition of Brazil, 1992–2019
Sources: *Censo Demográfico*, IBGE; *Pesquisa nacional por amostra de domicílios* (PNAD), IBGE.

over time. Identification refers one's subjective self-classification in a social category. Thus, while reclassification and identification are inherently related, the former is dynamic whereas the latter is static. Aggregate patterns of reclassification are evident in Figure 2.1, which displays the proportion of self-identified white and nonwhite (black or brown) populations between 1992 and 2019. Reclassification is by definition a microlevel phenomenon. But as is evident in Figure 2.1, when a critical mass of individuals chooses to reclassify, these behaviors can scale up to effect significant shifts in national-level demographic structures.

There are several features of note in Figure 2.1. First, the decade prior to the 2000 census is marked by relative stability. The size of white and nonwhite populations did not shift markedly over this period, remaining at roughly 54 and 45 percent, respectively.[1] Second, after the 2000 census, we begin to see notable and steady declines in the white population and corresponding growth in nonwhite populations. By 2007, nonwhite identifiers were estimated to outnumber white-identified Brazilians. And the 2010 census confirmed that between the 2000 and 2010 censuses, Brazil's population flipped from majority- to minority-white, from 54 to 48 percent. Third, after the 2010 census, we continue to observe a steady increase in the nonwhite population and a decrease in the white

---

[1] Though this is true for the last decade of the twentieth century, the mid twentieth century also saw instability in racial composition. See Carvalho et al. 2004; Lovell and Wood 1998; Wood and Carvalho 1994.

population.[2] By 2019, nonwhite identifiers represented a larger share of the population (56 percent) than had white identifiers in the prior three decades (a peak of 55 percent in 1996); and in 2019, white identifiers comprised the smallest share this group saw over this period, 43 percent. Overall, the empirical pattern is unmistakable: Brazil's population has been growing increasingly nonwhite since the early 2000s.

CENSUS ENUMERATION PRACTICES

It is not a foregone conclusion that these shifts in Brazil's racial composition are due to reclassification. Such changes could more simply be explained by changes in the practices employed by the census bureau to measure race and enumerate the population. By the turn of the twenty-first century, nearly every state carried out a decennial census (Loveman 2014). And though the state has been central to theories of the politicization and naturalization of social differences (Bourdieu 1985; Laitin 1986; Marx 1998; Scott 1998), census bureaus in particular have only more recently been scrutinized as mechanisms by which states exert such influence. Recent scholarship characterizes census bureaus as more than just technocratic and apolitical statistical agencies; these are sites where states actively shape social boundaries and identities, especially ethnic and racial ones (Hochschild and Powell 2008; Kertzer and Arel 2002; Loveman 2014; Nobles 2000; Waters 2002; Yanow 2002).[3] Scholars agree that census surveys do not merely reflect social differences, but actively shape, create, or reify them. Putatively objective "demographic" groupings are constructs naturalized by census enumeration, classification schemes, and the legitimacy endowed by state authority (Kertzer and Arel 2002; Loveman 2014; Nobles 2000). The implication of this line of argument is that apparent reclassification may simply be functions of changing enumeration practices on the part of the census bureau, which impact individuals' racial subjectivities.

This line of argument finds a seemingly clear parallel in the Brazilian context. Racial boundaries are generally regarded as weakly institutionalized, and racial categories and labels have been employed inconsistently

---

[2] Data for the 2020 census was set to begin in that year, but this was interrupted by the COVID-19 pandemic. Data collection began in 2021, but continued to be delayed through 2022. As of this writing, data collection had not yet been completed.

[3] Also see Lieberman and Singh (2017) for a discussion of the effects of census enumeration on social identification and subjectivity.

in the state's administration of its citizens, and official racial categories have not always reflected colloquial labels employed more commonly in society (Bailey et al. 2013; Loveman et al. 2012; Monk 2016).[4] Yet there is evidence to support the idea that classifications are sensitive to enumeration practices employed to measure race. Estimates of Brazil's racial composition are sensitive to the specific classification scheme (trichotomous vs. binary racial categories) employed,[5] as well as to whether respondents self-classify or are classified by third parties (Silva 1994; Telles 2004; Telles and Lim 1998). How Brazilians are confronted with the question of racial identification can make Brazil appear more or less white.

While these are valid considerations, any concerns pertaining to census enumeration practices can be allayed by the simple fact that the census bureau's practices have remained constant over the period in question, from 1991 to the present (IBGE 2003, 2016; Loveman 2014; Osorio 2004; Paixão 2009; Petruccelli 2002). Most importantly, the census bureau has consistently relied on a close-ended survey item asking respondents which category best describes their "race or color": white, brown, black, yellow, or indigenous.[6] Moreover, the census bureau has consistently relied on self-declaration to measure race (IBGE 2003, 2016), meaning that we can safely interpret racial classifications on census surveys as a measure of racial identification. This consistency in enumeration practices and racial measurement allows us to rule this out as an explanation for reclassification. We simply cannot explain change with a constant.

---

[4] See Lieberman (2009) on the institutionalization of social boundaries. There is a large anthropological literature on the multiplicity of racial terms employed in Brazil (e.g., Harris 1964b; Harris et al. 1993). For alternative views on the extent to which everyday usage deviates from official categories, see Sheriff (2001) and Telles (2004).

[5] For detailed examination of the census classification schemes in Latin America, see Loveman (2014) and Paixão (2009). See Yanow (2002) for an in-depth analysis of the construction of ethnoracial categories in U.S. public administration and the evolution of classification schemes. See Lee (2009), Masuoka (2017), and Davenport (2018) on how the altering the measurement of race in the United States led to major increases in identification in the mixed race-identified population. And see Irizarry et al. (2023) on the instability of Latino identification in the United States.

[6] In Portuguese, these are *branca, parda, preta, amarela*, and *indígena*. The indigenous category was added in the 1991 census round (Loveman 2014; Paixão 2009) and is included separately from an item inquiring about indigenous languages spoken. This is relevant insofar as it helps to separate those who identify as nonwhite as a result of indigenous, as opposed to African, heritage – both of whom might reasonably opt for the *pardo* (brown) category. See Supplementary Table A1 for detailed information on racial classification schemes employed in Brazilian censuses.

Demographic Trends

A second simple explanation that is harder to rule out completely relates to intergroup differences in demographic trends – in migration, fertility, and mortality. Historically, Brazil was a major destination for international immigrants, predominantly from Africa and Europe (Andrews 2004; Levy 1974; Skidmore 1993), though not exclusively (Lesser 1999). However, since the 1991 census, international migration has accounted for less than 1 percent of Brazil's resident population, and this figure has only since declined. Similarly, mortality statistics do not provide a logical explanation for reclassification. Nonwhite Brazilians are likely to die at similar or higher rates when compared to whites, suggesting that if anything their numbers should be declining in proportion. Fertility statistics, on the other hand, offer prima facie evidence in favor of a demographic explanation: on average, nonwhite women have more children than white women. But a longitudinal view reveals that the racial gap in fertility has been steadily declining for decades, suggesting that the relative proportion of nonwhites ought to be declining, not accelerating.[7]

Figure 2.2, which presents a simple analysis of birth cohorts between the 2000 and 2010 censuses, illustrates the shortcomings of demographic explanations more clearly. Each cluster of bars represents a birth cohort (individuals born in the same decade), and each bar shows the percentage change in the enumerated size of each racial group between the 2000 and 2010 censuses. Among individuals born in the 1990s, for example, the size of the self-identified white population declined by roughly 16 percent between the 2000 and 2010 censuses, and the brown and black populations grew by 23 and 49 percent, respectively. By excluding from these figures anyone born after the 2000 census, these simple comparisons control for any intergroup differences in fertility rates. If no reclassification were taking place, we would expect to see negative growth rates across all racial categories within cohorts, since over time individuals can only exit cohorts via mortality or migration. Yet several observations undermine demographic explanations.

First and notably, there are sizable and negative growth rates for self-identified whites in all cohorts. This means we cannot attribute the decline in the white population to exceedingly high mortality rates among elderly whites, for example, since white-identifiers decline at similar rates

---

[7] See Appendix A (available online) for descriptive statistics of all demographic trends.

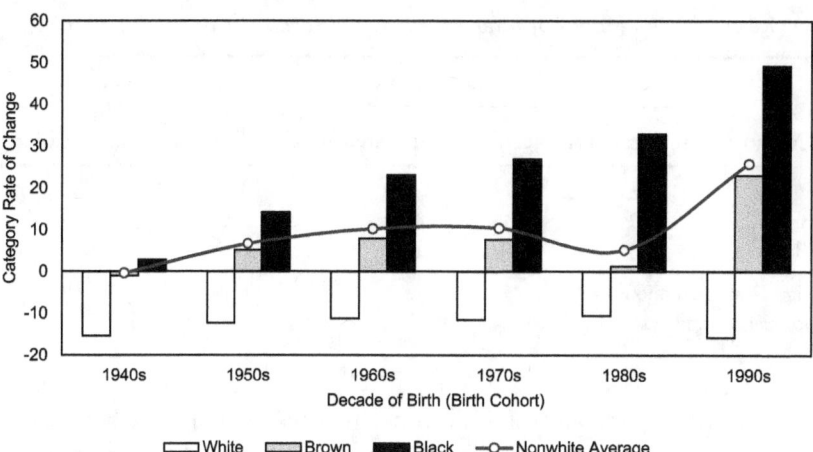

FIGURE 2.2 Percentage change in racial category between 2000 and 2010 by birth cohort
Source: IBGE. Each cluster of bars (1940s, 1950s, etc.) represents one cohort based on decade of birth. Each bar represents the percentage change in the size of each racial category between the 2000 and 2010 censuses, as determined by individuals' self-classifications.

regardless of age.[8] Second, there are positive and large growth rates among black and brown identifiers. This finding is difficult to square with mortality statistics, which indicate that nonwhite Brazilians die at much higher rates than white Brazilians. If anything, then, black and brown categories should see larger decreases over this period, and certainly not growth. Third, there is an ostensible relationship between decade of birth and the likelihood of reclassification into nonwhite categories, with higher growth rates among younger cohorts. One important caveat is that individuals born in the 1990s were likely classified by parents (or heads of household) in the 2000 census round, and are more likely to self-classify in the 2010 census round. The large increase in black and brown categories in this cohort, then, may not exclusively reflect changes individuals' self-conception per se; but this may nonetheless signal intergenerational differences in the logics of racial classification that are still germane to this study. Finally, remarkable as well is that the largest growth rates are found in the black category, historically the most stigmatized racial category.

---

[8] See Supplementary Table A3. This finding does not comport with mortality statistics, which show that the elderly die at much greater rates.

TABLE 2.1 *Estimates of inter-census racial reclassification, 2000–2010*

Category	2000 Enumerated	2010 (aged 10+) Projected	2010 (aged 10+) Enumerated	Change due to Reclassification	% Change due to Reclassification
White	92.0	88.1	77.8	−10.3	−12
Brown	65.8	62.6	68.8	6.2	10
Black	10.6	9.9	13.0	3.1	31

Figures are in millions.
Source: Miranda (2015).

In sum, simple cohort analysis does not bear out the predictions of demographic trends, something also confirmed by cohort component analysis presented in Table 2.1.[9] This more rigorous demographic method computes projections for the 2010 population based on demographic trends observed in the 2000 census, and compares these estimates against the populations enumerated in the 2010 census. This analysis bears out the same pattern as the simple cohort analysis earlier, showing the white population to be smaller and black and brown populations larger than expected. Specifically, this analysis estimates that roughly 10 percent of self-identified browns and 31 percent of self-identified blacks are comprised of reclassifiers. What these analyses make clear is that the apparent patterns of reclassification cannot be dismissed as artifacts of census practices or demographic trends. What demands explanation, then, is not *if* Brazilians are reclassifying toward blackness, but *why*.[10]

---

[9] This table is reproduced from Miranda's (2015) cohort component analysis. Also see Soares (2008) and Jesus and Hoffman (2020) for documentation of reclassification patterns in Brazil, as well as Loveman and Muniz (2007) and Seawright and Barrenechea (2021) for analogous studies of racial reclassification in similar contexts.

[10] Ethnic or racial reclassification is not unique to the Brazilian context, though the study of the phenomenon is far more common in sociology and anthropology than political science. This is partly due to the emphasis on boundary construction, maintenance, and decline in these disciplines (Barth 1969; Loveman 1999; Weber 1978), which lend themselves to problematize social boundaries. Political scientists, by contrast, more commonly treat boundaries as fixed in the short-term or constructed in the distant past. Such an approach enables the preoccupation with explaining the "political salience" of one type of social difference over another: linguistic over tribal differences, or racial over class differences (e.g., Huber 2017; Laitin 1986, 1998; Posner 2005). In any case, reclassification has been known to happen even in contexts with rigid and institutionalized ethnoracial boundaries, such as the United States. See, for example, Davenport (2018), Masuoka (2017), Nagel (1996), Saperstein and Penner (2012), and Waters (1990, 1999).

Subnational Variation?

Beyond longitudinal variation at the national level, rates of reclassification after 2000 appear to vary subnationally as well. Figure 2.3 displays the difference in the relative proportion of the white population by state, sorted by major geographic region in Brazil. The figure illustrates the wide variation in apparent racial reclassification across states in Brazil, ranging from a roughly 1 percent change in the northeastern state of Rio Grande do Norte to more than 8 percent in the central state of Goiás and southeastern state of Minas Gerais. At first glance, reclassification appears to vary greatly across states, but it is important to interpret these statistics with some care. First, many states with high rates of reclassification are located in the south and southeast regions. Historically, these states were majority white-identified, perhaps raising the ceiling on the

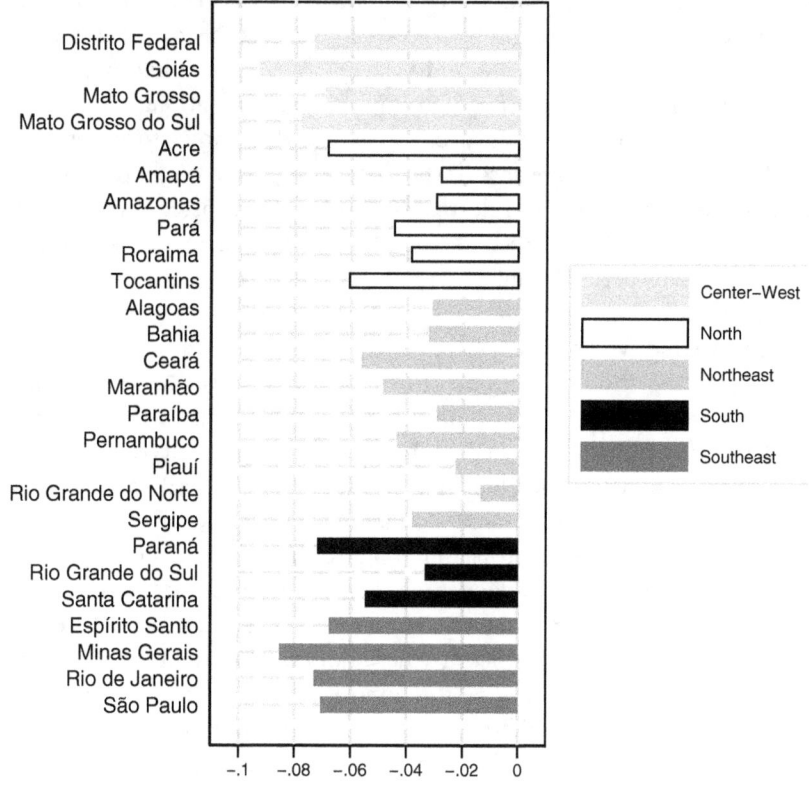

FIGURE 2.3 Inter-census difference in white population, 2000–2010
Source: IBGE.

possibility for reclassification into nonwhite categories. The reverse could be said of northern and northeastern states – historically home to majority nonwhite populations – though these states exhibit wider variation. These differences might simply be a function, then, of baseline proportions: given the same number of reclassifiers, states with a larger baseline share of nonwhites will exhibit smaller rates of reclassification, and vice versa.

Second, unlike national-level statistics presented in Figure 2.1, these statistics do not effectively control for patterns of migration within Brazil, likely a major source of state-level change in racial demography. Historically, the industrialization and economic growth of southeastern states, especially São Paulo (Weinstein 2015), attracted largescale migration from the impoverished northern and northeastern states, previously dominated by rural and slave economies. At the same time, however, since the 2000s there has been a significant trend of "reverse migration," in which southeastern residents have returned to northern and northeastern regions as these regions have seen greater levels of development and economic opportunities (Cunha 2015). We cannot rule out internal migration as a significant factor impacting subnational variation, but there is also reason to suspect this is not the whole story. On one hand, if we assumed no reclassification, then migration ought to produce increases in some states and decreases in others, but instead we observe growth across all states. Second, the phenomenon of reverse migration observed in this period (Cunha 2015) would suggest larger growth in the north and northeast and smaller growth in the south and southeast, but nor is this what we observe.

We perhaps should not place too much weight on these patterns, but they are still worth analyzing for two reasons. First, scholars have emphasized regional differences in racial boundary fluidity that do not map onto these patterns (McNamee 2020; Monk 2013; Telles 1993). Telles (2004) suggests that racial boundaries are less porous in southern regions of Brazil, where European immigration was more prevalent, and more porous in northern regions, where miscegenation was more widespread. Following this logic, we might expect reclassification to be especially prominent in the northeast, where boundaries are in theory easier to cross. But again, we observe the opposite trend, with states in other regions exhibiting the highest rates of reclassification. Second, this variation simply provides useful empirical leverage that can be used to test hypotheses about the causes of reclassification. Prevailing ideas about internal migration or regional differences in boundary fluidity may not, on their face, provide compelling explanations. But these patterns can nonetheless be mined for insights into the causes and timing of the reclassification reversal.

THE VIEW FROM ABOVE: THREE ERAS OF RACIAL STATE POLICY

Situated in historical context, the reclassification reversal can be understood as the most recent development in Brazil's racial politics, corresponding to major shifts in the state's posture toward the racial question. In the past, scholars have often pointed to the state's immigration and development policies, as well as its efforts at building national identity, as explanations for large demographic shifts in the Brazilian population. The state's posture toward the racial question thus becomes a natural point of departure for situating the reclassification reversal in its domestic context.

In the next chapter, I will argue that the reclassification reversal cannot be understood without consideration for the role of the state in processes of identity formation. Historically in Brazil, like elsewhere in Latin America, the state's posture on the racial question has evolved significantly, and at each step along the way has impacted the salience of racial boundaries and differences and the logics and strategies that inform individuals' racial identifications. Scholars have argued that this is especially true in the Brazilian case (Loveman 2014; Paschel 2016a), but the centrality of the state to such questions also finds parallels in cases across Latin America, including in the Andes, Mexico and Central America (Mattiace 2003; Yashar 2005). A key question with regard to the reclassification reversal, therefore, is how these patterns can be understood in relation to the state and the evolution of its posture toward the racial question. Placed in broader historical context, the reclassification reversal can be understood alongside shifting state policy, as simply the latest instance of racial change and transformation that has spanned three centuries in Brazil.

From the nineteenth to the twenty-first century, the Brazilian state evolved significantly in its approach to race. In the aftermath of abolition in 1888, Brazilian elites were heavily influenced by the international eugenics movement, which associated national progress and development with whiteness, and racial miscegenation with backwardness and perpetual underdevelopment (Loveman 2014; Skidmore 1993; Stepan 1991). Anxious about their large mixed-race population, state and scientific elites carved out their own racial theories of development that both subscribed to eugenic race thinking that cast European whites as categorically superior, and that elevated race mixture as a pathway toward whiteness (Stepan 1991). This racial thinking led to largescale immigration projects around the turn of the twentieth century, as well as the embrace of racial democracy in the mid twentieth century. But by the end of the Cold War, as international norms shifted toward the embrace of democracy and multiculturalism, the state shifted its posture once again, remarkably recognizing racial differences and implementing policies to redress racial inequities. In one sense, the Brazilian state has shifted quite dramatically in its approach to the racial question. In another, there has been continuity in the state's response and subscription to international norms in how best to become a modern – and now democratic – state.

Scientific Racism (1880s–1930s)

Current historical research estimates that forty percent of enslaved Africans arrived to Brazilian shores, making Brazil the single-largest destination of enslaved Africans in the slave trade (Andrews 2004). Following the peaceful abolition of slavery in 1888 (making it the last country in the Americas to do so) and the dissolution of the monarchy in 1889, Brazil's intense participation in the slave trade left the country with a large Afro-descendant population in the period of its first oligarchic republic. Data from Brazil's 1872 census place the combined black, mulatto, and Indian population at 62 percent, and the white population at 38 percent (Santos 2002). By 1890, the white population increased to 44 percent, but whites remained a numerical minority. As Brazil transitioned from monarchy to republic in 1889, the demographic picture, as elites saw it, was that the black and mixed-race populations outnumbered Europeans.

The numerical minority status of European descendants posed a dilemma to elites in the first republic, who had not yet consolidated state authority or a national community that could offer legitimacy or advance economic development (Centeno 2002; Marx 1998). Simultaneous to the forging of Brazil's nation-state, political and scientific elites – seeking to consolidate the state and pursue economic development for the nation – were heavily influenced by the international eugenics movement emanating from Europe, in which Latin American thinkers were not dominant players (Loveman 2014). The key idea of this movement, known today as scientific racism, was that national progress and civilization were functions of the inherent capacities of a population's racial stock. European nations were developed and civilized, the logic went, because of their inherent racial superiority. The human population was fundamentally understood as divisible into finite sets of mutually exclusive "races," which could be sorted into a clear hierarchy. Amerindians and Africans were placed near the bottom, yet worse still were the racially mixed, who eugenicists at the time believed to be degenerate. Thus, despite colonization by Europeans, Latin American populations were perceived as backward and undeveloped as a result of their large African, indigenous, and racially mixed populations. Brazilian elites, like others in Latin America, feared that their populations would pass on their racial unfitness to future generations, creating an insurmountable obstacle to national progress (Stepan 1991).

Facing these doomed prospects, state and scientific elites managed to both accept and innovate upon the basic tenet of the eugenics movement – that European whiteness was categorically and inherently superior to other races, more racially fit for economic development. Elites in Latin America embraced an alternative, neo-Lamarckian genetic logic (Stepan 1991) that viewed whiteness as the key to prosperity, but they also believed that whiteness was attainable through eugenic policies aimed at shaping the population's genetic stock. A prominent example of this view is the writing of João Batista de Lacerda, a prominent doctor and biomedical scientist who traveled to London in 1911 as the Brazilian delegate to the First Universal Races Congress – a conference of scholars and delegates from around the world to discuss issues of anti-racism.[11] At the time of the Congress, the prevalence of race mixture in Brazil had earned the country the ignoble title "the laboratory of the races" (Schwarcz 2011), an image that Brazilian elites hoped to reverse. In a paper titled "On the *mestiço* in Brazil," Lacerda put forth this logic:

Sexual selection always continues toward perfection by subjugating atavism and purging the descendants of *mestiços* of all the trace characteristics of the negro. Thanks to this process of ethnic reduction, it is logical to suppose that in one century's time *mestiços* will disappear from Brazil, a fact that will coincide with the parallel extinction of the negro race among us. (Schwarcz 2011, 239)

Lacerda's prediction contains the embrace of whiteness as "perfection," but also departs from prevailing race science by suggesting that race mixture was the *solution* to, not the cause of, the nation's racial backwardness.

---

[11] Participants included W.E.B DuBois and Franz Boas.

Though today it is obvious Lacerda's prediction would never come to pass, this idea that race mixture could produce a lighter, and eventually a white, population gave elites optimism about the future of their nation and instigated state policies of "whitening" (Loveman 2014; Skidmore 1993; Stepan 1991). Brazil was no longer doomed to perpetual backwardness. By *encouraging* race mixture, the population's less desirable (i.e., African) traits could be replaced by more desirable (i.e., European) ones, setting the nation on the path to progress. While according to Lacerda's logic Brazil was already firmly on this path, elites believed, or at least hoped, that his process of replacement could be accelerated by increasing the nation's share of European racial stock.

Immigration policy became a core piece of this strategy and sought, explicitly and implicitly, to encourage immigration from Western and Southern Europe and to limit immigration from countries that would not advance this goal. Even as early as 1891, immigration policy sought to restrict immigration by country of origin (Skidmore 1993, 197), and as the country entered the twentieth century, immigration policy succeeded in attracting European migrants to Brazil. The census of 1872 enumerated fewer than 400 thousand foreign residents in total. But between 1872 and 1903, nearly 2 million immigrated to Brazil, and a similar figure is reported for the period between 1904 and 1930. By 1972, an estimated 5 million immigrants had arrived to Brazil in the previous century, nearly 80 percent of whom hailed from Portugal, Italy, Spain, or Germany (Levy 1974). The result was at least a more European population, even if the neo-Lamarckian logic of whitening would not prove true.

In sum, the period of Brazil's first republic coincided with the prevalence of scientific racism in international epistemic communities, and the state's posture on the racial question reflected that. Responding to the initially pessimistic outlook for national progress, Brazilian elites accepted, but innovated upon, the eugenics movement to devise its own pathway to national progress. The belief that elites could eliminate African traces from the population by encouraging race mixture led the state to adopt immigration policies that would attract white Europeans and accelerate the eugenic process. Insofar as racial state policy had any impact on racial identification or demography in this era, it could be seen in immigration policy and the efforts to simply inject more Europeans into the national population. And, by encouraging race mixture, the state implored the population to participate in the eugenic process of absorbing and ridding the population of blackness. Eventually, scientific racism would lose international legitimacy, and the state's posture would shift in response to changing international norms around modern statehood. Race mixture, however, would remain central to Brazil's national image.

Racial Democracy (1930s–1980s)

Eventually, the state's posture toward the racial question would shift to embrace "racial democracy," or the notion that Brazil is a post-racial society born from the mixture of African, indigenous, and European peoples. Racial democracy is widely attributed to the writings of one academic, Brazilian anthropologist Gilberto Freyre, who hailed from the plantation societies of the Brazilian northeast and who studied under early critic of scientific racism, Franz Boas. Freyre's most influential work, *Casa-Grande e Senzala*, published in 1933 and translated to English as *The Masters and the Slaves*, is regarded today as a revisionist text arguing that Brazil experienced a benign form of slavery, bequeathing widespread race mixture, harmonious race relations, and fluid racial boundaries. Freyre's work departed from the biological fatalism of race science by bucking the view that racial mixture produced degeneracy. Instead, race mixture produced a "meta-race," a new human type that fused the best elements of African, European, and indigenous cultures. As Telles (2004) notes, Freyre's ideas did not fully depart from those of whitening; miscegenation was fueled by the hope that mixture would produce whiteness, and Freyre himself claimed miscegenation was leading Afro-descendants to disappear into the Brazilian population (Telles 2004, 34). Nonetheless, Freyre's ideas helped to establish the image of Brazilian society as racially harmonious, and that all Brazilians, regardless of their physical appearances, shared the same racial heritage. In Freyre's words, "Every Brazilian, even the light-skinned fair-haired one, carries about with him on his soul ... the shadow, or at least the birthmark, of the aborigine or the Negro" (Freyre 1986, 278).

The shift away from scientific racism and toward racial democracy was brought about by two changes in the international social and political environment. The first is the economic shock caused by the Great Depression in 1929, and the second was the aftermath of World War II. The Great Depression set off a period of economic and political instability in Brazil, culminating in the Revolution of 1930. In response to a collapse in coffee prices, an alliance of economic elites and the military brought an end to the oligarchic first republic, and installed populist leader Getúlio Vargas in power. Like many populist leaders of the time,

Vargas rose to power in an era of rapid urbanization and growing class conflict and sought to address economic turmoil through state intervention and labor-based populism (Collier and Collier 2002; Conniff 1981). In this context, Vargas sought national cultural symbols that could unify the population and serve his goals of economic growth and consolidated black and labor support (Andrews 2004, 165–68).

Adding to the economic and political imperatives was the second international change, the discreditation of eugenic race science beginning in the 1920s and finally in the aftermath of World War II. By the 1920s Mendelian genetics had come to challenge the views of neo-Lamarckians, but by this point Latin American elites were increasingly critical of race concepts altogether. At the First Brazilian Eugenics Conference in 1929, for example, participants debated whether miscegenation with black Brazilians would produce degeneracy. Though fears of degeneracy were still in circulation, the president of the conference argued against these deterministic predictions. Instead, ideas on the innate inequality of races were replaced by environmentalist theories that saw all individuals as innately equal and that recast "degeneracy" as products of social and economic forces – as acquired behaviors rather than inherited racial traits (Dávila 2003; Stepan 1991). Social policy addressing "the racial question" shifted away from eugenics and toward an emphasis on public hygiene and social policy (Telles 2004, 32–33). The final death knell for race science came in the aftermath of World War II, when the consequences of race science were brought to their logical and terrifying conclusions. Indeed, it was in the wake of World War II that the UN Educational, Scientific, and Cultural Organization (UNESCO) was formed. UNESCO released an official statement on the concept of race, which stated that "mankind is one," that race is a social myth, and that race mixture did not produce degeneracy (Loveman 2014, 219–20).

In the shifting international and domestic context of the 1930s onward, the idea of national unity through race mixture proved strategically useful to populist dictator Vargas, who again sought to unite political support from black and labor organizations. If Brazil's oligarchic first republic was defined by efforts at eugenic and cultural whitening, then Brazil's second republic under Vargas was defined by the incorporation of black and African cultural elements into a singular national culture. Vargas was the first leader to embrace many cultural traditions associated with African heritage and that continue to define international perceptions of Brazilian culture. *Carnaval*, *capoeira*, and African religions, all of which were repressed in the first republic, were now celebrated and elevated, displaying Brazil's racial conviviality for the world to see. Ideas about race mixture and Brazil's unique cultural fusion were also instilled in the public in the country's first national education curriculum, standardized and promoted through the newly formed Ministry of Education (Dávila 2003). At the same time, racial democracy also comported with the increasingly dominant view that race was a social and cultural product, rather than a biologically determined and deterministic one. Thus, for both political and scientific communities, racial democracy served the dual purposes of defining a national community and advancing Brazil's international status among civilized and modern nations (Andrews 2004; Loveman 2014).

In the mix of these forces and influences, myths of racial democracy took hold in Brazil and elsewhere in Latin America. Though they would later change their tune, even black intellectuals and activists in the mid twentieth century subscribed to and embraced the ideals of the racial democracy thesis (Alberto 2011). And through considerable political instability in the middle decades of the twentieth century, the idea of racial democracy offered a measure of continuity. Vargas, partly responsible for popularizing racial democracy by engaging in Brazil's earliest efforts at nation-building, was ousted from power in 1945. The following two decades were marked by leftist mobilization and right-wing reactionism, producing urban violence that often provided justification for military interventions and democratic interruptions. Political stability would arrive in 1964 in the form of a military coup, which installed the military in power until 1985. Through all of these major political changes and interruptions, governments and regimes would consistently maintain the myth of racial democracy.

From one perspective, racial democracy provided a ready-made basis for military regimes in particular to pursue what they likely saw as higher order concerns related to economic stability and national development. As for Vargas, the symbolic resources of a national community helped the state and regime maintain legitimacy and political support. Formal protections appeared, at least at first glance, to reflect this national image: constitutions of 1934 and 1946 stressed equality before the law regardless of color; a 1951 law outlawed racial discrimination; and in the 1950s and 60s Brazil ratified UN conventions that provided protections to victims of racism. Critics of racial democracy counter, however, that more than simply aiding national development goals, the national myth provided a ready-made discourse to disarticulate racial inequalities and discrimination, and permitted the state to pursue development while ignoring inequities. According to some, this "racial silence" (Fischer et al. 2018) also allowed the state to quietly continue promoting whitening and commonsense racial hierarchies that valorized whiteness. Black activists like Abdias do Nascimento, for example, deemed genocidal the unwillingness of the state to address issues that led to black suffering and mortality (Nascimento 2016; Nascimento 1989). Indeed, even under Vargas, who is so associated with Brazilian nationalism, the outward embrace of black culture coexisted with immigration policies that preserved the desire for whiteness: in 1945, shortly before his ouster, Vargas decreed that immigration should "preserve and develop ... the more desirable characteristics of its European ancestry" (Skidmore 1993, 199). Without any policy issued to replace it, Vargas's decree remained in force for much of the twentieth century, when successive governments simply inherited the racial democracy position.

By the end of the twentieth century, the era of racial democracy came to be defined by its contradictions. On one hand, the official position of the state and the perception of the international community was that Brazil had developed an enviable national identity rooted in racial unity born from race mixture. The state proudly promoted its image as a racial paradise that codified legal protections against racial discrimination – at least on paper. Brazilian elites, moreover, welcomed favorable comparisons to Nazi (Germany), Apartheid (South Africa), and Jim Crow (Southern United States), which buttressed Brazil's claims of superior race relations. At home and abroad, state elites from the military regime rejected notions of inherent racial differences or superiority, insisted that racism did not exist in Brazil, and elevated the racially mixed Brazilian as the symbol of the nation (Telles 2004, 40–42).

But on the other hand, the Brazilian state did little to realize the promises of racial democracy and suppressed efforts to publicize its shortcomings. Vargas' embrace of racial democracy culturally and in racial legal equality in his 1934 constitution was belied by his immigration policies, which sought to limit African immigration to the country and perpetuated the goals of whitening. And while the military regime proudly touted the racial democracy myth, it did nothing to address longstanding racial inequalities, banned discussion of race in Brazilian universities, and suppressed the black movement and civil society efforts to express dissent on the issue, driving many academics and activists into exile (Gonzalez 1982, 1985; Hanchard 1994). And in the 1970 census, the first census conducted under the military regime, racial classification questions were removed from the census questionnaire (Loveman 2014;

Nobles 2000). The regime cited the absence of racial discrimination as justification for not collecting racial statistics that could confirm or undermine this alleged fact. In the end, racial democracy would come to be praised for the world it imagined, and simultaneously derided for the harsh realities it disguised.

Democracy and Affirmative Action (1980s to Present)

Racial democracy, like the race science thinking that preceded it, would eventually give way to a third era of racial state policy characterized by multiculturalism and explicit recognition of racial inequalities and discrimination. By the 2000s, the Brazilian state and elites would not only move away from the homogenizing discourse of unity through mixture, but it would actively promote affirmative action policies for Afrodescendants. As has been well established, this sharp departure from the colorblindness of the racial democracy era tracks, once again, with shifts in international norms on "the racial question" and ideas of modern state and nationhood (Htun 2004; Loveman 2014; Paschel 2016a). But this shift was also the culmination of decades of activism carried out by black social movements in particular, who made it their mission to publicize hard truths about racial democracy, and to attempt to shift the state's posture in a direction that permitted dissent from the discourse that had become ingrained in the Brazilian imaginary.

Racial democracy began to come under attack in the 1970s and 1980s, as empirical data came to light that cast serious doubt on the realities of the national myth. Earlier studies, for example, by Florestan Fernandes (1965) and UNESCO researchers (Wagley 1952) examining Brazilian society had identified racial inequalities, but these studies contained a degree of optimism. For example, a team of UNESCO-sponsored anthropologists who set out to analyze Brazilian race relations after World War II indeed found patterns of racial stratification and discrimination in the countryside, but they cast these as secondary to the class structure of Brazilian society. Similarly, Brazilian sociologist Florestan Fernandes published his work *The Integration of the Negro in Brazilian Society* in 1965, which similarly documented persistent racial inequalities. But Fernandes attributed this to the legacies of slavery, and argued that these inequalities would disappear as capitalist development advanced.

A second wave of research, however, came to different conclusions. Pioneering research by Nelson do Valle Silva and Carlos Hasenbalg took more direct aim at racial democracy. Armed with sophisticated quantitative tools and census data, these authors identified deep racial inequalities in the labor market and in education, finding that black and mixed-race Brazilians suffered similarly to whites, and that income inequalities increased as nonwhites ascended socially (Hasenbalg 1979; Silva 1978).[12] Unlike prior scholarship on racial inequality in Brazil, these authors did not reduce racial inequalities to class structure or the residue of slavery; they centered race and discrimination as the causes of these inequalities, thus painting racial democracy in negative light. As Silva wrote in 1978, "the prospects for racial equality in Brazil seem to be quite remote, a fact that is reinforced by the extraordinary resilience of the 'racial democracy' myth in that country" (Silva 1978, 216). In light of this evidence, black movement activists who once were inspired by racial democracy had come to view it as a more nefarious force in Brazilian society, something they needed to rally against (Alberto 2011).

Such mobilization and dissent were also made possible by the timing of this new evidence, which corresponded to the *abertura* of Brazil's military dictatorship. Beginning in 1974, the military regime began allowing an officially sanctioned opposition party to compete in congressional elections, which began a slow transition toward democracy. In 1985, when the military regime lost its election to the opposition party, the military regime agreed to step down from power and restore civil rule. In the next four years, Brazil would hold a constitutional convention with the participation of social movements, ratify a new and progressive federal constitution, and restore democratic civil rights (Garay 2016). The political arena thus became significantly less repressive, allowing academics, activists, social movements, and international organizations to wage major campaigns against racial democracy (Bailey 2009; Hanchard 1994; Telles 2004). Alongside these domestic political shifts were also shifts in international norms around modern nationhood and multiculturalism. Whereas in the mid twentieth century homogenous national communities were seen as promoting modernization, recognition of ethnoracial (among other) differences and inequalities became marks of modern and democratic states (Loveman 2014).

This shift in domestic and international context once again provided an opportunity for elites to shift their posture on the racial question, and for civil society actors to push for this change from below (Htun 2004; Paschel 2016a). These pressures would be especially well received after

---

[12] Early studies scrutinizing racial democracy include Cardoso and Ianni (1960), Dzidzienyo (1979), Fernandes (1965), Hasenbalg (1979), Mitchell (1977), and Silva (1985).

Fernando Henrique Cardoso assumed the presidency in 1995. Indeed, Cardoso, who was driven into exile during the military regime, had a prior career as a sociologist at the University of São Paulo (USP). Though as a scholar he is best known for his work in international political economy (Cardoso and Faletto 1979) and arguably won the presidency on this basis, Cardoso studied under Florestan Fernandes at USP, and his early scholarship focused on race relations (Cardoso and Ianni 1960). Thus, it is no surprise that Cardoso's discourse on race marked a departure from the denialism and colorblindness of the military dictatorship. In his inaugural address in 1995, for example, Cardoso declared: "We will enthusiastically ensure equal rights for the equal: for women, who are the majority of our people and whom the country owes respect and opportunities for education and work; for racial minorities and near-minorities – for blacks, principally – who hope equality is more than just a word, but a portrait of reality" (Cardoso 1995a). Though it would be a stretch to say Cardoso was hostile to the ideas of racial democracy,[13] his discourse no doubt represented a symbolic break with the past. Under Cardoso, the state would no longer emphasize mixture to gloss over deep and persistent inequalities or discrimination; it now recognized racial differences and blacks, in particular, as deserving of equality and respect.

By the early 2000s, activist pressures from below converged with the political will of the state to produce watershed policy change in Brazil. The most stunning change occurred in advance of Brazil's participation in the UN Conference on Race and Racism held in Durban in 2001. Social movement actors – cognizant of the opportunity to present a new Brazilian posture on the world stage and of the state's desire not to suffer the embarrassment of international protest by activists – mobilized to apply pressure on Cardoso to reckon with Brazil's past (Htun 2004). Cardoso complied, and in the December before the conference in Durban, Cardoso gave a speech in which he formally endorsed race-targeted affirmative action policies, saying: "The Brazilian state recognizes the painful consequences that slavery caused in Brazil and will continue to aspire to repair them through public policies that promote equality of opportunity ... affirmative policies in favor of Afro-descendants" (Cardoso 2001).

Cardoso's statement shocked observers at home and abroad, few of whom expected a reversal of the state's racial democracy posture. But this was only the first of many institutional changes that would characterize

---

[13] Cardoso authored a glowing forward to the 2003 edition of Freyre's *Casa-Grande e Senzala*.

Brazil's new era of racialized democracy. Affirmative action policies would become a reality, beginning at the state level in 2001 and eventually federally in 2012. In 2003, federal law would mandate the teaching of African and Afro-Brazilian history as part of the national education curriculum. And by 2011, November 13th would be made a national holiday as Black Consciousness Day. These initiatives got their start under Cardoso and were continued and furthered under leftist Workers' Party governments beginning in 2003. Though not widely publicized, affirmative action and social inclusion would become institutionalized in a variety of educational policies and programs designed to increase educational access for the disadvantaged, such as federal grant and loan programs for private universities in Brazil (ProUni and FIES).

All in all, affirmative action policies, more than anything else, have come to symbolize the shift in racial state policy of Brazil's democratic era since the 1980s. Of course, Brazil remains one of the most unequal and racially stratified societies in the world. But as Brazil entered the twenty-first century, it has evolved in ways that positioned the country in sharp contrast to its past of scientific racism and the non-racialism of racial democracy. Insofar as state policy and discourse is a central component of reclassification, this recent era clearly tracks with the reclassification reversal, which made itself apparent in the 2000s. While such a state-centric perspective might seem to be explanation enough, such macro-level change leaves unanswered important questions that serve to sharpen the puzzle of the reclassification reversal. Above all, the question that the view from above does not address is how such macro-level change impacts the informal patterns and behaviors that have for so long been seen as central to the maintenance and reproduction of racial hierarchies in Brazil.

THE VIEW FROM BELOW: FLUIDITY, COLORISM, AND INFORMAL RACISM

While whitening may not have always been the publicly stated motivation of the Brazilian state, it has been a key force behind microlevel patterns of identification and reclassification. In fact, reclassification is not itself a new phenomenon in Brazil or Latin America, nor more broadly in the Western Hemisphere.[14] In comparative studies of racial politics, Brazil is often characterized in contrast to the rigid racial boundaries found in the United States

---

[14] See Carvalho, Wood, and Andrade (2004); Loveman and Muniz (2007); Seawright and Barrenechea (2021); Wood and Carvalho (1994). For analogous patterns in the United States, see Waters (2002) and Saperstein and Penner (2012). Masuoka (2017)

and South Africa (Davis 2001; Lieberman 2009). High rates of miscegenation and the absence of racial group membership rules were said to have produced a fluid system of classification in which Brazilians self-identify according to flexible phenotypical criteria, rather than rigid descent rules (Guimarães 1999; Harris 1964b; Nogueira 1998; Telles 2004). As a result, Brazilians possess rich lexicons to describe racial (or "color") differences, including labels that deviate from official census categories (Harris 1970; Harris et al. 1993; Silva 1996; Telles 2004). Moreover, the subjective understanding of race is intertwined with notions of class, what scholars refer to as "social race" (Degler 1971; Harris 1964a; Wagley 1965). As Nelson do Valle Silva describes, "given some phenotypic combination, the higher the socioeconomic position of the individual at the moment of classification, she will be classified that much closer to white" (Silva 1994, 70).[15] This complexity and ambiguity, therefore, enables individuals to place themselves in categories different from those ascribed to them, as well as to change their racial identifications over time.

But to the extent reclassification occurred in the past, it traditionally reflected practices known as whitening. Conventional wisdom holds and empirical analyses have shown that Brazilians traditionally capitalize on racial fluidity to reclassify in lighter categories.[16] Indeed, anthropology and sociology are replete with examples documenting the phenomenon, captured in the saying, "Money whitens." As Cardoso and Ianni write in their study of race relations in southern Brazil, whitening "is a 'universal' aspiration. Blacks, dark mulattoes, and many light mulattoes – all want to whiten" (Cardoso and Ianni 1960, 183; also see Schwartzman 2007). Given this context, an individual's racial self-identification may indicate a genuine self-conception, but it may also be a strategy for evading the

---

and Davenport (2018) also provide analyses of growing "multiracial" populations in the United States, enabled by institutional changes in racial measurement. These authors emphasize the ambiguity of racial identifications even in a context known for rules of hypodescent and rigid racial boundaries. Both authors emphasize subjectivity and identity choice in patterns of racial identification in this context and emphasize the centrality of individuals' subjective self-understandings behind the recent growth of multiracial identifiers in the United States.

[15] Author's translation.
[16] For microlevel analysis, see Silva 1994; Telles 2004, chap. 4; Telles and Lim 1998. For macrolevel analysis, see Carvalho et al. 2004; Lovell 1999; Wood and Carvalho 1994. It should be noted that these studies also uncover decreases in the white population, with net gain only in the brown population. Because the black population decreases by a much larger percentage (if not number), the authors conclude that lightening is more prevalent than darkening.

stigma associated with blackness. This aligns with the interpretation illuminated in Marvin Harris's ethnographic evidence from rural Brazil:

> The Negro in Minas Velhas attempts to 'pass' not by posing as white but by posing as anything but a Negro – as a dark *moreno*, or *chulo*, or *caboclo*, etc. If these categories do not suffice he is liable to invent new ones. For example, a Negro storekeeper named Antonio who is well educated by local standards, fairly prosperous and active politically, never refers to himself as *preto* [black], though physically he has every reason to do so. He prefers rather the original – and euphemistic – term *roxinho* [a little purple] and alludes to his son as 'that slightly purple fellow over there'. *Each individual twists as well as he can away from complete identification with the lowest echelon of the social order*. The Negro has the opportunity of saying first, 'My hair is not that kinky', or 'My lips are not that big', or 'My colour is not that black'; and second, 'I may look like that picture but I am not as poor, or as illiterate, as he probably is. Therefore, I am not like him'. (Harris 1952, 60. Emphasis added.)

Of course, Harris is referring to informal identifications and not official census categories, and this example suggests that, for some individuals, whiteness might be out of reach. But the important point is that even individuals who ostensibly meet phenotypical understandings of blackness can deploy any logics or strategies at their disposal in order to distance themselves from blackness, "the lowest echelon of the social order." More recent anthropological studies have uncovered a similar "yearning to escape all that is negatively associated with blackness" (Sheriff 2001, 31; also see Burdick 1998a; Twine 1998; Hordge-Freeman 2015). Fluidity and ambiguity of course permit such an escape. But we also should not lose sight of the fact that these individuals inevitably help reproduce racial hierarchies by reinforcing the view that whiteness is desirable and preferred.

The notion that racial identification can reflect a stigma-minimizing strategy finds broad support. Carl Degler (1971), for example, famously characterized mixed-race identification in Brazil as an "escape-hatch," and ethnographers have long documented the ways darker-skinned Brazilians are socialized to internalize racial hierarchies and participate in their reproduction.[17] Hanchard (1994), for example, argues that they fail to confront racism and tend to interpret discrimination as class-based; Sheriff (2001) documents how many Brazilians consider it "impolite" to refer to friends and neighbors as black (also see Nogueira 1998); and Hordge-Freeman documents how these dynamics play out even

---

[17] This is a dynamic that parallels Fanon's (2008) *Black Skin, White Masks*.

within families. "Afro-Brazilians," writes Hordge-Freeman, "engage in racial bargains, compromises that are often made ambivalently, in which [they] may comply with racial hierarchies in exchange for perceived payoffs that may be political, economic, psychological, or even affective" (Hordge-Freeman 2015, 6). What's more, not only have scholars documented rampant discrimination against the darker-skinned for decades,[18] but recent analyses reveal that Brazilian parents are more likely to invest in education for their lighter-skinned children (Rangel 2015), and that Brazilians earn higher wages when their employers perceive them as lighter-skinned (Cornwell et al. 2017). There are considerable incentives, therefore, for the potential targets of racialized discrimination to comply with racial hierarchies by approximating whiteness.

Some readers may question whether the emphasis on whitening and fluidity is overly academic or even well founded. After all, race may be socially constructed insofar as interpretations of physical attributes vary across time and space. But in a given context, these constructions are likely mutually understood and uncontested, and physical attributes – racialized or not – are presumably concrete and observable, which would seem to complicate, if not undermine altogether, efforts to lighten. This is certainly a view shared by many black movement activists in Brazil. While still recognizing "race" as an historical construction invented to serve political purposes (Nascimento 2016; Nascimento 2021), activists also bemoan the willingness of academics and citizens to invoke racial fluidity and other racial democracy discourse to obfuscate the violent and discriminatory practices inflicted upon Brazil's darker-skinned masses.[19] Discussion of and emphasis on racial fluidity, in this view, distract from the lived structural realities like police brutality, poverty, and a lack of access to health, education, and other forms of welfare. This is why those weary of the fetishization of fluidity are wont to offer the following retort: "If you want to know who is black or white in Brazil, just ask the police" (see Alves 2018). From this view, racial fluidity is an academic abstraction, and the ability to reclassify may be severely curtailed by one's physical appearance, which is visible to all.

---

[18] For seminal analyses, see Hasenbalg (1979) and Telles (2004). Also see Silva (1985, 2000), Andrews (1991, 2014), Lovell (1999, 2006), Lovell and Wood (1998), Monk (2016) and Telles (2014).

[19] Adding insult to injury, such discourse is commonly associated with Gilberto Freyre, whose *Casa-Grande e Senzala* is credited with establishing the racial democracy myth. Freyre received acclaim for his revisionist history of Brazil, but today activists view his work as a major disservice to the fight for racial justice.

This is an important critique, one that provides sometimes overly academic discussion with a healthy dose of reality. But there are two important points to remember before throwing the baby out with the bathwater. First, the widely and oft-touted idea of race fluidity in Brazil was established not via academic anecdote or mere impressions, but based on a long and rich body of empirical scholarship in anthropology and sociology. Scholars like Oracy Nogueira (1998), Donald Pierson (1942), and Marvin Harris (1952, 1970; also see Harris et al. 1993) contributed to this idea based on the documentation of ethnographic evidence. As Harris (1964b, 22) writes, "what is most distinctive about Brazilian race relations in comparison with other inter-racial systems ... [is] the plethora of racial terms and the abstract and referential ambiguity surrounding their application." Though in past decades much of this scholarship was confined to specific localities, more recent research employing ethnographic and quantitative survey methods also bear out similar ideas (see Silva 1994; Telles and Lim 1998). For example, Hordge-Freeman's illuminating ethnography of families in Salvador identifies common practices of anti-blackness within families, which contribute to ambiguity in racial identification (Hordge-Freeman 2015, chap. 4). And Robin Sheriff's seminal ethnography in Rio de Janeiro similarly documents how her interlocutors' "employment of race-color terms ... bespeaks a culturally articulated yearning to escape all that is negatively associated with blackness" (Sheriff 2001, 31). The implications of fluidity for racial identification, in short, are supported by empirical evidence from decades' worth of empirical social science scholarship.

Second, it is important to make clear the distinction between *identification* and *ascription*. In this study, I use the former term to refer to individuals' self-classifications in racial categories; I use the latter to refer to how individuals are read and classified by others. Ascriptions, therefore, are more pertinent to the activist's critique of how racialized citizens are unjustly treated, regardless of how they choose to identify. This point is not lost on scholars. For example, one seminal finding in the literature on racial inequality is Brazilian sociologist Nelson do Valle Silva's (1978) corrective to the notion of the "mulatto escape-hatch": through analysis of large household surveys, Silva showed that brown-identified Brazilians were no better off than black-identified Brazilians. Yet this does not inhibit the whitening effects Silva documents in other research (Silva 1994). The point here is a simple one: identification and ascription are different outcomes and are indeed the behaviors of different individuals. The nature of the reclassification reversal calls for analytical attention to identification

TABLE 2.2 *Comparing self-identification with racial ascription by interviewer*

		Racial self-classification				
		White	Brown	Black	Total (%)	N
Respondent as classified by interviewer	White	87.34	12.45	0.21	100	474
	Brown	23.62	64.47	11.91	100	470
	Black	9.76	31.71	58.94	100	123
	Total (N)	537	401	129	–	1,067

Shaded boxes indicate matches across both classifications. Cells located below or to the left of shaded boxes indicate lighter self-identification; cells located above or to the right indicate darker self-identification. Source: Pesquisa Social Brasileira, 2002. χ^2 (df = 4) = 681.91, $p < 0.001$.

over ascription. This does not mean that ascription is irrelevant – quite the opposite. As we'll see in Table 2.2, I rely on ascription as a proxy for individuals' attributes in my analyses. And in the following chapter, I discuss how individuals' subjective experiences of racialization contribute to the altering and politicization of their racial identifications and identities.

To show the continued importance of fluidity in this context, Table 2.2 cross-tabulates respondents' self-classifications in the official census categories with how they were classified by survey interviewers, indicating how the incentives discussed earlier can indeed shape patterns of identification. The likelihood of agreement between interviewer and respondent decreases monotonically as one moves from white to black (87 to 59 percent); among those classified as brown, mismatched respondents are twice as likely to opt for a lighter (24 percent) rather than a darker (12 percent) category; and 10 percent of those classified as black by interviewers self-identified as white. By contrast, almost none of those classified as white by interviewers self-identified as black.[20] Skeptics of racial

[20] For detailed discussion of classification mismatch, see Telles 2004, chap. 4. Also, Silva 1994; Bailey 2009; Telles and Lim 1998. Empirically oriented scholars problematize the ambiguity of racial identification to different degrees. Some characterize it as a kind of measurement error, complicating efforts to measure "race" and its related outcomes (Bailey et al. 2013; Guimarães 1999; Loveman et al. 2012; Telles and Lim 1998). In this view, measurement error in racial classification is an obstacle to precisely estimating intergroup inequality. If money does indeed whiten – if upwardly mobile Brazilians exit the black and brown categories – then it is likely that estimates of economic inequality between racial groups is biased upward. For others, any gesture at objective or "true" racial classification without mutually agreed upon criteria is inherently flawed (Harris 1970; Harris et al. 1993).

fluidity, in particular, should take note of these patterns. Other survey data collected by Telles (2014) indicate that racial ascriptions are reliable proxies for respondent skin tone.[21] Thus, rather than being most constrained by their physical appearances, darker-skinned individuals (those ascribed as black) exhibit the *lowest* level of overlap with survey interviewers, indicating *greater* capitalization on fluidity in the status quo.

This survey was conducted in the early 2000s, before the reclassification reversal became apparent in census data. Consequently, it's clear that at this point in time whitening was the dominant form of reclassification. Nonetheless, this cross-tabulation makes clear that many Brazilians have racial options. Among them are "exit" and "voice." Conventional wisdom leads us to expect racial exit: compliance with racial hierarchies and the pursuit of whitening to "defend [one's] welfare or to improve [one's] position" in society (Hirschman 1970, 15). Whitening also comports with expectations of social identity theory, which predicts exit from categories that do not contribute positively to the individual's self-concept. Without "positive group distinctiveness," individuals ought to exit this category, when possible (Tajfel 1974, 69). In contrast, the more recent patterns of the reclassification reversal suggest that growing numbers of Brazilians are choosing racial voice – "political action par excellence" (Hirschman 1970, 16) – by defying the social forces and commonsense logic that valorize whiteness. The reclassification reversal, therefore, presents a puzzle that conventional wisdom did not anticipate and cannot explain: Brazilians are seemingly and increasingly opting for voice over exit.

CONCLUSION

Stunning as it may seem to believers in the universal immutability of "race" or in the practice of whitening, the recent reversal in patterns of reclassification in Brazil is simply the latest development in a centuries-long evolution in the dynamics of race-making and racial identification in Brazil. Such a sudden reversal was made possible in part because of the racial and national projects undertaken by political and other elites over the course of the twentieth century. As the state's posture toward the "racial question" shifted from the pseudoscientific logic of eugenic race science toward the strategic logic motivating its nationalist project of racial unity, the state actively discouraged racial identification and promoted

---

[21] See footnote 10 in Chapter 4.

the dissolution, or at least weakening, of racial boundaries. One consequence was the shifting of racial identification dynamics in the informal sphere, enabling the state to maintain its officially colorblind posture while leaving in place the myriad forces that stigmatize and disincentivize certain racial categories. Under these conditions, commonsense racial hierarchies remained in place and whitening practices flourished.

As we shall see in the next chapter, it is no coincidence that the direction of net reclassification reversed in Brazil's democratic and more color-conscious era. Just as international norms influenced elite thinking on the racial question in the nineteenth and early to mid twentieth centuries, so too did they by the end of the twentieth century, when democratic institutions, respect for multiculturalism, and redress for social and economic inequities became marks of a modern state. Shifts in international norms, and the Brazilian state's continued adoption of those norms, provided space and legitimated a host of domestic institutional changes that would bring about an "inclusionary turn" in democratic Brazil (Kapiszewski et al. 2021). This, in turn, interrupted the status quo in patterns of racial identification. How and what lies behind such a dramatic shift in Brazil's racial composition are the subject we turn to next.

3

Theory

Racial Reclassification as Political Identity Formation

This book offers a causal and empirically verifiable explanation for shifting patterns of racial identification in Brazil, namely the newfound tendency for Brazilians to adopt nonwhite identities. In accounting for the reclassification reversal documented in the previous chapter, this book also leverages the exceptionalism of the Brazilian case as a rare opportunity to study the processes of identity politicization both empirically and systematically. I thus take up prominent calls in the identity politics literature to understand the ways in which identities "harden, congeal, and crystallize" (Brubaker and Cooper 2000, 1). To be sure, Brubaker and Cooper's sharp critiques have generated a surplus of scholarship aiming to rescue the study of identity in the social sciences.[1] Yet we still possess relatively few empirical and systematic analyses of how identities come into formation and take on political meaning at the individual level.[2] The empirical phenomenon of the reclassification reversal, therefore, provides meaningful variation that can be leveraged to shed light on what Taeku Lee (2008) has termed the "identity-to-politics link" – the processes that lead from social categories, to politicized identities, to group or collective politics.

Any satisfactory account of the reclassification reversal must account for why patterns of racial identification depart so starkly from the conventional expectations of whitening, as well as why the tendency to do so

---

[1] For responses within political science to Brubaker and Cooper's important critiques of the abuses of constructivism, see Abdelal et al. (2006) and Lee (2008).
[2] For a classic study in comparative politics, see Laitin (1998). Many studies of this sort focus on the United States. See Waters (1990, 2002), Saperstein and Penner (2012), Masuoka (2017), and Davenport (2018).

has become widespread so suddenly. In this chapter, I develop the argument that the reclassification reversal is the consequence of expanded access to education for the lower classes, which has led to the formation of racialized political identities. State-led efforts to better include lower-class sectors of the citizenry through educational expansion have increased the *exposure* of upwardly mobile citizens to information, social networks, and the labor market. Greater exposure, in turn, has led many to challenge commonsense racial hierarchies as they have come face-to-face with racialized inequalities in their pursuits of upward mobility. To be sure, whitening still occurs in Brazil, but this is no longer the dominant form of racial reclassification. Instead, formerly marginal and upwardly mobile citizens are increasingly choosing and politicizing blackness as an articulation of newfound, racialized, and politically meaningful identities. Ultimately, the account I develop in this chapter characterizes the reclassification reversal as a policy feedback effect – a new politics of identity generated by new and reformed social policy.[3]

Central to this argument is the notion of political identity – a concept that is commonly invoked but rarely defined. Before elaborating the causal argument and mechanisms, I offer a definition of the concept as I use it throughout this book, one that differs from related concepts like social identity and group consciousness. Briefly stated, I define political identity as a category of social membership that shapes how individuals make sense of power relationships. With this established, I move on to detail the argument from macro and micro perspectives, and situate this novel account in the literatures on ethnoracial and identity politics. More detailed and rigorous analysis of the theoretical propositions follows in Chapters 4 through 7. For now, I seek only to elaborate the argument and its hypotheses, and present evidence only to situate the institutional and macro-level context historically.

DEFINING POLITICAL IDENTITY

The formation of new "political identities," I argue in this book, is critical to understanding the reclassification reversal in Brazil. Through shifts in how individuals not only see themselves but understand their relative positions within their societies, many Brazilians have adopted new understandings of blackness and power that have motivated the newfound tendency to reclassify in darker racial categories. But what, exactly, is

---

[3] This chapter draws on arguments previously advanced in De Micheli (2021).

"political identity"? And how is this different from "identity" writ large, or related concepts like social identity and group consciousness? Despite the common invocation of the term, rarely, if ever, do scholars offer explicit definitions of the concept. Indeed, a number of prominent works in political science employ the concept to mean entirely different things, from the "common political identity" of Almond and Verba's (2015) civic culture, to the "Catholic political identity" of Kalyvas's Christian Democratic parties (1996), to the linguistic "political identities" of Laitin's (1998) Russian-speaking populations. Taken individually, one might not object to any one of these usages; but taken together, they range widely in their substantive applications and leave one to wonder what exactly makes any identity "political."

Throughout this study, I use the term "political identity" to mean categories of social membership that shape how individuals make sense of power relationships, broadly defined. To motivate this capacious definition, I briefly describe common usages in political science and detail their shortcomings for the theoretical task at hand – namely, problematizing identification and understanding the processes of politicization. I then elaborate on this conceptualization and highlight its theoretical utility for our purposes.

Prevailing Usages

Perhaps the most common prevailing usage ties "political identity" directly to the political arena via partisanship or political ideology (e.g., Kuo et al. 2017). The logic of considering partisanship and ideology as elemental to the concept is that they are central to politics as linkages to formal organizations of electoral competition or as those sets of ideas that shape voter preferences and worldviews (Campbell et al. 1960). This may seem logical enough, but restricting political identity to identity content – to membership in particular social groups, like political parties – is too narrow. This would limit political identities to memberships that emanate from the formal political arena and preclude those that do not. My point here is *not* that partisanship, for example, never constitutes political identity. Rather I suggest that we not automatically reduce political identity to specific categories due to presupposed linkages to formal politics. Doing so can divert our attention away from other, seemingly nonpolitical categories that take on political meaning from the subjective perspectives of group members. Our conceptions of political identity should be broad enough to capture identities that do not emanate from formal politics, yet shape it nonetheless.

The same can be said of another set of identities commonly classified as political based on their content, identities that define or constitute political communities generally as citizenries, nations, or states (e.g., Anderson 1983; Mouffe 1992). Unlike partisanship, these identities do not necessarily divide political arenas, but are said to unite them around attributes or values that encompass members of the community, rather than sort them. Moreover, because these identities tend to entail pluralities of individuals with some degree of spatial concentration, they symbolically homogenize communities by elevating shared characteristics and obscuring differences. As with partisanship, the inherently political nature of these identities may seem obvious at first glance. But similarly, these identities need not form the basis for political identities. Nor do we stand to gain theoretically or analytically by reducing political identity to these adequately labeled concepts. Additionally, by emphasizing unity these memberships can obscure other identities or cleavages within political communities that are in fact constitutive of political worldviews, in particular when constructed nations, states, and citizenries align with domestic political arenas. In other words, emphasizing unity can obscure identity politics itself, rendering such a concept useless for understanding how social differences become salient in the domestic political arena. This is not to deny that these boundaries can become politicized domestically (e.g., Theiss-Morse 2009). But again, these social memberships should not automatically be considered political identities because of their basis in political community. After all, many individuals may consider themselves members of these communities as simple matters of fact – according to legal status, place of birth, or residence. Whether or not these memberships are indeed identities at all or become the basis for identity politics is an empirical question, not a foregone conclusion (see Kalyvas 2003; Wilfahrt 2018).

A final approach to political identity extrapolates from social identity theory (SIT) and emphasizes the political consequences of identity. SIT, which was pioneered by Henri Tajfel and colleagues, defines social identity as "that part of an individuals' self-concept which derives from his knowledge of his membership in a social group together with the value and emotional significance attached to the membership" (Tajfel 1981, 255).[4] The SIT basis for political identity has been

---

[4] For finer distinctions between social identity and self-categorization theory, see (Huddy 2013).

articulated and popularized by Leonie Huddy, who defined the concept as "a social identity with political relevance" (Huddy 2013, 739).[5] This definition has proven an attractive framework for scholars, who need only hypothesize or assert that an identity is "relevant" to an outcome of interest to claim an identity is "political," without regard for the perspectives or subjectivities of group members themselves. In effect, this definition would seem to condone the scholarly treatment of political identities as "categories of analysis" rather than "categories of practice," one of the analytical sins bemoaned by Brubaker and Cooper (2000) in their critique of identity politics scholarship (also see Lee 2008).

Even setting this issue aside, this minimalist definition suffers from other weaknesses.[6] First, scholars are left to their own devices to determine what counts as "political relevance." Whether this is to be determined quantitatively or qualitatively, and in whose judgment (the analyst's or the research subject's), is far from clear. Second, such a definition leaves analysts to assess political identities in a post hoc manner, as explanatory factors for presumably obvious political outcomes. How are we to study political identities as dependent variables when that assessment is based on their "relevance" as an independent variable? How do we observe and measure political identity itself? The logic of this definition is circular, and it is difficult to see how such a definition can be useful for disaggregating the discrete identity processes of identification, politicization, and collective behavior, as scholars urge (Lee 2008). To be sure, SIT can be a useful framework for understanding the mechanisms of identity-driven behavior *once it has already emerged*. But to understand identify formation processes in their own right, we must be able to observe and identify "political identities" independently.

---

[5] Also see Huddy (2001) for a discussion of SIT's shortcomings for identity politics research agendas in political science.

[6] For a maximalist definition, see Smith (2004, 302). Smith's definition is not explicitly related to social identity, but it is one of the few explicit definitions in the literature. It supposes a "collective label ... by which persons are recognized by political actors as members of a political group." He goes on to specify that "political identities ... indicate the populations with which political actors expect that person to be affiliated in contests over governing power and its use." This definition does not specify who these supposed political actors are and whether or not these supposed group members also recognize these political identities as such. By linking political identities to "contests over governing power and its use," moreover, Smith also seems to be linking political identity to elections, though this too remains unspecified.

A Power-Centered Definition

The definition of political identity I employ throughout this book depends neither on identity content nor on a post hoc analysis of its relevance to something else deemed political. Instead, it is crafted with the goal of treating identities as "categories of practice," as an empirical assessment of the perspectives, meanings, and understandings that individuals themselves attribute to their identities, rather than categories deemed political by the analyst (Brubaker and Cooper 2000). I define political identities as *affirmed categories of social membership that shape how individuals make sense of power relationships, broadly defined*. In building this definition, I draw on social identity and group consciousness approaches, but ultimately advocate for a more capacious definition that is flexible enough to capture the myriad forms of politics in different contexts. What makes identities "political," in this view, is that these categories serve as a lens for subjective understandings of power relationships between groups. I highlight three analytical and theoretical elements of this definition that will aid our theoretical purposes.

Individuals in Groups. Implicit in this definition is an analytical focus on the individual, nested in the social group. This is similar to SIT's focus on the importance of group *attachments* for individual-level behavior, rather than taking the group, per se, as the unit of analysis.[7] This is a simple way to avoid the analytical sin that Brubaker has termed "groupism," which treats groups as preordained units of social analysis, as things in the world rather than ways of seeing the world (Brubaker 2004; Brubaker et al. 2004). Instead, scholars ought to consider the empirical referents of a given social category (who the presumed members are), and then determine empirically whether this membership has taken the form outlined earlier for group members.

A microlevel approach is also analytically appropriate for this study, since the goal is to explain individual-level variation in social identifications in a context where group boundaries are fluid and unstable. This kind of research question clearly requires analytical dexterity beyond the level of the social group. Moreover, situating individuals in groups also helps to distinguish the concept from the related concept of political cleavages. The latter can be viewed as the macro-level manifestation of microlevel political identities. In other words, if enough individuals

---

[7] According to Tajfel, one aim of social identity research is "to emphasise the role of 'men in groups' rather than of men *tout court*" (Tajfel 1974, 64).

assume political identities based on a social membership, then one might say members have cohered politically to form a cleavage (Bartolini and Mair 1990, chap. 9). Microlevel analysis offers analytical flexibility by allowing political identities to occupy a conceptual and empirical middleground between latent and politicized *cleavages*. Thus, the formation of political *identities* and *cleavages* ought to be considered empirically distinct, if related, phenomena, each potentially deserving its own set of theoretical explanations.

Affirmed Identification. Second, this definition centers "categories of practice," social categories deemed subjectively relevant by individuals themselves. Because I employ the concept of political identity in service of the theoretical agenda of understanding identity politicization, it is difficult to make the case for identities or categories that are imposed by the analyst ("categories of analysis"). However, it is a longstanding tenet of constructivism that individuals possess multiple identities, each of which might become situationally salient (Okamura 1981). Thus, more than simply a category that the individuals accepts or has internalized, I submit that identification must be positively declared and asserted by the individual – it must be meaningful – to be deemed political.

The emphasis on strength of identification borrows from related concepts like social identity and group consciousness, which rely on identification to varying degrees. On one hand, identification is the theoretical point of departure for SIT, which assumes a certain degree of internalization of social categories (Turner et al. 1987, 51–52). At the same time, however, the in-group bias and favoritism derived from social identities is also said to emanate from the individual's mere awareness of membership in a social category – the so-called minimal group paradigm (Tajfel 1981). Group consciousness, on the other hand, is conceptualized to entail not just awareness, but strong identification with a social group (Gurin et al. 1980; Miller et al. 1981). Unlike SIT, group consciousness theory explicitly hypothesizes within-group heterogeneity in strength of identification, which is said to explain divergent within-group attitudes.[8] This latter definition better comports with the notion of categories of practice, and lends further individual-level variation within groups

---

[8] Scholars, for example, have long studied "consciousness" and "linked fate" in order to understand within-group differences in salience/importance of a given social membership to the individual (Dawson 1995; Junn and Masuoka 2008; Mitchell-Walthour 2018; Wong et al. 2011).

that can offer empirical leverage in understanding microlevel processes of identity politicization.

Perceptions of Power. Classic conceptions of group consciousness also incorporate the idea that group consciousness relates specifically to the individual's beliefs about economic stratification and relative deprivation, namely the individual's blame of the system for distributive injustice, as well as the view that collective action is the best means of achieving the group's interests (Gurin et al. 1980; Miller et al. 1981). While such identity-based beliefs can certainly qualify an identity as political, I advocate for a more capacious understanding of politics that goes beyond stratification beliefs and does not preordain the type of political action or interest arena in which identities are articulated. Instead, I suggest political identities be identified based on subjective beliefs about intergroup asymmetries of power – power relationships. In assessing one's political identity, the empirical questions to be answered, then, are what identity (or identities), if any, serves as the basis on which one makes sense of power, or whether a given identity of theoretical interest has become imbued with political meaning such that it operates as a lens for the individual's interpretation of power.

Power, of course, is itself a contested concept, and I do not wade into the debates over its meaning here. But by taking a reasonably broad view of power – such as Lukes' (2005) three dimensions of power[9] – we can include and move beyond the economic sphere to center the individual's group-based understanding of power. Alternatively, other conceptions of power or status might justifiably be substituted instead; what matters in this conceptualization is that political identity be viewed as the individual's group-based understanding of power. Surely, relying on a contested concept will generate criticism, but it is precisely in the flexibility of the concept of power, as well as its centrality in the study of politics, that allows it to encompass the wide-ranging definitions of political identity currently in use in the literature. Indeed, struggles over power could just as easily describe electoral politics and competition for resources as it can social mobilization, nationalist violence, and interstate war.

As a final note, it is important to emphasize that understandings of power are perceptual and subjective, and individuals' beliefs about power may not find empirical support or conform to common views about

---

[9] These can be captured summarily as decision-making (Dahl 1957, 1961), agenda-setting (Bachrachand and Baratz 1962), and manipulation or hegemony (Gramsci 1971). See Gaventa (1982, chap. 1) for a useful discussion of Lukes.

which groups are marginalized or disadvantaged. The empirical basis for these views is less relevant than the individual's *belief* that they are true.[10] Thus, analysts may not agree that members of a given group suffer from power asymmetries, and even individuals belonging to groups not commonly seen as marginalized/dominated can develop the belief that they suffer from disadvantage due to changing contexts, norms, or values (e.g., Abrajano and Hajnal 2015; Cramer 2016; Hochschild 2016). Nonetheless, centering the study of political identities on individuals' group-based understandings of power can unite the varied usages of the concept around an elemental feature of politics itself, and helps to specify the empirical manifestations of political identity as a category of practice.

THE ARGUMENT: EDUCATIONAL EXPANSION, RACIAL SUBJECTIVITY, AND POLICY FEEDBACK

The ostensibly sudden reversal in patterns of reclassification, I argue, is the unintended consequence of expanded access to secondary and university education in recent decades, which has led many newly mobile citizens to develop racialized political identities. Beginning in the 1990s, state-led efforts to incorporate marginal sectors of the citizenry through social policy expansion granted lower-class sectors – many of whom are racially ambiguous and susceptible to internalizing racial hierarchies – unprecedented access to the benefits of social citizenship. Greater access to education, in particular, increased the exposure of lower-class citizens to new information, social networks, and labor market experiences. In turn, this greater exposure has brought many newly mobile citizens face-to-face with racial hierarchies and inequalities in their pursuit of upward mobility, altering the personal experiences and subjectivities that inform their racial identifications and their political identities, the bases on which they make sense of power relationships. So conceived, growing identification with nonwhite, and especially black, racial categories can

---

[10] Like Campbell et al.'s (1960) "perceptual screen," political identities can determine which facts and sources of information are deemed legitimate and true (Achen and Bartels 2016; Bartels 2002), thereby complicating so-called rational explanations for identity-based preferences and behavior (Cramer 2016); and groups who dominate halls of power, like oligarchic elites or ethnoracial minorities, might fear the loss of power due to numerical disadvantage, despite their status quo control. Such notions are central to elites' fears in formal theories of democratization (Acemoglu and Robinson 2006; Ansell and Samuels 2014; Boix 2003), as well as to group position theory and symbolic racism, in which groups sitting atop a social hierarchy seek to defend their symbolic status and relative positions (Blumer 1958; Bobo 1999; Kinder and Sears 1981).

be understood as an articulation of newfound and racialized political identities.

This argument is decidedly constructivist and thus embraces an understanding of "race" as a cultural interpretation of physical attributes, rather than a biologically ordained or self-evident and immutable set of categories. Instead, constructivism emphasizes that how race is understood is contingent on local and historical context, and is subject to reconstruction over time. By centering these central tenets as aspects of the research puzzle, this study contributes to our understanding of what Omi and Winant describe as "racial formation," or "the sociohistorical process by which racial categories are created, inhabited, transformed, and destroyed" (Omi and Winant 1994, 55). In doing so, this argument also contributes to the comparative ethnic politics literature by shifting attention away from the usual explanatory suspects in the study of identity politicization. Dominant theories have come to revolve around institutions and incentives as the primary determinants of the identities articulated in the political arena, often centering the agency of political elites and assuming stability in demographic structures.[11] Such assumptions, however, do not travel well to Latin America, where ethnic and racial boundaries are historically fluid and where discrimination has discouraged individuals from claiming and articulating stigmatized identities in the political arena (Contreras 2016; Madrid 2012). Instead, my account builds on Yashar's (2005) insight that reforms to citizenship institutions can politicize identities in unwitting yet significant ways. In contrast to Yashar's emphasis on decentralization and modes of interest intermediation, however, my account draws attention to the ways in which specific citizenship institutions like education policy can interact with racial hierarchies and inequalities to shape microlevel processes of identity politicization. By focusing on the consequences of educational reforms, I direct attention to what Marshall (1950) terms social citizenship rights in his classic essay on the subject. In contrast to civil (rights to individual freedom) and political (rights to exercise power) rights, Marshall conceptualized social citizenship as those rights that enable or empower citizens to live and participate in society as full-standing members. As Marshall put it, social citizenship is "the right to defend and assert all one's rights on terms of equality with others" (11). Marshall does not expound upon the range of rights or benefits that would lead to such equality, but he does identify education as a key right of social citizenship.

---

[11] I discuss this literature in greater depth in Chapter 6.

The emphasis on education as a right of social citizenship in my argument also broadens what political scientists refer to as "policy feedback effects," or the simple but impactful idea that "new policies create new politics" (Schattschneider 1935, 288). Rather than viewing policies as simple outputs of the political process (Easton 1953), policy feedback scholars emphasize that "policies can set political agendas and shape identities and interests. They can influence beliefs about what is possible, desirable, and normal" (see Mettler and Soss 2004; Soss and Schram 2007, 113). In turn, these reshaped identities, interests, and beliefs "feed back" into political and policymaking processes (Lowi 1964; Skocpol 1992).

Much policy feedback research on the mass public focuses on the (positive and negative) consequences of policy for political participation, engagement, and efficacy.[12] But other works emphasize the consequences for identity politics. Of particular note is Skocpol's (1992) study on the origins of the "maternalist" welfare state in the United States. Skocpol documents how the gender-based political exclusion of women in the nineteenth century fostered gender consciousness among middle-class women, who subsequently mobilized to demand social policies aimed toward mothers and children. More analogous to the argument I develop is Rose's (2018) analysis of how higher education policy aiming to incorporate women in the United States transformed their exercise of citizenship. Like Yashar's (2005), these studies illustrate cases in which citizenship policies play a central role in politicizing social identities and encouraging political action. My argument builds on these insights, but theorizes that social citizenship institutions can have even wider-ranging effects on identity formation and politicization processes. I detail how the state's allocation of social citizenship rights and benefits is capable of reshaping subjective self-understandings, shifting social boundaries, and imbuing newfound identities with political meaning. In this sense, the argument advanced in this book offers a causal account of the "interpretive" feedback effects of social policy on identity politics – that is, "the impact of

---

[12] Influential studies focus on the United States include Campbell 2003; Lerman and Weaver 2014; Mettler 2007, 2011; Skocpol 1992; Soss 2002; Soss and Schram 2007. Comparative studies focus overwhelmingly on advanced European democracies (Esping-Andersen 1990; Kumlin and Rothstein 2005; Larsen 2007; Lynch 2006; Lynch and Myrskylä 2009), though studies on countries outside advanced democracies are increasingly common (see Bleck 2015; Hern 2019; Hunter and Sugiyama 2014; MacLean 2011).

policies on the cognitive processes of social actors" (Pierson 1993, 610).[13]

To understand how educational reforms could possibly have such effects on microlevel identity processes, we first need to situate these reforms in their broader historical context. As such, I first detail the history of educational policy in twentieth century Brazil, the woeful state of educational access for much of this century, and the breadth of reforms carried out since the 1980s. With the macro-level institutional context established, I then elaborate microlevel causal pathways through which education has reshaped and politicized racial identities in Brazil.

MACRO-LEVEL CHANGE: STATE-LED EDUCATIONAL EXPANSION

The Brazilian state played an important, if indirect and unintentional, role in inducing the reclassification reversal with its unprecedented efforts to include "outsider" citizens through social policy expansion. These efforts followed a number of institutional changes in the late 1980s, most notably a democratic transition and the ratification of a new federal constitution. Democratization, of course, reinstated free and fair elections and made politicians more responsive to the public. But moreover, the new constitution codified universal social rights – including the right to education – and removed literacy requirements for political citizenship. With the return of elections and a newly expanded franchise, political elites suddenly found themselves competing for the votes of the poor masses (Garay 2016; Hunter and Brill 2016; Kapiszewski et al. 2021). Additionally, mainstream left and right-wing political parties vying for national office saw a shared interest in undercutting the clientelist politics of traditional parties by embracing programmatic appeals (Hagopian 2018). And finally, democratization created great space for civil society organizations to leverage international norms and alliances in their efforts to pressure the state into explicitly acknowledging racial differences, discrimination, and inequities (Htun 2004; Loveman 2014; Paschel 2016a; Telles 2004). In short, mainstream parties and politicians converged around the need to address the countries profound and persistent inequalities.

---

[13] Policy feedback scholars commonly distinguish interpretive effects from resource effects: incentives or material benefits that create interest groups/constituencies, or enhance the resources individuals require to participate in politics (Campbell 2012; Pierson 1993).

This array of institutional changes generated the incentives and political will for governments to create, expand, and reform social policies for the poor, unleashing unprecedented waves of upward mobility for the lower classes. Education was just one domain to which the state devoted its efforts. Particularly notable were efforts beginning in the 1990s to increase the quality of and expand access to public education at all levels (INEP 2016b; World Bank 2002). The consequences of these and other efforts are unmistakable. By the 2000s, education spending reached OECD levels, and enrollments in high school and university had significantly expanded. By the 2010s, more than nine million household (33 million individuals) were lifted out of poverty, leading to increasing awareness of the so-called "new middle class" (Klein et al. 2018; Neri 2011). Educational reforms were of course not solely responsible for this structural change, but it was during this period of aggressive action on inequality that the state was able to marshal the will and resources to reform public education and make it more inclusive.

In recent decades, Brazilian citizens may have witnessed dramatic improvements to the extent and quality of social policies and programs, and the domain of education was certainly no exception. But of course, that Brazil could witness such drastic improvements is a testament to both the committed action of the state and the impoverishment of social citizenship in the past. To make sense of the timing and extent of the reclassification reversal, we need to understand both sides of this coin and must situate recent patterns of education expansion in the broader history of uneven access to and punctuated expansion of social policy in the twentieth century.

For much of the twentieth century, education policy was shaped by institutions and directives established under Getúlio Vargas, the populist president-cum-dictator who governed Brazil off-and-on from 1930 to 1954. In the social domain, Vargas is most remembered for his creation of labor policy and control over state-sponsored unions (Collier and Collier 2002; Conniff 1981). But Vargas also set educational agendas and established agencies that continued to exist for decades. It was Vargas, for example, who created the Ministry of Education (MEC) and the National Institute of Education Research (INEP, tasked with coordinating education policy from basic through university education), both of which remain in operation today. The 1934 constitution, ratified under Vargas, made first mention of a nationally standardized education curriculum (Dávila 2003). Prior to Vargas, formal education was largely reserved for the children of elites. As a populist leader presiding over urbanization and industrialization, Vargas sought to improve education to guarantee the human capital needed for Brazil's growing economy. Accordingly, early educational initiatives focused on vocational and technical training and were targeted toward urban labor (Silva 1980).

Though politics outside of the educational domain was turbulent for much of the twentieth century, education policy was remarkably stable. Like Vargas, subsequent civil and military governments prioritized economic modernization powered by industrialization and thus counted on public schooling to endow the labor force with necessary skills. Education reforms in 1961 and 1971 marked advances in nationalizing education policy, but did little to interrupt this orientation. In 1961 the federal government passed the first law regulating education policy (*Lei de Diretrizes e Bases da Educação nacional*, LDB). Though education was delegated to state governments, the 1961 LDB established formulas for resource allocation and spending floors, and mandated school attendance at four years of age. However, schools remained few and far between, those that existed were under-resourced, teachers were undereducated and poorly paid, and widespread poverty meant few families complied with mandates to send their children to school (de Mello and Hoppe 2005). The military government modified the LDB in 1971 in response to continuing urbanization and industrialization, but this reform simply raised the age of mandatory school attendance to fourteen, added physical education to the curriculum, and made technical training the focus of high school education (Schwartzman 2016).

At the time, these new policies and agencies certainly marked advances in public education, but census data confirms that educational attendance and access were far from widespread. Figure 3.1 displays education rates identified in censuses between 1960 and 2010 (Minnesota Population Center 2018). By the 1960s, formal education remained a rare commodity, with the overwhelming share of the population (and nearly all of black and brown populations) failing to complete primary schooling. By 1980, only 20 percent of whites completed high school, and fewer than 5 percent completed university – and this is the best-case scenario. Access to education did improve over the course of the twentieth century, but a lack of resources meant that quality remained low, and major gaps in access continued to exist according to race and income (Castro 1989; Plank et al. 1996). By the end of the military regime in the 1980s, educational outcomes disappointed many, and public education was seen as a serious weakness that would undermine Brazil's efforts to join the ranks of high-income countries. Indeed, in the 1990s World Bank economists

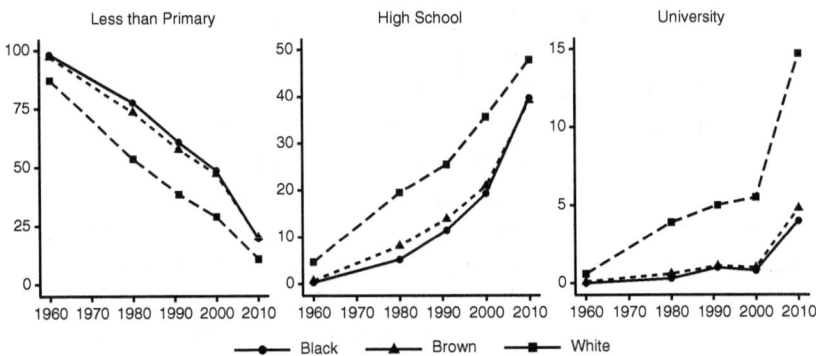

FIGURE 3.1 Education completion rates for Brazilians aged 22–26 by race, 1960–2010
Source: IPUMS, IBGE.

would characterize public education in Brazil as an "opportunity foregone" (Birdsall and Sabot 1996).

The period of educational expansion that led to the patterns of reclassification began with redemocratization, which ratified a new democratic constitution codifying the universal right to education and lifted literacy requirements for political citizenship. As Garay (2016) argues, the pairing of these institutional reforms meant that for the first time politicians found themselves competing for the votes of the poor masses, which gave politicians incentive and the political will to invest in social policies for "outsider" citizens (also see Hunter and Brill 2016). Adding to these pressures was the presence of the electorally competitive leftist Workers' Party (PT), which won increasingly large vote shares in national elections until capturing the presidency in 2002 (Hunter 2010). This electoral threat from the left raised the stakes for mainstream conservative parties in power in the 1990s, further incentivizing more moderate and programmatic policies that might undercut the appeals of leftist parties to large constituencies comprised of the poor (Garay 2016).

The first set of major education reforms came in the form of an updated LDB, passed in 1996 under President Fernando Henrique Cardoso of the center-right Social Democratic Party (PSDB). This new law entailed a number of reforms, but one set of reforms in particular took aim at the political bargaining between state and local governments that undermined resource delivery and education quality (Melo 2017; Plank et al. 1996). The 1996 LDB established FUNDEF (the Fund for Maintenance and Development of the Fundamental Education and Valorization of

Teaching), which reorganized the administration of basic education and created new incentive structures designed to circumvent this political bargaining and fund diversion between state and local governments. Specifically, FUNDEF mandated a spending floor of 25 percent of state tax revenue on education, as well as 18 percent of federal tax revenues. Of the state spending earmarked for education, 60 percent was required to be spent on teachers' salaries and training programs to improve quality (de Mello and Hoppe 2005). The 1996 law also stipulated that for ten years, 50 percent of federal funds be dedicated to addressing illiteracy and universalizing primary school coverage. And rather than leave local school funding to the discretion of state governors, federal funds would be transferred directly to local governments on the basis of student enrollments, creating incentives for local mayors to keep school enrollments high (Melo 2017).

In addition to increases in spending and improving resource allocation, the 1996 LDB took on a distinctly democratic character by incorporating elements of the philosophy of renowned Brazilian pedagogue Paulo Freire, author of such works as *Pedagogy of the Oppressed* (2014) and *Education for Critical Consciousness* (2005). Freire is best known for advocating a teacher–student relationship based on the shared transfer of knowledge, rather than authority and discipline. But Freire also promoted education as one of the best ways to combat inequity and intergenerational poverty. Freire saw education as critical to democratic citizenship because it would empower individuals to become critically aware of the world in which they lived and to develop agency. Freire's views initially led to his exile in Chile during Brazil's military dictatorship, the period during which he authored some of his most famous works. He later returned to Brazil, where his ideas would gain influence in policy circles and influence the 1996 LDB reform. The 1996 law states, for example, that the goal of national education is to prepare the student for "the exercise of citizenship and her qualification for work" (*Lei de diretrizes de Base da Educação Nacional*, 1996, art. 2), as well as that students should be educated on the basis of principles of "pluralism of ideas and pedagogical approaches" (art. 3, sec. 3) and "respect for liberty and appreciation for tolerance" (art. 3, sec. 4).[14] In addition to expanded access and resources, national education in Brazil became less vocational, technocratic, and elitist, and it incorporated pedagogical philosophies aimed at critical awareness and citizenship.

---

[14] A 2013 amendment (Law no. 12.796/2013) added to Article 3 of the 1996 LDB "consideration for ethno-racial diversity" (art. 3, sec. 8).

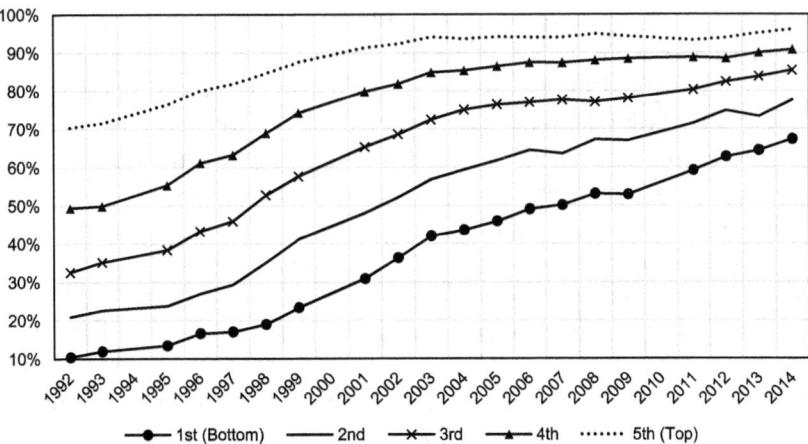

FIGURE 3.2 Population aged 15–18 with primary school completed by income quintile, 1992–2014
Source: PNAD, IBGE.

In any case, the effects of the 1996 LDB (which took aim at primary education) on attendance and completion rates was immediately apparent. Figure 3.2 shows primary completion rates for Brazilians aged 15 to 18 years of age by quintile of per capita household income. First, in 1992 there were massive inequalities in primary school completion rates by income quintile: whereas 70 percent of the wealthiest families saw their children complete primary school, only 10 percent of the poorest did. Over the following two decades, however, primary completion greatly improved for all income sectors: by 2014, two-thirds of individuals in the bottom income quintile had completed primary education. These improved outcomes were partly a function of the 1996 LDB, but they were undoubtedly also aided by conditionalities in Brazil's targeted cash transfer program, the *Bolsa Família*. This program offered cash payments to the poorest households conditioned on families' compliance with social requirements, notably children's school attendance. The program began as a state-level initiative during the Cardoso administration, but the program was scaled up to the national level in 2003 under Lula and greatly expanded in years thereafter, eventually reaching the households of roughly 30 percent of the Brazilian population by 2014 (Weisbrot et al. 2014).

The 1990s saw unprecedented attention paid to improving primary school outcomes and the reform of federal education policy to make

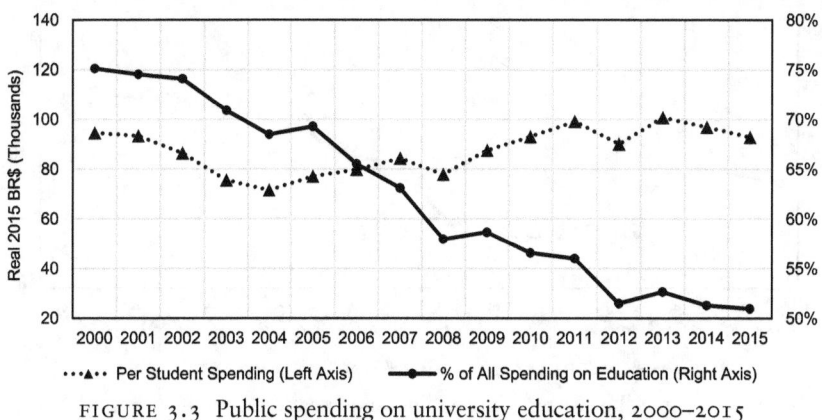

FIGURE 3.3 Public spending on university education, 2000–2015
Source: INEP/MEC

educational goals a reality. There was also remarkable continuity in this regard between the right-leaning Cardoso (PSDB) government of the 1990s and the left-leaning government of PT president Luiz Inácio "Lula" da Silva. Under Lula, FUNDEF was expanded to encompass secondary as well as primary schooling.[15] Additionally, FUNDEB, as it became known thereafter, earmarked additional federal funds for primary and secondary schools (Melo 2017; OECD 2011). Lula not only renewed commitments begun under Cardoso, but extended them to the domain of university education. Unlike primary and secondary education, which has historically been seen as low-quality and under-resourced, university education received the lion's share of public spending on education (Figure 3.3), and served a small and elite minority of the country's population (Artes and Ricoldi 2015; Gomes and Moraes 2012). The country's public universities are of exceedingly high quality and charge admitted students no tuition. The cruel irony, of course, is that students educated in public primary and secondary schools are dismally underprepared to compete for the scarce university slots in public universities (Artes and Ricoldi 2015; Heringer 2015; Schwartzman et al. 2015). Prior to educational reforms, the overwhelming share of public education spending was devoted to university students, who could gain admission by financing high-quality private educations in primary and secondary schooling.

[15] Federal funds are distributed to municipalities for primary schooling and to states for secondary schooling based on student enrollments. This policy was set to expire in 2020 but was passed as a permanent constitutional amendment prior to expiration (Conheça o novo Fundeb, que amplia gradualmente os recursos da educação 2020).

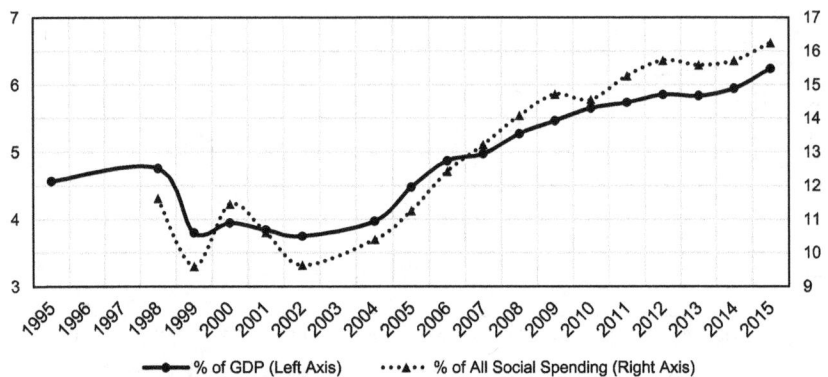

FIGURE 3.4 All government spending on education, 1995–2015
Source: UN Economic Commission on Latin America and the Caribbean.

These inequalities were apparent in educational spending priorities. Figure 3.3 shows public spending on university education across all levels of government. These figures indicate that even by 2000 – when fewer than 5 percent of the population completed university – public universities received 75 percent of government funds spent on education. By 2015, this figure dropped to just above 50 percent, meaning that the share of education spending on primary and secondary education doubled over this period. At the same time, however, there is no sign that this redistribution of priorities has meant a decline in the quality of public university education: between 2000 and 2015, per capita university spending has remained relatively stable.

The state was able to accomplish this more equitable distribution of education resources by simply increasing education funding overall. As Figure 3.4 shows, education spending as a percentage of GDP rose from roughly 4 to more than 6 percent between the late 1990s and 2015, on par with the OECD average for this period (OECD 2018; World Bank 2002). In addition, education came to occupy a significantly larger share of social spending overall, growing from roughly 10 to 16 percent of all social spending. This, of course, is not to suggest that there was no room for further improvement in terms of education quality and coverage in Brazil. Racial disparities also remained – and remain – a major issue in the domain of public education in Brazil and elsewhere in Latin America (Freire et al. 2018; Freire et al. 2022). But over this period, both domestic and international observers agree, Brazil made encouraging improvements in education quality and access (INEP 2016a, 2016b; OECD 2011).

Improvements in attendance rates for basic education eventually increased demand for university education, which was highly competitive even prior to efforts at educational expansion. PT governments thus similarly sought to expand access to university by expanding and creating resources to fund university education. In 2001, congress approved a national education goal of enrolling 30 percent of 18- to 24-year-olds in university, a goal that was increased to 33 percent in 2014. To meet these goals, Lula's administration: created 18 new federal universities between 2003 and 2014, including universities outside of state capitals to reach rural populations; created the federal Program for the Restructuring and Expansion of Federal Universities (REUNI), which awarded qualifying universities with up to BR$2 billion to invest in buildings, courses, and campuses, and to improve access and retention for vulnerable students; created the federal program Prouni, the University for All Program (*Programa Universidade para Todos*) in 2004, which awards full and partial scholarships to low-income and nonwhite students to attend private universities (a total of nearly 3 million scholarships were awarded as of 2016); nationalized and centralized the university entrance exam, creating a national exam analogous to the SAT in the United States (*o Exame nacional do Ensino medio*, ENEM) as well as a unified application system, allowing students to apply to multiple universities without the need to sit for separate entrance exams (SISU); and perhaps most famously, federal and state governments began to expand access through the active inclusion of low-income and nonwhite students through the creation of means- and race-targeted affirmative action programs (Gomes and Moraes 2012; Heringer 2015; Heringer and Ferreira 2009; Lima 2010; Melo 2017; Soares 2013).[16]

The impact of these policy initiatives – from FUNDEB to affirmative action – on high school and university completion rates are unmistakable. Figure 3.5 shows rates of high school completion from 1992 to 2014 among 18–24-year-olds by income quintile. In 1992 high school completion rates stood at 10 percent or less for the bottom 60 percent of the income distribution, and at just under 3 percent for the bottom quintile. Yet considerable gains in both access and completion are evident. By 2014, more than half of those in the middle-income quintiles had completed high school education. And those in the bottom quintile registered a tenfold increase, from 3 percent to 30 percent in 2014.

---

[16] Table 3.1 at the end of this chapter summarizes educational reforms.

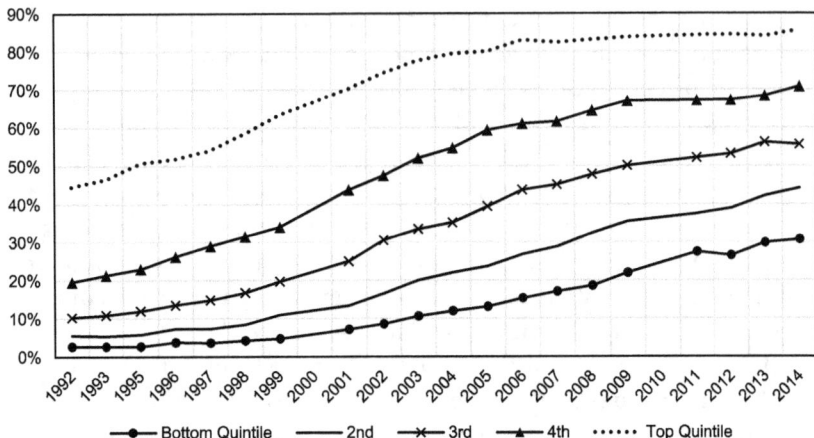

FIGURE 3.5 Population aged 18–24 with high school completed by income quintile, 1992–2014
Source: PNAD, IBGE.

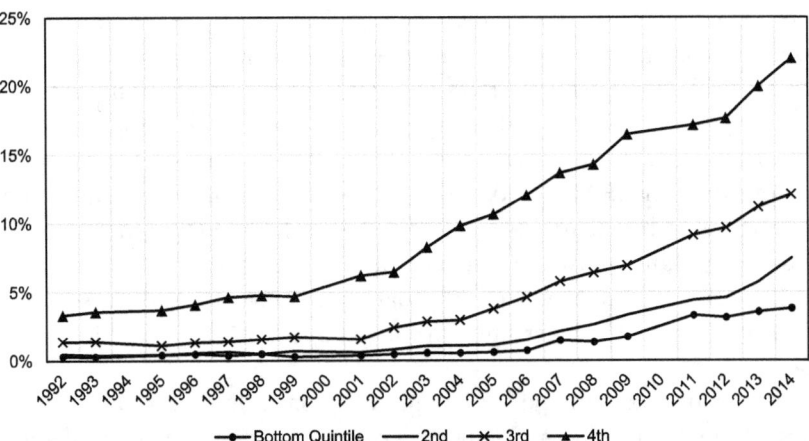

FIGURE 3.6 Population aged 18–24 with some university education by income quintile, 1992–2014
Source: PNAD, IBGE.

Rates of university access indicate a similar trajectory for all income sectors. Figure 3.6 displays the rate of those aged 18 to 24 with at least some university education by income quintile. The figure omits those in the highest income quintile, where university access is far and away the greatest (17 percent in 1992 and 47 percent in 2014). Among all levels of the income structure, access to university education expanded greatly over this period, particularly in the 2000s. Individuals in the two lowest income quintiles saw their access increase from virtually zero in 1992 to 4 and 7 percent, respectively, by 2014. Gains at this level of education are more modest than for primary and secondary schooling. And to be sure, stratification by income remains a challenge in efforts to democratize education. But considering that that the bottom forty percent of the income structure saw no access whatsoever to university in 1992, even these modest gains represent unprecedented access for the poor and disadvantaged in Brazil (Artes and Ricoldi 2015; Gomes and Moraes 2012; Senkevics 2021). These gains, moreover, represent the culmination of myriad institutional changes and policy reforms that have served to transform the experience of social citizenship in Brazilian society.

MICROLEVEL MECHANISM: EDUCATION AS EXPOSURE

The institutional changes detailed earlier help to explain the timing and macro-level context in which the reclassification reversal occurred. But to make sense of how and why individuals have begun to exhibit behavior so contrary to expectations, we must pay attention to the consequences of educational expansion for the lived experiences of the lower classes, those who only recently gained access to secondary and university education. Sociological research confirms that lower-income individuals are darker-skinned on average (Telles 2014; Telles and Paschel 2014). But as shown in Chapter 2, these individuals have considerable leeway when it comes to racial identification due to the multiple criteria that factor into this calculus (e.g., Harris et al. 1993). Though data indicate that a significant majority of Brazilians agree that physical attributes are the primary determinants of racial identification, this is followed by socioeconomic criteria (IBGE 2011, table 2.11; Silva et al. 2020). And ethnographic research has long documented whitening practices among lower-class Brazilians, who are socialized to comply with racial hierarchies and distance themselves from blackness (Burdick 1998b; Harris 1952; Hordge-Freeman 2015; Sheriff 2001; Twine 1998). Lower-class sectors, therefore, are likely *candidates* for self-darkening since they are well positioned to make plausible claims to nonwhiteness in phenotypical terms, and yet in the status quo are likely to comply with commonsense racial hierarchies by self-lightening.

For many in these sectors, greater access to education has interrupted this status quo by increasing the personal exposure of newly mobile citizens to racial hierarchies, discrimination, and inequalities. I build on the work of Gabrielle Kruks-Wisner (2018), who shows how increased social exposure and spatial mobility of the "have-nots" to the "haves" leads to greater citizen action and the exercise of citizenship in rural India. Though our contexts differ and the emphasis on spatial mobility in Kruks-Wisner's study differs from the one I describe, I argue that education can also operate as a form of exposure and play a role in reshaping individuals' racial self-understandings and the political meaning of these identities. Individuals, of course, pursue education for decades on end and with a variety of motivations, not least of which is upward mobility itself. But particularly for individuals from lower-class backgrounds, who previously saw scant educational access and who are often subject to – and might even participate in – informal institutional racism, unprecedented access to education can also entail sudden exposure to new information, social networks, and/or experiences in the labor market. In turn, these new forms of exposure can alter the personal experiences that inform how individuals understand themselves in racial terms and on what basis they make sense of power relationships – their political identities.

This argument parallels findings on racial consciousness and identity in the United States. Though the perennially salient racial cleavage in the United States has often been cast in stark contrast to the historically weak racial cleavage in Brazil, it is important to remember that the high degree of racial cohesion among U.S. blacks was not always seen as a foregone conclusion. Indeed, the period following the civil rights movement saw significant rates of upward mobility for blacks. Writing prior to the civil rights movement, Frazier (1957) predicted that the emergence of a "black bourgeoisie" would weaken racial solidarity and consciousness. When upward mobility led to greater class-based differentiation within the black community after the 1960s, scholars consequently predicted lower levels of racial consciousness among privileged black sectors relative to their lower-class counterparts. It was thus contrary to expectations that this upward mobility produced deepened racial consciousness among middle-class black Americans, who exhibited greater levels of racial linked fate and greater pessimism about the American dream, despite supposedly fulfilling its promises (Dawson 1995; Hochschild 1995; Tate 1994).

To be sure, black Americans are generally regarded as an exceptional case of group politics, even compared to other ethnoracial groups in the United States (McClain et al. 2009). It is therefore far from clear that such an experience would travel to other contexts, especially one seen as distinct from the United States. Adding to this, past studies of reclassification in Brazil tell us that it is the upwardly mobile who are most likely to adopt white identities (Silva 1994; Wood and Carvalho 1994). Yet, more recently, scholars have begun to uncover patterns and correlations that highlight parallels between these two cases, in particular with regard to the dynamics of race and class in the lived experiences of upward mobility. This is partly a function of higher-quality data that has become available as of late (e.g., Telles 2014).[17] In any case, scholars have found that better educated Brazilians are more likely to identify as black rather than mixed-race (Bailey and Telles 2006; Mitchell-Walthour 2018; Telles 2004, chap. 4),[18] even after controlling for physical attributes (Telles and Paschel 2014). Studies of parents' classifications of their children find that better educated nonwhite Brazilians were more likely to classify their children as white in the 1980s and 1990s, but that this pattern had reversed by the 2000s (Marteleto 2012; Schwartzman 2007). And a panel study of students at one university in Brazil finds that students are more likely to adopt black identities *after* enrolling in university, particularly those admitted via affirmative action (Francis-Tan and Tannuri-Pianto 2015).[19]

Taken together, evidence of a potential "darkening" effect is accumulating. Few studies, however, explicitly examine longitudinal dynamics in patterns of racial identification in Brazil,[20] and those that do only speculate on why education might correlate with black identification. Part of my objective, therefore, is to specify the theoretical mechanisms that link upward mobility via education with black identification. The development of a racialized political identity, or racial consciousness, is central to this relationship, I submit.

Before proceeding to the theoretical mechanisms, it is worth reviewing previous scholarship on racial consciousness in Brazil, which has generated lively debate and discussion. Perhaps no work has received more

---

[17] High quality data that allows for national and systematic analysis of racial dynamics in Brazil for the period prior to the 1990s is hard to come by. As such, many studies from previous decades rely on local-level surveys that raise questions about generalizability, or data collected in household surveys that – while informative – rarely contain the variables suitable for nuanced social analysis with adequate controls.

[18] Relatedly, Mitchell (1977) finds in his survey analysis that respondents with higher incomes were more likely to opt for the label *negro* over other color terms. This study, however, is based on a sample of "black association" members in the city of São Paulo, unlikely to be a representative sample.

[19] In a local study conducted in Recife, Miranda-Riberio and Caetano (2005) also identify darkening effects of education among women with more years of schooling.

[20] Notable exceptions include Schwartzman 2007; Marteleto 2012; Francis and Tannuri-Pianto 2012; Bailey et al. 2018

attention on this topic than Michael Hanchard's (1994) *Orpheus and Power*, which takes the absence of racial consciousness (and the failure to mobilize on the basis of race) as its point of departure.[21] Based on interviews with activists and observation of the Unified Black Movement (MNU) in the 1980s, Hanchard argues that the racial democracy myth has not instilled false consciousness, per se, but has led to a sense of "faint" (as opposed "strong") racial resemblance among the mass public. Similar to Vargas's (2004) notion of hyperconsciousness – in which Brazilian racial lexicons and a staunch resistance to discussions of racism belie any notions of colorblindness in Brazilian society – the faint resemblance common among the Brazilian public is more akin to situational affinity felt on the basis of racial similarity. This stands in contrast to strong racial resemblance, more akin to traditional understandings of racial (or group) consciousness. Hanchard's broad conclusion is that racial consciousness is weak in Brazil, and race is therefore unlikely to serve as a basis for successful mass movement mobilization. Hanchard is not alone in arriving to this conclusion. Other influential works by Burdick (1998a, 1998b), Marx (1998), and Twine (1998) all regard the likelihood of black mobilization as limited due to weak racial consciousness.

As some of the earliest prominent scholarship on the topic, these works set the terms of the debate on racial consciousness in Brazil, and provided later scholars with a foil in their arguments on black movements' ability to mobilize around race, the degree of racial consciousness in the mass public, and the salience of race, broadly speaking. Indeed, several scholars positioned their arguments squarely against the notion that Brazilians lacked racial consciousness and that racial movements and activism were unlikely to flourish in the Brazilian context. Based on interviews exclusively with *negras assumidas* (self-identified black women), Caldwell (2007) documents racial consciousness among activists and the processes of assuming a black identity, arguing that characterizations of weak racial consciousness paint with too broad a brush. Mitchell-Walthour (2018) similarly argues that Brazilians exhibit notable levels of "linked fate" – a form of racial consciousness characterized by the individual's inability to separate individual from group self-interest (Dawson 1995). Hordge-Freeman's (2015) powerful analysis of racial socialization within families charts more of a middle ground. While acknowledging that

---

[21] For vociferous debate of this work, see Bourdieu and Wacquant (1999) and French (2000). Also see Mitchell (1977) for an early work examining racial identity and consciousness in Brazil.

families largely socialize children to internalize and reproduce racial hierarchies, she also identifies a subset of interlocutors – many of whom are educated or are pursuing upward mobility in the labor market – who engage in "critical accommodation," or behavior that might appear to accommodate racial hierarchies (e.g., straightening one's hair) in order to ultimately further the goal of challenging inequality (realizing upward mobility or attaining positions of authority). In this latter view, dark-skinned Brazilians are neither free from the constraints imposed by commonsense racial hierarchies, nor passively compliant with them.

Scholars focused on activism and mobilization have strongly pushed back against the idea that Brazilians lack racial identities and consciousness. One point of contention in this literature is what counts as black mobilization. Hanchard's conclusions are based on the efforts of the Unified Black Movement, founded in 1978, as the main organization aiming to represent Afro-descended Brazilians and articulate and defend black interests in the country. Yet scholars have pointed to other, more localized forms of activism and mobilization (in which black Brazilians are protagonists) as evidence contrary to Hanchard. In her study of black women's participation in neighborhood associations in Salvador de Bahia, Perry (2013) argues that black women, in particular, are the "key political interlocutors ... the foot soldiers of the historical struggle for social and territorial belonging, participatory urbanization policies, and improved living conditions for black citizens in Brazil" (Perry 2013, 15). Moreover, because scholars like Hanchard and Twine focus attention on national black organizations like the MNU, "they fail to recognize the central role of community-based movements in black identity politics" (Perry 2012, 227). Central to these disagreements is the question of where to look and how to interpret the behavior of black or Afro-descended Brazilians. In response to this debate, Paschel (2016a, 49) distinguishes between "mobilizing while black" and "mobilizing as black." The distinction here, a la Marx, is whether movements (or individuals) articulate their goals, perspectives, or demands primarily in terms of race or something else. Ultimately, I agree with Paschel's compromise position that not all action or behavior carried out by black Brazilians can or should be reduced to or interpreted as racialized behavior or articulation.

One underappreciated aspect of these debates on consciousness is how methodological choices may help explain differences in scholarly findings. Notably, this debate is taking place between scholars who tend to employ qualitative and often ethnographic methods. All methods contain inherent strengths and weakness, and to be sure, qualitative approaches have yielded invaluable insights and offered important correctives that have inspired and informed later studies, including this one. But it's nonetheless worth reflecting on how a dominance of qualitative methods in studies of Brazilian racial consciousness may have contributed to the scholarly disagreements referenced earlier. First, while methods like ethnography are especially useful for gaining insight into the perspectives and logics of particular interlocutors, they are not the most appropriate method for resolving the empirical question of whether or to what extent racial consciousness is widespread among the mass public. Because they often rely on nonrandom sampling methods, such in-depth qualitative data are limited in their ability to generalize beyond particular locales, or overcome potential sampling or selection biases.[22] The consequence is that existing data on racial consciousness are unable to paint a broader, systematic picture of the nature and extent of racial consciousness *in the mass public*. One goal and contribution of this study, therefore, is to build on the insights of prior scholarship on racial consciousness and subject its insights to systematic empirical testing, as well as to assess the validity of these factors as causes of identification, consciousness, and reclassification. In the process, a more systematic approach might also help situate existing qualitative in broader context and potentially help rectify scholarly disputes.

Second and related, qualitative researchers tend to embed themselves in sites where they are likely to find relevant research subjects. By and large, these tend to be black movement and activist circles, that is, locales where individuals are likely to self-select into participation and are more likely than the general public to opt for black identification and exhibit racial consciousness. Again, this approach makes sense when the goal is to gain access to particular perspectives, logics, and mechanisms. But for the purpose of identifying *causes* of racial consciousness or identity change on a mass scale, selecting on the dependent variable limits our ability to infer, or even suspect, causality. Explanatory factors identified in this way may well be present in the cases of individuals who do not assume black identities or exhibit racial consciousness, which we cannot verify without empirical variation in

---

[22] One important exception is Mitchell-Walthour's (2018) recent analysis of black identities in Brazil, which combines interview and survey data. But even in this study, not all survey data analyzed are nationally representative and at times exclude white-identified respondents. While appropriate for particular research questions, this latter analytical choice directly impacts the relevance of findings for the present study, which seeks to understand shifts in identification away from whiteness and toward blackness. Eliminating white identification from the choice set in this way would be inappropriate here.

the dependent variable. Thus, beyond issues of representativeness or generalizability, selection of research sites where racial consciousness likely resides can raises doubts about the identification of causal factors.

And finally, debates on racial consciousness in Brazil generated by existing scholarship situated in particular times and places rarely, if ever, address longitudinal change in the nature of Brazil's racial politics. Notably, there is an underappreciated temporal trend in the conclusions scholars draw based on when data collection took place. Hanchard, Burdick, and Twine, the foils of later racial politics scholarship, conducted field research a decade or more before scholars like Caldwell, Perry, Mitchell-Walthour, Hordge-Freeman, Paschel, and Alves. If there is one fact or conclusion that readers should take away from this book, it is that a country's racial politics is not only capable of profound change over a period of three decades, but that this indeed occurred in the Brazilian case between the 1990s and 2020s. It is entirely possible, therefore, that what appears as theoretical or methodological disputes among scholars could simply be a function of collecting data at different points in time. Methodological bias is one possible explanation for these disputes. Contextual or political change is another.

I do not wish to suggest that any one method is inherently superior to another. Indeed, I employ qualitative methodology myself (see Chapter 4) and triangulate multiple methods and data sources in an effort to counterbalance the strengths and weaknesses of quantitative and qualitative methods. Instead, my purpose with this discussion is simply to highlight that one should not, and indeed I do not, take the existence of racial consciousness in the mass public for granted in the Brazilian case. At the same time, while there may be limitations to what we can infer from existing studies based on methodological choices, we also should not summarily dismiss consciousness as a plausible component of the reclassification I analyze and seek to explain. In later chapters, I rely on various forms of microlevel panel and national survey data to assess my claims. I provide evidence that greater education is associated with greater racial consciousness, and with movement from the white category into nonwhite, and especially black, racial categories. For the remainder of this chapter, however, I devote attention to one theoretical goal of my argument, which is to specify the causal mechanisms and pathways that link education to racialized political identities (racial consciousness) and reclassification in darker racial categories over time. I emphasize the interpretive feedback effects of education on racial subjectivity and identification, which operate via new and increased exposure to information, social networks, and the labor market.

Information

First, and rather directly, education can increase individuals' exposure to new facts, discourses, and understandings of race that can change their views about the significance of race in history and society, or lead them to alternative understandings of race, blackness, and their own self-conceptions. More specifically, new information and discourses, which one might acquire by pursuing courses of study in history, sociology, or education, can range from historical facts or narratives that complicate and undermine official histories, to processes of racialization and the reproduction of racial hierarchies, to alternative ways of conceptualizing "race" and blackness that lead to more expansive and inclusive nonwhite racial categories. In turn, this new information and these perspectives can change the way individuals see and make sense of present-day power asymmetries and inequalities, and change whether they interpret their own experiences as part of a larger or historically inherited social structure.

At first glance, this might strike readers as an argument premised on false consciousness, in which status quo Brazilians fail to recognize the "true" cause of their oppression and deprivation and only later come to identify race as the culprit. But one need not embrace characterizations of the status quo as a kind of false consciousness to accept the idea that education can simply introduce individuals to new ideas. Subsequently, these ideas can change how individuals see and make sense of their positions in society.[23] This more flexible view avoids the analytical pitfalls that some associate with false consciousness arguments (e.g., Bourdieu and Wacquant 1999; for rebuttal, see French 2000). And it avoids placing too much stock in scholars' assertions about the beliefs of the mass public, which had not, until recently, been

---

[23] Hanchard (1994) provides a thesis adjacent to false consciousness, in which the national myth of racial democracy distracts the darker-skinned from recognizing the significance of race and from prioritizing racial over class concerns. Also see Nascimento (2016) and Twine (1998). In her ethnographic study of a favela in Rio de Janeiro, Sheriff (2001) argues against the idea that individuals accept the myth of racial democracy wholesale, documenting beliefs in and understandings of racism and a general view that Brazil is less racially ambiguous than how it is often portrayed. Bailey (2009) analyzes nationally representative survey data and finds little support for widespread belief in the ideas of racial democracy among the public. For other useful discussions on this question in Brazil, see Hordge-Freeman (2015) and Paschel (2016a, 47–51). For other works debating the role of hegemony or false consciousness in other cases, see Gaventa (1982), Laitin (1986), and Scott (1985).

empirically and systematically tested. This is all-the-more important since studies of public opinion do not lend support to the idea that beliefs in the myth of racial democracy, per se, are widespread among the public. Moreover, these studies show that the public is aware of the extent of racialized inequalities in the country, and that they attribute this inequality to structural, rather than individual, causes (Bailey 2002; Telles and Bailey 2013). Such findings suggest that Brazilians' acceptance of ideologies or perspectives associated with the national myth may have been overstated, and that a lack of racial consciousness should not be equated with false consciousness.

But even without staking such strong claims, there remains a difference between knowing something exists or occurs in general and connecting this awareness to one's own personal experiences or making sense of perceived discrimination in racial terms. One of my interviewees, Roberta – who is high school–educated, darker-skinned, and identifies as black, but does not exhibit a high degree of racial consciousness – articulated precisely this point. When I asked Roberta to clarify a seeming contradiction in her views on structural inequality (which she acknowledges) and her own experience with racial discrimination (which she insists is due to her lower-class background), she explains, "You can see [racism] in the statistics. Does it exist? Of course it exists." But, she clarifies, "If I were to say that I've suffered from racism? No. There is racism, but I haven't suffered [from it]."[24]

Exposure to new information thus entails more than simply being made aware of racial inequalities, for example, as general facts or impersonal statistics. And it means more than simply being informed about things like slavery, abolition, or the national "myth of the three races" as historical events in the distant past. New information can make the difference between simple awareness of discrimination and inequality, and subjectively interpreting one's experiences or relative social position in racial terms. In this way, exposure to greater information can imbue racial categories with political meaning, alter the logic one employs to determine racial group membership, and strengthen ties to one's racial group.[25]

---

[24] Author interview, São Paulo, Brazil, February 1, 2017. Also see (Layton and Smith 2017).

[25] In an interesting parallel, see Hordge-Freeman and Veras (2020) for analysis of how access to information reshapes racial identities among Afro-Latinos in the United States.

Social Networks

The information pathway is likely to be relevant to students who pursue or enjoy courses of study in which topics of race, slavery, and inequality are centered. But of course, not all will do so. Yet a second way that education can impact racial consciousness and identification is by introducing individuals to new social contacts and networks, which then introduce individuals to new social spaces and locales. Like the information pathway, these new locales can also provide alternative ways of "seeing" and understanding race (Brubaker et al. 2004) that impact racial subjectivity. For lower-class sectors, who might be concentrated in peripheral communities, attending high school or university often entails frequenting new locales and neighborhoods that often expose individuals to new social spaces, contacts, and networks.

In one respect, university campuses have historically been elite spaces defined by high concentrations of wealth and whiteness. As sites that newly mobile citizens begin to frequent, therefore, school campuses can increase the firsthand exposure of students from marginal communities to specific or heightened forms of racialized inequality, especially as education has become more inclusive (Artes and Ricoldi 2015; Gomes and Moraes 2012; Silva et al. 2020). Indeed, several interviewees remarked on their experiences of being darker-skinned than many of their university peers, or being viewed as an undeserving *cotista* at university simply based on appearance. But at the same time, this racial disproportionality in university student bodies can also be found in high schools, as several interviewees noted. These interviewees also noted that they did not fully appreciate this fact until long after leaving these schools, until after they developed racial consciousness and reinterpreted their past experiences. Thus, while the disproportionate racial makeup of school campuses can come be meaningful to reclassifiers, it's difficult to conclude that this is a causal factor based on interviewees' own accounts.

More importantly, high school and university campuses can serve as organizational centers for student organizing, civic associations, and social movements that maintain presence on university campuses. At the same time, campuses bring together individuals embedded in different social and associational networks, and individuals with varying baseline propensities for participating in such organizations. By making new friends and social contacts, individuals can gain exposure to new social networks and associations. In turn, these networks can expose individuals to new interpretive frames that challenge racial commonsense or other ways of thinking unconducive to interpreting the social and political world through a racial lens.

It might be easier to envision university campuses as important centers for organizational activity, but high schools also provide students with important contact with civil society associations and organizations. In fact, many public schools across Brazil contain established student unions (*grêmios estudantis*), which provide opportunities for students to organize and participate directly in politics. In fact, resources to form such unions in primary and secondary schools was reserved as a right in the 1996 national educational directives implemented under President Cardoso and remained in place in subsequent renewals, making it relatively easy to create student unions where they do not already exist. Individual high school unions also form part of the umbrella UBES (*União brasileira dos estudantes secundaristas* or Brazilian Union of Secondary Students), which connects students in their local school unions to others within their cities, states, and even across Brazil.[26] Thus, as a function of pursuing higher education, students can find themselves in new locales, networks, and civil society spaces, or simply with new contacts who may bring about this kind of exposure.

This kind of exposure can also take place when students enroll in *cursinhos*, extracurricular courses to prepare students for the university entrance exam. Students in lower-class sectors often rely on low-cost *cursinhos*, which are often provided by local NGOs and other organizations. Beginning in the 1990s, black movements and other civil society actors recognized improved rates of high school attendance among popular sectors and began offering *cursinhos*, which naturally attracted students of modest means. The popularity of these courses quickly led to their spread across Brazil (Maggie 2001; Peria and Bailey 2014; Santos 2003). The connection to (often leftist) movements and organizations meant that these courses put a specific emphasis on race-related issues. But in addition to course material, these courses also helped foster ties between students and activism, and inspired students to participate in movement events and activities outside of the *curinsho* courses. In this way, even the mere aspiration of gaining admission to university could

---

[26] The organizational potential of this umbrella organization was on display in 2019, when student protests broke out in more than 200 cities across the country to oppose budget cuts promoted by the Bolsonaro government (G1 2019).

lead students to exposure to new racial perspectives and ways of thinking promoted by activists. Several interviewees described gaining exposure to these new discourses in this way, either through *cursinhos* or other student groups. Enrolling in these classes was often a first step that could generate interest in movement activities beyond the *cursinho*, and thus expose individuals to new discourses and perspectives.

Social movement scholars have documented these very kinds of network effects. Indeed, some influential studies challenge the idea that prior ideological or political worldviews lead to activism and movement participation, arguing that the direction of this relationship may be the reverse. For example, in a study of participation in the antiabortion movement in the United States – a movement commonly viewed as heavily influenced by ideology – Ziad Munson (2010) finds that many participants do not join the movement with preformed ideological commitments, values, or opinions on abortion, but rather adopt the movement's ideology *after* being introduced to the movement via preexisting social contacts. In this case, movement participation causes political worldview, rather than the reverse. Ann Mische's (2008) account of activist networks in Brazil indicates a similar process. In one strikingly relevant example, Mische describes an activist who developed a politicized racial identity by engaging in nonracial activism (Mische 2008, chap. 8). But through this activism, he gained exposure to new discourses and debate on racial issues in Brazilian society that resonated with him. In this case, drawing on networks to insert oneself into specific locales set this individual on a new path that led him to new ways of racial thinking and seeing. Civil and social movement spaces of all kinds, therefore, can be important locales where individuals first discover new racial discourses that ultimately shift racial boundaries and lead them to adopt politicized racial identities. Pursuing education can be the first step in altering the social contacts and networks that lead to this kind of exposure.

The Labor Market

A final indirect way that education impacts racial identity and consciousness is by altering one's trajectory and experiences in the labor market. Of course, many pursue education not simply to acquire information or knowledge but as a promised pathway of upward mobility and improved job prospects. In Brazil, one's level of education can (dis)qualify an individual for highly sought and lucrative public-sector jobs, which are awarded through an impersonal civil service exam and process (*concurso público*). But also in the private sector, high school and university education enable individuals to compete for these and other higher status jobs – which they may or may not attain – potentially exposing them to exclusivity, inequality, or discrimination in elite workplaces and public spaces. Indeed, sociological studies have long documented that the darker-skinned suffer the greatest wage penalties in high-status jobs (Andrews 1991; Campante et al. 2004; Lovell 1999; Soares 2000) – penalties they are likely to suffer even when attempting to distance themselves from blackness (Cornwell et al. 2017).[27] Evidence thus suggests that as darker-skinned Brazilians begin to compete for and even attain higher status job, they are likely exposed to greater racial discrimination.

Additionally, as one ascends the social ladder via education and higher-status or better-paying jobs, it becomes increasingly difficult to attribute any perceived discrimination or one's relative social position to class or status (Silva and Reis 2011; Souza 1983),[28] as one might prefer if both lower-class and darker-skinned (Hanchard 1994; Twine 1998). For Brazilians with racial options, greater education may not bring the economic success they anticipated, which may itself generate grievances that beg for new or additional explanation; alternatively, those who succeed may find themselves suddenly thrust into elite spaces overpopulated by the lighter-skinned. In fact, in a study of well-educated black-identifying professionals in Rio de Janeiro, Silva and Reis (2011) find that these individuals are most likely to identify experiences of racial discrimination in the workplace and other elite public spaces, where they report personal mistreatment or are denied recognition of their social status (also see Lamont et al. 2016). Similarly, Twine (1996) argues that gender differences in perceptions of racism can be explained by men's greater personal exposure to discrimination via higher labor market participation. And in a prescient ethnographic analysis of nonwhite university students in the 1990s (well before the affirmative action era), Teixeira (2003, 172) finds that the student "who has ascended in relation to other *negros* tends to broaden her vision of prejudice and discrimination," and that "it is as if

---

[27] These findings support arguments put forth by Fernandes (1969) on obstacles to the integration of nonwhites into Brazilian society.

[28] As Neusa Souza, a Brazilian psychiatrist who studied the psychological effects of racism in society, writes in her influential book *Tornar-se negro*, "The Brazilian *negro* who ascends socially does not deny a presumable black identity" (Souza 1983, 77). Perlman (2010) similarly argues that upward mobility and expanded opportunities have contributed to perceptions of marginality among the (formerly) lower classes.

this 'ascension' transforms, in some way, perception of the dimensions of prejudice and discrimination."[29] The experiences unearthed in these studies are also borne out in public opinion data, including a large survey conducted by the Brazilian census bureau. These studies find that greater education correlates with the belief that racial discrimination exists (Bailey 2002; Layton and Smith 2017), as well as the view that race is influential in shaping one's life (IBGE 2011, Table 2.5).

To be sure, labor market experiences are heterogeneous; but the broad point is that, by shaping trajectories of upward mobility and labor market insertion, education can significantly alter one's labor market expectations and personal experiences with racialized inequalities and discrimination – even among those with relatively good fortune in the labor market, those who land high-status or good-paying jobs. In turn, these experiences can lead individuals to question and rethink the significance of race and their own racial self-understandings.

SUMMARY AND OBSERVABLE IMPLICATIONS

The specific pathways through which education affects reclassification and the formation of racialized political identities are heterogeneous and often personal. These effects, moreover, unfold over varying periods of time: some individuals report that education impacted their identifications while they were still acquiring education; for others this process unfolded years after completing the highest level of education they would attain. The important point is that the pursuit of greater education, directly or indirectly, can alter racial subjectivities and political identities, and lead individuals to adopt nonwhite and often black identities. As mentioned earlier, systematic survey-based studies lend support to these mechanisms derived from my qualitative interviews, finding that greater education correlates with the belief that racial discrimination exists (Bailey 2002; Layton and Smith 2017), as well as that race is influential in shaping one's life (IBGE 2011, table 2.5). Existing qualitative studies also provide evidence of these causal pathways. Penha-Lopes's (2017, chap. 3) interviews with *cotistas* in Rio de Janeiro, for example, show that students' "racial self-classification has changed over time, especially after they entered university, by distancing themselves from the *branca* [white] and *morena* [dark] categories" (Penha-Lopes 2017, 74). And Teixeira's (2003, 245) rich interviews with nonwhite students in the 1990s provide

---

[29] Author's translation.

evidence that upwardly mobile and darker-skinned students "conserve the color that is socially associated with a situation of poverty and misery," that is, they decline to self-whiten. In this sense, the consequences of educational expansion – the new set of policies and policy reforms aimed at making public education more inclusive – can be placed under the rubric of interpretive policy feedback effects. These are new perspectives, logics, and cognitive frameworks through which individuals understand themselves, race itself, and their relative positions within society.

What sets the hypothesis of this argument apart from traditional expectations is the direction of education's effects. While conventional wisdom expects education (and other forms of upward mobility) to produce whitening, I expect education to produce "darkening," especially for those in the lower classes. The key observable implication that I test in the empirical analyses that follow, therefore, is that better educated Brazilians will be the most likely to reclassify in darker racial categories over time. While I do not strictly hypothesize that these effects are limited to individuals who meet certain phenotypical criteria, I do expect that lower-class Brazilians are likely *candidates* for reclassification partly because they are more likely to meet commonsense phenotypical criteria and are thus best positioned to make plausible claims to nonwhiteness (IBGE 2011; Telles 2014).[30]

While I emphasize the effects of targeted educational expansion on the reclassification patterns at the micro and macro levels, I also recognize the multicausal nature of racial identification and the complexity of factors that lead individuals to self-classify in different racial categories. Indeed, the rich social science literature on the myriad factors that impact racial identification has long served to debunk the essentialist and naturalizing notions of race as a purely biological and even strictly phenotypical phenomenon. To be sure, physical attributes are the most consistent and strongest predictors of racial identification in Brazil. Skin tone is the attribute most commonly invoked to explain identification (IBGE 2011, table 2.11; Monk 2016; Telles and Paschel 2014). Intersectional scholars also emphasize the outsized importance of hair in impacting self-esteem and racial identification, especially among women (Caldwell 2007; Gilliam and Gilliam 1999; Hordge-Freeman 2015; Means 2020). In short, there is no denying the effects of phenotype on patterns of racial identification.

Myriad additional factors, such as social class or occupation, participation in social movements, and exposure to art and media have also

---

[30] While physical attributes are central to Brazilian racial identification, Table 2.2 suggests all Brazilians are afforded considerable leeway in their identifications.

TABLE 3.1 *Federal education reforms, 1988–2012*

New policy or reform	Year	Description
Federal Constitution Ratified	1988	Codified education as a right for all citizens
Lei de Diretrizes Básicas (LDB)	1996	Reformed the national educational plan from 1971, incorporating teachings of Paulo Freire
Fundo de manutenção e desenvolvimento do Ensino fundamental e de valorização do Magistério (FUNDEF)	1996	• Created federal and state spending floors • Altered local incentives by allocating funds to localities based on student enrollments • Earmarked federal and state resources for teachers' salaries and teacher training • Incentivized administration by municipalities (by deducting funds for schools administered by states) to circumvent political bargaining between state and local governments
Exame nacional do ensino médio (ENEM)	1998, 2009	Initially created to assess the quality of high school education in Brazil (1998). Later reformed into a centralized university entrance exam (2009).
Fundo de financiamento ao estudante ao ensinso superior (FIES)	1999	Federal financial aid program for students to attend private universities
Fiscal Responsibility Law	2000	Imposed a host of requirements for transparency, monitoring, and reporting for subnational governments in Brazil, including spending by FUNDEF/FUNDEB programs
Federal Law 10.369	2003	Mandated teaching of African and Afro-Brazilian history and culture in school curriculum
Programa universidade para todos (ProUni)	2004	Federal program to awarded full and partial scholarships for students to attend private universities
Bolsa Família	2004	State-level initiative scaled up to national level; included children's educational attendance as a condition for receiving cash payments

New policy or reform	Year	Description
Sistema nacional de avaliação da Educação Superior (SINAES)	2004	Created a system for the assessment of the quality of public universities.
Fundo de Manutenção e Desenvolvimento da Educação Básica (FUNDEB)	2006	• Provides federal top-up for under-resourced localities • Expanded policy coverage to high schools • Mandated nationwide spending floors
Programa de apoio de reestruturação e expansão das universidades federais (REUNI)	2007	Expanded the number of federal university campuses and the number of slots offered at existing federal universities.
Sistema de seleção unificada (SISU)	2010	System operating jointly with the Enem to facilitate application and admission to multiple public universities
Programa nacional de assistência estudantil (PNAES)	2010	Program to improve retention of university students; Minimize effects of inequalities on completion rates; reduce dropout rates;
Federal Affirmative Action Law	2012	Means and race-targeted reservations in admissions to federal public universities

been shown to impact both racial identification and racial consciousness. Indeed, the very idea behind the concept of "social race" is that class position factors into one's calculus of racial identification (Silva 1994; Wagley 1965). And perhaps no greater organization or agent has received more attention in scholarship on racial identity in Brazil than black social movements (Alves 2018; Burdick 1998b; Hanchard 1994; Moura 1994; Nascimento 2016; Paschel 2016a; Perry 2013). Beyond these usual suspects, scholars have also identified more cultural influences on racial identification, such as hip hop (Mitchell-Walthour 2018; Pardue 2008; Santos 2016), theatrical performances (Smith 2016), and web-based content like YouTube (Mitchell-Walthour 2020; Silva 2020).

It is important to acknowledge the complexity of the social world, and to remember that in emphasizing the role of educational expansion I do not intend to discount or deny the importance of these factors in shaping racial identification. As we'll see in my analysis of interview data in Chapter 4, many of these factors are explicitly cited and discussed as relevant to interviewees' racial trajectories and their decisions. When and where possible I seek to incorporate these influences into my analyses as controls and alternative explanations. And where direct controls are not available, I rely on panel methods to control for unobserved confounders. In Chapter 5, I use time to control for recent developments in Brazilian institutions and culture by analyzing the identification patterns of cohorts who accessed university long before the recent affirmative action era. And in Chapters 5 and 6, I rely on fixed-effects analysis of panel datasets, which control for unobserved confounders that do not vary over time. But in any case, my analytical goals are not to comprehensively explain racial identification writ large, but to account for *change* in identification evident in the reclassification reversal and to show that education can increase the likelihood of nonwhite identification. My focus in the chapters that follow is on substantiating my argument empirically and systematically (in Chapter 5) and drawing out the implications for political behavior (in Chapter 7). But first, in the next chapter I seek to demonstrate the plausibility of this hypothesis and illustrate how this phenomenon manifests on the ground with firsthand accounts of identity change from reclassifiers themselves.

4

Education as a Mechanism of Exposure

> Being black is not a given condition, *a priori*.... To be black is to become black.
> —Neusa Santos Souza, *Tornar-se negro*

This chapter seeks to illustrate how expanded access to education can explain the reclassification reversal. To do so, I present qualitative interview data collected in two major cities, São Paulo and Recife, which helped to generate the hypothesis. The personal accounts of Brazilians of various education levels and socioeconomic backgrounds, as well as with reclassifiers and non-reclassifiers, make clear that individuals' racial self-conceptions and their explanations for identity change are informed, first and foremost, by their personal and lived experiences. But interviewees' accounts also indicate that the pursuit of education shaped those personal experiences, directly or indirectly, and interrupted the status quo beliefs and practices that have historically reproduced racial hierarchies and subjectivities traditionally based in colorism.

My goal in this chapter is to demonstrate the plausibility of this argument by empirically illustrating how education can operate as a mechanism of exposure at the individual level. My argument in this chapter builds on recent work by Kruks-Wisner (2018), who emphasizes how social and spatial exposure across villages in rural India shapes whether individuals exercise their citizenship rights to make claims against the state. The exposure I describe differs on both sides of this equation, but I want to emphasize the simple parallel that exposure to new experiences and locales can lead individuals to engage in political activities and behaviors that they otherwise might not. In this case, educational expansion granted lower-class sectors greater exposure to racial hierarchies and inequalities via access to new information, social networks, and labor market experiences. This greater exposure, in turn, altered racial subjectivities, led individuals to cross previously recognized racial boundaries, and imbued newfound racial identities with political meaning.

Qualitative analysis of interview data is particularly well suited for illustrating causal pathways of these complex and sometimes slow processes in greater detail. Interview subjects were sampled nonrandomly through my contacts at civil society and social movement organizations. This proved fruitful in many respects: it enabled me to find reclassifiers who could provide insight into these processes and it served the purpose of generating a testable hypothesis. But these interview data unto themselves are capable only of illustrating how these processes manifest on the ground, and cannot serve as systematic tests of the hypothesis. Nonetheless, such data are uniquely capable of demonstrating the processes of identity change and politicization at work. And they help specify observable implications that can be tested systematically with a variety of additional data, in this and following chapters. To overcome potential biases likely to arise from my sampling strategy, I conclude this chapter with analysis of randomly sampled survey data spanning 1986 to 2008.

Before presenting analysis of interview data, I first discuss my sampling strategy and other methodological considerations relevant to the analysis and interpretation of these data. I then present data to illustrate three main ways that education can increase exposure, via: new information, access to new social networks and movements, and new experiences in the labor market. Last, I present systematic tests of microlevel survey data.

INTERVIEW METHODS AND SAMPLING

Research Sites

The data presented in this chapter come from thirty-four in-depth interviews conducted with reclassifiers and non-reclassifiers between July 2016 and August 2017. These interviews were conducted in São Paulo and Recife, both capital cities of their respective states, but located in distinct regions of Brazil. Broadly speaking, these cities capture subnational cultural differences that scholars have previously argued impact the fluidity of racial boundaries (e.g., Monk 2013; Telles 1993). The city of São Paulo, located in the southeast of Brazil, is the country's most populous city and has long served as a symbol of the country's modernity (Weinstein 2015).

São Paulo is also known for receiving large waves of European immigration in the late nineteenth and early twentieth centuries (Levy 1974; Skidmore 1993), leading to a larger Euro-descendant population in this and other southern and southeastern states. Scholars have argued that this produced a starker white–nonwhite racial boundary. Comparatively, Recife, the capital city of the northeastern state of Pernambuco, was fertile ground for sugarcane plantations prior to abolition, and was the destination for large numbers of enslaved Africans. As a function of this larger Afro-descendant population, rates of interracial marriage and miscegenation have historically been higher in the northeast, and has been said to produce more fluid and/or ambiguous racial boundaries, relatively speaking (Telles 1993).

In addition to these differences, these two cities also provide empirical variation on the question of reclassification. I analyze subnational differences more rigorously in Chapter 5, but at the start of my field research, my selection of these two cities was also guided by the subnational variation in rates of reclassification these two states offered. In Seawright and Gerring's (2008) framework, these states represent "extreme values on Y," with São Paulo an above-average and Pernambuco a below-average case of reclassification into nonwhite categories. Leveraging variation in the dependent variable – rather than focusing on "average" cases – provides the opportunity to probe causal processes and to derive insights that can be tested more systematically with additional methods. This is the approach I employed. Armed with few satisfying hypotheses at the start, I engaged in inductive field research with the goal of generating a hypothesis that could account for the timing of reclassification, as well as individual-level variation in who chooses to reclassify and why (Martin 2013; Morse 1998, 1999).

Sampling Strategy and Sample Characteristics

In line with these goals, my main purpose was to recruit interview subjects who met the main criterion of being a reclassifier. This is easier said than done, for in Brazil one's physical appearance is a noisy signal of an individual's racial identification, let alone whether that person has changed her identification. I thus recruited interview subjects via snowball sampling, drawing on contacts I developed while conducting participant observation in civil society groups and organizations. As I began fieldwork in São Paulo, I was exploring hypotheses related to the symbolic and instrumental consequences of new affirmative action policies, which shaped my strategies for recruitment. Initially, I used my status as a visiting student at public universities to seek out students who had gained admission via affirmative action programs, as well as those who had not. I also sought out students not yet admitted, but who might seek to use affirmative action programs in the future. This led me to observing preparatory courses for the university entrance exam (*o vestibular*) – known colloquially as *cursinhos* – geared toward low-income students.

Enrolling in *cursinhos* is very common for Brazilians hoping to attend university. Upper and middle-class Brazilians typically enroll in expensive private courses with excellent track records, something that contributes to exclusion and inequality in university access. But thinking that the effects of affirmative action on racial identification might be stronger on those who face slimmer odds of admission led me to seek out free and low-cost *cursinhos* offered by local NGOs targeted toward popular sectors. Students enrolled in these courses were often part of the so-called "new middle class" (Klein et al. 2018; Neri 2011), individuals and families who had risen out of poverty in the prior two decades and many of whom were the first in their families to even try for university admission. As a consequence, many of my first interviews in São Paulo were with individuals who fit this general profile – high school-educated and familiar with affirmative action programs.

After the hypothesis regarding the link between greater education, specifically, and reclassification crystallized from my interviews, I began to seek out greater contact with individuals who were candidates for reclassification – that is, could make plausible claims to nonwhiteness – but did not have the same levels of schooling as the other interviewees I had recruited. Thus, in Recife, I began to observe free adult literacy courses offered at an NGO in a lower-class neighborhood. These courses were oriented toward basic skills like reading, writing, and arithmetic. This may sound extreme, but according to the 2010 census just over half of the Brazilian population did not complete primary schooling or was considered illiterate. Among those aged 50–59 and over 60, this figure rises to 57 and 75 percent, respectively. Though this subsample was limited in my interviews, observing this setting and conducting interviews with these students still offered insight into whether the logics and forces that shape identification might vary across educational strata.

Table 4.1 presents descriptive statistics of the interview sample, which is reasonably split by gender and city.[1] The majority of the individuals I interviewed were in their 20s and 30s, which was largely a function of my sampling current and recent students. Better-educated individuals are also

---

[1] For more on interview sampling and methods sequencing, see Appendix B (available online).

TABLE 4.1 *Basic characteristics of interviewees*

Variable	Mean	St. Dev.	Min.	Max.	N
Recife	0.47	0.51	0	1	34
Age	31.62	14.01	18	70	34
Female	0.59	0.50	0	1	34
Income	1307	1419.72	0	7666.67	34
Reclassifier	0.56	0.50	0	1	34
Education	3.15	1.02	1	4	34
(1) < Primary	0.15	0.36	0	1	34
(3) High School	0.41	0.50	0	1	34
(4) University	0.44	0.50	0	1	34
Racial ID	2.58	0.61	1	3	33
(1) White	0.06	0.24	0	1	33
(2) Brown	0.30	0.47	0	1	33
(3) Black	0.64	0.49	0	1	33

Income measures monthly household income per capita. Racial ID indicates the interviewee's self-classification in the official census categories. One interviewee declined to self-classify using census categories.

overrepresented as a result, but by virtue of seeking out *cotistas* and students from low-cost *cursinhos*, interviewees also tended to be lower-income than typical university students. Interviewees reported a mean monthly household income per capita between one and two minimum wages. Finally, at the time of the interview the vast majority identified as brown or black using official census categories, and roughly half reported having reclassified. It should be noted, however, that reclassification (toward blackness) is only available to individuals previously classified as white or brown, or who know their previous classifications for certain. In some cases, impacts on the political nature of racial identities is evident even without the possibility for reclassification, and at times interviewees were unsure of how they had been classified in the past. Where relevant, I note these details in my analysis.

Interview Setting, Conduct and Positionality

All interviewees participated voluntarily and without compensation,[2] and were informed that they were free to decline answering any question and

---

[2] This information was provided during review of IRB protocols and in the process of acquiring informed consent, which was audio recorded as part of each interview.

end the interview at any time. I personally conducted all of the interviews referenced in this chapter. Interviews were audio-recorded, transcribed, and analyzed without the use of qualitative software. In most cases, I conducted interviews in the offices of a local NGO with which the interviewee was familiar, in a private space on a university campus, or in the home of the interviewee at the interviewee's request. In some cases, interviews took place in public spaces (public parks or coffeeshops), also at the interviewee's request. Interviews lasted between one and two hours.

In conducting these interviews, I combined structured and semi-structured components. To collect basic information and establish a common baseline across interviews, I first asked interviewees to respond to a sixteen-item questionnaire comprised of demographic and socioeconomic information, as well as several questions related to racial identification, reclassification, and racial consciousness. After the questionnaire, I followed an interview guide that was organized around three major sections: educational background and experiences, racial identification and reclassification, and affirmative action.[3] Early interviews were less structured and focused on understanding the logic behind and history of each person's racial identification. Over time, I adopted a more standardized approach, which was conversational in tone and typically began with discussion of one's upbringing and family background before transitioning to educational experiences. If racial identification had not yet arisen in our conversation, I transitioned to this topic by asking them to elaborate on responses to close- and open-ended racial identifications provided on the questionnaire. I deliberately waited to bring up the topic of affirmative action myself until the end of our interview so as not to prime the interviewee to center these policies in our conversation. In some cases, however, these came up as part of our conversation about education and/or racial identification.[4]

As discussed in the introductory chapter, there is no doubt that my positionality was a factor that impacted who agreed to be interviewed and the information that interviewees provided. While there is little I could do to control or change my positionality, I did take measures to try to make my interviewees as comfortable as possible. For one, many of my interviewees were individuals whom I had met and with whom I had established some personal rapport prior to the interview.

---

[3] This semi-structured interview guide is available in Appendix B (available online).
[4] See Appendix B (available online) for reflections on and discussion of my positionality while conducting these interviews.

This meant that they not only knew me and what my research was about, but presumably also felt comfortable enough with me to agree to the interview. Because I also relied on snowball sampling to recruit additional interview subjects, I also relied on these contacts to vouch for me when recruiting individuals I did not personally know well. In these instances, I often addressed the strangeness of the situation with humor, acknowledging that it must be odd to encounter an American researcher in their hometown wishing to speak with them about something potentially mundane or bureaucratic. Openly discussing the situation, I found, helped put us both at ease, and doing so with some humor also helped to establish some rapport. Only in one instance did I receive explicit pushback against the idea of a light-skinned, foreign researcher conducting such research in Brazil; but this also ended up being one of the most illuminating and helpful interviews. Overall, without the power to control or alter my positionality, I found the best strategy was to address it, rather than to willfully ignore it. Because of this, the interview data I present are not free from this influence, but they are, to the best of my abilities, faithful representations of our conversations. Recognizing this potential bias, I cross-check and verify the insights from these interviews at the end of this chapter, as well as in other chapters.

Other Considerations

Though interviews were structured to focus on the relationship between education and racial identification, it's also important to acknowledge that not all interviewees fit neatly into the trajectory of education-induced racial change and politicization that I theorize. This is a probabilistic, not a deterministic, argument. Additionally, many interviewees also emphasized factors traditionally identified in the sociological literature: mixed-race parentage and family influence, physical attributes, interpersonal relationships and dating, and emotional factors. There is also the question of personality factors and internal efficacy that enter the equation and shape individual-level behavior.[5] I do not deny the importance of these factors, and discuss them where relevant. But my focus in this chapter is on demonstrating how exactly education can operate to reshape, change, and politicize racial identities – all in a direction opposite that

---

[5] One interviewee, for example, emphasized that while growing up she was always "big-mouthed" (*muito respondôna*) and always had a comeback for racist teasing or remarks.

theorized in traditional scholarship. As such, the data I present are not intended as tests of the hypothesis, but are intended to illustrate how I identified and observed reclassification on the ground and to demonstrate the plausibility of the hypothesis by illustrating the sequence of events and thought processes through which education, directly and indirectly, impacted interviewees' racial consciousness and, ultimately, their identifications.

MECHANISMS OF EXPOSURE: INFORMATION, SOCIAL NETWORKS, AND THE LABOR MARKET

Chapters 2 and 3 detailed and presented data on the institutional changes behind macro-level educational expansion, driven by the political will and incentives generated by redemocratization and the formal inclusion of the poor as full, *de jure* members of the Brazilian citizenry. Institutional change of this sort helps to explain the timing of the reclassification reversal, but understanding microlevel variation – why some Brazilians choose to reclassify and why – requires attention to the consequences of educational expansion for the lived experiences of those citizens gaining unprecedented access to higher education.

The effects of education on these lived experiences is likely to be different in this era in part because of the high correlation between income and skin color in Brazil, with lower-income sectors being darker-skinned on average (Telles 2014). Though much has been written on the complexity of racial subjectivity and the influence of socioeconomic criteria, survey data of the public indicate that a large majority of Brazilians nonetheless agree that physical attributes are the primary determinants of one's racial classification (IBGE 2011, Table 2.11; Silva et al. 2020). And ethnographic research has long documented whitening practices among lower-class Brazilians, those who most likely meet criteria for blackness but who are socialized to internalize racial hierarchies and thus distance themselves from blackness (Burdick 1998a; Harris 1952; Hordge-Freeman 2015; Sheriff 2001; Twine 1998). Lower-class sectors therefore, who traditionally self-whiten, are also more likely *candidates* for self-darkening. Individuals in these sectors are more likely to make plausible claims to nonwhiteness in phenotypical terms, and yet in the status quo are also likely to comply with commonsense racial hierarchies and engage in whitening.

For many in these sectors, educational expansion interrupted this status quo. Of course, education is an incredibly bundled "treatment."

Individuals pursue education for decades on end and with a variety of different motivations, not least of which is upward mobility itself. But for individuals from lower-class backgrounds, who previously saw scant educational access and who are often subject to – and might be participate in – informal, internalized, or institutional racism, access to greater education can also entail sudden exposure to new information and discourses, new social networks and movements, and/or new experiences in the labor market. In turn, these new forms of firsthand, personal exposure can alter the personal experiences that inform how individuals understand themselves in racial terms and on what basis they make sense of power relationships – their political identities. With greater personal exposure, I argue, race is more likely to form the basis of political identities among newly mobile citizens hailing from the lower classes.[6] I draw on reports from interviewees to demonstrate the plausibility of this argument and to illustrate more concretely how education can lead to racial identity change and politicization: through new and increased exposure to information, social networks, and the labor market.

Information

First, one of the more direct ways that education can impact political identity and racial identification is by exposing individuals to new facts, discourses, and understandings of race. Through certain courses of study in particular (but not exclusively), individuals can acquire new facts about history and official historical narratives, the nature and origins of inequality, or mechanisms of internalizing racial hierarchies. Consequently, this can change how individuals make sense of their relative positions within society and shape their broader conceptions of power and inequality. This does not require an assumption of false consciousness in the status quo. It simply entails a shift in individuals' subjective perspectives. Rather than depersonalizing facts or statistics or relegating racism to the

---

[6] Some interviewees reported similar experiences in terms of class instead of race. Two examples stand out: one light-skinned student and another medium-skinned student, both admitted via means-tested quotas. Both described how attending university deepened their awareness of class inequalities and affected how they understood their chances of getting ahead in life (Author Interview, São Paulo, Brazil, December, 12, 2016; Author Interview São Paulo, Brazil December, 21, 2016). Such reports suggest on one hand that the education–reclassification relationship is a probabilistic one, and on the other that the relationship between education and identity change may not be confined to racial identities alone.

distant past, individuals can come to subjectively interpret their experiences through a racial lens, and understand themselves as products of this history and durable social structure. Ultimately, exposure to new and more information can imbue racial categories with political meaning, alter the logic one employs to determine racial group membership, and strengthen one's ties to one's racial group. For any given individual, it's possible than any one – and even all – of these changes can occur, affecting one's racial classification, identity, and/or consciousness.

Differences between better and lesser-educated interviewees in their exposure to information was particularly stark, but interviewees with high school and university education indicated that gaining deeper knowledge of Brazilian history had a significant effect on their racial identities. Interviewees with low levels of education generally reported relatively little – and in some cases no – knowledge of major historical institutions like slavery. As a somewhat extreme example, lesser-educated respondents in the adult education course I observed in Recife reported that they learned about slavery only after the instructor designed a special unit to discuss slavery in Brazilian history. One student in the class, Raquel, later tells me: "I didn't know about that slavery thing. I used to see it in soap operas.… But I didn't know they had it for real, that there was this thing of blacks suffering so much."[7] Another student in the class, Joanna, reported knowing that slavery entailed coerced labor, but when I ask her from where the enslaved came when they arrived to Brazil, she responds "I forget." Among these informants, familiarity with historical institutions so formative of the Brazilian state and social structure was minimal at best. In some cases – especially among those with low levels of education – ideas about the role of race and/or slavery may be less a product of hegemony or the particular historical narratives in school curricula, and more simply due to a lack of exposure to Brazilian history in general.

By contrast, not only were interviewees with high school and university education much more familiar with historical institutions like slavery, but as a result of their familiarity with these topics they commonly griped about how these institutions were portrayed in national curricula and contributed to perceptions of black Brazilians in the present day that perpetuated racial inequalities and discrimination. Particularly common were complaints about superficial coverage of race-related topics or characterizations of slavery as a nefarious institution in the distant past that

---

[7] Author interview, Recife, Brazil, July 18, 2017. Interviewee names throughout this chapter are pseudonyms.

ceased to be relevant after the foundation of the Brazilian republic. One interviewee, Glória, a university student whom I met in São Paulo and who partially attributes her reclassification from brown to black to learning more about Brazilian history, reports the following about what she learned prior to university:

> In high school, I learned just that blacks were enslaved and that they [were beaten], and that's it. If you take a book from primary school, you'll notice they dedicate two paragraphs with a picture of a black man being whipped. And we learn that Princess Isabel freed [the enslaved] and full stop. That's what we learn and nothing more. You grow up learning that there was slavery in Brazil, but that's it.

To be sure, slavery and Afro-descendants are integral to Brazil's official historical narrative as a former Portuguese colony and a racially mixed – and united – people. And many interviewees reported learning more or less this version of historical events. However, as Glória's comments show, there is no guarantee that Brazilians learn, for example, that Brazil was the single largest and longest running participant in the slave trade, or that it was the last country in the Americas to abolish slavery in 1888; nor are they necessarily exposed to the idea that, as a racialized institution, slavery carries enduring consequences for present-day inequalities. Like Glória, interviewees often indicated that the insidious details of slavery were either downplayed or omitted from the official history they learned in public school, and that they came to a more profound understanding of these events either in university or while preparing themselves for the notoriously difficult university entrance exam.

Reports like these are especially notable coming from interviewees in their late teens and early twenties, that is, individuals who completed high school after the passage of federal law 10.369 in 2003. This law, which was heralded as a significant step forward in the state's recognition of racial differences and inequities, mandated the teaching of African and Afro-Brazilian culture and history in national curricula and was intended to correct the kinds of deficiencies that Glória emphasizes. Yet the accounts of interviewees, many of whom only recently left public high schools, convey that the law did little to focus more attention on facets of Brazilian history that run counter to the whitewashed story often told. This is perhaps not surprising, given that the few systematic analyses of this law that exist suggest it has not been well implemented (Almeida and Sanchez 2017; Negreiros 2017).

In any case, as someone who reclassified from brown to black, Glória exemplifies how exposure to greater information can impact racial identification. Another university student I interviewed, Paulo, reported a similar experience while studying for the university entrance exam, and emphasized the impact this had on his racial consciousness. Paulo, who has dark skin and kinky black hair that he wore in the style of an afro at the time our interview, reported that he had always identified as black. Paulo was therefore not a reclassifier, per se, but the substantive effects of greater information are still evident in how his racial identity came to take on political meaning as a result. Paulo reports that the salience of race in his own political worldview, and indeed the nomenclature he uses to describe his racial identity, changed as a result of exposure to information. His identification was stable, but the meaning of his racial identity changed.

Though at the time of our conversation Paulo considered himself a militant of the black movement, this activism was a relatively recent development in his life. Paulo hails from a peripheral community in the outskirts of São Paulo, but attended a public high school in Morumbi, one of the wealthiest neighborhoods in the city. Despite being one of a few darker-skinned students at the school and feeling socially excluded, Paulo says that at the time he "didn't notice" racial divisions and didn't believe his exclusion was racially motivated. Yet he reports this stands in contrast to his experience attending a prestigious public university in São Paulo that is also majority-white, which he describes as a source of discomfort. When I ask Paulo why this bothered him at university, but not at his largely white and wealthy high school, Paulo says it is because of his newfound "political and racial consciousness."

Paulo reports that this transformation into a racially conscious and politically active university student began when he enrolled in a *cursinho* to prepare for the university entrance exam. History courses, in particular, had a major impact on his racialized political consciousness because, he says, it was there that he first began to realize how little he had learned about the role of Afro-descendants and the enslaved in Brazilian history. In Paulo's words, "lessons on slavery and Africa opened my mind." Paulo cites in particular the greater depth of information he gained in this course:

[About] slavery I [had learned] a few things, but not much. Like, I knew that there was slavery, I knew more or less the time period, but it was very ... superficial, the lessons about this. I didn't know what slavery was like and a lot of times I never learned for example that there were [slave] revolts. For example, the most important was the Quilombo dos Palmares with Zumbi, and I didn't know about it. I came to know about it. I didn't know for example what happened after abolition, for example. After abolition came the Republic, and we heard nothing more about *negros* in the Republic. And the *negros* were there.

Like Glória, Paulo take issue with the superficial coverage of race-related issues in history lessons. Paulo's invocation of the *Quilombo dos Palmares*, the most well-known maroon community of escaped slaves prior to abolition, is one piece of information that commonly contradicts the sanitized narrative of Brazilian slavery, which revisionists describe as benevolent and humane (Nascimento 2021; Tannenbaum 1992; for critique also see Marx 1998). The presence of *quilombos* and the rebellions they often carried out are clear evidence of the desire to resist institutions of slavery, rather than submit to its "benevolence." Moreover, in Paulo's view black Brazilians are subjects of history only insofar as slavery is concerned. After abolition and the foundation of the republic, black Brazilians are absent from historical narrative.

Beyond the specific information that runs counter to what he previously was told, for Paulo learning a more detailed history of slavery was also about developing a point of view from which he could understand present-day inequalities and himself as legacies of historical institutions, rather than apolitical statistics. As Paulo describes, "I knew that slavery happened, but I didn't know how. I didn't know how much this legacy exists today. You learn what happened, but a lot of times it's that 'the past is just the past' and has no legacy today, or it's very small. We just think 'oh, that's alright, that was the past and it's not like that anymore.' But there is a great legacy from this now." Learning more about history was about more than "just the past," it was also about coming to understand the present as a product of the past, as a durable social structure with origins in slavery. Relatedly, Glória similarly describes how a misunderstanding of history can promote ideas that inculpate darker-skinned Brazilians for their subordinate positions, especially vis-à-vis European immigrants arriving in the late nineteenth and early twentieth centuries and with generous financial support from the state (Lesser 1999; Skidmore 1993):

The idea that's cultivated is everybody suffered, that everybody can get ahead if they want. 'Look where the Italians are. Look where the Germans are. Why haven't the blacks [accomplished this]? Because they didn't want to. Because they didn't want to work. Because they really are lazy bums.' And so you watch TV and the whole time they show this. Who's stealing, assaulting? Who's in jail? You see a black guy and think 'lord, black guys only.' So it's all a structural process, isn't it? Of alienation. Of trying to spread an image of something that really isn't how it was.

The perspective that Glória takes issue with – that Europeans and Africans faced similar migration experiences and conditions for social and economic integration – is similarly based on manipulation of historical fact. Failing to recognize the forced migration and labor exploitation experienced by enslaved Africans as juxtaposed to the subsidized passage and wages paid to European immigrants (Andrews 1991; Moura 1994; Skidmore 1993) generates a false equivalency that perpetuates negative stereotypes about black Brazilians, that creates "a structural process of alienation." Both Glória and Paulo describe how greater exposure to information led them to historically situate present-day inequalities and see themselves and others like them as part of a durable social structure.

For Paulo, this new perspective also fostered stronger and politically meaningful ties to his racial group. Recall that Paulo is not a reclassifier, per se, since he identifies as black and has always been classified as black by others in his family (on his birth certificate, for example). But the effects of this exposure on his racial identity are nonetheless evident in the specific nomenclature he prefers to describe his black identity. Instead of the term *negro* – which is increasingly common in Brazil and is promoted by the black movement to unite all Afro-descendants of various skin tones – Paulo prefers the term *preto* – the official census category, but also a term that can be deployed pejoratively and that carries a degree of stigma (Maggie 1994). Paulo explains that "there was always this idea of *preto* being bad ... 'ah, the *preto* was a slave.' [...] So that's why [I choose *preto*], to break the horrible stereotype that *preto* is bad." For Paulo, using the word *preto* to describe himself accomplishes several things. It of course indicates his racial identification. But at the same time, it carries with it the historical significance of slavery that is so central to his political consciousness, as well as his efforts to confront and challenge the racial hierarchies that convey that "*preto* is bad."

The accounts of Paulo and Glória illustrate how exposure to information in the form of historical facts can impact racial identities, but greater information can also entail exposure to new ways of thinking about and seeing race – what social movement scholars call "interpretive frames" (Snow et al. 1986). More specifically, by exposing individuals to alternative, more political understandings of blackness, individuals who previously subscribed to colorist logics of identification based on fine, color-based distinctions might take on a more expansive and political understanding of blackness rooted in shared experiences of racism and discrimination. This was a common theme among interviewees who could be described as falling in the middle of the color spectrum. These interviewees articulated a degree of uneasiness in identifying as black before altering their conceptions of blackness, something that could misalign with how they are read by others. These interviewees described a process of developing a new perspective which enabled them to assert a black identity.

Take, for example, Tiago, a university student in Recife who is classified as white on his birth certificate. He reports that, growing up, he thought of himself as *moreno* before eventually identifying as black while in enrolled in university. Explaining his logic for previously identifying as *moreno*, Tiago says:

I think it's because I never thought that I was so black. It's like, I'm dark, but [when] you look at me, do you say *'negro'*? Do you think 'he's surely black'? You look [at me] and you don't have that certainty. I think it was because of this. I used to say I was *moreno*, so I wasn't *negro*. People would say 'oh, because the *negros*,' so I [would think] 'Ok, the *negros*, is it? That's not me,' you know? I didn't identify, because – because of my color, which was a bit lighter.

Tiago previously thought of his racial identification as a simple matter of fact based on whether he was dark enough to qualify as *negro*, which he clearly understands to be distinct from, and not necessarily a euphemism for, *moreno*. Jorge, also a university student in Recife, explains a similar logic, but one that he employed with more anxiety than Tiago. Like Tiago, Jorge is classified as white on his birth certificate and would eventually come to identify as black. Jorge describes himself using the English word "colorblind" when he was growing up, though he also reports that he suffered from discrimination as a teenager. But, he tells me, "I didn't know to say it was racism, because I was a light-skinned *negro*, and I didn't know that I could be *negro*, self-identify as *negro*." At another point in our interview, Jorge says: "I had suffered racism and I didn't know to classify it as racism." Like other interviewees, Jorge also reports experiences that he came to understand as racist only years after the fact, since he "didn't know" he "could be" black. Going on to explain why, Jorge tells me:

If he isn't the totally darkest shade of black, [someone's] going to be like, 'oh, you aren't *negro*, you're *moreno*.' This happens since I have light skin. So for me it was impossible to identify as black, like, even today I have to fight to self-identify as black mainly among my white friends, who are the majority [of my friends]. And in some places, among *negros* too. Sometimes [*negros*] don't recognize me as black because of my light skin.

Clearly, Jorge does not equate blackness with specific physical attributes, which he recognizes might disqualify him as black in the eyes of some.

But also clear in Jorge's description is the battle he faces between this status quo discourse of colorism – in which blackness is defined as one end of a continuum – and a newer discourse (one also promoted by the black movement), in which blackness is understood in more encompassing and political terms.

For Jorge, arriving to this more expansive understanding of blackness took time and came about as a result of courses he took while in graduate school, specifically a course on black feminism. He began to read texts like Fanon's *Black Skin, White Masks*, introducing him to the ways in which the dominated internalize the norms and stigma of racial (or other) hierarchies, and may even help reproduce those hierarchies. Additionally, he describes the ways in which this classroom provided a forum for students to share their personal experiences. Jorge describes that he identified with and went through many of these same experiences himself, but was struck by how these students explicitly labeled those experiences as racialized and racist. When I press Jorge for a particular moment or turning point for his identification, he recounts a particular class session when a student in the class singled him out and asked to him to declare his racial identification:

[A student] was discussing a text in the front of the classroom and the conversation was going toward questions of racism. It had everything to do with the theme of the class, of the text and such. But like, people started giving personal accounts. Like there was a time when I said, "damn, I went through that, too," you know? And [then the student] pointed her finger at my face and said – like, she was far, you know, she was in the front of the classroom – and she asked like "do you identify as *negro*?" And I said ... [laughter] I didn't even know what to say. [...] So I said, I was there like, my heart beating fast, like, my adrenaline was [pumping], and I ... I said, "I'm discovering myself," I said. Because it was something I had felt my whole life, but with periods of horrible doubt. But like, it's ... it was also something that resonated with me and that I didn't know how to verbalize.

When I ask him if he can remember the first time he identified as brown (*pardo*) instead of white, he responds with "the only demarcation I have for certain to give you is from the time I had contact with the professor [of the black feminism class] and of the accounts of my peers in the classroom. That's when I was like 'I'm black [*negro*],' you know?"

Eventually Jorge would reclassify again as black, but during our first interview he had not yet done so, opting instead for the official category *pardo*. But in a follow-up interview, we had the following exchange:

Education as a Mechanism of Exposure 111

DD: Do you think there will come a day when you identify as *preto*?
JORGE: *Preto*? I think so. Honestly, I already want to.
DD: You do?
JORGE: Yeah.
DD: So why not [do it]?
JORGE: It's ... I even wanted to change that in the interview. [Laughter]
DD: You wanted to change it?
JORGE: I did. I wanted to talk with you to change it, because—but it's a question of—
DD: —well, it's recorded.
JORGE: [Laughter] Because it's a question of, like what I told you, that I don't see a problem of being a light-skinned *negro*, you know? I don't see a problem.
DD: So, two weeks ago, when I interviewed you the first time, I asked, like, 'if the IBGE [census bureau] arrived today for the census [and asked your racial identification].' [And] you would have said *pardo*. But today, like—today like right now—if the IBGE arrived, what would it be?
JORGE: The question today ... *preto*.
DD: It would be *preto*?
JORGE: It would be *preto*. What I was agonizing about was this—which was something that I talked about a lot with [my wife] too—that my son was going be born, and so I was with this doubt [of how to classify my son], you know? And so I said, 'I'm going to put *pardo*,' and then she was like 'No, don't put *pardo*. Put *preto*.' And then I [said] 'Dammit, that's right. I'm going to put *preto* for my son.' He's the son of *negros*, you know?

For Jorge the transformation of his racial self-understanding was a slow and ambivalent process. Of course, his self-classification as *preto* in this instance is due in part to my own prodding. But what is nevertheless clear from Jorge's personal trajectory is how his own reclassification required him to depart from the status quo racial subjectivity rooted in colorism and adopt an understanding of blackness rooted in shared experiences of racism. Previously, his own ambivalence about his racial identity and others' denial of his classification as black foreclosed the possibility of identifying as black. But exposure to new conceptions of blackness, in particular via fellow students' accounts in the classroom, led Jorge to embrace an understanding of blackness that was more resonant and inclusive. In the process of adopting this new racial subjectivity, Jorge reinterpreted his past experiences as racialized and racist, and came to reclassify first as brown and then as black.

Social Networks

The information pathway is likely to be relevant to students who pursue or enjoy courses of study in which topics of race, slavery, and inequality are centered. But not all will do so. A second more indirect way that education can impact political identity and racial identification is by introducing individuals to new social contacts and networks, which can then expose individuals to new social spaces, discourses, and perspectives. As locales that bring together individuals that might otherwise remain in disparate neighborhoods in large cities, high school and university campuses can serve as organizational centers for student organizing, civic associations, and social movements. Individuals of course vary in their baseline propensities or predilections for civic participation. But by making new friends and social contacts, even individuals who are not so predisposed can gain exposure to new social networks and associations. In turn, these organizations can introduce individuals to new ways of thinking and seeing – as well as new information – that might challenge racial commonsense or subjectivities that are unconducive to interpreting the social and political world through a racial lens. As described in Chapter 3, high school and university campuses contain networks of student unions, and black movement organizations became significant providers of university preparatory courses, both of which can set individuals on the trajectory summarized here. Thus, simply by frequenting school campuses, students become more likely to socialize with friends or pursue civic participation, which can result in exposure to new and resonant interpretive frames that reshape and politicize racial identities.

This inadvertent way that education can impact identification is illustrated well by Tiago, the university student from Recife who reclassified from white to black. As referenced earlier, Tiago says that he used to think of himself as *moreno* because he saw his skin tone as relatively light. Only later did he come to see himself as black and reinterpret his past experiences as racialized. Tiago reports that what triggered this change was a seemingly random chain of events set off by his friends. He describes his friends and girlfriend at the time, all of whom he met at university, as elites. Having grown up in a marginal community in Recife, Tiago is aware of these class differences but says he otherwise felt comfortable around these friends, whom he describes as political leftists who were very active in various activist and social movement circles. One day, Tiago reports, he went to meet his friends, who were planning to attend a social movement event that happened to be organized by the local black movement organization. Tiago identifies this event as the critical moment in his racial transformation:

So through [them] I went to one of their events, which was [during] the 'week of racial consciousness.' …And so I went to this event, it was a whole week, of panels, debates, there were things about the turban to, I don't know, discussions about the history of slavery. It was everything ... I arrived there and I identified, like, there were people who said 'you know, everybody's been through that moment [as a kid] where you're choosing a colored pencil [to color in] the skin color of your friend, and you [worry about] what color [your friend] is going to pick for you,' you know? Those situations that black people always go through? Always, always.... It was there that I started to realize. There I was like 'brother, all those situations had to do with the color of my skin. How had I not realized this before?' You know?

Tiago's experience is similar to the account of Jorge, who heard stories of discrimination that were similar to his own experiences that were being described as racist, and only then came to rethink his racial self-conception. For Tiago, too, what changed here was not his awareness of the experiences themselves, or the feelings they provoked for him in the moment. What was different was the interpretation of those experiences as racialized. He reports that hearing those experiences characterized in this way brought him clarity. Like Jorge, this ultimately changed his conception of blackness in ways that led him to see himself as black.

Prior to this exposure Tiago tells me that he scarcely thought about himself in racial terms. Recall that Tiago used to identify using the ambiguous term *moreno* and subscribed to a colorist logic of identification ("I'm dark, but [when] you look at me, do you say 'negro'?"). Describing himself as a child, he explains: "I didn't know that I was *negro*, like, I didn't have this perspective. I saw myself as strange and [only] after did I come to understand that I felt strange because I was *negro*." Attending this week of events organized by the local black movement was a turning point: "I used to think blacks were others ... but when I met the black people there I [said] 'I am [black],' you know?" He goes on:

It was more a feeling. It was really simple in reality. It was really – I looked [around] and said 'jeez, that all happened because I was black, because I *am* black.' It was really just like that. It was a discovery. It wasn't very, like, 'ah, if I'm black what's going to happen, if I say this?' It wasn't so explicit like that. I looked, like, I went through everything the people were talking about. They were saying that they're black and they went through this because they were black. It made a lot of sense ... [I thought] 'it must be right.' And so I started to think this.

Though Tiago's trajectory shares much in common with Jorge's, his process of reclassification was much faster and less anxiety-riddled. In his case, his new social contacts at university inadvertently led him to a social movement event that proved critical. He identified strongly with the recounted experiences of racism, which altered his understanding of blackness to a kind of shared experienced. Consequently, this changed the way he saw himself in racial terms and led him to reinterpret his past experiences as examples of racial discrimination. Though in Tiago's telling this happened in quick succession for him, it also unfolded as a multistep process, one that was set off by new contacts he made while at university.

Beyond altering racial subjectivity and shifting boundaries, exposure to social movements can also play a critical role in helping and empowering individuals to confront internalized racial hierarchies and the stigmatization of blackness that often disincentives black identification. Ethnographic researchers often describe beauty practices, especially around hair, as one of the primary ways Brazilians are socialized into racial hierarchies (Caldwell 2007; Hordge-Freeman 2015), namely through the expectation that those with kinky hair will either wear their hair exceedingly short (men) or straighten their hair via caustic treatments (women). To be sure, hair was a theme more commonly brought up by women I interviewed, but men also expressed anxiety around the appearance of their hair. And racially aware interviewees of both genders often opted to adopt natural hairstyles and afros in a style similar to the black power movement in the United States. As Tiago reports: "when I realized [I was black], I made a few decisions. First was [that] I'm going to let my hair grow." Jorge similarly began wearing his hair in the style of an afro as part of his reclassification, which he described as "painful." Reflecting on this, he tells me: "hair is as strong as [skin] color … for some even stronger than color. Hair – it's more meaningful, isn't it?" The question of hair, and the emotional baggage around it, was especially prominent among individuals with some contact with social movements. Many women, in particular, bemoan the pressure to engage in these practices either instrumentally (to maintain a job, for example) or for other reasons, and many also express concern and anxiety around decisions not to comply with these beauty practices.

Another role that social movements can play is drawing attention to these types of practices, and providing support to individuals who are making the decision to embrace what once brought them shame. The stigmatization of black features, especially hair, was very prominent among lesser-educated interviewees. As is common in Brazil, these interviewees did not necessarily refer to "black hair," but rather "bad hair" (*cabelo ruim*). When I would ask what they meant by "bad hair," those with kinky hair would point to their own heads. One such interviewee, Madalena, describes her son as light-skinned, but says he is not "really" white, because "he is white with bad hair," and "real whites have to have good hair."

Education as a Mechanism of Exposure

What set better-educated interviewees apart in this respect was not the absence of such stigmatization, but their ability to confront and overcome it, albeit painfully at times. Nina, for example, is a 19-year student who gained contact with the black movement through her *cursinho*, and who began wearing her hair in a natural style as she reclassified from brown to black. She tells me, "the process of assuming *afro* hair is painful, because you, like, you come up against the standard of beauty established in society." She reports that as a teenager, she used to have her hair straightened so routinely that her hair began to fall out and she was forced to adapt. But the idea of wearing her hair naturally provoked anxiety: "when the idea came up of wearing my *afro* hair, I even said 'No, I'd rather go with braids because can you imagine my natural hair? People, like, people are going to think it's ugly. I'm going to feel ugly.'" Nina attributes her ability to overcome those feelings and wear her hair naturally to the empowerment she felt by attending black movement events through her *cursinho*.

At one point in my interview with Jorge, I asked him how he felt after accepting his nonwhite identity, and he described this as "a moment of great pain because I remembered everything I went through. [...] Because being black isn't [a] good [thing] in Brazil, so like, you suffer a lot of racism, you suffer violence. You suffer all kinds of prejudice ... So who wants to be black, you know?" Similarly describing the pain and emotions around claiming blackness, a *cursinho* student in São Paulo, Isabela, relayed the following:

It's as if the person felt ashamed to admit it, you see? That they're black. Because it's associated with, I don't know, you being poor. Not everyone says it, you know? And people do [this thing] of saying *pardo*, just to not say the word *negra* ... People are afraid of saying the word *negra*, *preto*, you see? They don't like saying it ... It's like Harry Potter saying the name of Voldemort.

Lesser-educated respondents agreed with Isabela's sentiment. In one instance, during an adult literacy class in which the instructor was discussing issues of racial prejudice, one of the students in the class, Joanna, who is darker-skinned, was asked whether she would accept the label *negra* for herself. She replied: "I would not accept it, no! Why would someone call me that?" Her response was met with a burst of laughter from others in the class. After settling down the room, the teacher then asked Joanna if she would find the word offensive, to which Joanna replied: "If someone called me *negra*? Yes!"

Exposure to civil society and social movement organizations, in particular, can be a critical resource that helps Brazilians confront, manage, and overcome the personal challenges of contesting racial hierarchies rather than complying with them, of claiming rather than avoiding blackness. What set better-educated interviewees apart, from my view, was not the emotions they attached to blackness, per se, but their likelihood of encountering alternative perspectives on blackness that they would eventually adopt. Consider the case of Carol, a former university student in her late 20s whom I met at a public debate on the question of religious racism in Recife. Carol grew up and lives in a peripheral community in the greater metropolitan area of Recife. She describes her mother as black and her father as white, and reports that she used to self-identify as white before reclassifying as black. Explaining this change, Carol points to the importance of accepting her natural hair. She tells me that she used to routinely straighten her hair, but started to question this practice after a boyfriend began asking why she bothered. She hadn't yet begun to question her racial identity, but this prompted Carol to cut her hair short and let it grow back naturally. She reports that "initially I thought that—I thought I was going to [look] horrible with my natural hair." I ask her how it felt once she finally took this initial step: "The beginning was difficult ... because a lot of people started to criticize [my hair]. I would hear a lot of criticisms saying, 'what ugly hair' ... A lot of negative criticisms, you know?"

Despite Carol's showing early signs that she was able to buck the trend, her early efforts to do so were met with resistance from others. It was not until later, however, when she became more involved with social movements as a university student, that she came to accept and embrace her hair and, eventually, black identification. Carol, who as a public health student was broadly interested in social issues, began attending social movements oriented toward gender and women's issues. But, she describes, she quickly felt unsatisfied with the lack of attention paid to other forms of inequality. Eventually, she discovered organizations oriented toward racial and intersectional issues, and these spaces resonated more closely with her, especially around the question of accepting her hair:

Right when I started to participate in those spaces and I started to also see other girls with the same hair as mine. I started to frequent groups relating to hair. [I started] to leave [my] hair natural on Facebook, where there are some groups. Anyway, when it started a lot of people – a lot of women were assuming their hair and I started to see them and frequent those spaces. So I started to like it and I started to assume [my natural hair].

While the initial seeds of Carol's accepting her hair and claiming a black identity began long before she became active in social movements, her exposure to "black militancy," as she describes it, helped her to overcome the stigma and emotional challenges that can go along with contesting racial hierarchies, especially around hair. This militancy was something she stumbled upon as a result of her studies in public health. Carol's story is another example of the more indirect pathways through which education can impact identification through exposure to social networks and movements. Thus, in Carol's and the accounts cited here, education inadvertently brought students into contact with alternative discourses and perspectives that altered individuals' self-conceptions and racial identifications.

The Labor Market

A final indirect way that education impacts racial identity and consciousness is by altering one's trajectory and experiences in the labor market. Of course, many pursue education not simply to acquire information or knowledge but as a promised pathway of upward mobility and improved job prospects. High school and university education better position individuals to compete for competitive public sector and other jobs – at least in theory. In some cases, qualified individuals with desired skills may not attain employment they feel they deserve, generating a sense of status incongruity that begs for explanation. In other cases, individuals may succeed in attaining sought-after jobs, only to be thrust into professional environments of exclusivity, inequality, and discrimination toward the darker-skinned. Such discrimination – which can emanate from the combination of high education and darker skin, for example – can also spill out into other public spaces that these individuals can newly access as a result of upward mobility. Thus, personal exposure to discrimination continues to mount just as these individuals are attempting to realize the potential of their education. Moreover, as one ascends socially, it becomes increasingly difficult to attribute any perceived discrimination to one's class or status. To be sure, labor market experiences are heterogeneous. But by shaping trajectories of upward mobility and labor market insertion, education can significantly alter one's expectations and personal experiences with racialized inequalities and discrimination. In turn, these experiences can lead individuals to see the significance of race in their own lives and rethink their own racial self-understandings.

Several highly educated interviewees discussed experiences in the labor market as critical to their adoptions of politicized black identities. Relatively common was the view that the darker-skinned were expected to fulfill certain roles in society and that breaking free of this mold would require significant amounts of hard work and struggle. Carol, for example, in response to a question about what it means to her to be black, responds that "it's complicated" because "you have to enter the social fight, which is more a fight of accepting a job, employment. Because it seems like it's already determined that you're going to work in certain locales, isn't it? It seems like you're born and it's already predetermined that you'll have to [work] in domestic service work." As a master's student with humble origins, Carol says she's always looking for opportunities to pull in extra income and even considered domestic work as a side gig:

One day recently I started to ask myself, 'why don't I put up an add to be a domestic worker?' Because I thought like, I would get some good money, you know? One day of work at 100 *reais* per day as a domestic worker. I started to think about it. But then I – damn, I have a university degree! I have a bachelor's degree! I'm doing a master's! And so this feeling came, you know? Because it seems like it's something that's defined, that's predetermined for you. And the more you assume that identity the more you identify things, you realize racism, you realize all these nuances, like, I – when a person doesn't identify as much with her color she suffers racism but she doesn't realize it a lot of times.

For Carol, possessing high levels of education understandably changed her expectations of the *types* of jobs she should attain. And it's notable that when asked about the meaning of her racial identity, she quickly makes the connection to feelings of discrimination in the labor market. For her, being black is about identifying forms of structural disadvantage or subordination and interpreting that as racism. Her elevated status as a university graduate is central to that interpretation.

Gilberto, a 34-year-old doctoral student in Recife, reports a similar experience in which his status was not recognized, but this took place for him in the workplace. Gilberto couldn't tell me how he was classified on his birth certificate, but says that he used to think of himself as *moreno* ("a euphemism of nonrecognition" in his words), though his father used to call him *negão*, roughly translating to "big black guy" in English. Today, Gilberto proudly identifies as *negro* and *preto* and calls himself a militant of the black movement with an explicitly politicized black identity. Gilberto admits he had something of a predilection for participation in social movements and was always drawn to hot-button issues, but when he was younger he reports he was much more concerned with class than race. Gilberto says he did experience racism as a child and a teenager, but he didn't understand it as such until long after: "I came to understand that I was confrontational because of the racism I suffered, but ten years after I suffered it." At the time though,

You don't think about it. Because it's that thing, you naturalize. Thinking hurts. You create a self-defense mechanism to not feel pain. You don't think about that. [...] How can I say it? I never thought about it, you know? I knew that I wasn't the same, I knew that I was a minority. This was obvious, people call you black. But I didn't reflect on this, I didn't reflect in that way. And so, honestly it took a long time. It took me more than ten years to understand that these things had to do with being black. I took a long time.

Indeed, when he entered university, Gilberto tells me he participated in public debates, often taking the position of "the black guy against racial quotas." It wasn't until he began teaching high-school philosophy while in university that he began to see things, including himself, differently. He reports that "it was above all my experience as a teacher" that led him to adopt a politicized black identity. In his words, teaching "provoked me toward this because the students, on the first day of class they didn't think I was a teacher ... because I was black ... It's linked to teaching, [what] made me realize how black I was." He continues his explanation:

[It's] because I was black. But what they said is that it was 'No, professor, it's because [you] are really young,' and I said 'you don't have teachers as young as me?' They did. So what's left for us? 'ah no, it's the dreadlocks.' And I [said] 'The dreadlocks? The dreadlocks I get too. But let's say it, how many black teachers do you have besides me?' 'Ah, just [you].' So that was shocking. It was in 2004. It's linked to teaching. Work, which is the thing I love most in life – teaching, and research – work made me realize how black I was and [it] close[d] that cycle of what we in the movement today call empowerment. Of understanding blackness as a political position ... And so I start[ed] to look at my history and see 'oh, it was only me teaching while black.'

In addition to the students, Gilberto similarly reports that other school employees similarly did not respect his status and authority as a professional teacher:

[It] was thrust upon me because the doorman of the school didn't recognize me as a teacher. I got there, young. I was twenty-one, twenty. It was a while ago. And like, I went to go into the school and he opened the gate for a Portuguese professor, an old white lady, kind of old. And then when I went to enter he closed the gate. 'What do you want, young man?' And I [said], 'if you let me in I want to teach class.' And so that's when he looked at my face, 'oh, sorry, but I didn't recognize you.' I said, 'it's alright. Next time I'll wear a button-down shirt and old jeans and leather sandals, maybe then you'll recognize me as a teacher.' [...] I understood. It wasn't because I was young because there were other young teachers at the school. It was because I was black. So from that point forward [things] started to change.

The experiences working as a teacher in a high school were "a turning point in my life," according to Gilberto. They initiated the process of identity politicization, which he reports took more than ten years to unfold before he came to an "understanding [of] blackness as a political position." Later in our conversation when I prompt Gilberto again for a moment in time when he could identify this shift in the nature of his racial identity, he returns again to this experience teaching high school: "You're provoking me now to think about what that moment was. So, I chose that moment from 2004 because of that experience, but I had never thought, until now, that that experience was all of that. But it was, in fact. In fact, because 2004 was the year that I changed my position on racial quotas, that I started to change." In this case, attaining a certain level of education led Gilberto into a profession in which his status was neither recognized nor respected. By altering his expectations and giving him firsthand exposure to discrimination, this experience solidified his racial self-conception and imbued it with a "political position" based on discrimination and unjust treatment.

Yasmin, a 35-year-old in São Paulo with relatively light skin and bright, purple braids, similarly attributes her politicized black identity to this kind of exposure, which became possible through significant upward mobility she experienced after completing university. Yasmin was unsure when I interviewed her, but believed she was classified as brown on her birth certificate. When we spoke, however, she identified emphatically as a black woman (*mulher preta*). Like Paulo earlier, Yasmin specified that she prefers to use the "confrontational" word *preta* instead of *negra*:

Because people don't want to see me as black. Seeing me as black is already hard because they want to see me as *morena*.... And when I say I'm a *preta* woman it's heavier. They get uncomfortable when I confront [them] and say I'm a *preta* woman. I think that it's, I think the impact is greater in society when I say I'm a *preta* woman. It's more uncomfortable and they don't get to react. Sometimes when I say I'm a *negra* woman there's someone who says 'no, you're *morena*,' and I don't want them to have that response. I don't want to anymore because I'm in that phase, like, I don't want to just resist. I want to announce 'I am a *preta* woman in a racist society.'

Thus, today, Yasmin is eager to discuss her racialized worldview and political identity, but like others this was not always the case. She describes her teenage years as a period of compliance with racial hierarchies in which she attempted to "whiten" herself through hair straightening and other ways of courting romantic attention. When I ask her if she believed this to be racist at the time, she says: "we take a while to understand the process, you know? Of racism. But it – after a while you say, 'god, that was racism,' something like that. And I didn't at the time, obviously. At the time I was just thirteen. For me, it was just nothing."

To explain this racial transformation, Yasmin points to her great fortune landing a well-paid job at a public-sector bank in São Paulo – something she could not have qualified for without a university degree. This promotion entailed life-changing upward mobility for Yasmin, who grew up and worked in a marginal community in São Paulo's periphery. She worked in this majority-nonwhite community for years as a poorly paid public-school teacher: "I worked in a school where I also didn't suffer racism because the majority of educators were black women, poor." But when Yasmin landed the bank job, she suddenly gained exposure to a different kind of professional environment: "In the bank you have a different situation. Because in the bank where I work you see very few blacks in management positions." Suddenly, moving from the public school in São Paulo's periphery to the elite workplace of the bank, Yasmin came face-to-face with the underrepresentation of darker-skinned Brazilians in high status jobs, and their subordinate positions within these workplaces.

But in addition to experiences in the workplace, education and labor market mobility can also lead to new exposure to elite public spaces made accessible by greater disposable income. Yasmin explicitly cites her exposure to elite public spaces that she could suddenly access with greater disposable income as a significant factor:

And so at the bank I ... there I think the process was more difficult because you're more alienated, you know? In relation to this, because there you start to live another way of life, you know? So, for example, when I entered the bank, I think I escaped the cycle of economic violence. Obviously the racial [cycle] I can never escape, but from the economic [cycle] I think I escaped from the moment that I started to earn more [money], frequent other places. And then you start to notice, like ... we go to some places, there are no black people. You go to another, no black people. You got to a restaurant, no black people. You get on a plane to go to Europe, almost no black people. Families of all black people? Impossible, depending on the destination.

Yasmin's trajectory illustrates one pathway of reclassification, through which individuals might move from mixed-race identification or more euphemistic forms to an affirmed black identification. Yasmin's story illustrates how social ascension and experiences in the labor market made her cognizant of racial inequalities by granting her an enviable degree of upward mobility and showing her firsthand how poorly nonwhites are represented in elite spaces, professional or otherwise. Noticing the contrast of these spaces with the marginal areas with which she had been familiar, Yasmin develops an awareness of racial differences and starts to reinterpret her past experiences and practices she had been socialized to adopt. In short, by shaping individuals' expectations and trajectories in the labor market, education can increase firsthand exposure to inequalities and discrimination that inform racial consciousness and identification.

TESTING THE MECHANISMS: SURVEY ANALYSIS

Interviewees' accounts indicate a relationship between education and racial identification that runs counter to the conventional wisdom that upward mobility, and education in particular, is associated with whitening. But of course, the nonrandom sampling strategy and small number of interviews raises the question of whether this relationship is generalizable beyond the informants I met through educational and civil society networks. Moreover, if this relationship does generalize, it raises additional questions related to the whitening thesis. Do my interviewees' accounts differ because the whitening relationship was spurious, or wrong, in some way? Or did the direction of the education–reclassification relationship change over time? In the next chapter, I test the longitudinal implications of my argument more rigorously, but before concluding this chapter, I draw on randomly sampled survey data spanning 1986 to 2008 to assess these questions at the microlevel.

As Telles (2004, 96) notes, one important question to address is: "whitening in relation to what?" It may seem obvious that whitening refers to changes in self-identification, but many classic studies that reportedly document the practice do not study changes in self-identification, per se. Schwartzman (2007) and Marteleto (2012), for example, focus on parents' classifications of their children, and therefore do not address self-identification at all. Telles (2004) and Silva (1994) include self-classification in their analyses of whitening, but focus their analyses on the likelihood that self-identification matches racial ascription by survey interviewers.[8] The closest examples of studies of longitudinal changes in racial self-identification in Brazil are studies of census data by Charles Wood and colleagues (Carvalho et al. 2004; Lovell and Wood 1998; Wood and Carvalho 1994),[9] but these studies analyze net macro-level changes, and are less useful for identifying microlevel patterns.

One empirical question that demands interrogation is how or if the relationship between education, in particular, and reclassification has changed over time. I test this with microlevel survey data spanning three decades in Brazil, from 1986 to 2008. The timing of the four surveys I analyze is crucial as they span the period prior to democratization and educational expansion (1986 and 1989), as educational reforms were beginning (1995), and a point after noticeable improvement in educational access (2008). While surveys with racial identification variables are available in additional years, these four also include racial classifications of respondents by survey interviewers, a proxy for physical attributes.[10] Without this crucial control variable, respondents' education and other status variables will likely also capture phenotypical differences in the population as a function of racialized inequalities, and confound the estimated effects of these variables as a result. Only by controlling for physical attributes in some way can we reasonably isolate the effects of education on racial identification across decades.

A few caveats are in order pertaining to the 1986 and 1989 surveys. These are, of course, different surveys with samples taken in different years, though they are relatively close together and both prior to the period of educational expansion. They are also relatively small samples, containing 573 respondents in 1986 and 444 in 1989. I pool these surveys to compute more precise estimates, including a survey dummy to adjust for differences across surveys. More importantly, however, unlike the 1995 and 2008 samples these 1980s samples are *not* national in scope, and instead sample only select cities: the São Paulo Capital (1986 survey)

---

[8] In a recent analysis of labor market panel data, Silveira (2019) similarly focuses on the effects of status variables on the hetero-classification of respondents, similar to Saperstein and Penner (2012).

[9] Also see more recent studies by Soares (2008), Miranda (2015), and Jesus and Hoffman (2020).

[10] Telles's (2014) PERLA survey data indicate that ascribed racial classifications of Brazilian respondents are valid proxies for skin tone. On a scale from 1 (light) to 11 (dark), mean skin tones for ascribed racial categories are: white = 2.78, brown = 4.84, black = 8.31. Unfortunately, PERLA's sample size and the small number of darker-skinned and highly educated respondents in the sample render the data insufficient for the sectoral analysis I conduct here.

and Caxias do Sul in Rio Grande do Sul (1989 survey). Because these are located in southern regions with historically larger Euro-descendant populations, these samples might make it difficult to detect potential darkening effects of education. At the same time, however, these 1980s samples are more relevant for testing for potential whitening effects of education. A greater baseline probability of white identification might impose a lower ceiling on potential whitening effects, making this a difficult test for the whitening hypothesis. In any case, these are the best survey data available from this time period, and rather than dismissing these data altogether I believe it is worth taking care when interpreting estimates computed from them.

Figure 4.1 displays estimates of the effect of education on the probabilities of racial identification in each decade, after adjusting for the skin tone proxy and other control variables.[11] Though the 1986 and 1989 samples are drawn from southern regions, we find the correlations described in earlier scholarship on whitening. Even after controlling for income and skin tone, university education has a positive and significant effect on the likelihood of white identification, and negative effects on brown and black identification. High school education is similarly positively associated with white identification, though the corresponding decreases on black and brown Identification are insignificant.

By 1995, however, as educational access – especially high school education – begins to become more inclusive, we begin to see a reversal of the relationship between education and patterns of racial identification. The effect of university education on white identification becomes insignificant, and the effect of high school education is estimated to be *negative*. By contrast, the high-school educated are now more likely to identify as brown. The negative effects of education on black identification have shifted toward zero, and have no effect on this probability. Then, by 2008, we see signs of the reclassification reversal evident in the census data, and patterns that clearly correspond to the hypothesis that education is associated with nonwhite and black identification. By this point, there is a monotonic negative relationship between education and white identification, and a positive relationship with black identification. The brown category is unaffected by education, but seeing as this category falls between the two poles of the color spectrum, it is likely more difficult to detect net changes in this category.

---

[11] Full regression estimates are available in Supplementary Tables B3–B5.

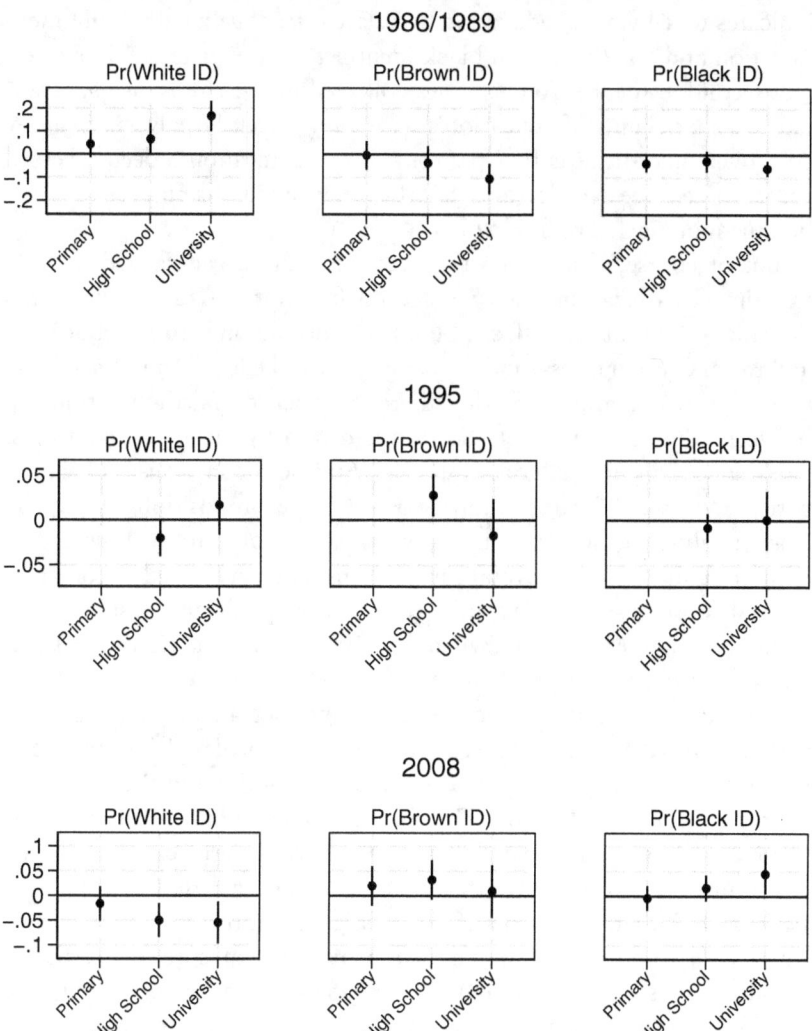

FIGURE 4.1 Average partial effects of education on Pr(racial ID), 1986–2008
Marginal effects are estimated relative to less than primary education and adjust for household wealth, age, gender, party ID, geographic region, and a skin tone proxy (racial classification by survey interviewer). The figure displays 90 percent confidence intervals.

Analysis of survey data across three decades provides two important takeaways. First, analysis of more recent survey data indicate that the darkening effects of education generalize beyond my nonrandom snowball sample. Systematic analysis of the nationally representative sample indicates that by 2008 education correlated *negatively* with white identification and *positively* with black identification, on average. However, and second, evidence from samples collected in the 1980s also substantiates earlier claims of education's *whitening* effects. Analysis of survey data over time suggests that patterns of reclassification indeed reversed across these three decades, and that this occurred just as public education became more inclusive in Brazil.

But of course, if interviewees' accounts can be generalized to fully explain reclassification, then we should find not only a change in the direction of education's effects, but also a correlation between education and racial consciousness, and consciousness and education in turn. That is, we need to examine whether there is evidence that the relationship between education and identification is driven by racial consciousness. Does education predict consciousness? And does consciousness predict patterns of racial identification? To test these propositions, I rely on closer analysis of the 2008 survey, which corresponds to the time period of interest and contains several survey items that can be used to construct a racial consciousness index that broadly corresponds to the substantive issues interviewees identified when discussing their racial trajectories and the content of their racial identities.

To measure racial consciousness, I construct an index from eight survey items that align with the dimensions articulated by interviewees when describing their politicized racial identities and the rationales for their racial identifications. The index includes a battery of questions probing respondents' subjective perceptions of experiencing race-based discrimination, awareness of the potential for internalizing or complying with racial hierarchies, a belief in the stigmatization and negative portrayal of Afro-descendants, and, as a proxy for exposure to alternative racial discourses, black movement participation. Race-neutral language would be ideal to measure consciousness inspired by any racial category, but this language at least suffices given the focus on reclassification into nonwhite categories. Each dimension is coded dichotomously and combined additively into a summary racial consciousness measure that ranges from 0 (low racial consciousness and disagreement with all items) to 4 (high racial consciousness and agreement with all items).[12] Self-identified black respondents exhibit the highest mean levels of racial consciousness (1.55), followed by self-identified brown (1.12) and white (1.03) respondents.

[12] See Supplementary Table B2 for item wordings and coding.

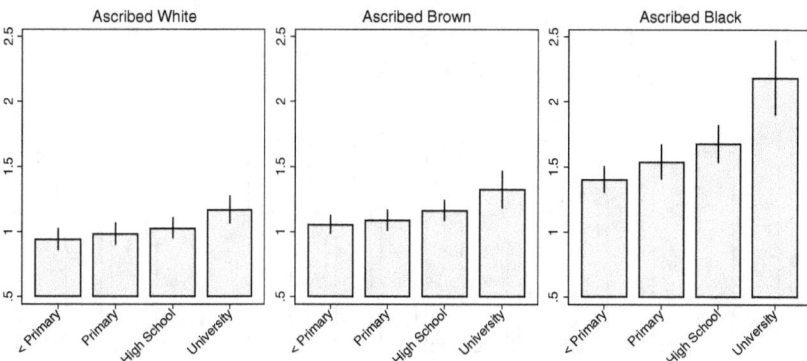

FIGURE 4.2 Predicted probabilities of racial consciousness by education and racial ascriptions, 2008

I test the propositions earlier in two steps, first analyzing the determinants of racial consciousness, and then assessing whether racial consciousness is associated with patterns of racial identification, as expected. Figure 4.2 displays estimates of racial consciousness according to respondents' education levels and how they are classified racially by survey interviewers. Unsurprisingly, we find that brown and black-classified respondents exhibit higher levels of racial consciousness compared to white-classified respondents. But among brown and especially black respondents, we also find a positive effect of education on exhibited levels of racial consciousness. And while we observe this relationship even among those classified as white, this relationship grows stronger as we move from white to black-classified respondents. Indeed, high school and university-educated respondents who are read as black by interviewers exhibit the highest levels of racial consciousness.

In turn, this racial consciousness also predicts patterns of racial identification consistent with the reclassification reversal. Figure 4.3 displays the predicted probabilities of racial identification at each level of racial consciousness. Controlling for other individual-level factors like skin tone and education, high levels of racial consciousness are associated with a decreased probability of white identification, and increased probability of black identification. Similar to the patterns we observed earlier with education, brown identification is unaffected by variation in racial consciousness. These findings may not be entirely surprising, but it is still important to establish this relationship with systematic analysis of randomly sampled survey data, given the inductive and nonrandom nature of the interview data collected.

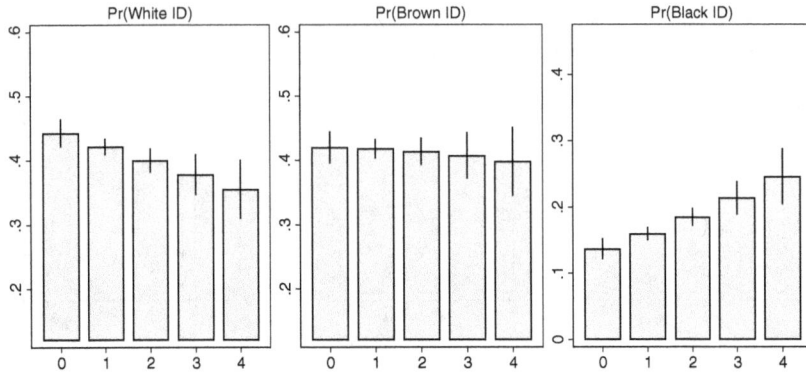
FIGURE 4.3 Probabilities of racial ID by level of racial consciousness, 2008

Table 4.2 separates the components of the group consciousness index and displays correlations of these items with the probability of racial identification, computed relative to brown identification. The individual items generally perform well in predicting patterns of identification, especially black identification. Of the four items, only attitudes about the stereotypical portrayal of blacks in media fail to correlate significantly with black identification. By contrast, discrimination, black movement participation, and awareness of internalized racism all correlate significantly with black identification. Indeed, respondents who report discrimination and who have participated in the black movement are roughly twice as likely to identify as black rather than brown. And respondents who exhibit awareness of internalized racism are roughly 40 percent more likely to identify as black. In a final model with all four items, these items retain their statistical significance, indicating their relevance to black identification. Of course, these items are highly collinear. But Table 4.2 helps us understand the varied dimensions of group consciousness, and provide some indication of the relative importance of each in patterns of identification.

One final doubt may pertain to how or if phenotypical variation might constrain the ability of certain individuals to capitalize on racial fluidity to reclassify. This could be true in for the adoption of darker or lighter identifications. Indeed, recall the common retort among black activists: "if you want to know who is black or white in Brazil, just ask the police." For activists, the discourse of fluidity elides the visibility of racialized features, which produce brutality and discrimination (Alves 2018). Some of my interviewees also articulated some of these phenotypical constraints

TABLE 4.2 *Estimated effects of group consciousness on racial ID*

	White ID vs. Brown ID					Black ID vs. Brown ID				
	(1)	(2)	(3)	(4)	(5)	(1)	(2)	(3)	(4)	(5)
Internalized Racism	0.87 (0.10)				0.91 (0.11)	1.38* (0.21)				1.31+ (0.21)
Blacks Stereotyped		0.90 (0.11)			0.91 (0.11)		1.00 (0.15)			0.93 (0.15)
Discrimination Index			0.74+ (0.12)		0.70* (0.12)			1.91* (0.30)		1.79* (0.29)
Black Movement				1.55 (0.59)	1.70 (0.68)				2.23* (0.83)	2.12+ (0.84)
Observations	2534	2353	2529	2533	2344	2534	2353	2529	2533	2344
AIC	3532.85	3277.65	3509.04	3533.16	3248.64	3532.85	3277.65	3509.04	3533.16	3248.64

+ $p < 0.1$, * $p < 0.05$. Exponentiated coefficients (odds ratios); standard errors in parentheses. All models are multinomial logit and control for interviewer-ascribed race, education, wealth, age, gender, region, and party ID.

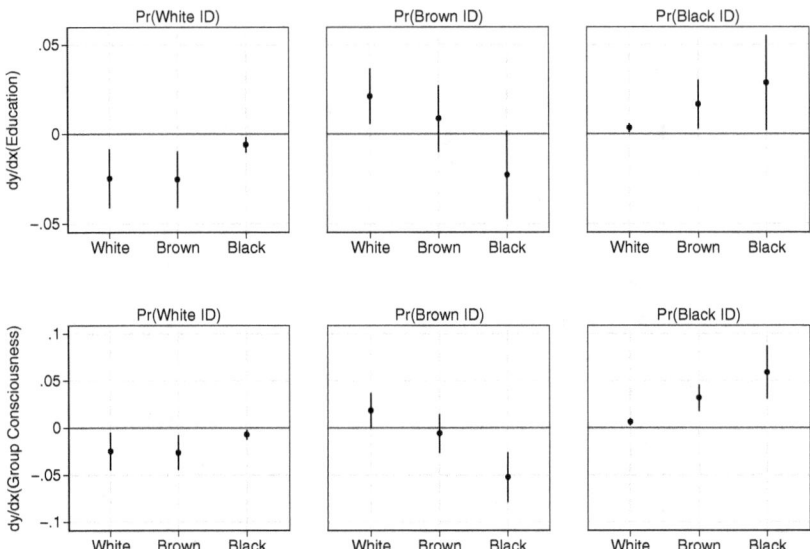

FIGURE 4.4 Marginal effects of education and racial consciousness by racial ascription, 2008

on their ability to reclassify. Jorge, for example, seriously struggled with rectifying with lighter skin tone with his black identity, and Paulo noted that because of his darker skin his identification was always invariably black. The question, then, becomes whether the effects presented earlier are limited to individuals of certain racial presentations, or if the oft-touted fluidity does in reality permit reclassification regardless of one's appearance. Table 2.2 suggested that even those individuals seen as black by others have significant latitude to opt for a different identification, even as white. But we can test this idea more rigorously by assessing whether the effects of education and consciousness I identify are limited to where one falls on Brazil's racial and color spectrum.

Figure 4.4. displays average marginal effects of education (top row) and racial consciousness (bottom row) on the probability of each racial identification, conditional on racial ascriptions (the skin tone proxy). Brown-ascribed individuals indeed fit the hypothesized pattern best: one-unit increases in education and consciousness significantly decreases white and increases black identification. Among black-ascribed respondents, the largest and most significant effects are on black identification, indicating that black identification is not a foregone conclusion among respondents of darker skin tones; there is room for education to exert additional effects. Among white-ascribed respondents, shifts tend to occur from the white to the brown category. The effects and patterns identified earlier do not appear constrained by, or limit to, particular phenotypical presentations. Overall, analysis of survey data collected across three decades helps to square the accounts of interviewees with the conventional wisdom and the broader Brazilian population. Microlevel survey data indicate that the relationship between education and racial identification changed over time, just as public education was becoming more inclusive. Moreover, survey data also identified correlations that bolster the idea that education impacts racial consciousness, which in turn impacts one's choices of racial identification.

CONCLUSION

This chapter has relied on qualitative analysis of in-depth interview data with reclassifiers to shed light on the pathways through which access to higher education can lead to racialized political identities and racial reclassification. Qualitative interview data were especially fruitful in this regard, helping to flesh out and illustrate what reclassification looks like on the ground. The narratives conveyed by interviewees revealed that these processes of identity change are heterogeneous and deeply personal. Yet the commonalities across personal stories highlighted the ways in which education, directly or indirectly, increased individuals' personal exposure to new information, social networks, and the labor market. In turn, these new experiences altered individuals' racial subjectivities and centered race as the basis on which they came to make sense of their relative social positions in Brazilian society. Analysis of national survey data buttressed these findings, showing how this relationship between education and self-darkening emerged over time, as well as how education and skin tone interact to shape political identities. By 2008, highly educated and darker-skinned Brazilians were those most likely to exhibit racial consciousness and *choose* black identification.

5

Education and Reclassification

Testing the Hypothesis

The previous chapter presented in-depth interview data and quantitative analysis of survey data to motivate the hypothesis that educational expansion lies behind the reclassification reversal. Firsthand accounts from reclassifiers indicated that access to higher levels of education, directly or indirectly, altered their personal experiences and led them to make sense of their relative social positions in racial terms. This chapter turns to systematic longitudinal analysis to test the observable implications that follow from this hypothesis – namely, that in recent decades individuals with higher levels of educational attainment have opted to self-darken. The evidence presented in the previous chapter helped to illuminate causal pathways and mechanisms and substantiated the significance and direction of this relationship via snapshot correlations. The analytical focus in this chapter is longitudinal, aiming to test more precisely whether the overtime changes in Brazil's racial composition can be attributed to educational expansion.

However, the temporal coincidence of several institutional changes related to education and racial policy or discourse presents inferential challenges to assessing the political identity hypothesis. I test these rival hypotheses more directly and rigorously in Chapter 6. But still relevant here is that many of the policy changes that have helped shed Brazil's image as a racial democracy – the endorsement and implementation of affirmative action, and reforms in educational resource allocation and incentive structures – were implemented or originated by President Fernando Henrique Cardoso in the mid to late 1990s, then later taken up or furthered by Workers' Party governments. All of these institutional changes related to educational expansion thus coincide with changes in racial subjectivity and identification. The challenge becomes how to isolate the effects of education from related policies and discourses, such as those surrounding affirmative action.

Though affirmative action policies are not the focus of this chapter, the analyses presented here take measures to address or control for these "contaminating" effects. More specifically, I rely on two panel datasets that offer strategies to remove or isolate the effects of affirmative action. In the first, a synthetic panel of birth cohorts built from microlevel census data, I strategically analyze cohorts who likely completed university education long before affirmative action entered national political debate and before the state's watershed shift in racial discourse in 2001.[1] By effectively removing affirmative action as an explanatory factor, we can examine whether the state's shift in racial discourse or policy was in fact a necessary condition for the reclassification reversal. In the second, a panel dataset of Brazilian municipalities between 2000 and 2010, I leverage subnational variation in the implementation of state-level affirmative action policies and the extent of educational expansion. Doing so provides an opportunity to pit these two variables against each other directly while controlling for confounders. In both analyses, the use of fixed-effects panel methods effectively controls for unobserved confounders that do not vary over time – especially important given the complexity of racial identification in this context, and the myriad factors excluded from census questionnaires.[2] Overall, the analyses in this chapter provide strong support for the political identity hypothesis and suggest that the reclassification reversal was not contingent on the presence of affirmative action policies.

THE POLITICAL IDENTITY HYPOTHESIS AND OBSERVABLE IMPLICATIONS

The previous chapter identified and tested three specific pathways through which education can impact group consciousness. I characterized these as forms of exposure to new (1) information, (2) social networks and civil society associations, and (3) experiences in the labor market. Qualitative

---

[1] Though 2001 is often cited as the momentous endorsement of affirmative action by President Fernando Henrique Cardoso, his support for expanded opportunities for *negros* can be traced to his earliest presidential address in 1995 (Cardoso 1995a).

[2] See Chapter 3 for discussion of the many factors shown to shape racial identification, including phenotypical attributes, social class, family socialization, social media, and other cultural factors.

interview data, which generated the hypothesis, helped demonstrate its plausibility and illustrated what reclassification looks like on the ground. Systematic survey-based studies lent support to interviewees' accounts, finding that greater education correlates with the belief that racial discrimination exists (Bailey 2002; Layton and Smith 2017), as well as the belief that race is influential in shaping one's life (IBGE 2011, Table 2.5). And my own analysis of microlevel survey data from 1986 to 2008 established correlations that supported these mechanisms as pathways through which education impacts consciousness and black identification, in particular.

The broad takeaway from my interviews is that the specific pathways through which education affects reclassification and the formation of racialized political identities are heterogeneous and often personal. Moreover, these effects unfold over varying periods of time: some individuals report that education impacted their identifications while they were still acquiring education; for others this process unfolded years after completing the highest level of education they would attain. Nonetheless, the important point is that interviewees consistently identified how the pursuit of greater education, directly or indirectly, altered their racial self-understandings and led them to adopt nonwhite and often black identities. While the analyses of microlevel survey data from the previous chapter established important correlations that substantiate the hypothesis, the goal of this chapter is to go further in systematically testing the observable implications of the hypothesis that expanded access to education leads to self-darkening over time. In other words, analyses of microlevel survey data *suggested* that the relationship between education and racial identification changed as the composition of high school and university education became more inclusive in class terms, but the focus in this chapter is on testing these propositions directly and systematically through longitudinal analyses.

In particular, I focus on testing what sets this hypothesis apart from the expectations of prior scholarship: the direction of education's effects. Conventional wisdom expects education (and other forms of upward mobility) to produce whitening, but I expect education to produce "darkening," especially for those in the lower classes. The key observable implication that I seek test in the empirical analyses, therefore, is that better-educated Brazilians will be the most likely to reclassify in darker racial categories over time, relative to their lesser-educated counterparts.

I do not strictly hypothesize that these effects are limited to individuals who meet certain phenotypical criteria. But I do argue that educational expansion matters because these sectors are likely *candidates* for reclassification – in part because they are more likely to meet commonsense phenotypical criteria and are thus best positioned to make plausible claims to nonwhiteness. Consequently, in the analyses that follow, I employ multiple strategies to assess and control for the effects of physical attributes on reclassification and the hypothesized processes. In a longitudinal analysis of demographic surveys, I use income to measure class and proxy for skin tone while testing observable implications (Telles 2014). And in the panel analysis of municipalities, I rely on fixed effects to control for time-invariant factors – like physical attributes – in assessing the impact of educational expansion of rates of reclassification. By isolating these factors, the focus in these analyses is on testing for one main observable implication: that better educated Brazilians are most likely to adopt nonwhite, and especially black, identities over time.

INFERENTIAL CHALLENGES

Of course, testing the longitudinal effect of education presents inferential challenges due to the presence and implementation of affirmative action policies. First, as a policy initiative, affirmative action itself seeks to expand educational access for segments of the population who previously were underrepresented in higher education. One consideration, then, is how to assess the impact of educational expansion without affirmative action, and how to consider whether the effects of education are in some way contingent on the presence of affirmative action policies even if these do not directly shape racial identification. Second, the timing of affirmative action policies coincides with the period of educational expansion that, I argue, has so greatly impacted racial subjectivities. This applies not only to the policies themselves, which might have generated new incentives for blackness (e.g., Francis and Tannuri-Pianto 2012), but also to the shifting discourse around racial difference and inequities that began in earnest during the presidency of Fernando Henrique Cardoso (Htun 2004; Paschel 2016a). Sociologists, in particular, emphasize the endorsement of affirmative action as a key way the Brazilian state has better institutionalized racial differences and shaped racial identifications (Bailey et al. 2018; Bailey and Fialho 2018). Thus, aside from the inclusionary effects of affirmative action, we also need to control for or remove other potential effects that might operate through distinct mechanisms, instrumental or symbolic.

To provide compelling evidence that educational expansion, per se, is behind the reclassification reversal, I employ several empirical strategies to remove or control for affirmative action. Both approaches are longitudinal; they explicitly measure and analyze change over time in rates of racial identification and reclassification. The first approach relies on what Angus Deaton termed a "pseudo-panel," which allows researchers to follow birth cohorts over time and analyze aggregated probabilities of behaviors within these cohorts. With annual microlevel data collected by the census bureau since 1976 (but more consistently since 1992), I am able to follow birth cohorts who plausibly completed university education *prior to* the implementation of affirmative action policies. This approach thus allows us to remove any "contaminating" effects of affirmative action. The second approach, which leverages subnational variation to further test these hypotheses, relies on a panel dataset of Brazilian municipalities to analyze change over time. The major advantage of panel data is the ability to control for unobserved confounders, which lends credibility to any analysis. But in this case, it also allows for the incorporation of affirmative action policies into the analysis as a control, and allows for direct comparison of localities in states that did and did not implement affirmative action. Beyond affirmative action, this approach also controls for other time-invariant confounders, like family socialization and phenotypical attributes. This second approach facilitates more direct examination of whether the effects of educational expansion are conditional on the presence of affirmative action policies.

ANALYSIS I: PSEUDO-PANEL ANALYSIS OF BIRTH COHORTS

The main hypothesis this chapter aims to test entails not only classificatory change, but a process that unfolds over time. Ideally, one would test the hypothesis with a microlevel panel dataset to allow for repeated observations of individuals' racial identifications over the relevant time period, in this case from 1992 to the present. But in the absence of such panel data, I rely on an alternative approach devised by economists. These synthetic panel, or "pseudo panel," methods rely on the construction of cohorts drawn from repeated cross-sectional surveys.

Though not common in political science, pseudo-panel approaches are regularly employed in other social sciences following Angus Deaton's (1985) pioneering application. In many cases, researchers are interested in testing hypotheses that would require panel data but are able to find only repeated cross sections of surveys, with samples annually drawn anew. Such surveys allow researchers to construct estimates of aggregated individual-level behavior by tracking cohorts, groups with fixed membership over time. In my application, I take a traditional approach and follow birth cohorts to estimate the aggregate likelihood that individuals in these cohorts will identify as nonwhite in each given year. Rather than estimate repeated individual-level probabilities of racial identifications over time – that is, direct observations of racial reclassification – the pseudo-panel approach replaces individual-level observations with aggregate cohort means as indirect estimates of individual-level change (Deaton 1985; Verbeek and Nijman 1992).

My analysis relies on the Annual Household Sample Survey (PNAD, *Pesquisa Nacional de Amostra de Domicílios*), a large demographic survey similar to the American Community Survey in the United States, commonly viewed as the census in census off-years. For consistency in the racial classification scheme employed, I analyze PNAD surveys for each year from 1992 to 2015.[3] Though ideally my analysis would extend beyond these years, changes in survey design and implementation make PNAD surveys incommensurate outside of this period. The PNAD survey has been conducted since 1976, but prior to 1992 a different racial classification scheme was employed, and racial identification data was collected inconsistently. After 2015, PNAD switched to a continuous (panel) format, but unfortunately in this design racial ID is considered a fixed characteristic that is not measured repeatedly in survey waves. In a supplemental analysis I include data from the 1976–1990 period, but as I discuss later these data present unique challenges. The main analysis focuses on the 1992–2015 period, since these surveys provide the sample sizes needed to construct adequately sized birth cohorts in each survey year to compute reliable estimates and pertain to the relevant time period.

While not ideal in certain respects, the pseudo-panel approach does offer one important advantage. Because the first survey suitable for this analysis was conducted in 1992, long before affirmative action policies became a salient topic of national political debate in Brazil, we can construct cohorts of individuals who likely completed university long before nonwhite identification offered any incentives or benefits. If instrumental motivations alone account for the observed changes in racial identification, then older cohorts – those highly unlikely to benefit from racial quotas in university admissions – ought to demonstrate stability in their racial identifications. This approach and these data, therefore, offer leverage on the political identity hypothesis by allowing me to isolate the effects of education in at least some time periods without potential

---

[3] PNAD was not conducted in 1994, or in the 2000 and 2010 census years.

TABLE 5.1 *Birth cohorts in PNAD sample*

Cohort	Birthyear		Age		Observations	
	Min	Max	1992	2015	Min	Max
1	1950	1954	37–42	60–65	8,877	11,403
2	1955	1959	32–37	55–60	10,252	12,674
3	1960	1964	27–32	50–55	9,962	14,496
4	1965	1969	22–27	45–50	6,722	14,135
5	1970	1974	17–22	40–45	2,058	13,472
6	1975	1979	12–17	35–40	104	12,610

"contamination" from affirmative action policies. At the same time, this is a difficult test for the political identity hypothesis.

Table 5.1 displays the cohorts constructed for this analysis, and illustrates the intuition behind this approach. Using respondents' birthyears, we can identify birth cohorts across successive surveys. Respondents born between 1950 and 1954, for example, fall into "cohort 1" and were between ages 37 and 42 in the first survey year of 1992, and between ages 60 and 65 in the final survey year, 2015. Pseudo-panel analysis requires assumptions as to the stability of cohorts over time (see Appendix C, available online, for further discussion), one of which is that cohorts be based on stable underlying populations (Guillerm 2017). This is relevant to older cohorts (whose mortality rates spike after age 55) and younger cohorts (who are likely to acquire additional education). Thus, in my analysis I place the greatest weight on cohorts 3 and 4: these individuals are able to have completed university education in the first survey year, but do not reach the age where mortality rates spike before the final survey year. In supplemental analyses, I include and leverage differences between all cohorts.

Dependent Variables

The dependent variables are coded from the close-ended racial identification questions employed by the census bureau. Respondents are asked "what is your race or color?" and asked to self-classify in one of five categories: white, black, brown, yellow, or indigenous. Because yellow and indigenous identification fall outside the scope of this study and comprise less than two percent of the total population, I exclude respondents identifying as such from the analysis. I analyze respondents' white, black, and brown identification in two ways. First, I construct a binary white/nonwhite variable by collapsing black and brown identification together. This coding reflects the understanding of blackness promoted by the black movement, in which *negro* is meant to unite all Brazilians of African descent, and is sometimes understood to describe one's "race" rather than one's "color." But it also captures the central tendency of the reclassification reversal, which is a shift away from whitening and toward darkening.[4] Additionally, I also analyze racial identification as a trichotomous variable, which, according to some, better reflects the panoply of racial identifications in Brazil, does not impose a black/white divide, and better reflects the choice set from which survey respondents are asked to choose. In the analyses later, I begin with analysis of the binary variable and follow with analysis of the trichotomous variable.

Independent Variables and Controls

The independent variable of interest in this analysis is education, measured as years of formal education completed and categorized into four categories: (1) less than primary education completed, (2) primary completed, (3) high school completed, and (4) university or more completed. In addition, the models also include controls for income, which is measured as the respondent's decile of household income per capita; and dummies for gender, and migration status at the municipal and state levels. In the case of migration, scholars have suggested that subjective understandings of racial classification vary across geographic regions of Brazil (Guimarães 1999; McNamee 2020; Monk 2013; Telles 1993), thus changes in classification might be shaped by movement across geographic boundaries by individuals with varying racial subjectivities. In this same vein, I include fixed effects for the respondent's state of residence, to control for these differences and any other state-level heterogeneity. Summary statistics of the independent variables are in Supplementary Table C4.

Models and Estimation

To capture changes over time, I estimate the likelihood of nonwhite identification with time-interactive, autoregressive, fixed-effects logit models.

---

[4] Supplementary Table C2 presents means of nonwhite identification by level of education for each survey year in the sample.

In keeping with the econometrics literature on pseudo-panels, I estimate fixed-effects models by measuring time with survey-year fixed effects (Deaton 1985). Additionally, to control for autocorrelation in the dependent variable, namely that Pr(racial ID) at time t depends in part on that probability at time $t - 1$, I include lagged means of nonwhite identification for each cohort. In the absence of individual-level fixed effects that can be controlled for in panel analysis, these models interact the survey-year and cohort-mean lags, which instruments for individual-level fixed effects (Moffitt 1993).

Because the proposition being tested here hypothesizes change over time in the relationship between select covariates and the probability of nonwhite identification, the survey-year variable is interacted with the full model.[5] In the case of binary dependent variables, models are estimated with logistic regression; in the trichotomous case, multinomial logit models are estimated. For the sake of clarity and simplicity, I later present substantive findings from fixed-effects models, focusing on the substantive effects of education on overtime change in the probability of identifying in a racial category. Full estimates for these models, along with predicted probabilities and difference tests of marginal effects, are presented in Supplementary Tables C6–C30.

Longitudinal Analysis of Nonwhite Identification

The left-hand panel of Figure 5.1 displays the substantive findings from the model estimated from the full sample and displays overtime changes in the probability of identifying as black or brown, relative to the baseline probability in 1993. As these are pseudo-panel estimates, they can be interpreted as changes in the aggregate probability that individuals in these cohorts will identify as nonwhite over time, given their levels of education. This model estimates a monotonic relationship between greater educational attainment and growth in the likelihood of nonwhite identification over time. As predicted, there is consistent growth in this

---

[5] I estimate models of the form

$$\log(Y_{i,c,t}) = \alpha_0 + year \cdot \tau_t \cdot (\bar{y}_{c,t-1} \cdot \lambda + educ_{i,t} \cdot \gamma + \sum_k X^k_{i,t} \cdot \beta_k + \delta_{i,t} \cdot \zeta),$$

where Y is the binary variable indicating nonwhite identification for individual i in cohort c in year t. Year is a survey-year fixed effect, $\bar{y}$ is the lagged cohort mean of Y, $educ$ is the categorical education variable, X is a matrix of control variables, and δ represents state fixed effects.

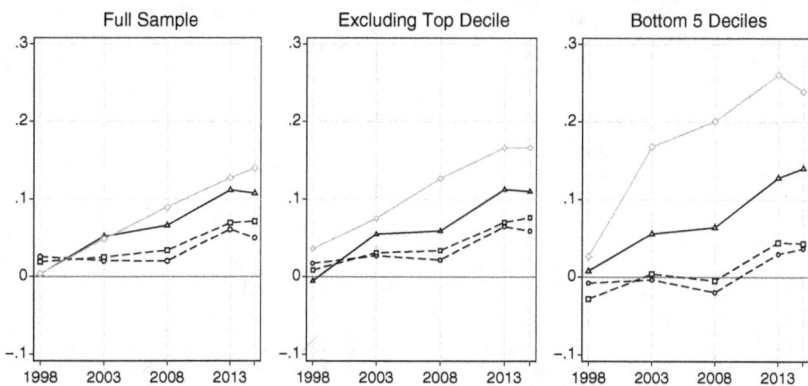

FIGURE 5.1 Pr(nonwhite ID) relative to 1993 by education and subsample, 1998–2015. Diamond = university, Triangle = High school, Square = primary, Circle = less than primary.

probability among the university and high school-educated, in particular. Between 1993 and 2015, this probability grew by 14 points (0.29 to 0.43, $p < 0.05$) for the university-educated and 11 points (0.41 to 0.52, $p < 0.05$) for the high school-educated.

Findings from the full analysis thus support the hypothesis that the adoption of nonwhite identities is associated with greater education. The hypothesis further expects the greatest tendency for reclassification among the lowest class strata. I estimate the model on income-based subsamples, intended to serve as proxies for skin tone (Telles 2014).[6] The middle panel of Figure 5.1 excludes those in the top income decile from the analysis and indicates a similar longitudinal pattern as in the full sample, suggesting that these findings are not driven by high-income (and, by proxy, lighter-skinned) individuals. As with the full sample, there is a monotonic relationship between greater levels of education and the overtime change in the probability of nonwhite identification.[7]

Probabilities estimated on respondents in the bottom five income deciles (the most likely candidates for reclassification) indicate that the

---

[6] Full model estimates are presented in Supplementary Table C9.
[7] Supplementary Tables C7–C8, C10–C15. Supplementary Table C19 also displays estimates for the top decile alone, which reveal no clear education-based pattern. Though there appears to be some change over time, a noisy picture emerges with no clear monotonic relationship between greater levels of educational attainment and overtime change in nonwhite identification.

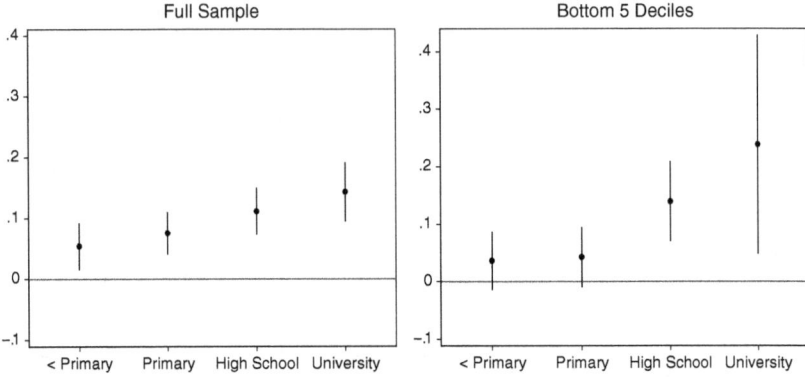

FIGURE 5.2 Change in Pr(nonwhite ID) between 1993 and 2015 by education

hypothesized relationship between greater education and overtime change in the probability of nonwhite identification is particularly pronounced. Among the better educated, there are consistent and substantial gains in the likelihood of nonwhite identification. For the university educated, this probability increased by 24 points between 1993 and 2015, from 0.36 to 0.6 ($p < 0.05$); among the high school-educated this increased 14 points from 0.51 to 0.65 ($p < 0.05$). By contrast among those with primary education and less, change in this probability is statistically insignificant and estimated at 4 and 3 points, respectively. Differences in the overtime differences by education strata are more clearly presented in Figure 5.2 for the full sample and bottom half of the income distribution. This pattern clearly displays a monotonic relationship between education and the probability of adopting nonwhite identities over time, especially among those in the bottom half of the income distribution.

Longitudinal Multinomial Logit Models of Racial Identification

The analysis earlier provides evidence in support of the main empirical claim of the political identity hypothesis. However the aggregation of black and brown categories might potentially obscure interesting variation that can shed additional light on the shifting patterns of racial identification over time in Brazil. In particular, while a decline in the probability of white identification is clear, one might wonder if the growth in nonwhite identification is a function primarily of identification as black or brown. From the perspective of the instrumental hypothesis, growth only in the brown category might be interpreted as suggestive evidence of instrumentality, as it is the white/nonwhite boundary one must cross to claim affirmative action benefits in most cases. Growth in the black category, by contrast, might be interpreted to suggest motivations beyond short-term calculations of material payoffs. And indeed, many of my interviewees indicated that the black category is especially relevant to racialized political identity.

I thus further test the political identity hypothesis by disaggregating the coding of racial identification into three categories and estimate multinomial logit models. In this analysis, I again focus again on cohorts 3 and 4 to maximize internal validity of the longitudinal analysis. I also focus on a sample that excludes respondents in the top income decile. While focusing on the bottom five deciles in the full sample led to strong findings in the binary case, further dividing the sample in the case of the trichotomous variable leads to too few observations among black identifiers. Thus, the estimates discussed here are computed from a sample that is relevant to the theoretical propositions, within reason.

Figure 5.3 presents the substantive findings of this analysis, displaying the change in the probability of identifying in each category relative to

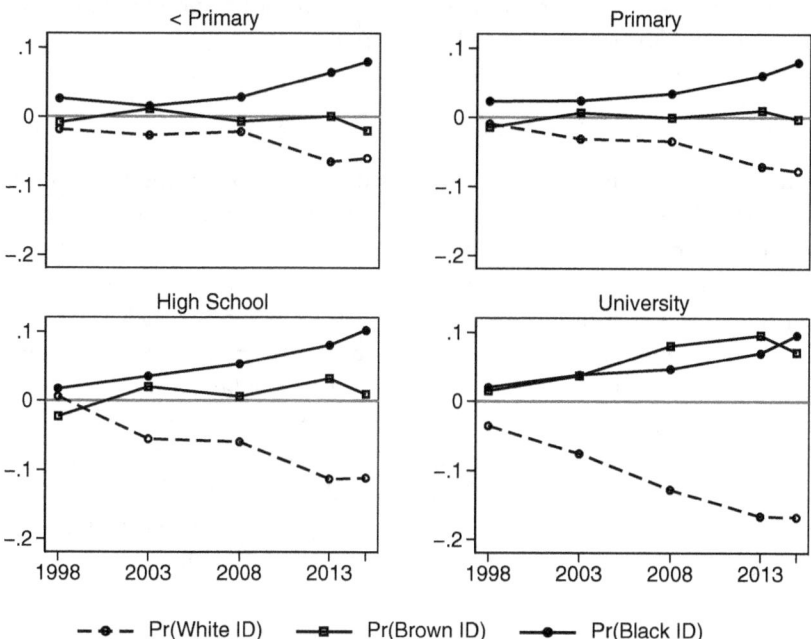

FIGURE 5.3 Change in Pr(racial ID) relative to 1993 by education, 1998–2015

the baseline probability in 1993.[8] Each quadrant shows these trends by level of education. First and again, clear from the plots is that the greatest decline in white identification over time is among those with high school and university education. Second, growth in both black and brown categories is most consistent over time among the most highly educated, those with university education. Third, growth in the brown category is rather uneven across education groups, while growth in the black category is more consistent. Individuals with less than high school education show no significant growth in brown identification. The high school-educated show inconsistent and substantively insignificant growth.

Of course, these pseudo-panel estimates are not indicative of individual-level movement out of the white category and into the black category, per se. Instead they suggest net changes in the likelihood of individuals moving in or out of these categories. The patterns nonetheless suggest that the greatest identifiable shifts in patterns of identification is away from whiteness and most consistently toward the black category. Analysis of these demographic data thus bear out findings from the analysis of survey data in the previous chapter, which also found that education and racial consciousness correlated specifically with black identification. In sum, this analysis supports the political identity hypothesis: not only are the better educated more likely to depart from status quo whitening and adopt nonwhite, especially black, identities.

Cohort, Age, or Period Effects?

Findings from these analyses are based on two birth cohorts chosen specifically to meet the assumption of pseudo-panel estimation and to avoid contamination from the presence of affirmative action policies. As a robustness check, I also estimate these models on an expanded dataset that includes four additional cohorts (two older and two younger). Full model estimates for these samples can be found in Supplementary Tables C16 and C19. These models estimate similar patterns as those restricted to cohorts 3 and 4: with the exception of respondents in the top income decile, there is a monotonic relationship between greater education and nonwhite identification, a relationship that grows stronger over time.[9] This additional analysis lends further support to the hypothesis. Due to stronger assumptions required to compute reliable pseudo-panel

---

[8] Full estimates from the multinomial model are available in Supplementary Table C26.
[9] See Supplementary Tables C16–C18 for full results.

estimates on these cohorts, the findings of this expanded sample should be taken with a grain of salt. The main empirical finding, that individuals with greater education are more likely over time to identify as nonwhite, does not appear to be limited to cohorts born in the 1960s.

But aside from expanding the sample, questions may linger as to whether these findings are the product of specific cohorts included in the sample. Two main questions need to be addressed. First, is reclassification common across cohorts of different ages in this period, or is reclassification toward blackness specific to educated Brazilians of certain ages? In other words, does this pattern hold across individual cohorts, or are they unique to specific cohorts? Second, is this pattern a cohort or a period effect? In other words, does this relationship exist among cohorts that accessed education prior to 1992?

One simple way to address the first question is to simply disaggregate the analysis and reestimate the models on cohort subsamples. Descriptive analyses show that there is a monotonic negative relationship between age and apparent rates of reclassification: the younger the cohort, the greater is reclassification (Jesus and Hoffmann 2020; Soares 2008).[10] It thus follows that we might expect such a trend according to age. Nonetheless, we can adjust for such differences across cohorts and test whether this relationship itself varies across cohorts.

Estimates computed from independent cohort subsamples (Supplementary Table C29) are displayed in Figure 5.4. Broadly, the

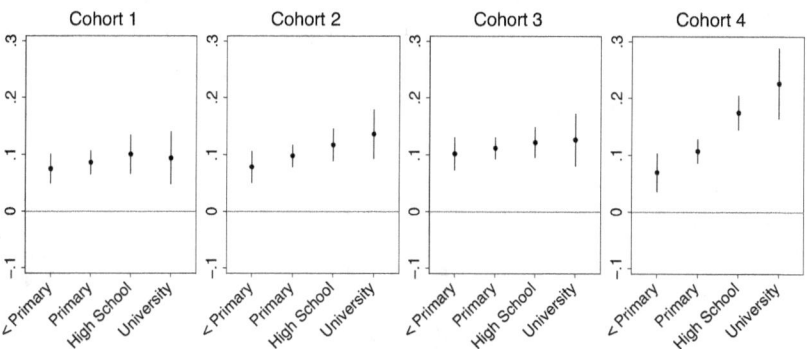

FIGURE 5.4 Change in Pr(nonwhite ID) between 1993 and 2015 by education and cohort

---

[10] See Figure 2.2 in Chapter 2. Also see Sansone (1993, 2003) on intergenerational differences in racial identifications.

hypothesized relationship holds across cohorts, with education correlating positively with the average over time change in the probability of nonwhite identification. The relationship is strongest in cohort 4 (the youngest cohort), but it is not specific to this cohort. Cohort 2, also displays this positive and statistically significant relationship. The relationship is more modest in cohort 3, and less clear in cohort 1. Given the strength of the relationship in cohort 4, there is suggestive evidence that age is a factor that contributes to these patterns. But seeing as the pattern is clearer in cohort 2 than in cohort 3, it's not obvious that the relationship between education and reclassification is contingent on, or heavily influenced by age.

The second question presented earlier requires additional data to disentangle whether these patterns are effects unique to certain cohorts, or a function of the time period in which they gained access to education. To assess this, I draw on earlier waves of PNAD survey data collected between 1976 and 1990. Several important caveats are in order regarding these data. First, the census bureau's classification scheme changed beginning with the 1991 census: earlier PNAD surveys do not include an indigenous category, which might affect estimates pertaining to nonwhite categories. Second, the collection of racial identification in these surveys was inconsistent, and the need to control for autocorrelation with a lagged dependent variable means that we can only analyze the period between 1982 and 1990.

Third, and importantly, the stratification in access to education in this earlier period makes analysis of income-based subsamples less reliable due to scarce observations with high education and low income. At the same time, however, this can also be considered a point of leverage in determining whether the specific period of educational access matters in whether education might produce darkening or whitening. Figure 5.5

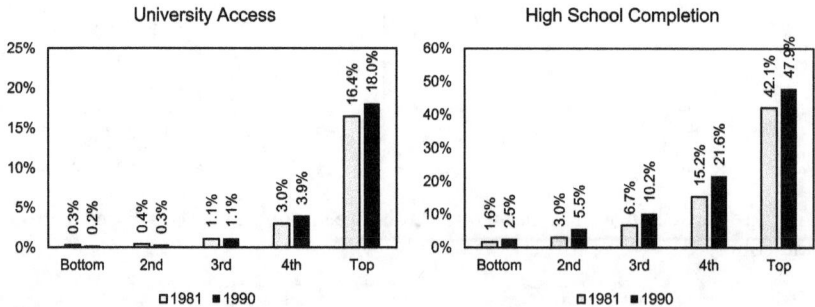

FIGURE 5.5 Educational access by income quintile, 1981–1990
Source: PNAD.

displays statistics on high school completion and university access derived from these PNAD surveys, and shows that access was highly stratified by income, and changed little over this period. Brazilians in the bottom 80 percent of the income structure saw virtually no access to university education in this period; high school completion rates in these sectors are not nearly as dire, but are still dismal for the bottom 60 percent. Conversely, in 1990 individuals in the top income quintile comprised 75 percent of those with some university education, and 53 percent of those who completed high school. Corresponding figures for the top 40 percent of the income distribution are 93 and 80 percent, respectively. Thus, with less representation of lower-class sectors in higher levels of education, we might not expect to find the same relationship, or a similarly sized relationship, especially among the university educated.

Figure 5.6 displays over time changes in the probability of nonwhite ID between 1982 and 1990. Estimates from the full sample somewhat corroborate the findings from the later samples. Estimated effects are substantively smaller in this period compared to the later period, though one should remember these changes are being computed over a narrower window of time. With the exception of the high school educated, the probability of nonwhite ID increases between 2 and 4 percentage points over this period. We do not see the same monotonic relationship between education and reclassification over this period. Only the high school educated stand out: they are 6 points more likely to identify as nonwhite over time ($p < 0.05$). The effect of university education, by contrast, is substantively small at only 2 points ($p < 0.1$).

Disaggregating by income, we do not find evidence of the hypothesized pattern. As expected, respondents in the top income decile exhibit

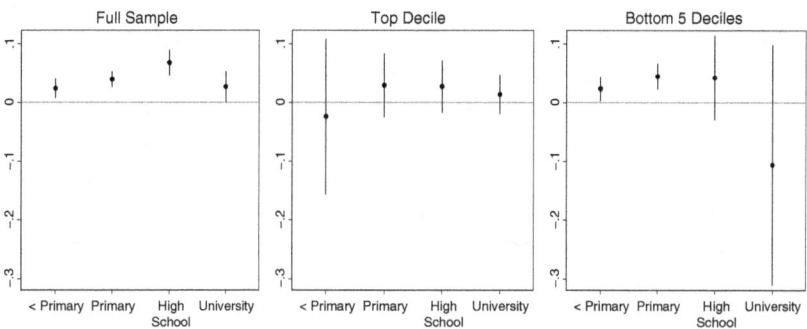

FIGURE 5.6 Change in Pr(nonwhite ID) between 1982 and 1990 by education and income

stability in their racial identifications. But respondents in the bottom half of the income structure are less stable, but do not exhibit the hypothesized pattern. Significant effects are estimated only for the least educated, though these effects are modest in size (3 and 4 points $p < 0.05$). Due to the scarcity of these observations, high school and university respondents are estimated less precisely. The effect of high school education is insignificant but correctly signed; the estimated effect of university education, however, is negative in this period.

To be sure, evidence from this earlier period is scarce, complicating efforts to pin down precisely and rigorously the direction of education's effects and if or when this changed. But considering the sum total of this evidence, it is difficult to conclude that the relationship between education and reclassification was strong or present in the earlier period when lower-class sectors saw scant access to education. We still must be cautious in interpreting these findings, seeing as these sample lack the number of low income and highly educated respondents needed to compute more reliable estimates. Nonetheless, two important takeaways can be drawn. First, even during this earlier period evidence still does not indicate a whitening effect of education on a mass level. To the extent there is any change, it still occurs in a darkening direction. And second, when analyzing subsamples of theoretical interest, the darkening effect of education is not identified. I consider this suggestive evidence that the relationship between education and reclassification changed as access to higher education became more inclusive.

IS RECLASSIFICATION GENDERED?

Gender is also relevant to this analysis in at least two major ways. First, and simply, the strategy of analyzing self-identification by restricting the sample to heads of households leads to gender imbalance in the sample. Men are more likely than women to be considered head of household in Brazil, and as a result the average findings presented earlier are based disproportionately on estimates of men. One obvious empirical question, then, is whether the results presented earlier are specific to men (or women), and whether Brazilians of both genders exhibit similar behavior over this time period. This question can easily be answered by computing estimates on separate subsamples.

But a more complex question that will likely be asked by interdisciplinary scholars of race and gender pertains to the distinct ways that gender may impact processes of identification or reclassification, and if there is quantitative evidence to support what has been found in qualitative research, including my own. Indeed, anecdotes often relayed to me by activists and other interlocutors suggested gender would impact reclassification in different ways. On one hand, darker-skinned women were sometimes portrayed as more likely candidates for reclassification because of perceived higher rates of participation in activism. Indeed, among the growing number of black movement organizations that have emerged in Brazil in recent decades are many black *women's* movements, which can be found in nearly all major cities. According to Perry (2013), part of what contributes to this activism is the especially vulnerable position of women in society, which better motivates them to organize on a racial (and gender) basis through neighborhood associations. More anecdotally, it was not uncommon for activists to suggest to me that women were simply more solidary than men, and therefore exhibited greater propensity to organize and influence each other.

Such arguments are in line with intersectional theorizing (Carneiro 2004; Crenshaw 1991), which in its broadest strokes emphasizes the differential impact of race by gender. But another intersectional view also articulated by activists, more line with Crenshaw's (1991) notion of invisibility deriving from multiple marginalities, is that darker-skinned women would be *less* likely to reclassify. The logic here is that multiple oppressions create greater barriers to self-acceptance for women. Burdick (1998a), for example, provides evidence that, facing competition in dating markets, women engage in practices that comply with and reproduce racial hierarchies, like hair straightening and pursuing mates to "lighten the family" (*clarear a família*). Caldwell (2007, chaps. 3, 4) describes the normative value placed on white beauty in Brazilian society, which creates a sense of inferiority among women who do not fit that mold. Her interviews with women who adopted politicized black identities reveal women's need for "reconstruction of [their] self-image" and "to address [their] sense of being unattractive" (117). Hordge-Freeman (2015) similarly emphasize aesthetic norms and socialization as influencing racial identification. My interviews with men reclassifiers suggest they go through their own gendered version of this process (see interview with Jorge in previous chapter). But nonetheless, intersectional analyses maintain that this burden falls harder on women.

Yet a third way of thinking about this issue is to concede that reclassification or racial subjectivity are gendered in qualitative, but not quantitative, terms. In other words, gender differences might be differences in kind but not degree. For example, it was not uncommon for men and women interviewees to emphasize different aspects of their personal experiences when discussing their racial trajectories. As much research would suggest (Burdick 1998a; Caldwell 2007; Hordge-Freeman 2015), women often discussed struggles with hair straightening or feeling sexualized. Men, on the other hand, were more likely emphasize interactions with police or security guards, or discipline in other settings like schools (Bruch and Soss 2018). These are different and gendered experiences, but all of them were cited by interviewees as important experiences that led to racial consciousness and reclassification, and it's at least unclear from my analysis of interview data whether these gendered experiences lead to differential *propensities* of reclassification by gender.

We can attempt to leverage these data to address two distinct questions related to gender. First, are the main effects presented earlier driven more by men than by women? Second, are women more or less likely to reclassify than men? To assess these questions, I reestimate the models on gender subsamples of the dataset. Several caveats for cautious interpretation of these findings are in order. One caveat here is simply that, due to the gender imbalance in the sample, sample size is severely curtailed when analyzing women. This means that estimates are less precise for women than for men, but also that due to limited sample size computing estimates on income-based subsamples is not feasible. Additionally, because we are analyzing heads of household, and gender dynamics surely play a role in determining head of household, we might be cautious about generalizing from women heads of household to the broader population of Brazilian women.

That said, Figure 5.7 display the average overtime change in rates of reclassification between 1993 and 2015. Clearly, the main effects

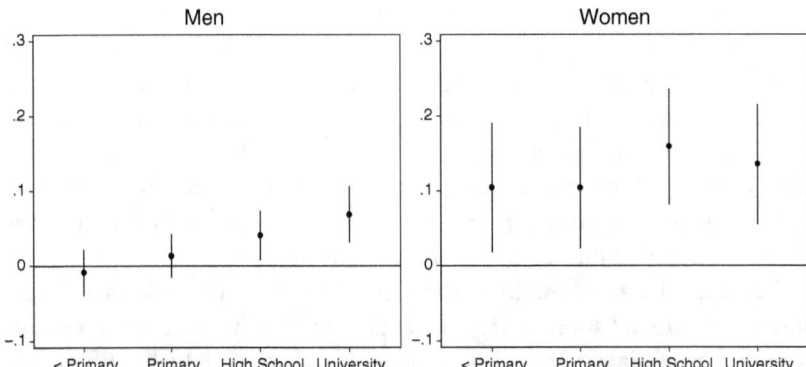

FIGURE 5.7 Change in Pr(nonwhite ID) between 1993 and 2015 by education and gender

displayed earlier are driven by men heads of household in the sample, who fit the hypothesized pattern very neatly. Women, on the other hand, do not exhibit the same monotonic relationship between education and reclassification, though they are likely to reclassify at all levels of education. We can cautiously conclude that there may in fact be gender differences in reclassification at lower levels of education, where women are more likely than men to reclassify. If anything, therefore, evidence from this analysis provides modest support for the intersectional hypothesis that women are more likely than men to reclassify.

Is Reclassification Region Specific?

Additionally, we might also ask whether the effects presented earlier vary, or are contingent on, a specific geographic region of Brazil. Anthropologists and sociologists have long pointed to subnational variation in racial subjectivities within Brazil as evidence for the claim that "race" is a social construct. The two major geographic regions of Brazil, the industrialized southeast and the lesser developed northeast, are said to represent distinct poles of Brazilian racial subjectivity.

As Monk (2013) notes, the hypothesis that regional variations in racial subjectivity shape identifications has a long history in interdisciplinary scholarship, though this notion has not been centered or well integrated into studies of regional differences in racial identification. Early influential studies by Pierson (1942), Frazier (1942), and Degler (1971) all describe more fluid racial boundaries and lesser racial prejudice in the northeast, compared to the south and southeastern region. But Telles (1993) and Guimarães (1999) both criticize these arguments about regional differences in this early scholarship as impressionistic and inappropriate, arguing that these studies tend to situate research in a single locality and do not rigorously incorporate cross-regional comparisons. Aiming to test this notion, Telles's (1993) regional study of intermarriage indicates that much of the perceived regional differences in prejudice are driven by differences in the historical distribution of racial groups and miscegenation across regions.

More pertinent to the question of reclassification, in his later seminal study Telles (2004) offers the impression that due to European immigration to southern and southeastern Brazil, racial boundaries are brighter in these regions and less ambiguous compared to the northeast, where historical miscegenation has blurred boundaries to a greater extent. Telles argues that the whitening hypothesis is overblown, but concedes that classification into white and black categories is less ambiguous in São Paulo compared to Bahia. But, he adds, that classification in the brown category is more ambiguous in São Paulo (also see Muniz and Bastos 2017).

Monk (2013) and McNamee (2020) similarly argue that regional differences in the distribution of African and European (forced) migrants in the northern and southern regions, respectively, explains a starker racial binary in southern regions and more fluid racial boundaries in northern regions. McNamee goes further, suggesting that status variables (like education) ought to predict whitening in regions predominated by European settlers, such as southern and southeastern Brazil. Silveira's (2019) analysis of racial reclassification in Brazil finds that reclassification into the brown category is more common in the northeast, but Jesus and Hoffman (2020) document reclassification across all major geographic regions. As a counterpoint, in her analysis of parents' classifications of their children, Schwartzman (2007, 957) interacts education and region and does not find significant whitening effects, but does find that education has a smaller whitening effect on women in the northeast and center west compared to other regions.

Though many scholars make reference to these regional differences, clear patterns or variation is not easily discernible from this scholarship. But we might still ask whether the patterns identified earlier hold across all regions in the sample. And, if not, do we observe differences across regions as suggested by early and more recent scholarship? If arguments pertaining to regional differences are correct, we ought to find the pattern is driven by respondents in the north or northeast where racial boundaries are fluid, and less boundary crossing in the south and southeast where there is a starker racial binary. However, if my hypothesis is correct, we ought to find the relationship between education and nonwhite identification holds across regions in Brazil. I reestimate the models earlier on separate regional subsamples. Once again, a caveat pertaining to this analysis is that dividing the sample in this way does limit sample size for certain regions (the north and center-west in particular) that limits our ability to compute precise estimates. Nonetheless, the subsamples for the northeast and southeast - the two largest regions, and the two seen as most distinct in racial terms (Weinstein 2015) - provide an opportunity to assess these regional effects.

Figure 5.8 presents the overtime change in nonwhite ID by education and geographic region. The pattern expected by the political identity hypothesis holds in four out of five regions. Two of these, the north

Education and Reclassification 153

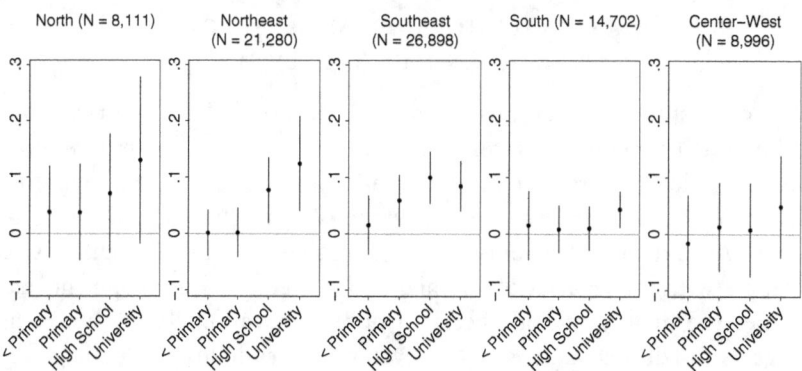

FIGURE 5.8 Change in Pr(nonwhite ID) between 1993 and 2015 by education and region

and center-west, are estimated imprecisely due to sample size; but the size and direction of the points estimates indicate a positive and monotonic – if insignificant – relationship between education and nonwhite identification over time. In the northeast and southeast – the two regions commonly thought to be most distinct within Brazil – the pattern is clear and statistically significant. In both regions, the highest educated respondents are the most likely to adopt nonwhite identifications over time. In the northeast, lesser educated respondents are estimated to be stable in their racial identifications. In the southeast, the same can be said of those with the lowest levels of educational attainment. Only the south does not fit the pattern so neatly. Yet while the high school-educated are not estimated to change racial identifications over time, those with university education are more likely to do so.

Analysis of regional subsamples indicate that the patterns identified from the full sample do not appear driven by any one geographic region in particular. And perhaps even more striking, the northeast and southeast are the two regions that exhibit the most similar patterns, defying the common perception that boundaries are more fluid in the northeast than in the southeast. Of course, this evidence does not indicate directly that prior scholarship is wrong about regional differences in racial boundaries. But even so, differences in boundary fluidity clearly do not impede, nor are they necessary for, the darkening effects of education. And last, this analysis also suggests that in no specific region of Brazil does education have a whitening effect. As Telles (2004) finds in his analysis, education darkens in this period.

ANALYSIS II: PANEL ANALYSIS OF BRAZILIAN MUNICIPALITIES

Beyond testing whether this microlevel pattern holds across regions, subnational variation in rates of reclassification provides an additional source of leverage to test the observable implications of the hypothesis. Like many countries with a history of extractive colonial institutions (Acemoglu and Robinson 2013), present-day Brazil continues to grapple with the legacies of colonial and postcolonial development that shapes the quality of and access to public education. In a country as large as Brazil, inequalities in the level and accessibility of public goods also varies greatly across the territory (Arretche 2016). Among the most notable variation is the commonly cited contrast between the wealthy southeast and the impoverished northeast (Weinstein 2015). If the political identity hypothesis is correct, then territorial inequalities of this sort ought to offer empirical variation in educational access and expansion that can be probed as correlates or causes of reclassification.

Figure 5.9 depicts the rate of change of the white population in each state between 2000 and 2010. Indeed, there is significant subnational variation in apparent rates of reclassification. Two points are worth highlighting. First, in every state there is a decrease in the *relative proportion* of white identifiers, suggesting, as the national data do, that the net tendency of reclassification decidedly shifted toward self-darkening in every state and region of Brazil.[11] Second, there is considerable variation across states in the size of these declines. States like Goiás and Minas Gerais registered declines of nearly 8 percentage points between 2000 and 2010. In other states, like the northeastern states of Rio Grande do Norte and Piauí, white populations decreased by only one and two points, respectively. Third, states in two geographic regions – the southeast and the center-west – cluster at one end of this variation. States in these regions experience the largest declines in the white population. By contrast, states in the northeast, north, and south all exhibit wider variation.

These patterns more or less map onto the subnational patterns identified by Jesus and Hoffman (2020) in their thorough analysis of subnational patterns in reclassification over this period. Employing cohort

---

[11] This does not mean that the absolute size of the white population has declined in every state (see Figure C1). Some states register decreases and others large increases, though large increases appear to be a function of population size. States with smaller populations register larger growth rates.

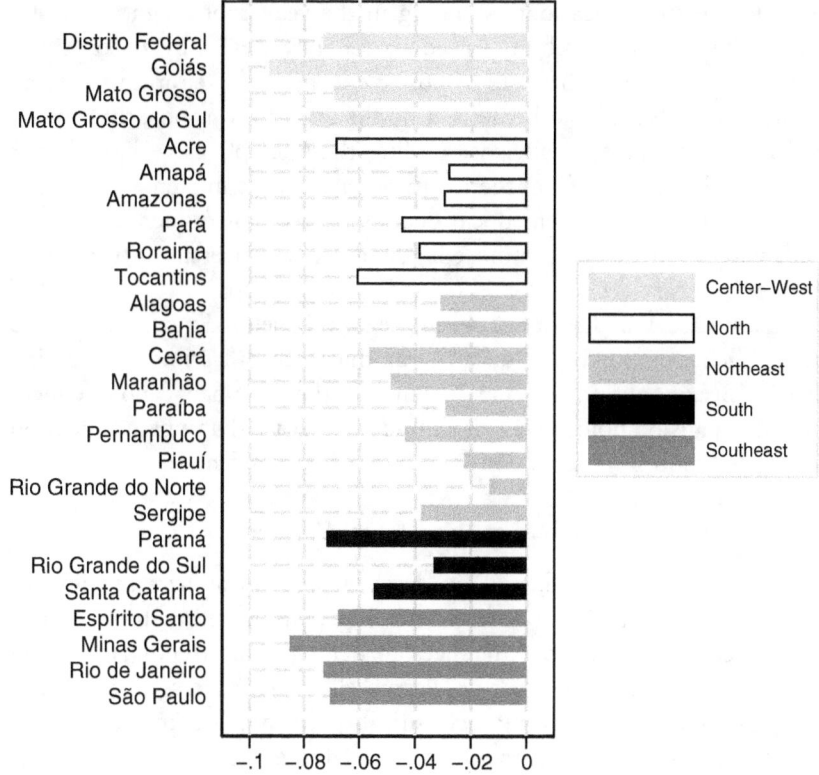

FIGURE 5.9 Inter-census difference in white population, 2000–2010
Source: IBGE.

methods similar to those employed earlier, these authors show that reclassification is occurring across all major geographic regions, with some variation in degree. Similar to what Figure 5.9 suggests, these authors find that the southeast exhibits the highest rate of reclassification (5.5 percent), followed by the south (3.75 percent) and center-west (3.7 percent) in the middle, and the north (2.63 percent) and northeast (2.64 percent) at the low end.

This regional variation in where patterns of reclassification appear greatest deepen the puzzle at the heart of this book and provides another opportunity to test whether these subnational patterns can be explained by variation in educational expansion. It is not immediately clear that they do. On one hand, the wealthy and modernized southeastern states might provide better opportunities for upward mobility via better public goods provision and higher baselines of educational access or quality.

But their better educational standing in the year 2000 might impose a low ceiling on the possibility for educational *expansion* by 2010. At the same time, seeing as the state of public education – even in the wealthy southeast – left much to be desired by the end of the 1990s, these modernized states and the citizens residing there simply have been better positioned to benefit from the institutional changes implemented in the 1990s and beyond. Given educational expansion, lower-income individuals may simply have been more likely to access university if they reside in the southeast.

In any case, whether or not certain regions benefitted more than others from educational expansion, it's clear that reclassification is occurring across Brazil, but to varying extents. If the argument about educational expansion holds water, it should be the case that where education expanded more, we also see greater rates of reclassification.

Sources of Subnational Variation

Rigorous analyses conducted by demographic researchers are invaluable for helping to rule out knee-jerk explanations for reclassifications attributed to intergroup differences in demographic trends (Jesus and Hoffmann 2020; Miranda 2015; Petruccelli 2002; Soares 2008). But to fully explain what is causing reclassification toward blackness, and why this trend is so much greater now compared to earlier decades, a satisfying account must be able to account for this subnational variation within Brazil. Variation in educational access and expansion provides this explanation, I argue, since the question of educational access necessarily raises the question of territorial inequalities within Brazil. Earlier analyses addressed the former questions, but testing two additional observable implications can further strengthen the argument regarding educational expansion. First, given that reclassification patterns clearly vary within Brazil, rates of educational expansion should vary too, if the hypothesis is correct. And second, the spatial correlation of educational expansion and racial reclassification should stand up to rigorous scrutiny.

The first point is demonstrable and should be uncontroversial. Sokoloff and Engerman (2000) offer a broad historical narrative for the underdevelopment of Latin America as a whole based on the rich resources in the colonial period which led to extractive institutions (also see Acemoglu and Robinson 2013).[12] Brazil is no exception. Brazil was by far the largest

---

[12] For similar subnational patterns identified elsewhere in Latin America, see Dell (2010), Acemoglu et al. (2012), and Sanchez Talanquer (2017).

recipient of enslaved Africans in the trans-Atlantic slave trade, and coercive labor institutions formed the backbone of the colonial economy. But historical economic evidence is mixed on the local-level consequences of slavery for long-term patterns of development or public goods provision (Naritomi, Soares, and Assunção 2012; Papadia 2017; Summerhill 2010). Beyond local prevalence of slavery, historic patterns of immigration and development are an additional source of local variation in public goods provision. Localities associated with European immigration (and postcolonial resource booms, like coffee) around the turn of the twentieth century have been shown to possess better quality public schools (Filho and Colistete 2010; Musacchio et al. 2014; Naritomi et al. 2012).

To those familiar with Brazil or other former colonies, this should come as no surprise. But the relevant question is not just whether public goods provision varies locally, but how *change* in that provision has varied across space. In Chapter 3, I detailed state-led efforts to increase educational spending and enrollment and the efforts to circumvent political interference that might undermine federal spending. But the question remains as to how prior territorial inequalities have shaped the *expansion* of education in the contemporary period, seeing as localities are likely starting from vastly different baselines.

This variation is displayed in Figures 5.10 and 5.11, which display municipal-level rates of high school and university attendance between

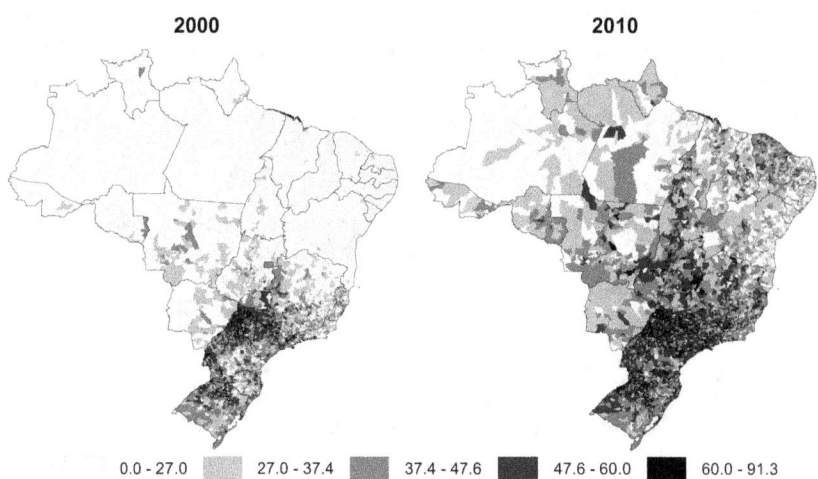

FIGURE 5.10 Municipal-level high school attendance rates among Brazilians aged 15–17, 2000 and 2010
Source: Atlas Brasil

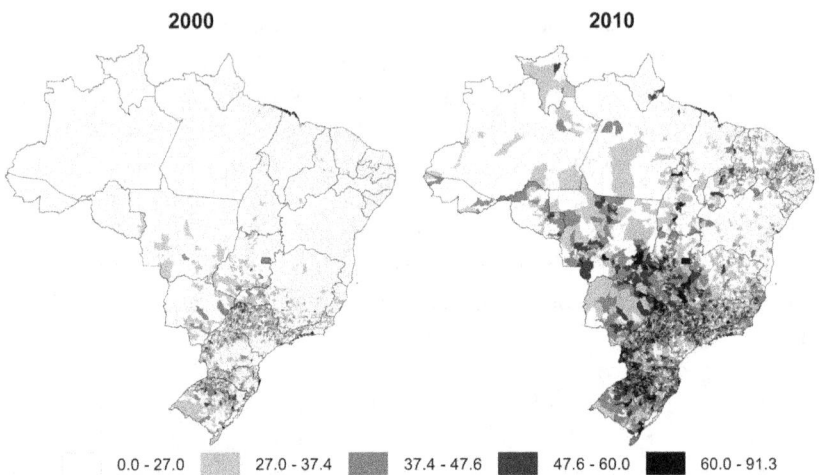

FIGURE 5.11 Municipal-level university attendance rates among Brazilians aged 18–24, 2000 and 2010
Source: Atlas Brasil

2000 and 2010. First, the degree of territorial inequality in 2000 is strikingly clear. High school attendance is heavily concentrated in the wealthier south and southeast states, but even within these states there is considerable variation at the local level. Patterns are more uniform in the north and northeast, but rates of both high school and university attendance are dismal in these regions in 2000. By 2010, however, there is striking improvement in high school and university attendance across nearly all of Brazil. To be sure, educational attendance rates in the south and southeast continue to outpace those in other regions and university attendance lags behind high school rates. But localities in every region and state register notable improvements in secondary and tertiary education. Looking more closely at *expansion* in education, then, it seems that local rates of educational expansion broadly map onto observed state-level variation in Figure 5.9.

Is This Just Affirmative Action?

A second important consideration relates again to affirmative action policies, which are especially pertinent when examining the period between 2000 and 2010. The federal affirmative action law was not passed until 2012, but state-level initiatives were implemented as early as 2001. Rio de Janeiro was the first state pass affirmative action policies of any kind for higher education, starting with a 50 percent quota for public-school students in Rio de Janeiro's state-run public universities.[13] The first race-targeted policy was also passed in Rio de Janeiro in 2001 (Law 3.708/2001) and established a 40 percent quota for black and brown students in state universities.[14]

Soon after Rio de Janeiro, other states and individual universities began implementing affirmative policies in a similar mold, by combining racial and class-based criteria to determine eligibility for admission via quotas. Though affirmative action policies generate surprising levels of support among the Brazilian public (Bailey et al. 2018), these policies continue to receive politicized coverage in the media and have mobilized conservative backlash (e.g., Daflon and Feres Jr. 2012) due to perception that the targeting of racial criteria is unfair and "un-Brazilian," and due to the thorny issues of how and where to draw "the color line," so to speak. Yet despite all the controversy, Peria and Bailey (2014) find that applicants' ability to use affirmative action policies is more restricted than public debate would suggest. Indeed, these authors find that of the ninety-five public universities in Brazil (at the time of their writing), seventy-three had an affirmative action policy of some kind (77 percent). However, of these only thirty-nine target applicants on a racial basis (41 percent), and thirty-three target race only in conjunction with socioeconomic criteria (35 percent). This leaves only six public universities that target race without consideration for other criteria (6 percent). Closer inspection of the nature and extent of affirmative action policies reveals that the incentives for blackness may not be as strong, or as easily pursued, as they initially appear.

Nonetheless, the presence of affirmative action policies must be accounted for in analysis of subnational variation of racial reclassification, given that such policies represent an important institutional change between 2000 and 2010, and their hypothesized effects extend beyond instrumentality (see Chapter 6). Table 5.2 sorts Brazil's twenty-seven states according to the timing and targeting of affirmative action laws passed in this period. Six states – Amapá, Minas Gerais, Rio de Janeiro, Paraná, Mato Grosso do Sul, and Goiás – passed laws prior to 2010 that reserved at least some slots for Afro-descendants, most in proportion

---

[13] This is in contrast to the *federally* run network of public universities, which exist throughout Brazil.
[14] See Peria and Bailey (2014) for review of the controversy over, backlash against, and evolution of affirmative action policies in Rio de Janeiro.

TABLE 5.2 *Affirmative action policies by state and year of passage*

Policy	State (Region)	Law / Year	Targeted beneficiaries / University issuing decree
States with race-targeted affirmative action law before 2010	Amapá (N)	1.022/2006, 1.023/2006, 1.258/2008	Afro-descendants among others; Universidade do Estao do Amapá (UEAP)
	Goiás (CW)	14.832/2004 20.249/2018	Negros among others; Universidade Estadual de Goiás (UEG)
	Mato Grosso do Sul (CW)	2.589/2002, 2.605/2003, 3.594/2008	Negros (20%) among others; Universidade Estadual de Mato Grosso do Sul (UEMS)
	Minas Gerais (SE)	15.259/2004, 13.465/2000	Negros (20%) among others; Universidade do Estado de Minas Gerais (UEMG), Universidade Estadual de Montes Claros (UNIMONTES)
	Paraná (S)	14.274/2003, 13.134/2001	Afro-descendants (10% in *concurso publico*); indigenous quotas in state universities
	Rio de Janeiro (SE)	4.151/2003, 3.708/2001	Negros (20%) among others; Universidade Estadual do Rio de Janeiro (UERJ), Universidade Estadual do Norte-Fluminense (UENF), Centro Universitário Estadual da Zona Oeste (UEZO)
States with race-targeted affirmative action by university decree before 2010	Alagoas (NE)	2003, 6.542/2004	Negros by decree, public-school quotas by law; Universidade Federal de Alagoas (Ufal), Universidade Estadual de Alagôas (UNEAL)
	Bahia (NE)	2004, 15.353/2014	Negros by university decree (2004); Universidade Federal da Bahia (UFBa)
	Distrito Federal (CW)	2003	Negros (20%); Universidade de Brasília (UnB)
	Maranhão (NE)	2006, 9.295/2010, 10.404/2015	Negros (10%) by decree in 2006 (UFMA); Universidade Federal do Maranhão (UFMA), Universidade Estadual do Maranhão (UEMA)
	Pará (N)	2005	Negros (20%) among others; Universidade Federal do Pará (UFPA)

State	Year(s)	Description
Piauí (NE)	5.791/2008	Negros (15%) by university decree (2008) and public school by law; Universidade Estadual do Piauí (UEPI)
Rio Grande do Sul (S)	2007, 11.646/2001, 14.631/2014	Negros (10%) among others; Universidade Federal de Santa Maria (UFSM)
Santa Catarina (S)	2007	Negros (10%) among others; Universidade Federal de Santa Catarina (UFSC)
São Paulo (SE)	2006	Bonus system for negros, public school; Universidade de São Paulo (USP)
Sergipe (NE)	2008	Negros among others; Universidade Federal de Sergipe (UFS)

States without any race-targeted affirmative action before 2010

State	Year(s)	Description
Acre (N)	–	–
Amazonas (N)	2.894/2004	Indigenous; Universidade do Estado do Amazonas (UEA)
Ceará (NE)	2014, 16.197/2017	Negros among others; Universidade Estadual do Ceará (UEC), Universidade Regional do Cariri, Universidade Estadual Vale do Acaraú, among others
Espírito Santo (SE)	2007	Public-school quotas by decree; Universidade Federal do Espírito Santo (UFES)
Mato Grosso (CW)	2011, 2003	Cotas for negros approved by university decree in 2003, but not implemented until 2012; Universidade Federal do Mato Grosso (UFMT)
Paraíba (NE)	2006	Public-school quotas by decree; Universidade Estadual da Paraíba (UEPB)
Pernambuco (NE)	2004, 2010	Public-school quotas by decree (UPE in 2004, Univasf in 2010); Universidade de Pernambuco (UPE), Universidade Federal do Valé do São Francisco (Univasf)
Rio Grande do Norte (NE)	8.258/2002	Public-school quota (50%); Universidade do Estado do Rio Grande do Norte (UERN)
Rondônia (N)	12.990/2011	Negros (20%) in *concurso público*
Roraima (N)	2012	Disability quota; Universidade Estadual de Roraima (UERR)
Tocantins (N)	2004, 2013	Indigenous quotas (2004) and quilombolos (2013) by decree; Universidade Federal de Tocantins (UFT)

Policies are implemented in the year following passage. See Albuquerque and Pedron (2017) on the case of Mato Grosso.

TABLE 5.3 *Pearson's correlation coefficient of change in high school attendance and change in relative proportion of racial group in municipality, 2000–2010*

	All municipalities	Without AA	With AA
Black Population	.34*	–.18	.38*
Brown Population	–.34*	–0.23	–0.31
White Population	.20*	0.28+	0.15*

High school attendance is measured as the percentage of the population aged 15–17 attending high school in municipality. $N = 5,565$. $^* p < 0.05$, $^+ p < 0.1$.

to the Afro-descendant population in the state. Five additional states – Piauí, Bahia, São Paulo, Mato Grosso, and the Federal District – contained at least one university that implemented racial quotas by decree. The remaining sixteen states have either still not implemented affirmative action policies, or implemented these policies after 2010.

While on the one hand the implementation of these policies complicates efforts to make inferences about the effects of educational expansion, the timing and state-level variation of these policies also present an opportunity to test their effects. But here, I control for and leverage this variation in my analysis to assess the impact of educational expansion on racial reclassification at the local level.

Casual observation of the differences in rates of reclassification in states with and without affirmative action policies does suggest that affirmative action may shape, or is a contingent factor in spurring or boosting, reclassification toward blackness during this period. Table 5.3 displays correlation coefficients between the increase in high school attendance rates in each municipality and the change in the relative proportion of each racial group, divided by states with and without affirmative action. For our purposes, I choose high school attendance rates, since it is likely the high school-aged and -educated who are in a position to manipulate their racial identifications to take advantage of affirmative action in university admissions. First, it's clear that educational expansion correlates with shifting racial demographics at the local level in Brazil overall. Second, correlations indicate that the positive correlation between high school attendance and reclassification is driven by municipalities in states with affirmative action policies, either by law or university decree. Also noteworthy is that the bivariate correlation with the black population is negative in states without affirmative action. But third, in these municipalities, there is a positive correlation with both black *and white* identification, which is not what we might expect if opportunists are thought to manipulate their identifications to benefit from affirmative action. In this case, we might expect high school attendance to correlate negatively with white identification, and positively with brown identification. If anything, it seems that affirmative action may have had a chromatically polarizing effect on racial identification, increasing identification with the poles of the black–white color spectrum. This is in line with what Bailey has argued regarding the effects of affirmative action in this purely chromatic sense (Bailey 2008). However, we should be careful not to place too much weight on these correlations, which do not adjust for potentially confounding differences across municipalities.

Panel Analysis of Brazilian Municipalities

To test this relationship more rigorously, I rely on fixed effects analysis of a panel dataset of Brazilian municipalities between the 2000 and 2010 census rounds. These years not only correspond to the major period of educational expansion, but they also provide the most comprehensive municipal-level data available from the census bureau. This enables the construction of a dataset of municipalities to directly analyze subnational variation in patterns of racial reclassification. Panel analysis accomplishes this through repeated observations of single units over time – in this case, the municipality. As of the 2010 census, Brazil was divided in 5,565 municipalities across twenty-seven states. The dataset analyzed here was built to analyze changes in the relative sizes of racial categories in each municipality, corresponding to the observed variation presented in Figure 5.9.

I analyze these changes with fixed effects regression, which enables controlling for time-invariant, unobserved characteristics that might otherwise confound estimates. For example, we might suspect that observed subnational variation might be driven by cultural factors that distinguish localities like São Paulo or Salvador, which might make individuals in these localities more or less likely to reclassify. But, with repeated observations of the same units over time, we can assume that such characteristics will have constant effects across time periods. Fixed effects analysis instead estimates how time-varying characteristics – like rates of school attendance – correlate with the time-varying outcome of interest, reclassification. Thus, beyond any time-varying controls included in the model, we can assume that potential time-invariant confounders are absorbed and controlled in a time-constant error term for each unit.

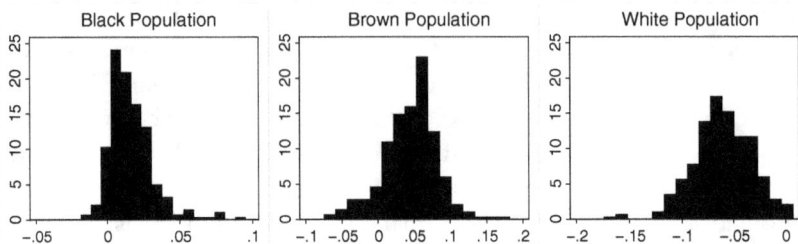

FIGURE 5.12 Histograms of change in relative racial group size, 2000–2010

Figure 5.12 displays histograms of the change in the relative size of each racial category between 2000 and 2010, which is the dependent variable in this analysis. First, it's clear that nearly every municipality in Brazil saw a decline in the *relative* size of white identifiers between 2000 and 2010. These figures do not account for fertility rates, so this does not necessarily mean that the absolute size of white identifiers decreased. More simply, their share of the population declined between 0 and 10 percentage points. Conversely, the vast majority of municipalities saw increases in the black and brown-identified populations. In the vast majority of cases, the relative size of the black population grew between 0 and 5 percentage points, and the brown population grew between 0 and 10 percentage points.

The observable implication of the hypothesis I seek to test with this analysis is whether such variations between and within municipalities can be attributed to differences in educational expansion in these municipalities. I test this with multiple independent variables derived from the Atlas Brasil, a dataset of local-level development provided by the UN Development Program. I consider three main educational variables of interest: rates of university, high school, and primary school attendance at the municipal level. For each level of education, attendance rates are measured as the proportion of the age-relevant population that attends schooling. For primary school, this includes those aged 6–14; for high school, those aged 15–17; and for university, those aged 18–24. The models later estimate whether *changes* in these rates of attendance at each level of schooling correlate with shifts in the relative size of racial groups.

My analysis also takes into account the population size of the municipality to account for potential scope conditions of the hypothesis. While I do not explicitly hypothesize that the theorized relationship holds only in urban, or densely populated localities, there is good reason to expect variation across these types of municipalities. First, though governments have made great strides in expanding educational access in rural areas, the reality is that most opportunities for education, especially university education, are to be found in major urban centers and capital cities. Second, the primary mechanism I theorize relates to exposure, which alters personal experiences and subjective interpretations. In geographically large and sparsely populated municipalities, there may be fewer opportunities for exposure via civil society, or types of labor market experiences that my interviewees in urban areas identified. And third, as Touchton and Wampler (2013) argue, as of 2010 more than 80 percent of Brazil's population resided in an urban area, a significant portion of which resided in municipalities with populations over 100,000. I thus follow Touchton and Wampler and separate the sample into municipalities above and below 100,000 residents. The theoretically relevant subsample of municipalities with more than 100,000 residents ("urban" municipalities) includes 282 municipalities, which is just 5 percent of the 5,565 municipalities. These municipalities, however, contain 55 percent of the total 2010 population. As we will see, accounting for population size in the analysis helps to further specify the conditions under which the political identity hypothesis holds.

Different from the pseudo-panel analysis – in which I sought to control for affirmative action by removing its potential effects – in this analysis I measure affirmative action laws directly and incorporate these as a control. I code municipalities based on whether they are located in states that *implemented* race-targeted affirmative action laws or with at least one university with a race-targeted university decree implementing affirmative action prior to 2010. Coding is based on the data presented in Table 5.2. After estimating models with affirmative action as a control variable, I interact affirmative action status with rates of educational attendance to assess conditional effects.

Fixed effects regression is a powerful tool for controlling for time-invariant characteristics, assuming that these factors are indeed time-invariant as well as the magnitude and direction of their effects. These aside, I also control for time-varying factors. Two important demographic factors are the birth and death rate in the municipality. These will of course control for any intergroup differences that might emerge in changes in fertility or mortality over this period. A third related demographic factor is domestic migration between municipalities. Unfortunately, fine-grained data on municipal-level migration is not available in the year 2000, and I am unable to control for this factor in the analysis.

However, it's somewhat reassuring that Jesus and Hoffman's (2020) analysis of reclassification by geographic region finds that the effects of interregional migration are negligible. Similarly, bivariate correlations of the 2010 migration rate[15] and the change in relative group size for the black (ρ = 0.1) and brown (ρ = 0.03) populations are weak. Last, I also control for economic factors that might impact the capacity of states to implement educational expansion, as well as factors that might inhibit individuals' uptake or pursuit of education. For the first factor, I include a measure of the municipality's GDP per capita. For the second, I include the Gini coefficient of income.

Results and Discussion

Table 5.4 presents estimates from fixed-effects models estimating the change in the relative size of each racial category. Models 1–3 present estimates from the relevant subsample of urban municipalities. Control variables have inconsistent effects across racial categories and according to population size. Affirmative action policies correlate significantly with white and brown, but not black, change. These correlations are similar in magnitude, but are differently signed. Compared to the effects of the high school and university attendance variables, these effects are substantively small. Across all models, increases in fertility are associated with decreased black populations and increased white populations. The reverse is true for death rates, though neither demographic factor consistently correlates with changes in relative racial group size. Finally, increases in income inequality and GDP per capita correlate with larger white groups, and smaller brown groups.

Turning to the variables of interest, there are two consistent trends across the first three models. University attendance is signed as expected and statistically significant across all three racial categories. Changes in primary school attendance have no identifiable effect on the relative size of racial categories in urban municipalities. In model 1, which estimates change in the black population, the estimates for high school and university attendance are positive and statistically significant, indicating that expansion of both high school and university education correlate with growth in the black population. In model 2, university has a similar and substantively larger effect on the relative size of the brown population.

---

[15] This is measured as the proportion of the municipal-level population residing in the municipality for less than ten years.

TABLE 5.4 *Fixed-effects estimates of change in relative racial group size, 2000–2010*

	Population > 100k			Population < 100k		
	(1) Black	(2) Brown	(3) White	(4) Black	(5) Brown	(6) White
Primary	−0.0304 (0.0395)	−0.00121 (0.0969)	0.0406 (0.0813)	−0.0326* (0.00853)	0.0977* (0.0198)	−0.0383* (0.0163)
High School	0.0795* (0.0132)	−0.100* (0.0324)	−0.0000196 (0.0272)	0.00267 (0.00414)	0.0219* (0.00959)	−0.0378* (0.00787)
University	0.0600* (0.0237)	0.126* (0.0582)	−0.213* (0.0488)	−0.0166 (0.0123)	0.150* (0.0285)	−0.163* (0.0233)
Racial Affirm Action Law	−0.000229 (0.00207)	0.0302* (0.00508)	−0.0265* (0.00427)	0.00473* (0.00107)	0.0331* (0.00247)	−0.0360* (0.00203)
Birth rate	−0.0835* (0.0314)	−0.130+ (0.0771)	0.190* (0.0647)	−0.0533* (0.0114)	0.00773 (0.0263)	0.0402+ (0.0216)
Death rate	0.258+ (0.139)	−0.460 (0.342)	0.179 (0.287)	0.0771* (0.0322)	0.0464 (0.0742)	−0.149* (0.0610)
Income Gini	−0.00241 (0.0313)	−0.211* (0.0767)	0.212* (0.0644)	0.00141 (0.00804)	−0.153* (0.0186)	0.143* (0.0153)
GDP per capita	−0.104 (0.113)	−0.558* (0.277)	0.562* (0.232)	−0.0991 (0.0815)	−0.401* (0.189)	0.463* (0.156)
Constant	0.0564 (0.0390)	0.566* (0.0955)	0.374* (0.0802)	0.0928* (0.00874)	0.389* (0.0202)	0.491* (0.0167)
Within-group error	0.0438	0.192	0.223	0.0455	0.237	0.265
Overall error	0.0103	0.0253	0.0213	0.0278	0.0644	0.0532
ICC	0.947	0.983	0.991	0.728	0.931	0.961
N	564	564	564	10,464	10,476	10,497
Within R^2	0.596	0.633	0.803	0.0244	0.262	0.388
Between R^2	0.124	0.00252	0.456	0.000	0.445	0.526
Overall R^2	0.0249	0.00559	0.0580	0.00242	0.0901	0.121

Standard errors in parentheses. $^+ p < 0.10$, $^* p < 0.05$.

But the effect of high school education on the brown population is negative. This suggests that the effect of high school attendance on municipal-level black growth results from shifts away from brown identification. Finally, model 3 estimates that only university education impacts the relative size of the white population, exerting a statistically significant and substantively large negative effect on the relative size of the white population.

In less densely populated municipalities (models 4–6), there are several notable differences. First, the effect of high school education on the brown population is positive and significant, unlike in urban localities. Second, unlike in urban areas, primary education also impacts relative group sizes. Expansion of primary attendance is associated with a decrease in white and black identification, and a growth of brown identification. At higher levels of education, however, the negative association with black identification disappears. Whereas in urban areas there is a clear tendency for the highly educated to opt for black identification, in rural areas it appears that the educated are more likely to opt for brown identification at the expense of black and white groups.

We also want to know not only if the effects of education are robust to controls for affirmative action policies, but also whether the effects of education are contingent on the presence of affirmative action. In other words, affirmative action and educational expansion are not mutually exclusive, and indeed the purpose of affirmative action is to increase the representation of social groups historically excluded from higher education. Thus, one question is whether the effects of educational expansion hold only in the presence of an affirmative action law, or whether these effects are contingent on their presence, as Table 5.3 suggests.

Figure 5.13 presents substantive findings from interactive models that estimate the conditional effects of educational attendance and affirmative action (see Supplementary Table C33 for full estimates). By and large, substantive findings presented in Figure 5.13 do not estimate significant conditional effects of educational expansion by affirmative action status, nor do they show that affirmative action boosts the effects of educational expansion on black or brown identification. Only in rare instances do affirmative action policies alter the direction or substantive significance of the effects of educational attendance, though not to the level of statistical significance. In other instances, point estimates do not vary significantly across affirmative action status. Consideration for conditional effects reveals, therefore, that the effects of educational expansion on subnational variation in reclassification are neither conditional nor contingent on affirmative action. If anything, evidence suggests the opposite is true.

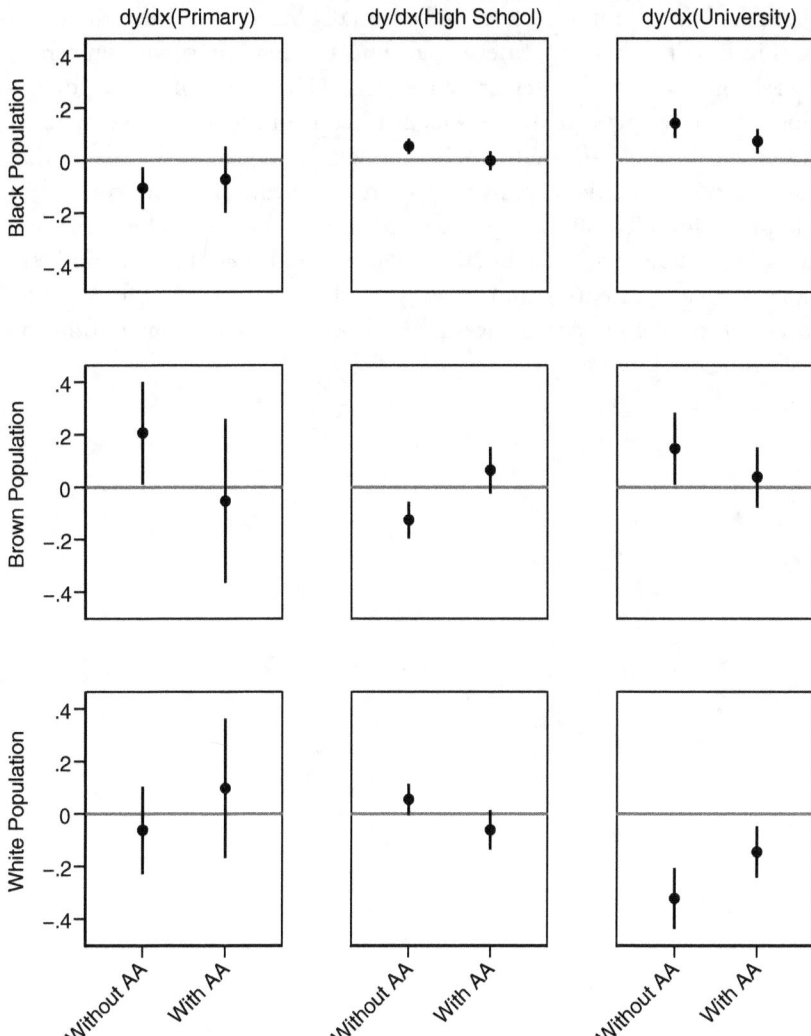

FIGURE 5.13 Average partial effect of change in education attendance rate on relative racial group size by affirmative action status, 2000–2010

CONCLUSION

This chapter focused on testing the longitudinal implications of the political identity hypothesis. Rigorous and systematic panel analyses of microlevel and municipal census data provided consistent support for the hypothesis: over the period in question, better educated Brazilians were more likely to adopt nonwhite, and especially black, identities; and localities in Brazil that saw greater expansions of high school and university education also saw greater growth in the relative size of black populations. Analyses presented here sought to control for or remove the confounding effects of affirmative action policies, and provided evidence that the effects of educational expansion on reclassification are not contingent on, or confounded by, such policies. Of course, the political identity and rival hypotheses are not mutually exclusive, and these latter hypotheses deserve greater attention and scrutiny. In the next chapter, I focus direct attention on the impact of race-targeted policy and state institutions on reclassification.

6

Affirmative Action and Reclassification

The preceding chapters developed and tested a theory of identity politicization that emphasizes how citizenship institutions and social structures interact to shape individuals' personal experiences, and in turn the logic and political content of their racial identities. A number of structural, historical, and institutional factors converged to provide the conditions under which this form of identity change could occur on such a wide scale and at particular points in time.

No other form of institutional change has become centered in recent debates about Brazil's shifting racial politics like affirmative action policies. As these policies were first passed and implemented in the early 2000s, political debate and contestation quickly ensued. These policies were supported by many in the public and across a number of political and academic domains. Indeed, the passage and implementation of affirmative action has been attributed to work by black movement activists inside and outside of formal elected office (Benedito 2015; Moehlecke 2002), and analyses of public opinion have generally shown public support for such policies, though nonwhite support is greater than white support (Bailey 2009; Bailey et al. 2018; Mitchell-Walthour 2015; Turgeon and Habel 2022).[1] This did not, however, prevent opponents of affirmative action – comprised of politicians, activists, journalists, public intellectuals, and academics with expertise in race and race relations – from criticizing these policies on a number of fronts,

---

[1] Along similar lines, Kay, Mitchell-Walthour and White (2015) find that while there is public support for race-targeted affirmative action, support is higher for class-based policies.

including: how a state that once promoted and celebrated race mixture and ambiguity would go about implementing race-targeted affirmative action; the merits of addressing myriad social inequalities by targeting race; the risk of hardening and politicizing racial differences; and how, given racial fluidity, such policies could be implemented to deliver more equitable outcomes.

Aspects of the controversy and backlash that affirmative action caused in public debate also raise questions about how these policies factor into the reclassification reversal. To what extent are the effects of educational expansion contingent upon, or really driven by, affirmative action policies? Analyses in previous chapters sought to address the possibly confounding effects of affirmative action in various ways. Nonetheless, affirmative action predominates as a kind of folk wisdom in public debate and in scholarship, and its impact on the reversal deserves undivided attention.

Two affirmative action-based explanations predominate in the social science literature. The first casts affirmative action as a new benefit that generates incentives for nonwhite identification. In this view, the reclassification reversal is a function of material incentives, namely highly competitive slots in Brazil's public universities. The second explanation derives from the sociological literature on symbolic state institutions, which are said to shape ways of "thinking and seeing" and in turn shape individuals' behavior. Affirmative action, therefore, may have caused the reclassification reversal by signaling the state's embrace and acceptance of blackness, previously downplayed through national myth and efforts to whiten the population.

This chapter seeks to empirically assess the extent to which the reclassification reversal can be attributed to the advent of affirmative action policies in Brazil. The two affirmative action-based hypotheses previewed here are not easy to disentangle, and I do not pretend to settle this here. But I nonetheless present a series of empirical tests designed to assess the causal validity of the claim that affirmative action impacts racial identification and explains the reclassification reversal. First, I draw on secondhand and original survey experiments to probe for effects of affirmative action and to disentangle these competing hypotheses. These include priming experiments conducted in 2002 and 2018, as well as a list experiment probing for evidence of instrumental manipulation. Second, I turn to panel analyses of Brazilian municipalities and federal university students to assess the impact of state and federal affirmative action laws on reclassification. Overall, there is evidence to conclude that affirmative action was a relevant part of educational reforms that encouraged nonwhite identification in Brazil. But findings from these analyses are also mixed and at times inconclusive, suggesting that the effects of affirmative action policies may be less straightforward than public debate or parsimonious theorizing would suggest. Before I turn to these analyses, I provide a brief overview of the affirmative action controversy in Brazil and detail these two distinct hypotheses related to race-targeted policies.

THE CONTROVERSY

It is difficult to overstate the splash that the advent of affirmative action policies made in Brazil, this once-celebrated racial democracy whose claim to superiority on the racial question was based on its purported racial harmony and colorblindness. In the wake of the atrocities of World War II and in comparison to the Jim Crow (Southern United States) or Apartheid (South Africa), the informality of Brazilian racism was considered by many to be a better alternative (Wagley 1952) – even by black intellectuals at the time (Alberto 2011). But in light of sociological studies examining the extent and depth of racial inequalities in Brazil,[2] it became clear that the national myth served to veil the commonsense racial hierarchies and informal practices of discrimination that reproduced profound racial inequalities. In terms of socioeconomic outcomes, the lived experience of darker-skinned Brazilians did not appear to differ greatly from that of African Americans, and indeed African Americans experienced greater upward mobility in the decades following the 1964 Civil Rights Act than did their Brazilian counterparts (Andrews 1992; Andrews 2014). Consequently, scholars and activists began calling for affirmative policies to redress racial inequities.

Though efforts at implementing such race-based policies can be traced to the 1960s (Moehlecke 2002), the first prominent effort at implementing affirmative action was made by federal deputy and well-known black movement activist Abdias do Nascimento in 1983. Nascimento proposed "compensatory action," which would create mechanisms and funds to implement quotas for *negros* (Afro-descendants, or black and brown Brazilians) in public sector jobs, educational scholarships,

---

[2] The literature examining and undermining Brazil's myth of racial democracy is large. See Andrews (1991, 1992), Hasenbalg (1979, 1985), Lovell (1999), Paixão et al. (2010), Paixão and Carvano (2008), and Silva (1978, 1985, 2000).

incentives for private firms to eliminate discriminatory hiring practices, and curricular reforms to alter the stereotypical representation of the darker-skinned in primary schools, as well as the inclusion of African history (Freire et al. 2022; Nascimento 1989, 2016). This effort did not succeed, but it nonetheless marks a significant advance in efforts to acknowledge and redress racial inequalities in Brazil. In time, redemocratization and the new federal constitution in the late 1980s created greater political space to address issues of descriptive representation and for federal deputies and senators to push for greater recognition of racial inequalities. Prominent black representatives Benedita da Silva, Paulo Paim, and Luiz Alberto all pushed for affirmative policies in the 1990s (Benedito 2015; Johnson III 2006; Moehlecke 2002). These efforts also did not lead to legislation, but they were taken up by social movement actors outside of formal political institutions. In 1995, for example, social movements mobilized to commemorate the 300-year anniversary of the death of *quilombo* activist and rebel fighter Zumbi dos Palmares. As part of this mobilization, activists submitted to the federal government a wide range of affirmative action policy proposals (Marcha Zumbi 1996).

Scholars have identified the presidency of Fernando Henrique Cardoso, who assumed office in 1995, to be a major turning point in the effort to install affirmative action in Brazil. Cardoso, who holds a doctorate in sociology and who previously published a book on race relations in Brazil (Cardoso and Ianni 1960), departed from the characteristic silence on racial issues from the earliest days of his presidency. Indeed, in his inaugural address, Cardoso proclaimed: "We are going to energetically ensure equal rights for the equal ... for racial minorities, and some quasi-minorities – for *negros*, principally – who hope that equality will be more than words, a portrait of reality" (Cardoso 1995a; also see Cardoso 1995b). Here, Cardoso not only explicitly acknowledges racial differences in society, but encourages redress of racialized inequalities. However according to scholars, the bigger splash came in 2001, when in the run-up the 2001 World Conference against Racism in Durban, Cardoso explicitly endorsed race-targeted affirmative action policies (Cardoso 2001; Htun 2004; Paschel 2016a). This marked the first time that affirmative action had received such unequivocal and public endorsement from the highest levels of the federal government. As I detail in Chapters 3 and 5, the federal affirmative action law would not be passed until 2012, but states began to implement these policies in the early 2000s (Peria and Bailey 2014). The first state to do so was

Rio de Janeiro in 2001, which implemented a 40 percent quota for black and brown students in state-run universities (Law 3.708/2001).[3] Soon after, other states began to pass similar laws, though these were targeted toward low-income and public-school students, and many targeted race only in conjunction with socioeconomic criteria.[4]

In any case, these policies are among the most celebrated recent accomplishments of the black movement in Brazil, but the advent of affirmative action also met with significant backlash and criticism.[5] Some proponents of affirmative action portray this response as the result of privileged groups losing their advantaged position in the status quo (Guimarães 2005), and there is evidence to support this view (Daflon and Feres Jr. 2012; Turgeon and Habel 2022). But critics of affirmative action – a group that includes prominent politicians, celebrities, academics, and public intellectuals – criticize these policies for a number of reasons.[6] As Paschel (2016a, 215) details, criticisms tend to fall into three broad types: that the policies (1) were designed as top-down initiatives with little input from the public or civil society; (2) were simply a U.S. import, likely bringing with it U.S.-style racial divisions; and (3) violate Brazilian colorblindness and could not be rationally implemented in a context of profound racial ambiguity. Proponents of affirmative action equally push back against critics. They argue that redress of racial inequities requires the state to offer protections against discrimination in society and the economy; that Brazil's national myth and racial fluidity has never prevented discrimination against the darker-skinned; and that, far from a mere import from abroad, affirmative action has been proposed and debated in Brazil for decades.

Political disagreement aside, this third critique raised a thorny practical issue that would impact the rational and effective implementation of affirmative policies once these policies were eventually enacted. Simply

---

[3] In addition to state-run public universities, Brazil also maintains a high-quality network of federal universities, which are not subject to state affirmative laws even when located in states where these laws are implemented.

[4] In an analysis of affirmative action policies, Peria and Bailey (2014) find that only 6 percent of public universities targeted race without consideration for other criteria at the time of their writing. See Table 5.2 for information on state affirmative action laws.

[5] For general histories of the Unified Black Movement in Brazil, especially in the period of its resurgence during the military dictatorship, see Gonzalez (1982, 1985), Nascimento (2016), and Hanchard (1994).

[6] Many of these dissenting views are contained in the volume *Divisões Perigosas* (or *Dangerous Divisions*) edited by prominent anthropologist Peter Fry (2007). For an early prominent critique, see Fry and Maggie (2004).

put, the question is who is "black enough" to benefit from race-targeted policies in Brazil (Santos and Anya 2006; Schwartzman 2008). After all, the "myth of the three races" provides Brazilians of all skin tones with a ready-made discourse enabling claims of some African heritage, an idea enshrined in the common saying that all Brazilians "have a foot in the kitchen."[7] The absence of clear criteria for racial membership, the celebration of racial fluidity, and the state's policy of relying on self-declaration to measure racial identity render the target population imperfectly defined. Universities implementing these policies acknowledge this reality. Like the census bureau, many universities rely on self-identification to racially classify students and applicants. To provide some degree of oversight, some universities have instituted councils to assess the eligibility of applicants, in addition to or instead of self-identification. But such methods have produced their own controversies (Maio and Santos 2005). At the University of Brasília, for example, the first federal university to implement quotas by decree, a case of light-skinned identical twins seeking admission through racial quotas caught national media attention: one was deemed eligible for racial quotas by the council while the other was not (see Paschel 2016a, 213–14).

This example is perhaps an instance of extraordinary ambiguity that highlights the subjective nature of racial classification in this context. It also raises the question of how and whether such policies factor into the logics or calculations of racial identification. A view common among scholars and the public casts affirmative action as a material benefit that incentivizes nonwhite identification, either as "fraud" or via instrumental manipulations of racial ambiguity. A second view emphasizes the symbolic significance of these policies, suggesting that the state's embrace of affirmative action ought to legitimate and encourage nonwhite identification. I motivate each of these hypotheses in turn.

AFFIRMATIVE ACTION AS INCENTIVE

Beyond media hype and scandal, the notion that affirmative action policies will impact identity politics is supported by dominant theories in the comparative politics literature. These theories, which derive mainly from the ethnic politics literature, attribute identity change and salience to material incentives altered by institutional change, often in conjunction

---

[7] This reference to the kitchen alludes to the fact that many black women, before and after slavery, worked in kitchens.

with demographic structures. Posner (2005), for example, argues that elites politicize different axes of ethnic identity based on whether various ethnic groupings form minimum-winning coalitions under shifting electoral rules (also see Huber 2017). Even more explicitly, Chandra (2012) identifies "institutions that structure incentives" as one prototype of identity change in her overview on constructivist approaches to identity politics. In this view, identity change and salience are the product of means-ends calculations made in contexts of resource scarcity (Bates 1974; Laitin 1998) – such as when competing for highly sought admission to free public university. Affirmative action policies have featured explicitly in this literature. In her analysis of the resurgence of Native American identification in the United States, for example, Nagel (1996) argues that affirmative action for Native Americans incentivized identification as such and encouraged collective action. Similarly, Chandra (2005) argues that in the case of India these policies incentivized excluded ethnic groups to mobilize and demand inclusion as policy targets.[8] And Hoddie (2006) argues that "ethnically preferential" policies incentivized ethnic identity change in China and Australia.

Institutional and instrumental explanations of this sort are attractive for their parsimony: the logic is simple and straightforward, and the empirical predictions are clear. Upon closer inspection, however, there are reasons to doubt whether such policies are compelling explanations for the reclassification reversal – that is, whether they explain the sustained and newfound patterns of nonwhite identification evident in the census. First, affirmative action benefits are not awarded based on individuals' identifications on the census questionnaire, which are anonymous by law. In order to attribute census patterns to affirmative action, we must therefore assume that individuals change their racial identifications instrumentally, and continue to do so in all contexts and facets of their lives. This is a more stringent assumption than is commonly acknowledged. Second, and related, it may be true that affirmative action created incentives for nonwhite identification where there perhaps were none (or few) before, but this does not mean that such policies have fully supplanted the status quo incentives for whiteness and disincentives for blackness in particular. Indeed, scholars have long documented the ways in which racial hierarchies are reproduced and blackness is stigmatized through *informal* institutional racism (Cornwell et al. 2017;

---

[8] See Skocpol (1992) for a less materialist account of how exclusion leads to identity politicization.

Soares 2000), even by the darker-skinned themselves (Hordge-Freeman 2015; Sheriff 2001; Twine 1998). We might concede that fluid racial boundaries permit savvy opportunists to manipulate their declared race when and where necessary, but such individuals likely also prefer to reap the rewards of whiteness whenever it pays to do so.

Third and finally, the misuse or abuse of affirmative action policies also carries serious risks for individuals who pursue that path. As mentioned earlier, implementing these policies in a context of profound and celebrated racial ambiguity has raised thorny questions of where to draw "the color line," so to speak (Bailey 2009; Fry 2007; Schwartzman 2008). Both critics and proponents of affirmative action have called for greater regulation and oversight of such policies to prevent fraud (light-skinned individuals disingenuously claiming black or brown identification) and manipulation (racially ambiguous individuals who could or did identify as white, but opt for brown or black identification). Black movement activists refer to these manipulations as "Afropportunism." In response to criticism and the exposure of cases widely deemed fraudulent, some universities have created councils to determine the eligibility of applicants admitted via racial quotas with the goal of preventing misuse (e.g., Oliveira 2016; Sperb 2017; Unesp 2017). But even in the absence of such councils, students who are deemed guilty of fraud when using racial quotas can face expulsion from university, and often undergo public scrutiny in the media (e.g., Martins 2018).

There is empirical support for these misgivings. In a series of panel studies of university students at the University of Brasília before and after the implementation of quotas, Andrew Francis-Tan and Maria Tannuri-Pianto find evidence that applicants manipulate their identifications for admission. But these authors also find that students are likely to revert to lighter identification after matriculation (Francis and Tannuri-Pianto 2012). These studies reveal that upward of 20 percent of students exhibit inconsistency in their racial identifications, but that the majority of these cases consist of darker-skinned students who reclassify from brown to black *after* matriculation. Such changes would not impact eligibility in most cases, and thus suggest motivations beyond crude instrumentality (Francis and Tannuri-Pianto 2013). These students were also more likely to adopt the colloquial racial label *negro* (promoted by the black movement) within five years of completing university (Francis-Tan and Tannuri-Pianto 2015). In a similar analysis, Senkevics and Mello (2022) finds that students who repeat the university entrance exam multiple times do indeed adopt nonwhite racial categories; but they also finds that exam repeaters adopt white identification as well, complicating this picture. Finally, there is evidence that backlash to affirmative action has, to some extent, stigmatized program usage (see Penha-Lopes 2017). Findings from a list experiment show that – contrary to the United States, where leftist white respondents exhibit social desirability bias in favor of affirmative action (Sniderman and Carmines 1997) – in Brazil it is Afro-descendants who exhibit social desirability bias against affirmative action (Turgeon et al. 2014). It appears likely, then, that rather than doing away with the complex racial incentives of the past, affirmative action policies have become caught up in them.

In sum, explanations for racial reclassification based on new institutional incentives resonate with the comparative ethnic politics literature and the broader public. There are reasons to doubt whether these policies are compelling explanations for the sustained reclassification reversal that is evident in the census. But despite these misgivings, this hypothesis holds currency in public discourse and merits assessment nonetheless. The main observable implication of this hypothesis is simply that affirmative action policies have disincentivized white identification and incentivized nonwhite identification. We might also examine whether these policies encourage brown identification in particular, as this category typically qualifies for affirmative action benefits, but does not carry the same stigma as the black category. Moreover, to conclude that such policies help explain census patterns, these policies must be associated with longer-term patterns of nonwhite identification, rather than short-term, opportunistic behavior.

AFFIRMATIVE ACTION AS STATE-CENTERED RACE-MAKING

A second affirmative action-based explanation for the reclassification reversal focuses on the ways in which states "make race" by naturalizing or making salient social boundaries and differences (Bourdieu 1985; Marx 1998). In one vein of this literature, scholars point to censuses, in particular, as sites where states not only seek to make the mass public "legible" (Scott 1998), but also institutionalize and actively shape social boundaries and identities (Hochschild and Powell 2008; Kertzer and Arel 2002; Lieberman and Singh 2017; Omi and Winant 1994). The idea is that censuses do not simply reflect preexisting or naturally derived social differences, but actively create, reinforce, and reproduce them by instilling them with the authoritative legitimacy of the state. Such arguments find a clear parallel in the Brazilian case. Black movement activists in Brazil, for example, have long bemoaned the state's official racial classification scheme – which, according to activists, separates Afro-descendants into black (*preta*) and brown (*parda*) – as a way to inhibit race-based collective action and political consciousness (Hanchard 1994; Nascimento 2016; Nobles 2000). More recently, Loveman (2014) shows how Brazilian and Latin American states use census enumeration and classification schemes to whiten, or at least lighten, their populations in service of "modernizing" the nation (also see Skidmore 1993).

Though scholars have in fact pointed to the census as a mechanism by which the state impacts racial subjectivities among the mass public, a close reading of this hypothesis does not gain much traction in the Brazilian case. Lieberman and Singh (2017), for example, argue that the salience of social differences depends on whether states decide to enumerate those differences. Loveman (2014) makes a similar point, but emphasizes in the case of Brazil that it's not simply whether the state enumerates, but how the particular classification scheme the state chooses can impact identification and subjectivity. Both arguments require a shift in census enumeration practices or classification schemes to explain the reclassification reversal. Yet, as described in Chapter 2, Brazil's census has remained constant since 1991, and between 1950 and 1991 it changed only with regard to the indigenous category. Without any variation on these variables, the census itself cannot explain the reclassification reversal.

But while the census may not have changed in Brazil, another approach might be to think of the census simply as one piece of a bundle of policies that signal the state's shifting posture toward the racial question and its efforts to recognize and redress racial inequities. We might thus view affirmative action as a kind of symbolic institutional change that impacts racial subjectivities and identifications. From this perspective, affirmative action policies are not reducible to concrete benefits or material incentives; they are a symbolic institution that can lend legitimacy to alternative racial discourses or make salient altered racial boundaries and identities, similar to the ways that scholars argue censuses can (Paschel 2016a). From this perspective, affirmative action policies can be viewed within a broader array of institutions such as the state's official racial discourse, cultural policies, and inter and transnational cultural influences (Loveman 2014; Paschel 2016a).

There is reason to view affirmative action policies in this way. After all, this was not the only striking shift in racial policies that occurred in Brazil since the 1990s. Indeed, years before his watershed endorsement of affirmative action, Fernando Henrique Cardoso openly discussed racism, explicitly acknowledged racial differences, and espoused policies seeking to redress inequalities (Cardoso 1995a, 1995b). In the years after passage of state-level affirmative action laws, other significant steps were taken that signaled a major shift in the state's approach to race: the national education curriculum was modified in 2003 to mandate the teaching of African and Afro-Brazilian teaching in public schools (Law 10.369/2003), and a national holiday (Black Consciousness Day) was created to commemorate racial struggles in Brazil. The specific and direct impact of these individual changes is yet to be seen, but at the very least they signal the state's changing willingness to recognize and address racial inequality and inclusion in Brazilian society.

Additionally, affirmative action might also convey to the public the state's priorities. While affirmative action is often bemoaned by its opponents in any context, the reality is that these policies are part and parcel of the broader educational reforms that have greatly expanded access to education (Artes and Ricoldi 2015; Heringer 2015), unleashed waves of upward mobility for lower-class and darker-skinned Brazilians, and have sought to better incorporate marginalized sectors of the citizenry. Moreover, much of the affirmative action discussion has focused on the quota system used in admission to public universities, but quotas have also been incorporated into other policies, such as PROUNI (full and partial scholarships for private university tuition) and SISU (the national system for admission to public universities), which also incorporate quotas. The consequence is that affirmative action policies have expanded a number of avenues through which students can access university education (Feres Jr. et al. 2015). Citizens might interpret these new policy commitments as part of the institutional change that signals a broader symbolic shift in the state's racial discourse and priorities.

As with the instrumental hypothesis, there are also reasons to question this argument. First, the argument is vague with regard to the timing of when we ought to observe the effects of changing state discourse, and which segments of the population ought to be affected. Prominent arguments regarding affirmative action by Htun (2004) and Paschel (2016a) point to Cardoso's 2001 speech endorsing the policy. But Cardoso's discourse had shifted years prior, from his first day assuming the presidency (Cardoso 1995a). Moreover, affirmative action laws trickled out slowly over the course of the 2000s, and the federal law remained stalled in congress until 2012. All in all, this is a large swath of time, and one that happens to coincide with the period of educational expansion I detail in Chapter 3. Additionally, longitudinal analysis of microlevel census data in Chapter 5 revealed that reclassification is not widespread across all social sectors. Particular combinations of education and class background help to determine which individuals are likely to reclassify, and others not. Yet symbolic institutional explanations present the effects of such change as more diffuse and cultural, without specifying who is likely to respond by reclassifying.

Second, the symbolic institutional argument is underspecified in how exactly changes in state institutions "trickle down" to shape mass subjectivities uniformly and on such a wide scale. While it may seem obvious that turnabouts in state discourse are noticed by the public, past studies on racial democracy urged caution against placing too much weight on the effects of official discourse. For example, in her ethnography of favela residents in Rio de Janeiro conducted in the era of racial democracy, Sheriff (2001) found little evidence that individuals subscribed to the tenets of racial democracy, which scholars argued was hegemonic among the mass public (e.g., Hanchard 1994). Similarly, systematic analyses of public opinion found that beliefs in racial democracy and related views were not particularly widespread among the public (Bailey 2002; Telles and Bailey 2013). An important implication of these findings was that the link between state discourse and public opinion was perhaps more tenuous that scholars previously acknowledged. Whether this remains true in the post-racial democracy era is perhaps an empirical question, but it is something one still should not take for granted.

This is not to say that the empirical predictions of this argument are entirely without merit. Notably, a recent study by Bailey and colleagues (2018) tests the effects of symbolic institutional change, assessing whether Brazilians became more likely to identify using the state's official ethnoracial nomenclature, rather than more colloquial labels that have historically been common in Brazil. The authors find that between 1995 and 2008 the tendency to use official labels did increase, which they interpret as support for their argument. Yet because we only confirm change over time in this study, we cannot exclusively attribute this change to the symbolic mechanism instead of, say, instrumentalist or educational exposure mechanisms. This literature would benefit from more clearly specified claims and empirical predictions, and finer-grained empirical analysis.

In any case, like the instrumental hypothesis, the symbolic hypothesis nonetheless merits assessment. This hypothesis is difficult to test in a rigorous way. If we believe symbolic institutions impact identification and lie behind the reclassification reversal, we would expect growing nonwhite identification over time. We already know that this is occurring; the question is who chooses to reclassify and why. Admittedly, I possess few tools to isolate this mechanism from other mechanisms bundled with affirmative action policies. In the analyses later, I will attempt to probe for evidence of the symbolic hypothesis using originally designed survey experiments.

SURVEY EXPERIMENTS: DOES AFFIRMATIVE ACTION IMPACT RACIAL IDENTIFICATION?

Both the instrumental and symbolic hypotheses predict the same behavioral outcome: individuals should be more likely to identify in nonwhite categories as a result of affirmative action, and less likely to identify as white. It is thus important to establish whether there is evidence that affirmative action policies have systematically impacted patterns of racial identification – separate and apart from educational expansion, to the extent this is possible. I leverage a variety of empirical tools to try to shed light on two main questions. First, what evidence is there to suggest that the reclassification reversal is directly attributable to affirmative action policies, as opposed to educational expansion? And second, if we find this evidence, is there evidence to support either the instrumental or symbolic mechanisms? I first analyze a series of survey experiments to test whether information about race-targeted benefits impacts how individuals choose to racially identify, and to probe for evidence that individuals manipulated their identifications to access benefits. I then turn to panel analysis to assess the real-world impact of these policies on patterns of identification over time. Where possible, I discuss possible inferences that might help us to adjudicate between instrumental and symbolic mechanisms.

Priming Experiment I

It can be difficult to simulate the real-world conditions under which individuals might manipulate their racial identifications in response to affirmative action. On the one hand, individuals might only do so when they believe their anonymity is protected (as when census data are collected). On the other, they may do so temporarily or situationally, as when they complete their applications for university admission to qualify for quotas, for example. In this latter case, opportunists may be keenly aware of when strategic manipulations of racial identification are worth any potential risk. Savviness might thus bias against finding effects in survey experiments conducted by non-state interviewers among the randomly sampled public.

Nonetheless, an important baseline to establish is whether information about affirmative action benefits has a causal effect on racial identification. To assess this, I analyze two priming experiments embedded in randomly sampled surveys, conducted in 2002 and 2018. The 2002 Brazilian Social Survey (PESB, *Pesquisa Social Brasileira*) was national survey of 2,365 respondents conducted by the Ford Foundation and the Universidade Federal Fluminense in Rio de Janeiro. The survey instrument included a split-ballot design, in which half of the respondents were randomly assigned to receive primes alerting them to the implementation of affirmative action policies in recent years. In the control condition, before collection racial identification and other data, respondents were told "Now I'm going to change the subject and ask questions about the color and race of the Brazilian population." In the treatment condition, the following was added to this transitional text:

The topic of color and race is very important in Brazil. The government is already reserving slots in public sector jobs for *negros*, because they have had fewer opportunities than *brancos* to get good jobs. Before this change, to get these jobs people had the same tests or competitions, and those that had the best results got the job. Now *negros* are guaranteed some good public-sector jobs, even if their results on the tests and in the competition aren't the best.

Immediately following this prime, respondents were asked to classify themselves racially, first in an open-ended format and then using the close-ended census categories.

While it is a stroke of luck to stumble upon a national survey with a survey experiment relevant to one's research question, the downside here is that this prime is written with regard to public sector jobs, rather than university admissions, which are far more widespread in Brazil. However, public-sector jobs are among the best paid and most stable in Brazil, and as such are highly desired and competitive. Individuals seeking white-collar jobs in state bureaucracies as well as those seeking jobs as bus drivers, for example, compete for jobs through the *concurso público*, the civil service exam. Insofar as we wish to signal material benefits or symbolic change, this prime meets the minimum conditions for such a test. Another point to highlight is that the wording of this prime does not allow us to disentangle the instrumental and symbolic hypotheses. The prime contains language that recognizes that *negros* "have had fewer opportunities than *brancos* to get good jobs," the type of symbolic recognition by the state that sociologists argue can legitimate and encourage greater nonwhite identification. At the same time, the prime clearly indicates that these new policies have created an advantage for *negros*.

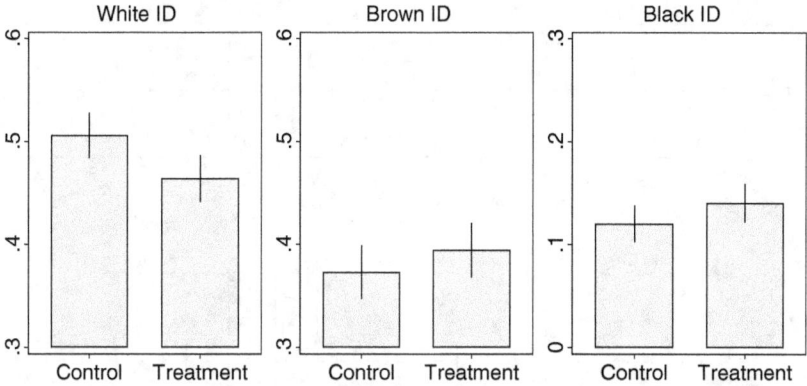

FIGURE 6.1 Regression-adjusted estimates of treatment effects on Pr(racial ID)

While the language does not specify which census categories would benefit, respondents might reasonably understand *negro* to refer to either brown (*pardo*) or black (*preto*) categories.

A major benefit of analyzing this survey is that we can assess the impacts of this information during the time when these policies were first implemented in Brazil. I estimate treatments effects on the probability of identifying as white, brown, and black. Balance tests indicate that randomization was successful; there is no significant difference across treatment groups in age, gender, wealth, party ID, religion, education, region, racial ID of the interviewer, or respondent skin tone.[9] Responses to the close-ended racial ID question are dichotomized and analyzed as linear probability models.

Figure 6.1 displays estimated treatment effects of the survey prime on respondents' racial identifications. After adjusting for covariates, treated respondents are 4 points less likely ($p < 0.05$) to identify as white relative to the untreated, and 2 points more likely to identify as brown and black. In the case of black and brown identification, these estimates are not distinguishable from zero. These effects may not be as substantial as expected given the attention paid to this issue in the Brazilian media, and given the incentives ostensibly contained in the survey prime. Nonetheless, the negative effect on white identification is identified in this analysis.

One reason for these modest effects might be that not all respondents might believe they have racial options – they may feel constrained by

---

[9] Skin tone is inferred from the racial category ascribed to respondents by survey interviewers. See Supplementary Table D1 for balance tests.

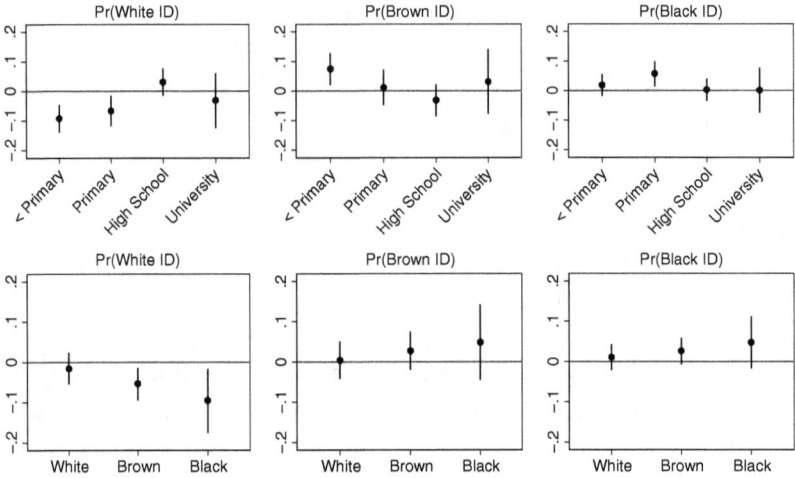

FIGURE 6.2 Treatment effects conditional on education and skin tone

their phenotype, for example. Though the controversy surrounding the so-called fraud has focused on light-skinned Brazilians with very tenuous claims to blackness, these individuals may also feel the most constrained in opting for anything but the white category. Alternatively, given the emphasis on public sector jobs in the survey prime, respondents of different educational background may understand the potential opportunities differently. On one hand, lesser-educated individuals who might be competing for lower-status public jobs might be most receptive to the opportunity for a leg up; on the other, higher-educated individuals who are competing for highly sought-after white-collar jobs might be more aware of the possible payoffs of manipulating their identifications.

To assess these possibilities, I estimate conditional treatment effects by the respondents' level of education, as well as their skin tone – proxied by the racial category ascribed by the interviewer. Conditional treatment effects are presented in Figure 6.2. The top row presents treatment effects according to respondent education. Again, the effects on white identification are clear and negative, but vary across education levels. The average negative effect estimated from the full sample is driven by lesser-educated respondents. Indeed, those with less than primary education are an estimated 9 points ($p < 0.05$) less likely to identify as white and 7 points more likely to identify as brown ($p < 0.05$). Those with primary education are 7 points less likely to identify as white ($p < 0.05$) and, by contrast, 6 points more likely to identify as black ($p < 0.05$). Among the high school- and university-educated, there are no significant treatment effects on racial identification. These null findings for the higher-educated – the presumed fraudsters – may well be a function of the survey prime, which did not emphasize university admissions. At the same time, the effects among the lesser-educated are somewhat surprising, given that analysis of microlevel census data found that these individuals were least likely to reclassify over time.

The bottom row of Figure 6.2 displays conditional estimates according to respondent skin tone. Only effects on white identification are identified and exclusively among those in the middle to the darker-end of the color spectrum. Individuals classified as white by survey interviewers do not respond to treatment by altering their racial identifications. Among those classified as black, treated respondents are 10 points less likely to identify as white ($p < 0.05$). Among those classified as brown, treated respondents are 5 points less likely to identify as white ($p < 0.05$). Effects on brown and black identification among these respondents, however, are not distinguishable from zero.

These conditional effects do provide some clarity on the question of how affirmative action shapes racial identification. These data indicate that lesser-educated and darker-skinned respondents are more responsive to the symbolic or instrumental effects of these policies. However, this finding does not fit the portrayal of affirmative action "fraud" commonly portrayed in the media and bemoaned by critics, in which university applicants (the highly educated) with light skin manipulate their declarations to gain admission to competitive programs. Nor do they fit the patterns in census data, in which the better-educated reclassify over time. Of course, the caveats stated earlier apply to these findings, especially the difficulty of simulating real-world stakes of affirmative action in the context of a survey experiment. But insofar as these data provide evidence of major effects of affirmative action, it appears to be the most vulnerable members of Brazilian society who respond to these policies by altering their racial identifications. Whether this ought to raise questions about the prevalence of fraud as it is publicized, or whether the emphasis on public sector jobs in this experiment does not capture the reality of education-focused affirmative action, is far from clear.

Priming Experiment II

The 2002 survey experiment cannot distinguish between material and symbolic motivations of the respondents. As discussed earlier, this is due to the bundling of these two treatments in the original survey design. To address and improve on this design, I modified the priming experiment earlier with an original face-to-face survey of 1,000 respondents in São Paulo and Recife in 2018. While useful as an effort to replicate the findings earlier, I must also urge caution in directly comparing findings from both surveys. First, the 2018 survey did not sample nationally like the 2002 survey. Second, the sample size of the 2018 survey was smaller than the 2002 survey, reducing the efficiency of computed estimates. Nonetheless, the 2018 survey was designed to parse the effects of the two forms of institutional change. While casual observation of the longitudinal patterns would suggest that one or both of these factors are responsible for the observed reclassification, such claims require further scrutiny and firmer empirical foundation.

To attempt to disentangle the effects of both hypotheses, I employ a survey-based priming experiment in which respondents are randomly primed about different aspects of affirmative action policies prior to providing racial self-identification. The experiment is a 2 × 2 factorial design with four experimental conditions, displayed in Table 6.1. Respondents in the control condition are simply told that the interview will turn toward questions of racial identification. These respondents are then asked to self-identify in racial terms in an open-ended format, followed by the close-ended census question. Respondents in one of the three experimental conditions, however, are informed that the survey will turn toward questions of racial identification and are read one of three survey primes before self-identifying. In the "instrumental" and "symbolic" conditions, respondents are informed of affirmative action benefits for blacks and browns (*pretos e pardos*) in Brazil and the state recognition of racial suffering, respectively. Respondents in the combined ("both") condition receive both of these primes. This conjoint design will thus allow for testing of the causal validity of these two hypotheses, independently and together.

Means of independent variables and balance tests are provided in Supplementary Table D3. Balance tests indicate that randomization was successful. Like in the first priming experiment, I analyze close-ended racial identification questions, which have been dichotomized. Figure 6.3 displays predicted probabilities of self-classifying in each racial category across treatment conditions. Respondents are most likely to self-classify as brown (roughly 45 percent), followed by white (roughly 30 percent), then black (20–25 percent). There is no significant variation in the likelihood respondents will decline to self-classify in any of the racial categories based on whether they were informed of the presence of race-targeted affirmative action benefits, the shift in the state's posture toward the racial question, or both.

TABLE 6.1 *Survey primes*

		Instrumental treatment	
		Control	Treatment
Symbolic Treatment	Control	Control Now I am going to ask specifically about your color and racial identification.	Benefits Now I am going to ask specifically about your color and racial identification. <u>In recent years, the government began reserving slots for *pretos* and *pardos* in public universities and the civil servant exam.</u>
	Treatment	Recognition Now I am going to ask specifically about your color and racial identification. **In recent years, the government recognized the inequality and discrimination suffered by *preto* and *pardo* populations in history and present-day Brazil.**	Both Now I am going to ask specifically about your color and racial identification. **In recent years, the government recognized the inequality and discrimination suffered by *pretos* and brown populations in history and present-day Brazil.** <u>Also, the government began reserving slots for *pretos* and *pardos* in public universities and the civil servant exam.</u>

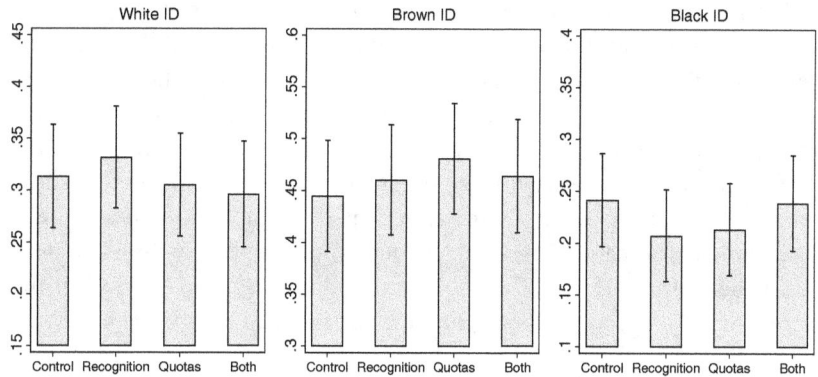

FIGURE 6.3 Predicted probabilities of racial ID by experimental condition
The figure displays 90 percent confidence intervals.

Simple estimates of the differences-in-proportions across treatment groups does not yield evidence that material incentives or discursive changes alter individuals' racial identification. To test the robustness of these null effects, I estimate regression-adjusted treatment effects to enhance precision and ensure that these null findings are not simply an artifact of statistical inefficiency. Supplementary Table D4 presents regression-adjusted estimates of treatment effects, each relative to the baseline control group. For each racial category, respondent classification is regressed on the treatment indicator variable, first in a univariate model then in a regression-adjusted model. These estimates show little change in the standard errors of the estimated treatment effects, suggesting that the null effects observed in Figure 6.3 are not simply due to inefficient estimates. There is also little movement in the estimated magnitude of the treatment effects in the regression-adjusted models, and the effects remain statistically insignificant.

Another possibility is that estimating average treatment effects on the full sample obscure potentially significant effects for specific subgroups within the sample. Any heterogeneity that is apparent across levels of education would be relevant in this case, as affirmative action benefits in Brazil are most relevant for individuals of higher levels of education. The same can be said of heterogeneity by respondent skin tone. The instrumental hypothesis in particular suggests that at least some reclassifiers might alter their racial identification without meeting commonsense (phenotypical) understandings of blackness, even in a context of racial ambiguity such as Brazil. I test for both of these possibilities, though there is little evidence to suggests treatment effects vary at all across subgroups in the sample.[10]

Overall, the priming experiments conducted in these two surveys provide inconsistent support for either hypothesis. In the case of the 2018 survey, neither informing respondents of either the material benefits newly available to Afro-descendants nor of the state's shifting posture toward the racial question had a statistically discernible impact on respondents' identifications consistent with the predictions of these hypotheses. These findings thus run counter to the idea that the patterns of racial reclassification in the census can be reduced simply to savvy opportunists, or to the diffuse effects of changing state discourse. But of course, the 2002 survey did provide some support for the idea that lesser-educated

---

[10] For analysis of heterogenous treatment effects, see Supplementary Tables D5 and D6 and Supplementary Figures D1 and D2.

respondents would respondent to information about affirmative action. To be sure, there is always a chance that (null) findings are a function of design effects. But another possibility is that any potential impact of affirmative action was made shortly after the advent of these policies, and ceased to have an effect later on. The evidence I presented here is far from conclusive on this point, but it is one possible explanation. More importantly, because of the null findings from the 2018 survey, this analysis did little to disentangle the instrumental and symbolic explanations for earlier findings.

LIST EXPERIMENT

The null results of the priming experiment sharpen the question of whether such an approach is the best way to probe for evidence of strategic manipulation of racial identification. First, as with anonymous responses to census questionnaires, savvy opportunists who seek to take advantage of affirmative action policies are likely aware of the fact that their responses to a survey questionnaire are unlikely to yield any material benefits. With this in mind, respondents have little reason to engage in the kinds of strategic calculations that they might under other circumstances. One reading of the null results of the priming experiments is that they failed to replicate the conditions under which individuals are incentivized to manipulate their racial identifications.

To probe for additional evidence of instrumental behavior, I also analyze a list experiment in which survey respondents are provided with anonymity to reveal whether or not they have in the past manipulated their identifications in pursuit of material benefits. List experiments have become a common technique for eliciting honest responses regarding practices or attitudes that might be seen as socially undesirable, and that thus might lead individuals to conceal their true responses. While affirmative action policies remain controversial in Brazil, the so-called "fraud" in the use of affirmative action has provoked criticism and outrage from folks of all political stripes (albeit for different reasons). Respondents who have in fact engaged in such manipulation may then respond dishonestly to direct questioning about the strategic use of affirmative action, leading to biased estimates of such behavior.

I employ a list of ethically questionable behaviors and instruct respondents to inform the interviewer not which behaviors that have done in the past, but rather *how many*. Treated respondents are randomly assigned to receive an additional list item, which is the sensitive behavior of interest.

TABLE 6.2 *List experiment design*

Assignment	Behaviors
Control	I used a fake ID to get discounts or free items
	I used the internet to watch TV or movies without paying
	I tipped a civil servant to get something I needed
Treatment	**I changed my declared color to qualify for a racial quota**

The list items are displayed in Table 6.2. The selection of these list items follows common practice in the literature on list experiment design. First, the nonsensitive items are on a topic similar to that of the sensitive item: engaging in ethically questionable behaviors to gain something of material value or in one's own interest (Droitcour et al. 1991). Second, nonsensitive list items include both high- and low-prevalence items. Using the internet to watch TV or movies without paying, for example, is a common practice in Brazil, whereas engaging in direct bribes by tipping a civil servant is less common. Including high- and low-prevalence items reduces variance and mitigates ceiling effects (which can undermine the anonymity intentionally provided to the respondent) and improves statistical efficiency (Glynn 2013).[11]

I analyze the list experiment in various ways, including standard difference-in-means tests, regression-adjusted estimation of average treatment effects, and other multivariate statistical methods to analyze item counts and to exploit information provided by covariates to attempt to understand subgroup heterogeneity in the sample. Following Glynn (2013), Supplementary Table D8 shows the proportion of responses falling in each item count by control condition. There is some suggestion of possible design effects, whereby the presence of the sensitive item affects respondents' responses to control items; but difference-in-proportions tests show no significant differences across treatment groups, and Blair and Imai's (2012) likelihood-ratio test for design effects (Table D9) in their "list" statistical package fails to reject the null hypothesis of no design effect (Bonferroni-corrected p-value = 0.43).

Figure 6.4 presents mean values of respondents' reported item counts across treatment and control groups. The left panel shows mean values

---

[11] The standard deviation among baseline respondents was 0.73. For other sample descriptives and balance tests, see Supplementary Tables D7–D9.

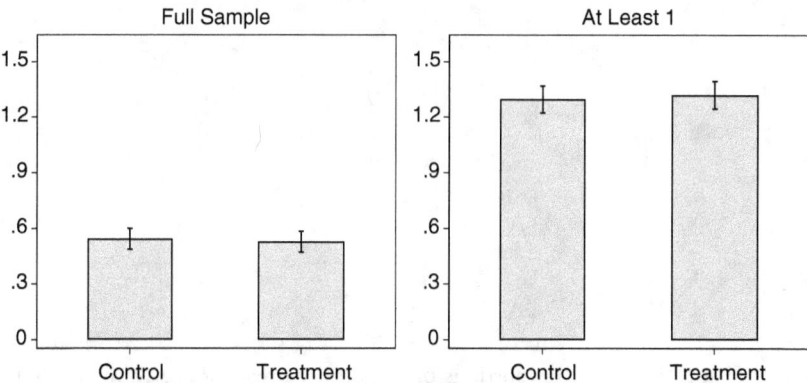

FIGURE 6.4 Comparison of means of item counts by treatment group
The figure displays 90 percent confidence intervals.

for the full sample of respondents, with a slight difference of −0.01 items in the treatment group (T-test p-value = 0.76). The mean count for both groups is just above 0.5, which is rather low given the inclusion of a high-prevalence item. Indeed, roughly 59 percent of the sample reported having participated in zero activities on the list. Such a high rate of non-participation raises concerns over prevalence of satisficing and/or nonresponse bias in the sample. Following Glynn (2013), I attempt to mitigate this bias in the sample by restricting the analysis to those respondents who reported participation in at least one activity. The comparison of means in this subsample is displayed in the righthand panel. This analysis also reveals no difference in the estimated mean number of activities participated in across treatment groups. The estimated difference is 0.02 (T-test p-value = 0.70). Analyses in the appendix (available online) do not indicate heterogeneous treatment effects; adjusting for covariates adds little precision to estimated treatment effects; and negative binomial estimates (more appropriate for analyzing item counts) also estimate null effects.[12] Estimated in a variety of different ways and after accounting for potential satisficing and nonresponse bias, the list experiment provides little evidence of instrumental behavior.

Finally, I also analyze responses to the sensitive item by taking Imai (2011) and Blair and Imai's (2012) multivariate approach to list experiment analysis, estimating how the probability of answering affirmatively to the sensitive item varies according to respondents' characteristics, as

[12] Supplementary Tables D11–D14.

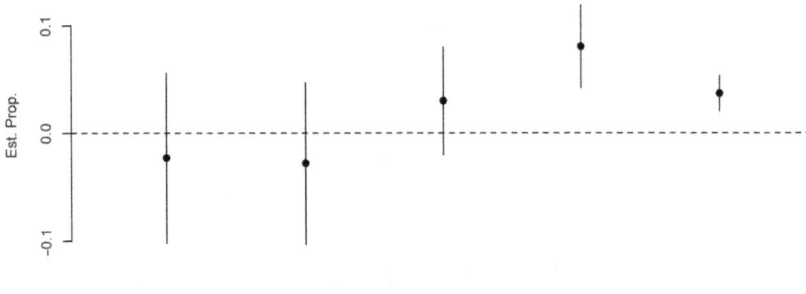

FIGURE 6.5 Estimated proportions of respondents responding affirmatively to sensitive item

well as leveraging covariate information to more efficiently estimate the proportion of respondents who respond affirmatively. Given the particular concern for "fraud" in the use of university quotas, I estimate these probabilities according to various levels of educational attainment and respondent skin tone.[13]

Figure 6.5 plots the predicted proportions of sample respondents who responded affirmatively that they have in the past manipulated their racial identifications to use affirmative action benefits. Predictions from each model are presented alongside a simple difference-in-means estimate. Three of five specifications, the difference-in-means and two linear models, estimate that no respondents in the sample responded affirmatively to the sensitive item. The maximum likelihood models, however, estimate small, but statistically significant, proportions of the sample responded affirmatively, roughly 8 percent in the constrained model and 4 percent in the unconstrained model. Supplementary Figures D5 and D6 compute heterogeneous treatment effects from the same model. Like with the full sample, however, results are inconsistent.

The overall picture that emerges from analysis of the survey experiments is unclear. There is evidence that respondents have, indeed, manipulated their racial identifications to take advantage of race-targeted affirmative action benefits. This evidence, however, is not robust to model specification, and simple difference-in-means calculations do not provide

---

[13] Because estimates from these models are difficult to interpret, I focus on the substantive findings on these analyses, though Supplementary Table D15 presents full estimates from four models: linear and nonlinear least squares models, and constrained and unconstrained maximum likelihood models.

any such support. Moreover, the constrained maximum likelihood model provides evidence that lighter-skinned and better-educated respondents were most likely to respond affirmatively to the sensitive item; but this pattern is not borne out in any other specification. Taken together, these survey experiments appear to lend additional empirical support to the findings of Francis and Tannuri-Pianto (2012, 2013) and Francis-Tan and Tannuri-Pianto (2015). While there is some discernible evidence that individuals will act strategically to manipulate their racial identifications, questions remain regarding the prevalence and longevity of such change in racial identifications. For greater insight into such patterns, we turn to analysis of affirmative action's effects in the real world.

AFFIRMATIVE ACTION IN THE REAL WORLD

Survey experimental evidence is inconsistent on the question of whether affirmative action policies impact racial identification, either via new material incentives or symbolic legitimation. But of course, survey experiments may not be an especially appropriate tool to probe for the effects of affirmative action. Since much of the controversy around affirmative action has centered around who qualifies for such benefits, manipulating one's declared race may be seen as risky, and something one is not willing to do for a public opinion survey. On the symbolic side, it's unclear when and on whom we should observe these effects. In this sense, the weak support from the survey experiments might be dismissed as a function of tools inappropriate for identifying these effects.

Absent randomized data collected in a real-world setting, observational data may actually provide more compelling evidence of the effects of affirmative action on racial identification. In the final set of analyses, I probe for these effects by leveraging the implementation of state and federal affirmative action laws. If arguments related to affirmative action are to hold any water, we must be able to show, first and foremost, that affirmative action policies correlate with greater rates of reclassification into black or brown categories, and out of the white category. I test this idea with two types of data: first, I return to the panel dataset of Brazilian municipalities (introduced in Chapter 5) to compute difference-in-differences estimates of the effect of affirmative action on relative group proportions in municipalities. The second test introduces a new panel dataset of university students that includes racial identifications in high school, at the time of registration for the university entrance exam, and after university matriculation. Leveraging the same state-level variation in affirmative action policies, we can assess whether the behavior of students applying for university – the target population of affirmative action policies – reflect behavior in line with the expectations of the instrumental hypothesis.

State-Level Affirmative Action Laws: Difference-in-Differences Analysis of Municipalities

First, I analyze the impact of affirmative action policies on demographic structures in Brazilian municipalities between the census rounds of 2000 and 2010. The sample includes 5,565 municipalities across 27 states.[14] Leveraging subnational variation in the implementation of state-level affirmative action laws, I estimate the impact of these institutional changes on the relative proportions of racial groups by comparing the rate of racial change in municipalities in affirmative action states to that of municipalities not located in affirmative action states. To be sure, this approach is imperfect. It presumes that individuals residing in a given state will not migrate to another to attend university, which is a perfectly common occurrence.[15] Additionally, while the federal affirmative action law was not passed until 2012, other federal university programs, such as ProUni (*Programa Universidade para Todos*) did use racial criteria to allocate scholarships for students studying in private universities. Such policies might introduce a conservative contamination effect into the "treatment" of affirmative action policies by boosting rates in non-affirmative action states. Nonetheless, given the emphasis on the role of affirmative action *laws* in shaping identification patterns and the weakness of national-level experimental evidence, it's worth testing for these effects subnationally.

Difference-in-differences (DID) analyses are typically employed in observational settings to mimic randomly assigned treatments. DID analyses rely on two identifying assumptions. The first is that assignment to treatment is not caused by the measured outcome, in this case

---

[14] For additional descriptive statistics on the sample, see Chapter 5.
[15] Though not safe, this assumption is required since relevant municipal-level migration data is not available to include as a control. But as discussed in Chapter 5, bivariate correlations of the 2010 migration rate, measured as the proportion of the municipal population residing in the municipality for less than ten years, and the change in relative group size for the black ($\rho = 0.1$) and brown ($\rho = 0.03$) populations are weak. Since this is a fixed-effects analysis, time-invariant characteristics are absorbed by the unit-specific error term. Assuming time invariance in migration rates, parameters of interest remain unconfounded by this unobserved heterogeneity.

relative racial group size. This is a reasonably safe assumption in this case. First, while the decision to implement these policies had much to do with racial inequality and politics, it is far from clear that these had to do with *reclassification*, per se. As others have argued, the decision to implement affirmative action was heavily influenced by a number of national and transnational actors, who were carrying out and influenced by international norms regarding ethnoracial culture and inequality (Htun 2004; Loveman 2014; Paschel 2016a; Peria and Bailey 2014). Scholars have found that university faculty and students viewed one purpose of such policies as encouraging greater acceptance of blackness or racial consciousness among admitted students (Schwartzman and Silva 2012; Silva 2006). But that laws were passed or policies adopted as a function of *reclassification* is far from clear. This is bolstered by a second key piece of information, which is that subnational patterns of reclassification were not explored until fairly recently in scholarship (Jesus and Hoffmann 2020), and were not explored systematically at the state- or municipal-level until *after* the publication of 2010 census data. Earlier analyses of reclassification, namely that by Soares (2008), focused on national trends. Seeing as the 2010 census data were generated after treatment, it is a reasonably safe assumption that such information could not have impacted quota adoption.

The second identifying assumption of DID analysis is that trends in the dependent variable do not vary between treatment and control groups *prior to treatment*. This "parallel trends" assumption allows us to determine that differences we observe in the rates of change between groups posttreatment are due to the intervention, rather than prior or unobserved forces that confound the treatment effect. State-level policies took a variety of forms in the period between 2000 and 2010, including a combination of socioeconomic and racial criteria, exclusively socioeconomic criteria, and policies implemented by law versus those implemented by university decree. I consider all of these possibilities, but for the majority of them we cannot reasonably assume parallel trends prior to treatment.

Figure 6.6 displays DID estimated effects of various affirmative action treatments on white identification between 1991 and 2000, that is, prior to the implementation of any affirmative action policies. If the parallel trends assumption held, we should find null effects over this period. But as is clear, in most cases there are significant differences in the trend lines for most treatments and subsamples. Fortunately, we can safely assume parallel trends in two instances relevant to our hypotheses: in urban

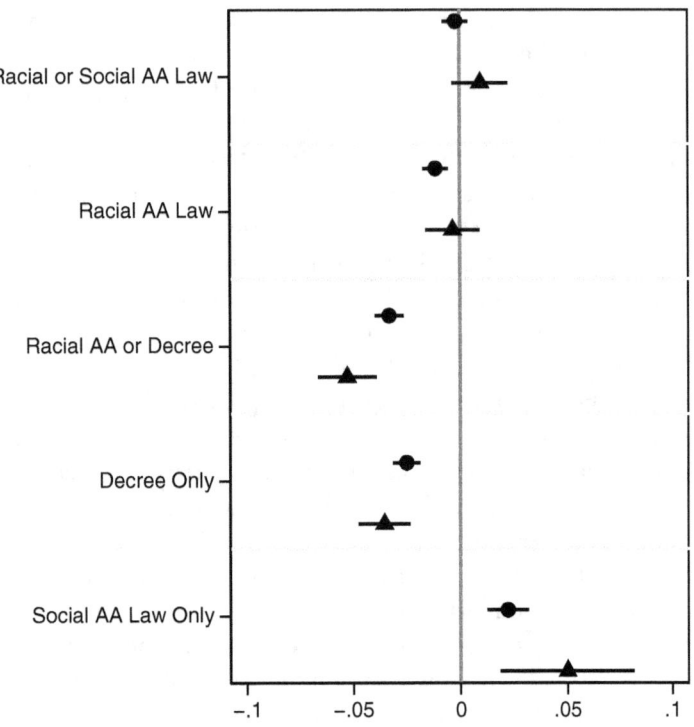

Circles = Full Sample, Triangles = Population > 100k

FIGURE 6.6 Parallel trends violations based on difference-in-differences estimates of affirmative action prior to implementation (1991–2000)

municipalities in states (1) with a race-targeted affirmative action law, and (2) with a race-targeted or means-tested law. My analyses restrict the sample to urban municipalities (those with populations over 100,000), and consider treatment effects of either a social or racial affirmative action law, and exclusively racial affirmative action laws.

Figure 6.7 displays estimated effects of affirmative action policies on relative group size. The effects of both treatments are estimated to be relatively similar in size. In states with affirmative action laws, the relative proportion of white and brown populations is estimated to decrease and increase, respectively, by between 2 and 3 points ($p < 0.05$) between 2000 and 2010. By contrast, the effects on the relative size of black populations is statistically or substantively insignificant. There is no effect of racial or social affirmative action laws on this population. The effect of the exclusively race-targeted treatment is statistically significant at the 5

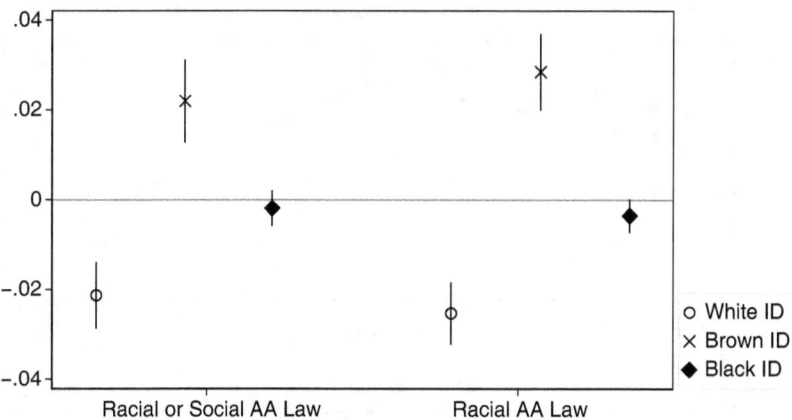

FIGURE 6.7 Difference-in-differences estimates of state-level affirmative action on relative group size, 2000–2010
Models control for municipal birthrate, mortality rate, Gini coefficient of income, human development index, and rate of university attendance.

percent level. But the effect is not estimated to be substantively significant at less than half of a point, and this effect is *negative*. Thus, difference-in-differences estimates indicate effects that conform to the hypothesized expectations: municipalities in states with race-targeted affirmative action laws saw a roughly 3-point decrease in the size of the white population and a corresponding increase in the brown population.

As a robustness check, I estimate the effect of the race-targeted treatment using the synthetic difference-in-differences (SDID) estimator (Arkhangelsky et al. 2021), which integrates synthetic control and DID estimators to compute doubly robust estimates. Figure 6.8 displays SDID estimates, as well as treatment group trends prior to treatment. Estimates from this analysis indicate a similar pattern: race-targeted affirmative action is estimated to decrease (increase) the size of the white (brown) population by 2 points ($p < 0.05$), and is estimated to decrease the black population by 0.6 points ($p < 0.05$). Also evident in Figure 6.8 is the extent to which the patterns of racial demographic change occur in both states with and without affirmative action. Indeed, for both white and brown populations, there is a reversal of the trajectory prior to 2000. Yet for black populations, it is clear that these populations had been experiencing a steady upward trajectory since 1991, one that appears uninterrupted by the implementation of affirmative action policies. Considering that the black category is that most associated with racial

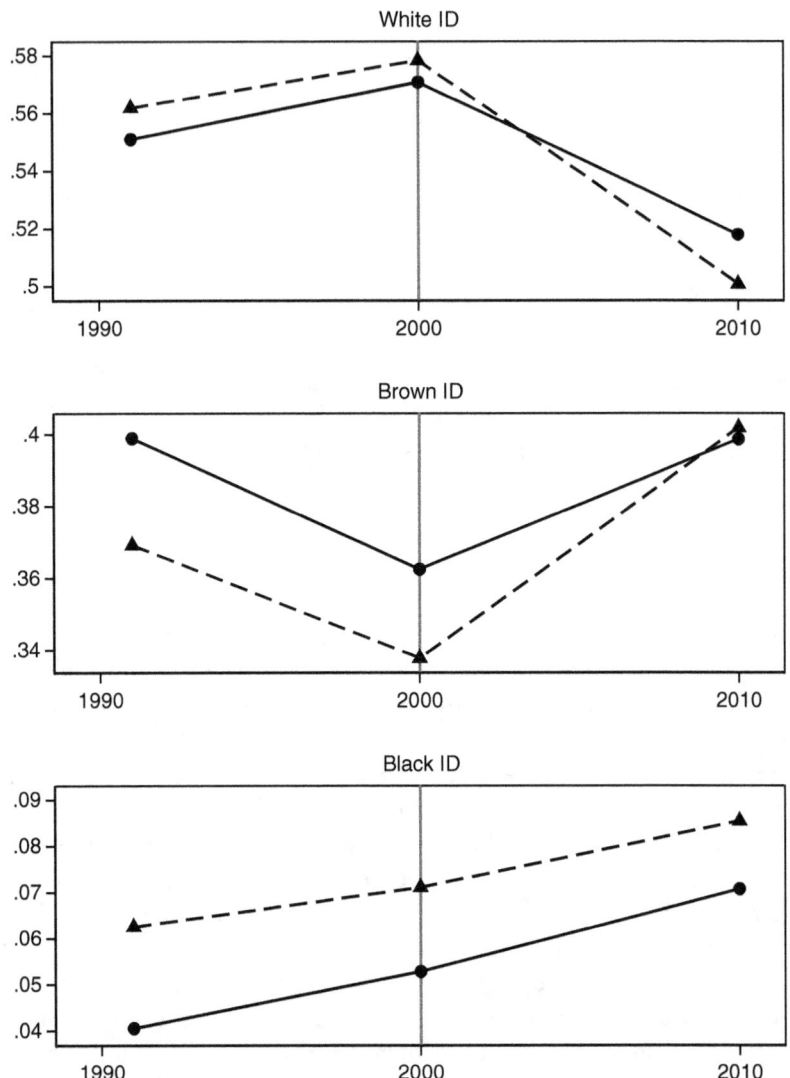

Circle = Control, Triangle = Treated

FIGURE 6.8 SDID estimates of racial affirmative action on relative population size in census, 2000–2010
Estimates do not adjust for covariates.

group consciousness (Chapter 4), this is a noteworthy difference, and one that potentially suggests that the effects of affirmative action and education may not be competing as strongly as it may initially appear. On the one hand, black identification is significantly less impacted by affirmative action than is white or brown identification. On the other, the estimated effects of affirmative action policies are small when compared to the estimates of educational expansion in Chapter 5. One tentative conclusion we might draw, then, is that the consequences of affirmative action and educational expansion for patterns of identification may simply differ across racial categories.

Federal Affirmative Action Law: Panel Analysis of University Students

Analysis of municipalities provides compelling evidence that affirmative action has indeed played a role in the reclassification reversal, even if this is not the only factor at play and it does not appear to be a necessary condition for such change. Yet aggregate analysis, again, tells us little about who reclassifies, and if the effects of affirmative action are indeed on the targeted beneficiaries, or the broader population. In a final effort to gain leverage on this question, I conduct a panel analysis of the racial classifications of university students, from their time in high school through university. To do so, I rely on an original panel dataset of federal university students, constructed *post hoc* from three independent databases held by Institute of Educational Study and Research (Inep),[16] a subagency of the Ministry of Education.

Inep conducts two censuses of all students enrolled in accredited educational institutions, public and private: a school census comprising primary and secondary schools (*censo escolar*) and a university census (*censo da educação superior*). Both surveys are conducted annually and collect racial identifications. In addition, Inep administers the Enem (*exame nacional do ensino médio*), which is the exam many students now take to compete for university admission. Relying on unique identifiers akin to social security numbers in the United States,[17] I am able to identify unique individuals across these three databases and construct a panel. These data sources also provide other useful information. First, the university census collects data on students' quota usage: whether they were admitted via socioeconomic or racial quotas, both, or neither. Leveraging

---

[16] The complete name of this agency is the Instituto Nacional de Estudos e Pesquisas Educacionais Anísio Teixeira.
[17] The analogue in Brazil is the CPF (*cadastro pessoa física*), which is not sensitive like American social security numbers. Inep masks CPFs, as well as two additional identifiers assigned internally by Inep. For more information on data availability and gaining access to protected data, see "Serviço de Acesso a Dados Protegidos" (2018).

this variation, we can assess how quota usage impacts racial trajectories over time. Second, these surveys provide multiple observations of racial identification in three distinct periods relevant to affirmative action: (1) in high school, before incentives or the symbolic significance of affirmative action may have crystallized for students and/or their parents; (2) when they register for the university exam, closely corresponding the time period when racial identification may (dis)qualify students for race-targeted policies; and (3) after matriculating at a federal public university, ostensibly after one no longer stands to gain from manipulating one's racial identification. Fixed effects analysis, again, will provide a powerful tool to make causal inferences.

Analyzing data from these distinct educational periods might also shed some light on the competing mechanisms to explain responses to institutional change. With respect to timing, if reclassification is due to opportunistic behavior then we ought to see an increase in nonwhite identification when students register for the university exam. Furthermore, to provide a compelling explanation for patterns observed in the census, the probability should not decline after the fact; in other words, temporary increases in nonwhite identification *only* during the time of registering for the university exam would suggest instrumental, but short-term, behavior. In contrast, if other mechanisms are at play, we might observe delayed or greater increases in nonwhite identification only after students enroll at university. Similarly, we can assess how these time periods interact with quota usage to impact racial identification. If the instrumental hypothesis is correct, we should find that increases in nonwhite identification are specific to individuals who ultimately entered university using racial quotas, and that this increase should be observed when registering for the university exam. But if other mechanisms are also at work, students admitted via other means might also exhibit increases in nonwhite identification.

Two important caveats are in order pertaining to this analysis. The first is that observing racial identification via the Enem is not a perfect measure of the manipulation of racial identification. While this corresponds to the time period of quota usage, one's identification matters when completing university admissions applications (*Sisu*), rather than when registering for the exam.[18] Insofar as the anticipation of university

---

[18] As we'll see, students who registered for the exam as white later reported to have entered university using racial quotas. It is not entirely clear how to interpret this. While it may at first glance sound like evidence of "fraud" or manipulation, it is hard to see choosing

admissions impacts identification, we should nonetheless observe effects on racial identification, but these may be conservative estimates. Second, while racial identifications in high school provide a useful baseline against which to compare later changes, it is not clear that these reflect the self-identifications of students. These are based on responses completed in administrative forms, which may have been completed by parents. Thus, we can only assume that changes in identification at the time of the Enem reflect changes in self-identification.

The sample is restricted in other ways as well to ensure internal validity, which may limit the generalizability of findings. First, this analysis exclusively examines students enrolled at federal public universities, which means they are students of high caliber and potentially not representative of the Brazilian student body as a whole. Second, the sample includes only those students who could be identified in each of the three surveys, and who opted to declare a race or color in each survey.[19] This means that it exclusively analyzes students who completed high school, registered for the entrance exam, and chose to enroll in a federal university. These students, again, are not representative of high school students writ large. And finally, the sample includes data from the year 2013 onward, so as to be able to assess the impact of the federal affirmative action law passed in 2012. Insofar as the university experience, or the behavior of students, is different in the post-affirmative action period, we cannot draw inferences about the effects of university prior to the implementation of affirmative action.[20] Overall, the constraints imposed

---

white identification as an attempt to defraud the system by disingenuously declaring one's race. Opportunists are expected to identify as brown or black, not white. Since many Enem registrants are teenagers, there is always the question of whether identifications are self-identifications, or the classifications of the students by parents.

[19] Rates of color non-declaration are significant. Nearly half of high school students did not declare a race, whereas fewer than 10 percent of students registered on the university exam and roughly 20 percent of university students did so. In this analysis, I calculate relative proportions of racial identification that adjust for missingness, so as to prevent estimates from being skewed by attrition in the sample. Beyond measurement concerns, the large variation in willingness to declare at different points in time suggests that simple administrative pressure might play some role explaining patterns of reclassification. Color declaration is highest when it is required on the university exam; though this recedes after matriculation, university students remain more likely than high school students to declare a race. One possibility is that simple administrative requirements entailed in matriculation lead individuals to consider their racial identification more carefully than they had prior.

[20] See Teixeira (2003) for an ethnographic study of the experiences of dark-skinned students in a public university in Rio de Janeiro in the 1990s, when universities were the near-exclusive domain of elites.

on this sample mean these respondents are unlikely to be representative of the population overall. Nonetheless, this analysis enables us to compute internally valid estimates of the effects of affirmative action usage over time.

The final dataset contains 4,932,722 observations, comprised of 436,972 individuals. Each individual's racial identification is measured at least three times (once per survey period), following the official classification scheme employed by the census bureau: white, brown, black, yellow or indigenous. This analysis includes only white, brown, and black identifiers. Responses in each category are dichotomized and analyzed individually with linear probability models, and these proportions also account for missingness in the racial identification variable – an important factor not to ignore given that the decision to opt out is somewhat prevalent at various stages (footnote 19 in Chapter 6). Given the panel structure of the data, estimates are computed with individual fixed effects and adjust for age and gender, as well as state and year fixed effects.

Difference-in-differences estimates are presented in Table 6.3. These estimates are computed relative to the baseline categories of high school and no quota usage. Thus, each estimate indicates the average probability of color identification at each period of time given some type of quota usage vis-à-vis individuals with no quota usage. Model 1, which estimates the probability of identifying as white, indicates that across all treatment groups and time periods, these respondents are less likely to identify as white relative to students who did not enter university via affirmative action. However, there is variation over time. Across all treatment groups, the effect of quotas on white identification is a decrease of, at most, 1 percentage point at the time of the university exam. However, after matriculating in university, the impact of quotas on white identification is more sizable: a decrease 3 points for SES quotas and 13 points for either type of racial quotas. There are two important findings here. First, both means- and race-targeted quotas are associated with decreases in white identification. But second, the effect of race-targeted quotas is notably larger *after students matriculate at university*.

Another relevant question is to which racial categories these respondents are being diverted. Comparing models 2 and 3, which respectively estimate brown and black identification, indicates interesting variation across types of quota usage in terms of whether these individuals are more likely than nonquota users to reclassify as brown or black. For SES quotas, these students are roughly 4 points more likely to reclassify

TABLE 6.3 *Difference-in-differences estimates of effects of affirmative action usage on racial identification*

	(1) White ID	(2) Brown ID	(3) Black ID
SES Quota × Exam	−0.000864+ (0.000)	0.0360* (0.002)	−0.0132* (0.002)
SES Quota × University	−0.0257* (0.001)	0.0410* (0.002)	−0.00484* (0.002)
Racial Quota × Exam	−0.0105* (0.001)	−0.0711* (0.005)	−0.0154* (0.006)
Racial Quota × University	−0.127* (0.002)	−0.0860* (0.005)	0.0889* (0.007)
Racial and SES Quota × Exam	−0.00553* (0.000)	−0.0816* (0.002)	0.0142* (0.002)
Racial and SES Quota × University	−0.134* (0.001)	−0.106* (0.002)	0.140* (0.002)
Exam	0.0264* (0.000)	−0.0662* (0.001)	−0.0181* (0.001)
University	0.221* (0.001)	−0.143* (0.001)	−0.101* (0.001)
Age	−0.000272* (0.000)	−0.00625* (0.000)	0.00386* (0.000)
Female	−0.00297* (0.001)	−0.00674* (0.002)	0.0146* (0.002)
State Fixed Effects	Y	Y	Y
Year Fixed Effects	Y	Y	Y
N	5,246,102	5,246,102	5,246,102
Panel N	499,308	499,308	499,308
ICC	0.272	0.632	0.558
Within R^2	0.139	0.0591	0.0125
Between R^2	0.140	0.127	0.181
Overall R^2	0.139	0.0896	0.0936

Standard errors in parentheses. $^+ p < 0.1$, $^* p < 0.05$. Estimates computed relative to No Quota Usage and High School. Treatment base categories are omitted estimates.

as brown – and this effect holds even after matriculation in university. However, these *cotistas* are 1 point less likely to identify as black in both time periods. These findings indicate that SES quotas have a "browning" effect more than a "blackening" effect. Such behavior would comport with the predictions of the instrumental hypothesis – except that these students do not use race-targeted benefits. Similarly, the symbolic hypothesis emphasizes the race-targeted nature of such policies as doing work that might encourage nonwhite identification. It's also worth remembering that these data contain no measures of physical attributes that might provide some phenotypical basis for reclassification. Assuming physical attributes are constant, fixed effects control for such factors. But we still cannot rule out that the racial subjectivities of individuals who could plausibly identify as white or brown simply changed.

The effects of racial quotas on brown and black identification differ from those of SES quotas. For both types of racial quotas, usage consistently decreases brown identification by between 8 and 11 points at the time of exam registration and after matriculation in university. By contrast, the effects on black identification are largely positive, with a notable increase *after matriculation*. The effects of racial quotas on black identification is inconsistent at the time of the exam. Those using race-exclusive quotas are 2 points less likely to identify as black; indeed, looking across all three models, these students appear less likely to declare any race at all at the time of exam registration. By contrast, those using combined quotas are 1 point more likely to identify as black on the exam. The substantively larger effects of these quotas, however, appear to occur after matriculation. Exclusive and combined racial quotas are estimated to increase black identification by 9 and 14 points, respectively, after matriculation.

At first glance, these findings would seem to confirm both hypotheses: quota usage leads to decreases in white identification in favor of nonwhite racial categories. But upon closer inspection, it is far from clear that the behavior exhibited by federal university students comport with such predictions. On one hand, even beneficiaries of nonracial quotas exhibit shifts in racial identification, suggesting that there is something at work beyond means-ends, cost-benefit calculations. And while it's true that race-targeted quotas have significantly larger effects on reclassification, these quotas increase *black* identification. This departs from how we might expect a savvy opportunist to behave: by manipulating racial identification and moving from the white into the brown category. Moreover, analysis of national survey data in Chapter 4 indicated that black identification among the highly educated, more so than brown identification, is associated with racial group consciousness. In light of this and the fact that these shifts occur *after* matriculation, these findings suggest that either non-instrumental processes are at work altogether, or are perhaps bolstered by quota usage.

The negative effects of racial quotas on brown identification is also noteworthy considering that the analysis of Brazilian municipalities earlier found that these state laws positively impacted brown identification, and did not impact black identification in the aggregate. How to square these macro-level and microlevel patterns is not clear. But the answer to this question might depend on the implicit comparisons made in these analyses. In the municipal analysis earlier, we compared the public in states with and without racial quota laws; in the microlevel analysis here, we compared university students based on quota usage. It is entirely possible that affirmative action laws impact students – those most directly impacted – and the public at large in different ways, and these results indicate as much. Unfortunately, how and why this is the case my data cannot speak to. More broadly, despite my best efforts to assemble various types of data from multiple sources, the task of assessing the impact of affirmative action policies has proven far more difficult and complex than predominant arguments about these policies would lead one to expect. In any case, this matter is far from closed, and ought to be the subject of additional research.

CONCLUSION

This chapter has devoted considerable attention to the question of how and if affirmative action policies impact systematic and widespread patterns of racial identification in Brazil. Results from these analyses proved mixed and inconsistent. Attempts to use survey experiments provided little evidence that information about affirmative action causes major shifts in racial identification, and certainly not among the populations commonly thought to respond – high school-educated respondents of medium or light skin tone, for whom manipulating identification might provide benefits. Observational municipal and microlevel panel data analyzed with rigorous nonparametric methods offered greater support for these hypotheses. But these findings were also mixed. Aggregate census data indicates that race-targeted state affirmative action laws led to a decline in the white-identified population, growth in the brown-identified population, and no effect on the black population. However, panel analysis of quota usage in federal universities indicates similar patterns only for students using means-tested quotas. Among those using racial quotas of some kind, usage led to greater black identification *after matriculation in university*.

Overall, then, one can conclude that affirmative action plays some role in these processes. But it is difficult to reach the conclusion that these policies are decisive, or even central, factors behind the reclassification reversal. Instead, one might simply view them as one piece of the broader initiatives of social and educational policy expansion (Senkevics and Mello 2019; Senkevics and Mello 2022; Vieira et al. 2019). Apparent effects of such policies casually observed in Brazilian society may simply be confounded by the recent era of social policy expansion, or other kinds of effects. As I hope is clear, these are conclusions made tentative by the extraordinary difficulty of isolating the effects of affirmative action on students, let alone the population at large. Better designed analyses, especially ones that can tease apart the instrumental and symbolic explanations for affirmative action, would be valuable additions to the literature.

7

Implications for National Politics

Previous chapters established educational expansion as a driving force behind the reclassification reversal. This chapter shifts its focus to consider the consequences – rather than the causes and mechanisms – of racial reclassification and consciousness by situating these processes in the broader context of Brazilian national politics. In other words, this chapter considers reclassification as an explanatory independent variable, rather than a dependent, or outcome, variable. Shifting the focus in this way serves two purposes. First, doing so is central to the main theoretical framework I apply and build on in this book, the "identity-to-politics link," which implores scholars to disaggregate and isolate the processes of identity formation and politicization, and to separately consider the political arenas in which politicized identities are articulated. In keeping with this theoretical agenda, I aim to identify how and if the electoral arena serves as a venue in which racially conscious Brazilians articulate their newfound political identities. At the same time, this chapter will also shed light on whether the reclassification reversal is a predominantly sociological phenomenon – simply the result of shifting racial boundaries and subjectivities – or whether these newfound political identities find expression in a more overtly political arena.

Second, in following this theoretical framework, the analysis of this chapter also provides a more complete account of the ways in which Brazil's racial politics have shifted over the past three decades. Analyses of racialized electoral behavior in five consecutive general elections situate these racial and sociopolitical developments within the country's electoral and party politics. I show that highly educated black voters have emerged as an overlooked electoral constituency and that these voters are increasingly important to the electoral base of the leftist Workers' Party (PT), the dominant electoral party in the country. In sum, this chapter shows that the reclassification reversal is political in both its causes and its consequences.[1]

Conventional wisdom on the "relevance" of race in Brazil's political arenas would have expected few electoral consequences to be uncovered. Following redemocratization in the 1980s, scholars of political behavior and party systems remarked on the low salience of race and other social identities in Brazil's electoral arena (e.g., Mainwaring 1999; Mainwaring et al. 2000; Samuels 2006; Samuels and Zucco 2018). In contrast to the United States and South Africa (Carmines and Stimson 1990; Ferree 2006; Marx 1998), Brazil's deep and racialized structural inequalities did not translate into durable voting blocs, group-centered political parties, or patterns of partisanship in Brazil. Even after Brazil's weakly institutionalized party system stabilized around the programmatic agenda of the Workers' Party (Roberts 2014), scholars continued to argue that race was not a salient feature of Brazilian electoral politics (Samuels and Zucco 2018).

The findings I present here thus run counter to scholarly wisdom. A key finding of earlier chapters is that racial consciousness cannot be assumed among members of any racial category, but that education predicts greater racial consciousness, especially among those who *choose* black identification. One implication of these findings for political behavior is that racial identification and education should interact to shape voter behavior. Highly educated black-identified voters should be those with highest levels of racial consciousness, and consequently should be most likely to incorporate racial considerations into their electoral calculations. By closely analyzing electoral and protest behavior during five presidential election cycles between 2002 and 2018, I show highly educated black voters are more consistently leftist than other voters – more *ideologically* leftist than their lesser-educated black counterparts and more reliable leftist *voters* than their highly educated white counterparts. Overall, my analyses reveal that racial identification and education interact to shape electoral preferences and behavior, and highlight the electoral arena as one venue in which reclassifiers articulate their racialized political identities.

---

[1] This chapter expands on insights developed in De Micheli (2023).

To be sure, the consequences of the reclassification reversal for political behavior should be understood as secondary to, or situated within, the broader political developments and transformations that have shaped Brazilian national politics over the past two decades: the rise of the PT as a dominant electoral force and the politics of corruption. Though the PT was initially elected with the support of highly educated white voters in the south and southeast of Brazil, these voters became the most ardent opponents of *petismo* following the 2005 *mensalão* corruption scandal, which embroiled Lula's first term in office. But whereas white educated voters were quick to abandon the PT in light of the scandal, educated black voters remained loyal leftists. These voters are not always willing to look past allegations of corruption, but as we'll see, this cross-pressure on educated black voters was never so great as to compromise support for the left or the PT. This remained true even in 2018, when anti-PT sentiment reached fever pitch and was a major force that helped elect far-right populist leader Jair Bolsonaro to the presidency.

Finally, this chapter makes an empirical and methodological contribution to the analysis of ethnoracial electoral politics in Latin America. Relying on the interaction of racial identification and educational status to proxy for racial consciousness demonstrates an empirical strategy for more nuanced analyses of ethnoracialized patterns of behavior. This is especially pertinent in Latin America, where quality and reliable measures of racial identification, let alone racial ascription or group consciousness, are not always readily available on high quality domestic surveys. I show how more nuanced quantitative analysis of racialized behavior can still be conducted with items commonly found in public opinion surveys, and that this can, when applied appropriately, yield insightful findings. This approach can easily be applied to studies of other Latin American contexts, which increasingly focus on the region's complex ethnoracial politics. In short, the contributions of this chapter extend beyond the theoretical imperatives of the identity-to-politics link, and provides an empirical illustration of how scholars might conduct more contextually appropriate analyses of ethnoracial politics in the region.

In what follows, I first make the case for renewed attention to the role that race plays in Brazilian elections in light of the fact that the reclassification reversal suggests significant flux in the country's racial politics. I then draw out observable implications of this book's central argument for political behavior and evaluate these propositions by closely analyzing the period of transformation and tumult that has characterized Brazilian national politics over the past two decades.

RETHINKING THE IRRELEVANCE OF RACE IN BRAZILIAN ELECTIONS

Though in recent decades Brazil has taken a number of policy strides that have helped shed its image as a so-called "racial democracy," scholarly wisdom has continued to hold that few social identities or differences – and certainly not race – had become significant bases of the party system or electoral competition. Brazil's open-list system of proportional representation is said to favor candidates who can individually amass as many votes as possible, incentivizing personalities over parties (Carey and Shugart 1995). Moreover, low seat allocation thresholds in the lower house of congress (1.5 percent historically, and 2 percent more recently) has been associated with party system fragmentation and electoral volatility (Mainwaring 1999). One might expect low thresholds to permit the formation of niche parties around relatively small constituencies, such as Brazil's black population. Yet in the decade following redemocratization, few social cleavages or identities were channeled into partisan affiliations or strongly predicted vote choice, let alone served as the basis for group-centered parties (Mainwaring 1999; Mainwaring et al. 2000; Samuels 2006).

To explain the low electoral salience of race in Brazil, scholars pointed to the usual suspect of racial democracy. Though social scientists have long denounced racial democracy as a myth that obscures the country's deep and enduring racial inequities, many have nonetheless claimed that the myth is responsible for fluid and ambiguous racial subjectivities, the primacy of class-based considerations over racial ones, and the relatively low politicization of racial differences in the electoral arena more generally (Bailey 2009; Guimarães 1999; Hanchard 1994; Marx 1998; Telles 2004). To be sure, more recent scholarship has identified significant forms of race-based political activism and mobilization outside of the electoral arena (Bueno and Fialho 2009; Caldwell 2007; Perry 2013; Smith 2016). But by and large political scientists have maintained that, likely as a result of racial democracy, race has played no major role in Brazilian politics.[2]

---

[2] See Fialho (2021) for a recent example of this view. For exceptions, see De Micheli (2018) on racial differences in the effects of CCTs; Mitchell (2009) and Oliveira (2007) on the implicit role of race in campaign strategies; and Janusz (2018, 2021) for evidence of racial discrimination in voting and strategic instability in elites' racial identifications. Bueno and Dunning (2017) find in an experimental study that Brazilians do not necessarily prefer voters of the same race/color, but Aguilar et al. (2015) find they do when faced with ballots with many candidates.

However, there are good reasons to question conventional wisdom on the electoral irrelevance of race in Brazil. First, many empirical studies that established the "political irrelevance" of race in Brazil were conducted before significant shifts in the Brazilian state's posture toward the racial question, or in the context of an unconsolidated democratic regime and considerable political and economic instability. Indeed, 1990s Brazil saw severe hyperinflation and the impeachment of the first president democratically elected in nearly three decades. The situation stabilized by the late 1990s, but it was by studying the aftermath of this tumult that important work by Mainwaring (1999) and Samuels (2006) established the purported electoral irrelevance of race and other social identifications. In one instance, Mainwaring and colleagues (2000, 200) conclude the irrelevance of race based on the absence of racial data altogether, writing that "limited politicization of race even surfaced in survey questions: the 1988 and 1991 surveys [we analyze] did not ask respondents to identify their race." More recently, Samuels and Zucco find in their analysis of Brazilian partisanship that "the proportions of [PT supporters] who self-identify as white is always lower than for [PT anti-partisans], and often by a large margin." Nonetheless, they reach the conclusion that "[r]ace has never been a key political divide in Brazil" (2018, 37–38). This scholarly rush to judgment on the race question is striking seeing as literacy requirements denied large swaths of the poor (and darker-skinned) population the right to vote until 1988 (Berquó and Alencastro 1992; Love 1970). With this in mind, it's unclear why one would expect unseasoned voters to emerge from two decades of military rule with fully formed electoral preferences, familiarity with the country's voting process and complex electoral institutions, or established partisan sympathies that mapped cleanly onto racial or other lines.[3]

Second, that race was electorally irrelevant has not always been a consensus view, and findings from analyses of the 1990s did not always comport with studies of earlier elections or elections at different levels of government. Indeed, even studies conducted at the height of the state's embrace of racial democracy – that is, when one might expect race to be especially irrelevant to voters – identify racial identification as a significant correlate of electoral preferences in in national and state-level elections across several decades. Studies by Castro (1993), Soares and Silva

---

[3] Though South Africa's "racial census" emerged immediately upon democratization, this transition was shaped by the dissolution of apartheid – a form of institutionalized racial oppression with no equivalent in Brazil (Marx 1998).

(1987) and Souza (1971) all find that nonwhite voters are more likely than their white-identified counterparts to support leftist candidates or parties. At the very least, we must acknowledge this empirical variation.

And third, even if we grant that race was irrelevant in the decade following redemocratization (the 1990s), Brazil's electoral arena has since undergone significant realignment around the electoral dominance of the PT. In 2002, the PT won the presidency with support from myriad social sectors, though its greatest support was concentrated in the industrialized southeast region. But following the 2005 *mensalão* corruption scandal – which embroiled the PT and cost the party support from educated, middle-class (and white-identified) voters – the PT's base of support swung toward poorer voters in the northeast, who greatly benefitted from the PT's social program agenda (Hunter 2010; Hunter and Power 2007). Given the high correlation between race, region, and class in Brazil, the shift in the PT's electoral base also shifted support toward black and brown voters who disproportionately populate the northeast and lower-class strata (De Micheli 2018; Telles 2004). The collinearity of race and class of course does not foreclose the possibility of interpreting this realignment as class-based. But the more important point is that since the election of the PT to the presidency in 2002, Brazil's electoral arena has been stabilized and realigned around this partisan divide (Roberts 2014; Samuels and Zucco 2018) in ways that had not yet occurred when conventional wisdom on the irrelevance of race was established.

Analysis of general election survey data supports these misgivings. Figure 7.1 presents estimates of the effect of black and brown identification on presidential vote choice from 2002 through 2018. It is true that race does not significantly predict vote choice in 2002. But racial identification has consistently proven to be a robust and significant determinant of voter behavior in national elections since 2006 after the shift in the PT's electoral base. It's also clear that *black* identification has been a more consistent and significant predictor of vote choice than has brown identification. Notably too, race did not emerge as a significant predictor in 2018, when some scholars argue the inflammatory racist rhetoric of Jair Bolsonaro arguably gave nonwhite voters reason to oppose him (Layton et al. 2021; Silva and Larkins 2019). The difference in 2018 was not the apparent salience of race, but rather that the preferred candidate of black voters did not prevail. Given the scholarly emphasis on the irrelevance on race, the consistent correlations between racial ID and vote choice might come as a surprise. But it's also clear in Figure 7.1 that while racial identification does have a significant substantive effect on the

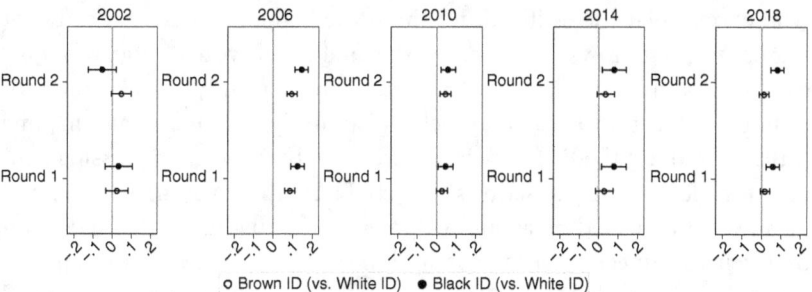

FIGURE 7.1 Average partial effect of racial ID on electoral support, 2002–2018
The figure displays 90 percent confidence intervals. Estimates indicate support for second-round winner in each year (Lula 2002–6, Rousseff 2010–14, and Bolsonaro in 2018). Estimates are regression-adjusted and control for age, sex, region, income, education, religion and party ID in all years except 2006, which did not collect party ID and religion. Full model estimates in Supplementary Tables A7.1a–A7.1e.

probability of voting, racial ID does not singularly determine vote choice as in other contexts, such as black identification in the United States or in the more extreme case of South Africa's "racial census" (Dawson 1995; Ferree 2006). We know from Figure 7.1 that race is indeed relevant for some, but not all, voters. Thus, the question is not *if*, but *for whom*, racial identification is a relevant factor.

One reading of Figure 7.1 might reduce these correlations to collinearity between race and class. In this view, racial ID and class position overlap and nonwhites are disproportionately targeted as beneficiaries of the PT's conditional cash transfer program (De Micheli 2018). Thus, race appears to predict vote choice, but this is the spurious effect of lower-class support for the Workers' Party. A different perspective is derived from the shifting racial politics and new racial subjectivities indicated by the reclassification reversal. From this view, it is important to remember that the black racial category is heterogeneous (e.g., Silva and Leão 2012), comprised of individuals who subscribe to traditional (i.e., colorist) understandings of race, as well as race-conscious and politically oriented identifiers (i.e., the highly educated) who may less clearly meet phenotypical criteria for blackness but identify as such nonetheless as a function of racial consciousness. The implication in this case is that both education and racial identification matter for hypotheses regarding whether voters will incorporate race into their electoral decisions. Because previous chapters have shown that highly educated Brazilians who choose black identification exhibit the highest degree of racial consciousness, it follows that highly educated black voters ought to view electoral politics through a racial lens. Consequently, black voters of different education levels may behave similarly at some points in time (rallying around the PT) and differently in others (when expressing support for ideological alternatives to the PT). At the same time, we should also expect educated black and white voters to diverge in their electoral preferences, especially after corruption emerged as a major campaign issue: due to their beliefs regarding racialized social structures, educated black voters ought to exhibit distinctive leftist tendencies vis-à-vis educated white voters, who are more likely to lean conservative.

DATA AVAILABILITY

Before proceeding to analysis, it's worth taking a moment to address a real limitation in the study of racialized political behavior in Latin America, which is the inconsistency in the collection of racial data in national political surveys. One of the greatest challenges of conducting this research has been the relative scarcity of high-quality public opinion data that includes information on racial identification, let alone additional measures that would permit deeper analysis of racial consciousness or other attitudes. Even in Brazil, where the census has consistently measured racial identification since 1980, public opinion researchers have not always followed suit. Many surveys conducted by sociologists, such as the *Pesquisa Social Brasileira* or the Project on Ethnicity and Race in Latin America (PERLA) survey, include a wealth of race-related survey items, but these surveys often do not measure outcomes of interest to analysts of political behavior. Surveys that do include both sets of questions, such as the Latin American Public Opinion Project (LAPOP) or Latinobarometer, collect data many months prior to elections and can lead to inaccurate findings (see Zucco and Power 2013). But even when this is not the case, small samples make the type of within-group sectoral analysis called for here infeasible due to the limited number of highly educated black respondents.

What I present in this chapter is part of an effort to reassess this scholarly wisdom and to contend with the very real limitations in data availability. I have assembled what are, to my knowledge, the highest quality data of political behavior in Brazil that permit analysis of racial identification. These data include general election data from 2002 to 2018 and surveys of historic protests in 2013, 2015, and 2016. Table 7.1

TABLE 7.1 *Surveys for analysis of general elections*

Year	CESOP No.	Survey	Total N	Black ID N	Black ID × Univ. N	Data collection	1st round	2nd round
2002	1838	ESEB	2,514	300	18	October 31–December 28	October 6	October 27
2006	2551	Datafolha	12,561	1704	195	October 27–28	October 1	October 29
2010	2717	IBOPE	3,010	426	42	October 11–13	October 3	October 31
2010	2718	IBOPE	3,010	410	33	October 22	October 3	October 31
2014	3928	ESEB	3,136	375	43	November 1–19	October 5	October 26
2018	4577	Datafolha	9,137	1366	299	October 24–25	October 7	October 28

summarizes the election surveys I use to analyze general elections, and illustrates the dilemma of data scarcity. In identifying surveys appropriate to analyze, I prioritized surveys that provide larger numbers of university-educated and black-identifying respondents, since these are of greatest theoretical interest and are often the most underrepresented. In several election years, the best-case scenario provides relatively few black identifiers with university education. Though not always ideal, these samples still manage to demonstrate that race has been a relevant factor in Brazil's complex political arena. One goal of these analyses is to show that more consistent collection of racial data in Brazil and Latin America is worthwhile, and to encourage scholars to approach the study of ethnoracial politics in these contexts with the nuance and sensitivity it demands.

THE RISE OF THE LEFT'S BLACK CONSTITUENCY, 2002–2010

Scholars argue that as the PT began moderating its program in the 1990s in order to win national elections, the PT relied on firm support from well-educated voters, predominantly from the wealthier and higher developed regions of the country in the south and southeast (Hunter 2010; Hunter and Power 2007). Conversely, conservative parties have historically counted on lesser developed regions and rural areas, where they were able to maintain power through clientelism and patrimonialism (Mainwaring et al. 2000; Hagopian 1996). This dynamic largely held following Collor's impeachment in 1992. In the 1994 and 1998 elections, wealthier voters and more developed regions were more likely to vote for a *leftist* party, contrary to the patterns observed in Europe by Lipset and Rokkan (1967). As Samuels and Zucco (2018) find in their analysis of the PT cleavage from 1989 to 2014, PT partisans were significantly wealthier and better educated than nonpartisans up through the 2002 election. But by 2002, the PT had secured support from voters of all stripes and was delivered a resounding victory in 2002. Multivariate analysis confirms that the PT received broad support from across social sectors, as displayed in Figure 7.2. Majorities of all racial and educational combinations supported Lula in the second round of voting, and near-majorities in the first.

However, the PT's electoral bases began to shift following the *mensalão* corruption scandal. In 2005, federal deputy Roberto Jefferson (PTB) publicly reported to the national newspaper *Folha de S.Paulo* that the PT had

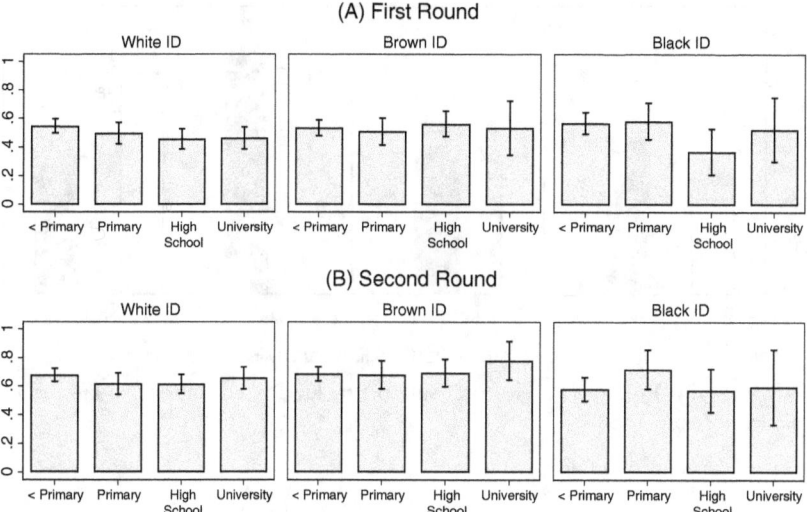

FIGURE 7.2 Predicted probabilities of PT support by racial ID and education, 2002

been funneling state funds to legislators in the form of monthly payments in exchange for political support for its legislative agenda. The scandal was particularly damaging to the PT's image and reputation since the party had long promised to bring "the PT way of governing" (*o modo PT de governar*) to the presidency, presenting itself as above party politics and accountable to organized civil society. As has been well documented, the scandal cost the PT the electoral support of many educated and middle-class voters on whom it relied to elect Lula in 2002. But, Lula was able to survive this scandal due to his social program agenda, especially the targeted cash transfer program *Bolsa Família*, which shifted the PT's electoral support from the industrialized south and southeast regions toward the poorer and lesser developed north and northeast (Hunter and Power 2007; Zucco 2008).

Scholars argue that education leads to punishment of corruption either because educated voters possess the political interest and awareness that make them better able to discern and punish corruption (e.g., Weitz-Shapiro and Winters 2017) or because they are less tolerant of patrimonialism and abuses of political power (Hunter and Power 2007). At first glance, examination of PT support among educational sectors bears out these predictions. Figure 7.3, which presents first-round PT support in elections between 1994 and 2006, shows a reversal in the relationship

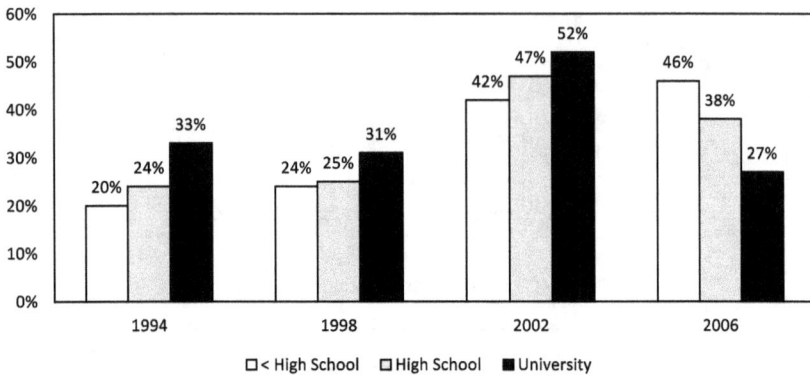

FIGURE 7.3 Round 1 PT electoral support by level of education, 1994–2006
Source: Zucco 2008

between education and PT support after 2002. Considering education alone, the PT consistently received its highest levels of support from the best-educated between 1994 and 2002. In 2002, the PT even received an outright majority from this group (52 percent). But in the first election after *mensalão*, there is a clear decrease in support for PT among the highly educated. Among those with university, support falls by nearly half, from 52 to 27 percent; among the high school-educated, support declines by 20 percent, from 47 to 38 percent. By contrast, among the least educated the PT gained an additional 4 points of support, making this sector the most supportive of Lula and the PT for the first time.

However, these averages belie a more heterogeneous pattern that emerged in 2006 and that becomes apparent only when considering the interaction of education and racial identification. Figure 7.4 displays conditional probabilities of PT support in the 2006 election by racial ID and education. Panel A indicates that in the first round of voting, there is a clear negative relationship between education and PT support across all racial groups.[4] At the same time, white voters are categorically least likely to support the PT, black voters are most likely, and brown voters fall in between. Despite this negative relationship in the first round of voting, the PT continues to win the majority of university-educated voters among black and brown voters, but not among white identifiers. The picture in the second round of voting is different (panel B). The negative relationship between

---

[4] Within each racial group, differences in the predicted probabilities of less than primary and university voters is statistically significant at $p < 0.05$.

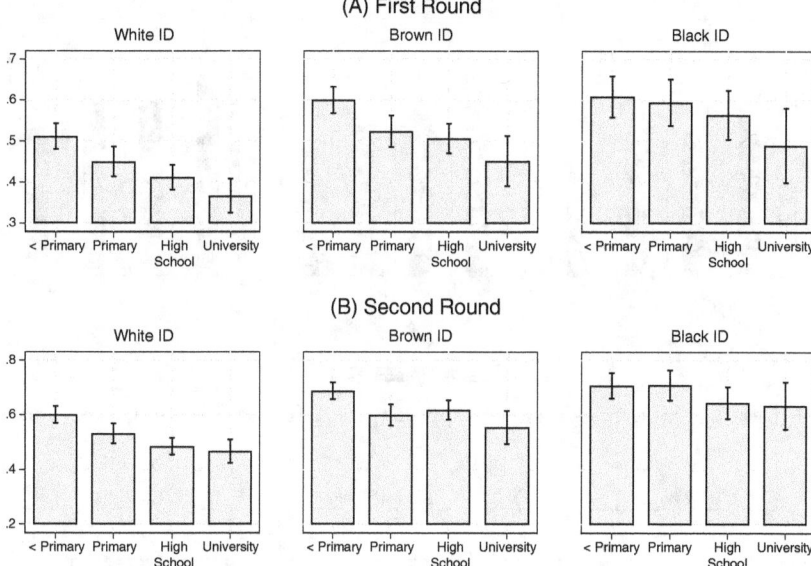

FIGURE 7.4 Regression-adjusted estimates of PT support by racial ID and education, 2006
Data collected by Datafolha (CESOP-Datafolha/02551) on October 27 and 28, 2006, on the eve of the runoff. N = 12,561. Multivariate models include controls for age, gender, region and income. Party ID was not captured in this survey. Estimates are survey weighted.

education and PT support holds for white and brown voters, but not for black voters. Not only are black voters more likely to support the PT than those in other racial categories, but they are likely to do so at all levels of education. It has since become well known that the least-educated – likely to be beneficiaries of the PT's social program agenda – are the most loyal PT supporters (Hunter 2010; Hunter and Power 2007). But what emerges from this analysis is an overlooked conditional effect: in 2006, black identification blunted the negative effects of education on PT support.

Closer examination of the shifts in the PT's electoral support further reveals racial differences in the effects of education. Figure 7.5 compares simple means of first-round PT support in 2002 and 2006 by race and education. Among white voters, the negative relationship between education and PT support in 2006 is driven by large drops in support among the highly educated. By contrast, among black voters the PT registers only a marginal decrease in support among the university-educated, and increases among all other education groups. Brown voters fall in between, registering

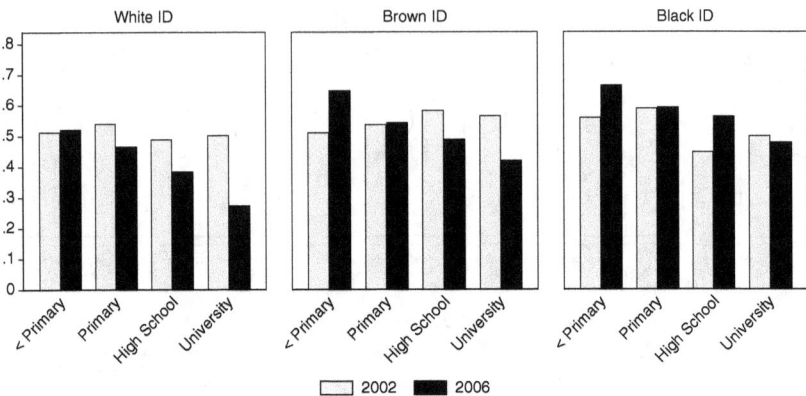

FIGURE 7.5 Mean first-round PT support by racial ID and education, 2002–2006

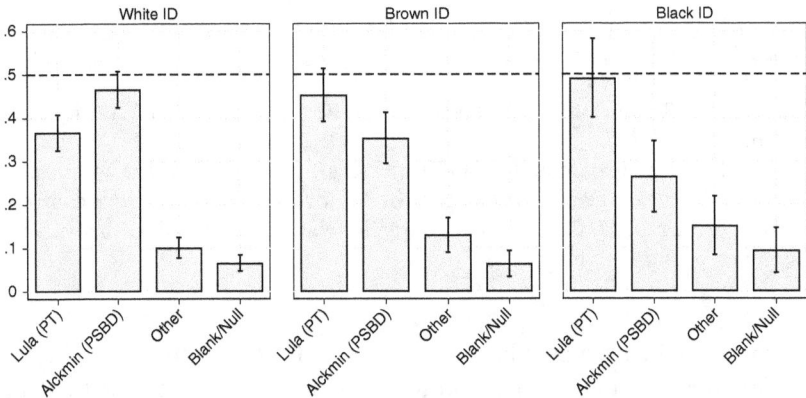

FIGURE 7.6 First-round vote choice of university-educated voters by racial ID, 2006

more modest increases and decreases. In light of these comparisons, it's clear that the negative effects of education that appear in panel A of Figure 7.4 derive from different electoral shifts: among white voters this is a function of decreased support among highly educated voters; among black voters, this is due to the increased support of the least-educated. Education undoubtedly played an important role in explaining change in PT support over time. But this relationship was conditioned by racial identification.

Racial identification appears to impact not only *whether* highly educated voters defected from the PT in 2006, but also to which other candidates or parties that support was diverted. Figure 7.6 presents regression-adjusted estimates of first-round the vote choices of university-educated voters by racial ID. University-educated white voters abandoned the PT in favor of Lula's conservative rival, Geraldo Alckmin of the PSBD, preferring him outright over Lula. Brown voters, again, fall between white and black voters, preferring Lula but also supportive of Alckmin. Black voters, by contrast, remain significantly more supportive of Lula in the first round, and black PT defectors are significantly less likely to translate their preferences into support of the conservative Alckmin. These voters are more likely to support alternatives to these two mainstream candidates, and marginally more likely to spoil their ballots. Unlike white voters, then, opposition to the PT among educated black voters did not translate into support for the PT's conservative rival.

The relative scarcity of highly educated black respondents in survey samples makes it difficult to pin down consistently or with a high degree of confidence any change in this sector's ideological leanings over this period. But there is suggestive evidence that this racial divide that emerges in 2006 among highly educated voters is explained in part by ideological differences among university-educated voters, a potentially more politically engaged sector of the electorate. Data from the 2002 ESEB election survey suggests that 45 percent of university educated black voters place themselves on the ideological left, compared to 40 and 35 percent of white and brown, educated Brazilians. However, the number of educated black respondents in this sample is small, and unfortunately reliable estimates are not available again until 2014. But these data, presented in Figure 7.7, indicate that in later years university-educated black voters lean even further left relative to their counterparts in other racial groups. Approximately 30 percent of university-educated black voters place themselves on the left, nearly twice the rate of white and brown university voters ($p < 0.1$). Survey data thus indicate an ideological gap among voters that is conditioned by race and education.

The conditional effects of education and race suggest that the dominant narrative regarding the realignment of Brazil's electoral arena around the PT best fits the behavior and responses of educated white Brazilian voters (conservatives) and poor nonwhite voters (social program beneficiaries and PT loyalists). White educated voters were more likely to support the PT in 2002 as it made its economic moderation clear to voters, but were quick to abandon the PT in light of the 2005 corruption scandal (Hunter 2010). Lesser educated nonwhite voters, many of whom are *Bolsa Família* recipients (De Micheli 2018), remained loyal to the PT as a result of the targeted social spending that greatly benefitted low-income

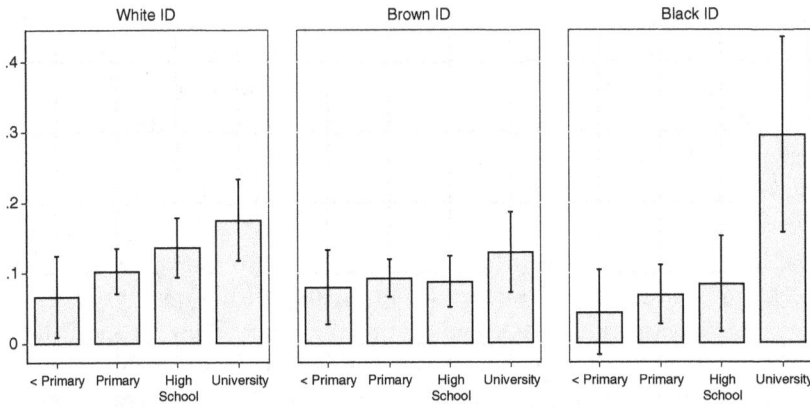

FIGURE 7.7 Left self-placement by education and racial ID, 2014
Data come from the 2014 ESEB. Estimates are predicted probabilities from a multinomial logit model, controlling for age, gender, income, region, religion, and party ID. The dependent variable is coded as (1) nonpartisans, (2) left, (3) center, and (4) right self-placement.

(and disproportionately nonwhite) households. Highly educated black voters do not fit neatly into this dichotomy. In the elections that follow, these voters continue to distinguish themselves from their lesser-educated black counterparts and highly educated white counterparts.

CRACKS IN BLACK SUPPORT FOR THE PT?

While in 2006 educated black voters remained loyal to the PT, this should not necessarily be construed as a lack of electoral accountability over or as apathy toward the issue of corruption. While Lula was able to win a resounding victory in 2006 due to overwhelming support from black and low-income voters, by 2010 the electoral loyalty to the PT among these voters had begun to wane. Scholars have debated the extent to which Lula's handpicked successor, Dilma Rousseff, was elected by riding Lula's coattails in the 2010 election. Rousseff, who had not previously run for political office before capturing the presidency, was largely unknown to the public and had served in Lula's administration as energy minister and chief of staff. Given Rousseff's reputation as tough on and intolerant of corruption, her selection for such a prominent political role in Lula's administration was intended in part to signal a greater commitment to anticorruption in the wake of the *mensalão* scandal (Souza 2011).

Though Rousseff won the 2010 election, this strategy arguably failed to change the PT's image. On one hand, it's striking that a political neophyte such as Rousseff could win the presidency in her first ever political run. But on the other, it's unlikely she would have won without Lula's endorsement, and her second-round vote share (56 percent) fell short of Lula's approval rating upon leaving office (83 percent) by a wide margin, and was short of Lula's vote share in 2006 (61 percent). Samuels (2006) argues that a significant proportion of *petismo* can be explained by personalistic attachment to Lula himself. From the coattails perspective, Rousseff clearly underperformed in 2010 as a politician without name recognition or personal attachments to voters. Another view attributes Rousseff's underperformance to late-hour corruption allegations within Lula's cabinet and Rousseff's staff, likely undermining the strategy of choosing a staunchly anti-corruption successor like Rousseff (Balán 2014). Though Rousseff certainly worked to cultivate her anticorruption credentials with voters, it's possible that many educated voters would not look past her proximity to alleged improprieties. Lest we forget, a third important but difficult to prove possibility is gender bias against the first viable female candidate to Brazil's presidency.

Within this broader political context, the question remains as to how and whether black voters respond to these issues, and if they do so in ways that are distinct from other voters. Figure 7.8 compares first-round electoral support in the 2006 and 2010 elections. In only one surprising instance – white university-educated voters – is support for Rousseff noticeably higher than it was for Lula in 2006. Seeing as these voters were the ones who abandoned the PT in light of the 2005 corruption

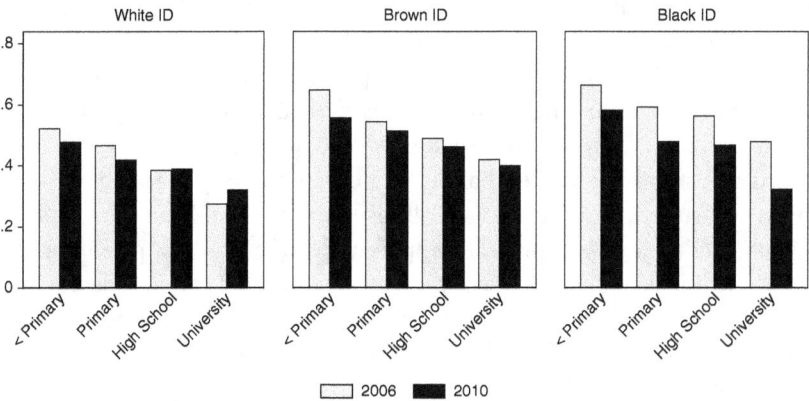

FIGURE 7.8 First-round PT support by racial ID and education, 2006 and 2010

scandal, there is some evidence they were swayed by Rousseff's anticorruption image, or potentially by the possibility of the first female president. Across all other sectors, support for the PT candidate declines in 2010, most precipitously among educated black voters. It's tempting to interpret this as a response to the late-hour corruption allegations in Rousseff's office, potentially a final straw for these voters who did not punish the PT in 2006. But data from the 2010 ESEB survey indicate small differences across racial and educational groups in the importance voters place on corruption. Roughly 40 to 50 percent of all respondents list corruption as one of the top three issues facing Brazilian society. Educated black respondents are more likely place greater weight on issues like social spending (67 percent) when compared to white respondents (44 percent). But given the similar anticorruption values across racial groups, it's not immediately clear why this would translate into decreased support for the PT candidate among black voters, and increased support among white voters.

Upon closer examination, the decline in support for Rousseff among educated black voters is not driven by an abandonment of the left, but rather by these voters' diverting support from the mainstream and increasingly centrist PT toward more ideological leftist parties. One of the several surprises of the 2010 election was the late-hour surge in support for Marina Silva of the Green Party (*Partido Verde*, PV), a former minister of the environment in Lula's government. As a nonwhite, evangelical candidate from a small and left-wing party, Silva was able to appeal to diverse sectors in the electorate, including evangelicals and the highly educated with greater post-material concerns (Norris and Inglehart 2003). In the end, analysts concluded that Silva's surprising support from a variety of social sectors denied Rousseff a first-round victory (Balán 2014; Souza 2011). Figure 7.9 shows the marginal effect of university education on vote choices. First, across all racial groups, university education increases support for Silva. Among white and brown identifiers, this support comes from a combination of Rousseff support (roughly 8 points), as well as a decline in blank or spoiled ballots (4 points). Among black identifiers, however, support for Silva comes almost entirely from Rousseff support, which declines by 19 points. The apparent decrease in PT support among educated black voters in 2010 is driven by support for the ideological leftist alternative. The emergence of a viable leftist alternative to the PT – something that would have been a formidable challenge in 2006, given Lula's personal popularity – obscures the committed leftist leanings of educated black voters. Educated nonwhite voters remained committed

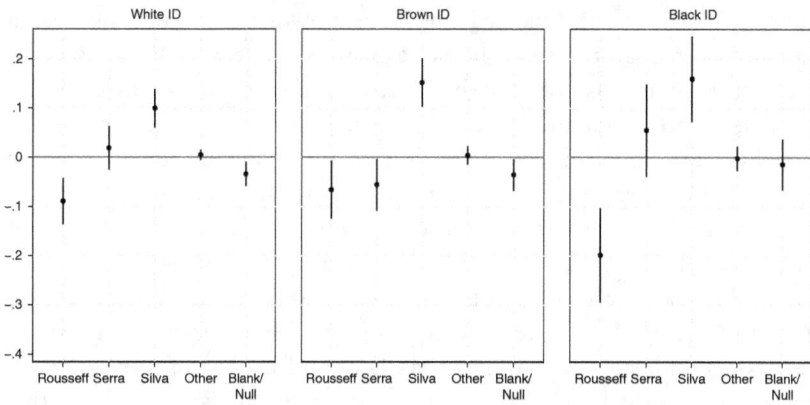

FIGURE 7.9 Marginal effect of university education (vs. less than primary) on first-round electoral support, 2010
The figure displays 90 percent confidence intervals.

to leftist candidates, but for the first time they begin to divert their support away from the PT and toward more ideological leftist alternatives. Whereas in 2006 black identification blunted the negative effects of education, in 2010 it appears to boost the effects of education.

With the luxury of hindsight, these cracks in electoral loyalties of leftist voters toward the PT help to make sense of the burst of disenchantment that emerged in the waves of protest that shook Brazil in 2013 and that in some ways likely helped to set the stage for Rousseff's impeachment in 2016. To be sure, few saw the protests coming in 2013 despite the corruption scandals that had emerged and disillusioned Brazilian voters. By this point, the outlook for Brazil was optimistic after three consecutive presidential victories for the PT: the Brazilian economy weathered the 2008 financial crisis without major catastrophe; 81 percent of Brazilians reported that they expected their personal economic situations to improve or remain the same; and 57 percent of Brazilians rated Rousseff's government as good or great, compared to only 9 percent rating it bad or terrible. Many were caught off-guard when routine increases in federally regulated bus fares inadvertently catalyzed major protests in several of Brazil's major urban centers.

These protests were initially organized by the *Movimento Passe Livre* (MPL, free fare movement), a fringe movement originating in the southern city of Porto Alegre that has long demanded free public transportation. Despite the movement's long lifespan, the MPL had not received considerable national attention in Brazil until June 2013, when its protests began to draw increasingly large crowds and created significant disruptions in major cities. Why these protests suddenly galvanized wide-scale participation is not entirely clear, since the protests seemed to coalesce disparate social and political groups. Some observers argue that the fare hike was ill-timed for the middle of the academic semester, when they would anger university students – many of whom rely on public transportation to frequent campuses. But participation in the movement exploded only after violent clashes with the police during a protest in São Paulo. Following a series of disruptions in São Paulo, governor Geraldo Alckmin deployed the state's military police to keep the protests in check. Protesters and the police quickly clashed, and images of violent police repression of largely middle-class university students went viral, igniting participation in subsequent protests in cities across Brazil.

The profile of protesters in many ways fits conventional predictions of political participation – the protesters were overwhelming middle-class, university-educated, or enrolled in university. But unlike the right-wing protesters that would mobilize against Rousseff in 2015, these protesters were much more ideologically heterogeneous. Protesters articulated grievances that ran the gamut from general political disenchantment, to police violence, to corruption. Despite being the initial mobilizing issue, demands for free public transportation motivated few participants. Without a clear center of gravity or shared grievance, these unexpected protests seemed to indicate a broader crisis of representation and disillusionment that set in during successive PT governments. Some of the protesters were surely comprised of anti-*petistas* or conservatives who were tired of the PT and its electoral dominance; but the ideological heterogeneity of the protesters makes it difficult to reduce these protests to conservatives capitalizing on a moment of political vulnerability for the PT.

Despite ideological heterogeneity, data from a Datafolha survey conducted during the June 20th protests suggest that protesters were overwhelmingly comprised of young, white, university-educated Brazilians. Figure 7.10 shows the racial and education breakdown of protesters at the 20 June protest, compared to the Sao Paulo population (per the 2010 census). On the left-hand side, the educational disparities are striking. Nearly 80 percent of protesters were university graduates or students, roughly triple the rate of the broader population. Lesser educated Brazilians, by contrast, are almost entirely unrepresented. Racial disparities in protest participation are also apparent: 65 percent of protesters self-identify as white (compared to 48 percent of the population), and 22 and 8 percent identify as brown and black, respectively, below their

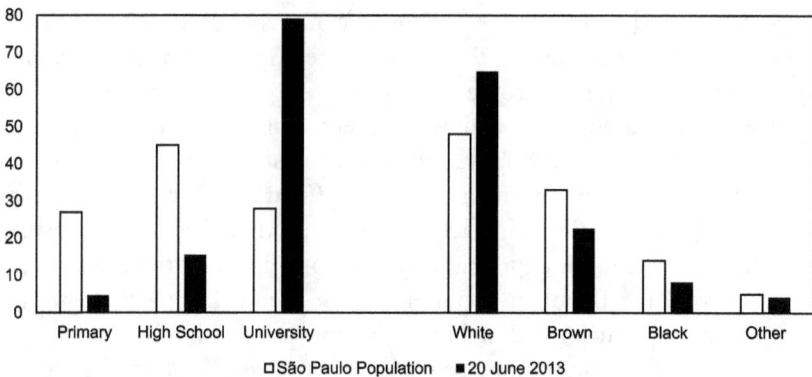

FIGURE 7.10 Racial and educational profile of June 2013 protesters, Sao Paulo Data provided by Datafolha (CESOP survey no. 0377).

population proportions. Once racial disparities in access to education are accounted for, this racial gap in participation might not seem as large. But whether this is due to differences in rates of participation or a function of racial inequality in university access, it's clear that white identifiers largely comprised these protesters.

On the one hand, it might make sense that these protests, which revolved around increases in bus fares, might overwhelmingly mobilize students who report often relying on public transportation to attend universities. On the other hand, however, universities remain socially exclusive domains in Brazil, despite state-led efforts to expand access. University students tend to come from privileged families, and despite recent efforts to racially diversify student bodies, campuses are overpopulated by the lighter-skinned. Considering the degree of advantage and privilege traditionally required to gain admission to universities, then, it would seem that university students are among the better positioned to withstand fare increases in public transportation. This latter interpretation of the 2013 protests find suggestive support in self-reported household income data from Datafolha surveys of protesters: participants report family incomes significantly higher than the median. In light of these structural considerations, it is no small wonder that these protests surprised observers, who ultimately came to see them as an outcry of frustration after more than a decade of PT governance, rather than as motivated by material concerns like the bus fare hike.

Such an interpretation no doubt gave the conservative opposition, electorally centered on the PSBD, some hope that this disenchantment could be capitalized upon to finally unseat the dominant PT. But how or if the broad and heterogeneous discontent that coalesced in 2013 could translate from the protest to the electoral arena was far from clear. For while the socioeconomic profile of the protesters was well known (young, university educated), the protesters were politically heterogeneous. According to Datafolha surveys taken of protesters, significant proportions of the protesters reported no partisan affiliation (84 percent on June 17th, and 72 percent on June 20th), suggesting that these protests were not the overwhelming expression of partisanship or anti-partisanship. One study of the Brazilian population even found that partisanship in the general population declined after these protests, a finding one might expect to be more acute among protesters themselves (Winters and Weitz-Shapiro 2014). Additionally, roughly one-third of protesters identified as ideologically centrist, and another third as leftist. At only 20 percent of protesters, self-identified conservatives were a clear minority, but there was no dominant ideological center of gravity among the protesters, whose demands included reversing bus fare hikes, police repression, and general political disenchantment. None of these themes mapped clearly onto the policy programs of the PT or PSDB, or major issues that had come to dominate national political debate, such as the minimum wage or affirmative action.

This disconnect between mainstream parties and 2013 protesters is evident in the protesters' preferences ahead of the general election in 2014. Figure 7.11 displays preferences from protesters on the night of June 20th according to racial self-identification. First, disenchantment with all candidates (blank or null ballots) is exceptionally high across all protesters. Election returns historically report blank and spoiled

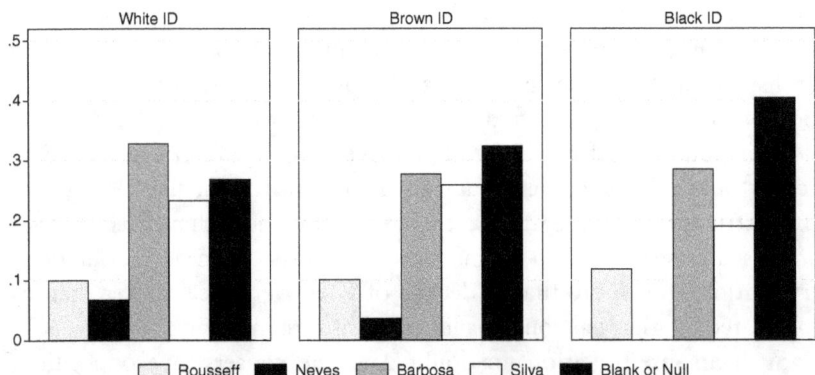

FIGURE 7.11 Preferred 2014 presidential candidate of June 2013 protesters, São Paulo

ballots in the single digits, compared to an average of 29 percent among protesters. This number varies, however, by racial ID, with 40 percent of black identifying protesters likely to express this disenchantment, compared to 27 percent of white identifying protesters. Second, neither Rousseff nor Neves – the two mainstream candidates who would advance to the 2014 runoff – appear competitive among this group. Rousseff performs better than Neves, but sees her peak support from black protesters at only 12 percent. Third, protesters voice considerable support for then–Supreme Court Justice Joaquim Barbosa. Barbosa, who retired in 2014, presided over many trials tied to the *mensalão* scandal and developed a confrontational reputation on the high court. Notably, as the first black justice to serve on the court, he is also known for writing the supreme court decision that unanimously upheld Brazil's 2012 affirmative action law. In some ways, strong electoral support for a justice presages what was to come in the aftermath of the historical *Lava Jato* corruption scandal, in which judicial actors are exalted as national saviors by conservatives and others. But in any case, insofar as protesters prefer a candidate, all place Barbosa at the top of the list. In second is Marina Silva (PV) – the leftist spoiler to Rousseff's first-round victory in 2010. The overwhelming support for alternatives to the mainstream lends credence to the idea that these protests represented disillusionment with incumbent politicians. Insofar as the proportion of protesters opting for spoiled ballots indicates disenchantment, these educated black protesters exhibit the highest levels.

ROUSSEFF'S REELECTION, *LAVA JATO*, AND IMPEACHMENT

Despite signs that the public was growing weary of PT governance, Rousseff ultimately prevailed in the 2014 election by a narrow margin of 3 points – at the time, the closest margin since the 1989 election and much narrower than Rousseff's 12-point margin in 2010.[5] Rousseff managed to eke out this win by once again relying on support from lower-income voters and educated black voters, despite the disillusionment they exhibited in 2013 protests. By 2014, these voters were much more likely to identify as ideologically leftist than their nonblack counterparts (see Figure 7.7) and were less likely than other highly educated Brazilians

---

[5] Fernando Collor de Mello defeated Lula by 7 points in 1989. Lula defeated Bolsonaro by 2 points in 2022.

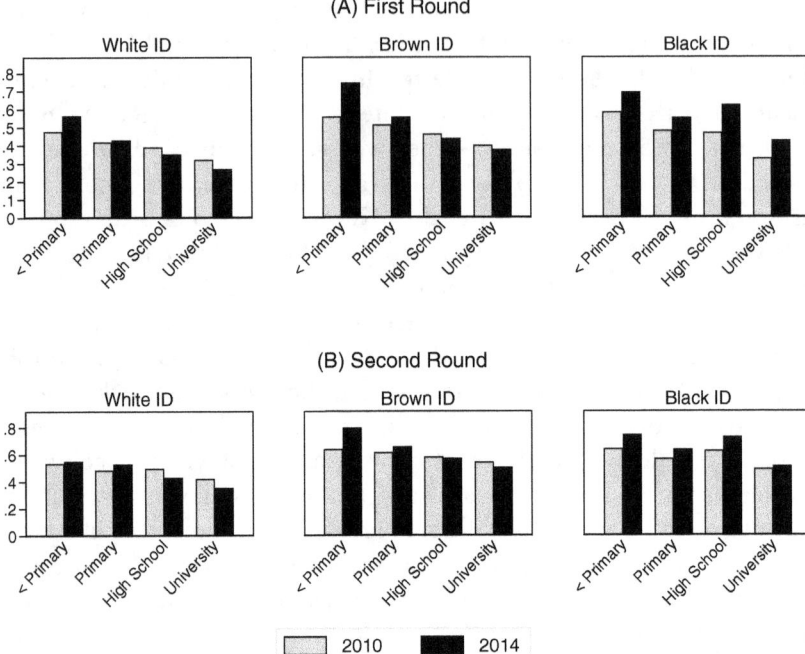

FIGURE 7.12 Electoral support for Rousseff by education and racial ID, 2010 versus 2014

to participate in the 2013 protests. Thus, although among protesters black Brazilians showed signs of greater dissatisfaction, highly educated black voters appear less likely than their highly educated counterparts to appear among protesters.

Figure 7.12 compares PT electoral support between 2010 and 2014. Among white and brown identifiers, Rousseff registers marginal increases among lesser educated voters, and marginal decreases among better educated voters in both election rounds. Among black identifiers, however, Rousseff improves her margins across all education levels and in both rounds of voting. What exactly is behind this improvement is unclear; it could easily be Rousseff's demonstrated intolerance for corruption (Balán 2014) or the continuity with Lula's social program agenda immensely popular with low-income beneficiaries and educated black voters who prefer leftist policies. The 2010 election may also have been a function of uncertainty regarding continuity with Lula, or fatigue with the incumbent PT. What is clear is that with each passing election the PT is relying on an increasingly narrow electoral base anchored first and foremost by the poor beneficiaries of its social program agenda. The 2013 protests did little to weaken the PT electorally despite clear dissatisfaction, or to upset the PT–PSDB rivalry that has characterized Brazilian elections since 1994. Educated black voters did not appear to enthusiastically support the PT in 2010, opting instead for the leftist alternative in the first round; but the rebound in support for the PT in 2014 suggests 2010 might have been a blip in the transition from Lula, the standard bearer of the PT, to his successor. Indeed, it's not clear that the 2010 dip in PT support among educated black voters is driven by any specific factor. Trends in PT partisanship over this period indicate no major decline in *petismo* among educated black voters. And their rates of anti-*petismo* were at their lowest level in 2010, before ticking up in 2014 (see Supplementary Figures E7.1a and E7.1b).

Thus, the leftist tendencies of educated black voters reemerged in 2014, and these would only deepen in the face of the corruption scandal that engulfed Brazil in 2015, discrediting mainstream political parties in the eyes of voters, and laying the foundation for mass disenchantment and distrust that Jair Bolsonaro would ride to power in 2018. Indeed, the corruption scandal known as *Operacão Lava Jato*, or Operation Car Wash, named for a money laundering scheme that was first discovered operating through car washes in Brasília, was a true turning point in Brazilian politics. This investigation was first revealed in early 2014 well in advance of Rousseff's reelection, and would eventually come to implicate a large proportion of politicians across all major parties.

Operation Car Wash consisted of a bribery scheme in which politicians exercising control over the allocation of public contracts, notably the in state-owned energy firm Petrobras, would solicit bribes from a cartel of engineering firms in exchange for lucrative public contracts. News of this scheme initially broke early in 2014, when a notorious money launderer was arrested. But what at first seemed the isolated improprieties of select individuals was soon revealed to be a major operation in which politicians, engineering firms, political parties, and bureaucrats participated for personal and partisan gain. Trial and adjudication of charges brought during these investigations are ongoing, but as of this writing it is estimated that more than 900 individuals and more than 160 politicians participated, and an estimated BR$42 billion were diverted, in this scheme (Bertran et al. 2022; Macedo et al. 2015). The implicated politicians include former senate leader Renan Calheiros (PSDB) and former leader of the chamber of deputies Eduardo Cunha (PMDB). The latter was removed from his post by the supreme court and later convicted and imprisoned for accepting more than US$5 million dollars in bribes. Also among the political casualties of the scandal was former president Lula, who – despite later having charges overturned by the supreme court – was convicted and sent to prison for allegedly accepting a condo as a bribe in the scheme.

Though PT politicians were not the only ones involved – and despite the lack of any evidence to implicate Rousseff personally – Rousseff and the PT were among the worst damaged. As a party that grew out of union organizing and protest during the military dictatorship, part of the PT's electoral appeal was its ethical commitments as a party above politics. Moreover, by boasting *o modo PT de governor*, the party insisted that it would be responsive to the public and would be held accountable to organized civil society. The scandal also emerged during the PT's fourth consecutive presidential term and after the public had already expressed weariness with PT governments in the 2013 protests. Opponents of the PT thus found it easy to portray the PT as the focal point of the bribery scheme.

The scandal would do little to win back electoral support from white educated voters, who abandoned the PT a decade prior. But whereas these voters primarily took to the electoral arena in 2006 to express their disillusionment, in 2015 these opponents of the PT took to the streets in massive numbers with a clear message: *impeachment já*, or "impeachment now." Indeed, in March 2015, an estimated 2.5 million Brazilians turned out in unprecedented numbers in over 200 cities to demand Rousseff's impeachment, sending a clear message that public outrage over corruption had reached fever pitch (Mapa n.d.). Rousseff would not be removed from office until more than one year later, after her fraying coalition with congressional allies finally unraveled (De Micheli et al. 2022). But over the course of the next year, protesters would continue to fill the streets. In March 2016, one year after the March 2015 protests, massive protests were again organized across the country, voicing outrage over the corruption scandal and the PT, in particular.

This wave of protests was unlike the 2013 wave, which was ideologically heterogeneous and failed to articulate a clear message or demands. The 2015/2016 wave, by contrast, was heavily populated by the conservative right – white, highly educated, and wealthy voters – sectors that were already least likely to support the PT and that exhibited highly levels of *antipetismo*, negative partisanship toward the PT (Samuels and Zucco 2018). By 2014 – even before the corruption scandal broke – 35 percent of white university educated voters rejected outright the possibility of supporting the PT (Supplementary Figure A7.1b), a nearly one-third increase over this group's 2010 level of anti-*petismo* (27 percent).

Implications for National Politics

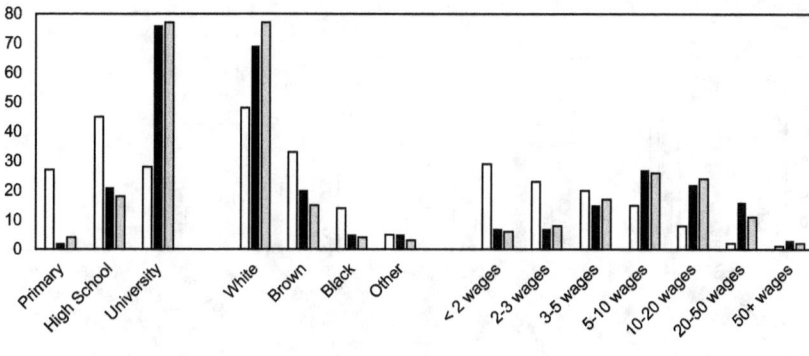

FIGURE 7.13 Socioeconomic profile of pro-impeachment protesters, Sao Paulo 2015–2016

The racial and class disproportionality in these pro-impeachment protests is clear. Figure 7.13 displays the sociodemographic profile of pro-impeachment protesters in Sao Paulo. Once again, protesters were disproportionately white, wealthy, and university-educated. Black identifiers comprise 5 percent or less of pro-impeachment protesters in 2015 and 2016.

These protests became a clear symbol of how racial, class, and regional divides in Brazilian politics were increasingly becoming channeled into the partisan cleavage around the PT. As massive and historic protests demanding the removal of a democratically elected president, these protests garnered significant international attention. Brazil was painted by international media as a once-rising star now falling from grace, an erstwhile BRICS powerhouse capable of hosting major international events (the Olympics in 2016 and the World Cup in 2014) that had descended into chaos. But perhaps unexpectedly for the pro-impeachment protesters, this attention also shined a light on the enduring challenges and inequalities that prevented Brazil from fulfilling its promise on the global stage. A photo first published in the newspaper *Correio Braziliense* was circulated in international media, capturing a wealthy, light-skinned family attending the protest and trailed by their darker-skinned nanny tasked with pushing the baby stroller (e.g., Nolen 2016).[6] This image seen around the world encapsulated Brazil's racialized structural inequalities

---

[6] In fact, the photograph captured the family of the financial director of CR Flamengo, one of the most successful clubs in Brazil's professional soccer league.

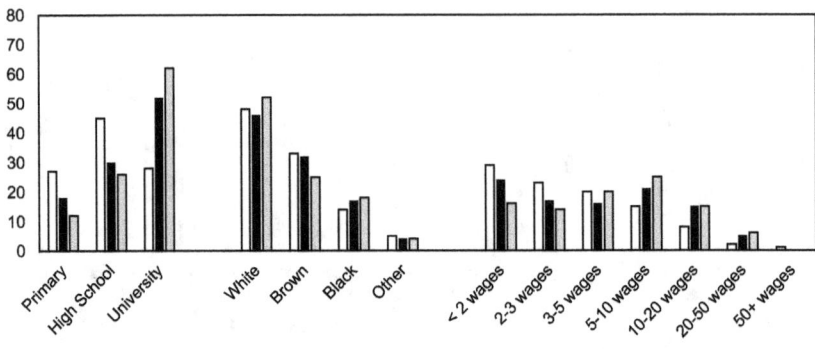

FIGURE 7.14 Socioeconomic profile of impeachment counterprotesters, Sao Paulo 2015

and the less-than-obvious ways these social structures are channeled into the political arena.

The 2015/16 protest wave was also met with counter protests. To be sure, the size of these protests was no match for the pro-impeachment protests. But the differences in social composition of counterprotesters illuminates the extent to which social structures or inequalities get channeled into other salient cleavages and identities. Figure 7.14 shows the demographic composition of counterprotesters compared to the broader Sao Paulo population. Once again, we see a disproportionate rate of university participation in the protests, though this is not nearly as pronounced as in 2013 or pro-impeachment protests. In August 2015 protests, for example, those with less than high school comprised nearly 20 percent of protesters, and the university educated only half of protesters. Similarly, lower-income groups are significantly better represented in these counter-impeachment protests. Counter protests were also significantly more racially representative than pro-impeachment protests. In fact, black-identified protesters were slightly overrepresented at counter protests. This may not seem surprising at first glance, seeing as the PT's electoral success has increasingly depended on running up its margins with low-income and lesser-educated voters. But it was highly educated nonwhite voters who turned out to defend Rousseff in counterprotests, highlighting this constituency's place in the base of political support for the PT.

Despite the efforts of counter protesters, Rousseff was officially removed from office in august 2016 and replaced by her vice-president and erstwhile ally, Michel Temer of the PMDB. Though many on the left partially blame Temer for Dilma's impeachment for coordinating with opposition forces to oust her, Temer was not exactly welcome by impeachment protesters. Motivations for Temer's disapproval are difficult to discern from available public opinion data, but one thing is for certain: Temer consistently had some of the lowest approval ratings of recent Brazilian presidents. Indeed, by the time he left office, the number of Brazilians rating his government as good or great stood at 3 percent. Temer was not well liked by PT partisans and sympathizers who, though disillusioned by the corruption scandal and the PT's ideological moderation, were not eager to welcome a conservative politician in her place, not to mention someone personally implicated in the corruption scandal. For conservatives who disproportionately blamed the PT for corruption, Temer likely seemed an improvement. But considering the never-ending series of scandals paired with economic recession, Temer inspired little optimism in the public. By the end of Temer's tenure, all Brazilians seemed to agree that Brazilian politics was due for a change.

ENTER BOLSONARO

The context of the historic corruption scandal, divisive impeachment, and economic recession set the stage for the rise of the far-right populist campaign of Jair Bolsonaro, a scarcely known political firebrand from Rio de Janeiro who would capitalize on widespread disenchantment to defeat the PT and win the presidency in 2018. With mainstream parties largely discredited by the corruption scandal, the 2018 election would be the first since 1994 that would not feature the political rivalry between the mainstream PT and PSDB parties. Instead, PT candidate Fernando Haddad would face Bolsonaro of the PSL, who waged an electoral campaign based on a message of anti-corruption, law and order, and antiestablishment politics. Like many populist figures, his claims to outsider status was rather tenuous, having served as a federal deputy for nearly three decades by 2018. Outside of his home state, Bolsonaro was mostly known to voters for his penchant for making denigrating statements about women, Afro-descendants, and gays. In the years before announcing his presidential bid, Bolsonaro attracted media attention for insulting a female politician who said he encouraged sexual violence, saying "I wouldn't rape you because you aren't worthy" (Calgaro 2014). In addition, when voting in favor of Dilma Rousseff's impeachment in 2016, Bolsonaro dedicated his vote to the military officer that tortured Rousseff during the dictatorship. Bolsonaro also once told black movement protesters to "go back to the zoo," and said that residents of *quilombos* (maroon communities of former runaway slaves) "do nothing" and "aren't even good for procreation" (Congresso em Foco 2017; Pragmatismo 2013). Bolsonaro has also described himself as proudly homophobic, and said he would be "incapable of loving a homosexual son" (Phillips 2018).

This offensive rhetoric positioned Bolsonaro well to launch a "tell it like it is" campaign focusing on security and corruption. Bolsonaro would capitalize on public disillusionment in the aftermath of the corruption scandal and historic levels of *antipetismo*. Bolsonaro's campaign garnered international attention as part of the global wave of right-wing populism and because Bolsonaro's politics was antithetical to the socially inclusive agenda of the PT, once celebrated abroad as the steward of a rising Brazil.

Observers of the 2018 election also offered two competing narratives on Bolsonaro's appeal, or lack thereof, to nonwhite voters. In one view, 2018 was seen as yet another example of the country's paradoxical racial politics: significant shares of black and brown voters were said to support Bolsonaro despite his inflammatory racial rhetoric targeting Afrodescendants and progressive racial policies like affirmative action (Caleiro 2018; Calgaro and Caram 2017; G1 Rio 2017). Journalists in particular remarked on the surprising levels of support Bolsonaro managed to garner from these voters (Agence France-Presse 2018; Sousa 2018; Spektor 2018). According to two such journalists, Bolsonaro was "the top candidate" of nonwhite voters, who were "entranced" by Bolsonaro even "while [he] insult[ed] them" (Faiola and Lopes 2018). Thus, 2018 was "business as usual" – race was deemed irrelevant to electoral preferences or outcomes, even among the ostensible targets of racism.

In contrast, others have argued that the 2018 election was a significant departure from the past. In this view, Bolsonaro's candidacy and his racial rhetoric signaled an unprecedented electoral salience of race in Brazilian elections (Avendaño and Gortázar 2018; Layton et al. 2021; Silva and Larkins 2019). Previously, political scientists argued that few social cleavages or differences found expression in the political arena (Mainwaring 1999; Samuels 2006), and that campaign strategies of courting votes along racial lines have led to electoral defeat (Mitchell 2009; Oliveira 2007). Bolsonaro's rhetoric therefore signaled that 2018 was different, and consequently voters had good and inescapable reasons to factor racial identities into electoral calculations. From this perspective, race was relevant to voters in 2018 in ways it simply was not before.

There is no denying that Bolsonaro was able to garner significant levels of support from Brazilians of all stripes, due to several factors. First, Lula, was disqualified from the election after being convicted for corruption – charges that were overturned only years later. This was a boon to Bolsonaro, who consistently trailed Lula in polls. Lula's replacement, former Minister of Education and São Paulo Mayor Fernando Haddad (PT), failed to generate similar levels of name recognition or enthusiasm from voters and consistently underperformed Lula. Second, the context of crisis, scandal, and the discrediting of mainstream political parties was fertile ground for an outsider politician to win office. Whether voters felt Bolsonaro truly represented their political preferences, or simply saw in his candidacy the opportunity to send a message to the political establishment, many voters found something to like in Bolsonaro's right-wing populist campaign. Third, and in particular for black voters, though Bolsonaro's rhetoric is often deemed racist, Bolsonaro denies that he himself is racist (Bolsonaro nega ser racista ao dizer que salvou colega negro do Exército 2019) and maintained public relationships with prominent black (and conservative) politicians, such as Hélio Negão (PSL), a federal deputy from Rio de Janeiro. Additionally, when prominent *capoeirista*, Moa do Katendê, was killed in a politically motivated stabbing during the 2018 campaign, Bolsonaro was quick to lament his death and condemn the use of violence (Bolsonaro comenta 2018). This public posturing may have shored up support among conflicted Bolsonaro sympathizers or ambivalent PT defectors, or at the very least introduced noise into the relationship between racial ID and Bolsonaro support. For all of these reasons, black support for Bolsonaro may well appear higher in Brazil than one might expect given characterizations of his campaign and presidency as racist.

While black voters did not reject Bolsonaro wholesale, neither characterization of the 2018 election – that race remains irrelevant or was newly salient – accurately captures the role of race in this election, or prior elections for that matter. Some black voters exhibited surprising support for Bolsonaro, but not all; and it would not be accurate to characterize nonwhite voters as "enchanted" with Bolsonaro. Figure 7.15 displays predicted probabilities of first-round Bolsonaro support in 2018 according to racial ID and education.[7] Bolsonaro receives his greatest levels of support from white and brown identifiers, especially those with

---

[7] See De Micheli (2023) for further analysis of racial voting in the 2018 election.

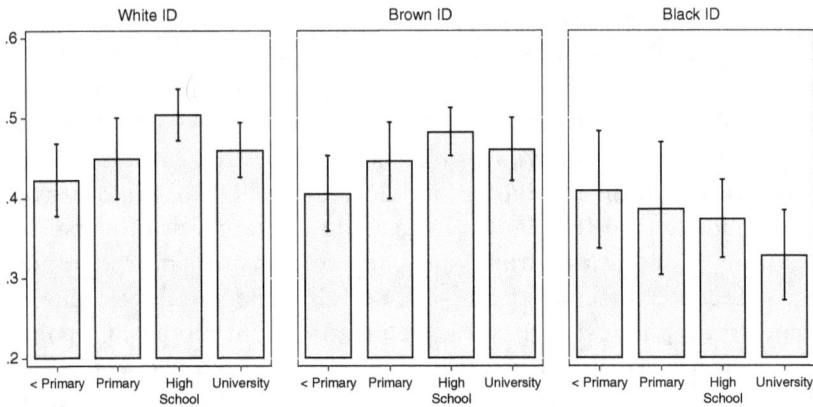

FIGURE 7.15 First-round Bolsonaro support by education and racial ID, 2018 Probabilities account for blank/null votes and control for age, sex, party ID, income, religion, and region.

high school education.[8] In this election, brown voters behaved more similarly to white voters than black voters. Among white and brown voters, there is a positive relationship between education and Bolsonaro support, though this is not monotonic. Among black identifiers, by contrast, education has a negative effect on Bolsonaro support in the first round of voting, decreasing this probability from 41 to 33 percent ($p < 0.1$) among

[8] The peak support for Bolsonaro among the high school-educated is noteworthy. And while by and large university-educated voters fit the broader educational trend for white and brown voters, in this election there is a noticeable dip in Bolsonaro support among the university educated. It is not entirely obvious why this is the case. One possibility is that the university-educated are more likely to reject populist campaign strategies. But this does not explain why Bolsonaro received such high support from the high school-educated. One possibility that this group was in a more precarious economic position and less able to weather the series of economic problems that ensued after 2014. Based on ethnography conducted in the predominantly white state of Rio Grande do Sul, Pinheiro-Machado and Scalco (2020) argue that voters who attained self-empowerment and efficacy from the economic success and poverty-targeting of the PT years are Bolsonaro supporters. They argue economic prosperity turned to disillusionment as upward mobility came to a halt in the face of economic crisis. Men in this previously ascendant sector were especially likely to support Bolsonaro, who offered simple solutions to the complex and chaotic problems that had been roiling Brazil for years and inspiring unending pessimism. A similar argument is made by Junge et al. (2023), who find that individuals who experienced upward mobility prior to 2015 and downward mobility after exhibited higher levels of *antipetismo*. Though it can't be verified with my data, it's possible that the high school educated fit these profiles. Either way, as with prior narratives around major events in Brazil's electoral arena, this story may be true for white and brown voters, but not necessarily for black voters.

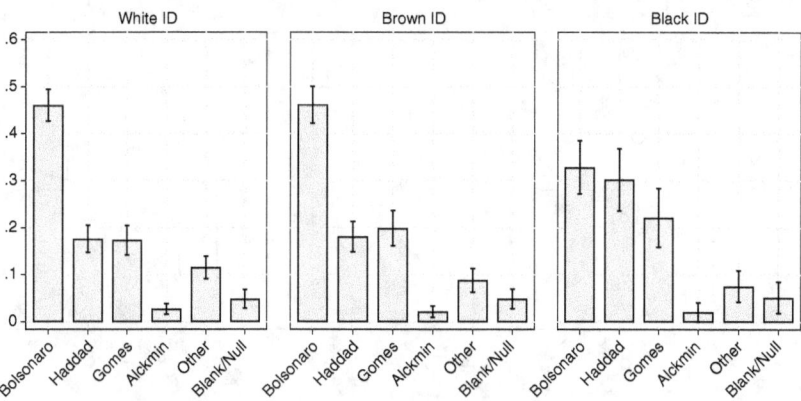

FIGURE 7.16 First-round vote choice of university-educated by racial ID, 2018

the least and most educated, respectively. Because the effects of education move Bolsonaro support in different directions, differences *between* racial groups are significant only among the highly educated. Only highly educated black voters are (13 points) less likely to support Bolsonaro relative to their white counterparts ($p < 0.01$). Not all nonwhite voters responded similarly to Bolsonaro's candidacy. Once again, racial identification and education interacted to shape electoral support, this time between and within racial categories.

Black opposition to Bolsonaro is even more evident when considering the full choice set available to first-round voters. Figure 7.16 displays the first-round preferences of university-educated voters by racial ID. At first glance, this figure appears to show Bolsonaro as the clear favorite of all university-educated voters. This is clearly the case for white and brown identifiers with university education, near majorities of whom prefer Bolsonaro outright. By contrast, university-educated black voters are split in their preferences. First, Bolsonaro support is significantly lower among black voters (33 percent) than among white and brown voters (roughly 45 percent, $p < 0.001$). Second, educated black support for Bolsonaro and Haddad are statistically indistinguishable, meaning that Bolsonaro is not the clear first preference among these voters. Third, trailing Haddad in third is Ciro Gomes of the Democratic Workers Party (PDT), a former cabinet official to Lula and leftist rival to the PT. The fracturing of support for Haddad and Gomes obscures the leftist loyalties of these voters in a dynamic similar to 2010, when they were split between PT candidate Rousseff and leftist alternative Marina Silva of the Green Party. In 2018, combined black support for both leftist candidates amounts

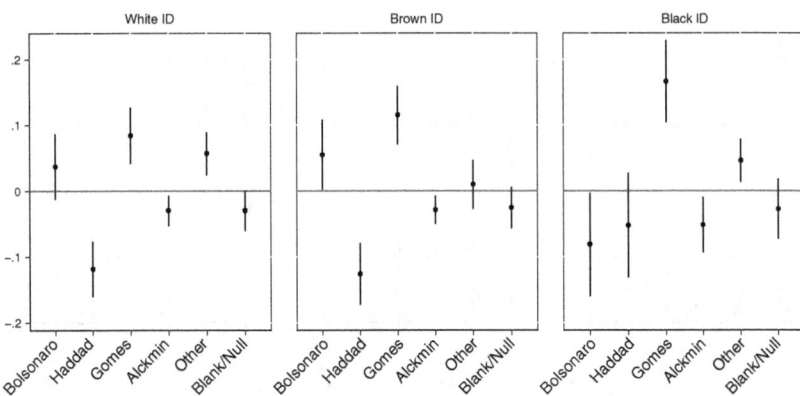

FIGURE 7.17 Average marginal effect of university education on first-round electoral support by racial ID, 2018
The figure displays 90 percent confidence intervals.

to 52 percent, 20 points higher than black support for Bolsonaro and 17 points higher than the combined support for Bolsonaro and Geraldo Alckmin (PSDB), the mainstream conservative alternative to Bolsonaro. On balance, university-educated black voters prefer a leftist candidate outright, unlike their white and brown counterparts.

Leftist preferences are not entirely absent among white and brown voters, of course. But examining the marginal effects of education on the preferences of different racial groups, as displayed in Figure 7.17, highlights the conditional effects of education on support for the left or the right. Among white and brown identifiers, university education (vis-à-vis less than primary education) shifts support from both mainstream parties (Haddad of the PT and Alckmin of the PSDB) toward Gomes, but has little effect on the probability of supporting Bolsonaro. Among brown identifiers, there is suggestive evidence that Bolsonaro benefits, but this estimate falls shy of statistical significance. The net effect of education among these groups, then, does not chip into Bolsonaro's formidable support among these groups, and therefore does not disrupt the left–right balance in electoral preferences. By contrast, among black identifiers, university education has little impact on support for the PT candidate Haddad, while decreasing support for Bolsonaro and Alckmin, the two conservative candidates. Among black identifiers, then, the net effect of university education in this election shifts support away from conservatives and toward leftists.

The fragmentation of left support among black identifiers thus obscures continuity in the relationship between education and leftist

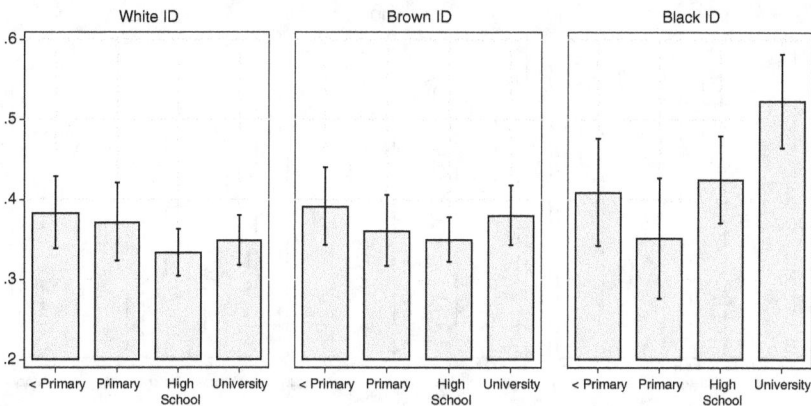

FIGURE 7.18 First-round support for leftist candidate (Haddad or Gomes), by education and racial ID, 2018

preferences among black identifiers. Figure 7.18 presents predicted probabilities of support either Fernando Haddad or Ciro Gomes in the first round of the 2018 Election. Among white and brown identifiers, education appears to decrease support for leftist candidates, if anything. The high school-educated are least supportive of leftist candidates, mirroring their support for Bolsonaro earlier; but support ticks up slightly among the university-educated. Among black identifiers, voters with primary education appear less supportive of leftist candidates – likely a function of their loyalty to the PT and only the PT. But there is a positive, if non-monotonic, relationship between education and leftist support among black voters. With combined support over 50 percent, university-educated black voters exhibit the highest support for leftist candidates in the first round of voting. Indeed, they are the only slice of the electorate that prefer the left in a majority, and they do so in significantly larger numbers (52 percent) than university-educated voters of other racial identifications (35 and 38 percent among white and brown identifiers, respectively). Analysis of combined support for Bolsonaro and Alckmin, the alternative and mainstream conservative candidates, mirrors these patterns (see Supplementary Figure E7.2).

As in previous elections, black voters overcome their disagreements on the left and exhibit a greater degree of electoral cohesion around the PT candidate in the second round of voting. Figure 7.19 presents predicted probabilities of Bolsonaro support in this round. Highly educated white and brown identifiers prefer the conservative candidate – though

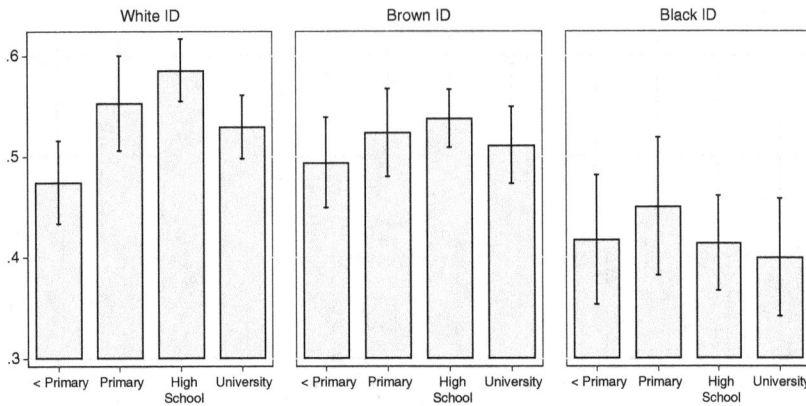

FIGURE 7.19 Second-round Bolsonaro support by education and racial ID, 2018

this relationship is again non-monotonic: the high school-educated are the strongest supporters of Bolsonaro. Bolsonaro captures 59 and 54 percent of white and brown voters with high school education, respectively – 14 and 19 points more than black identifiers with the same education (40 percent, $p < 0.01$). Though Bolsonaro support dips among university-educated white and brown voters, Bolsonaro still captures majorities. Black voters, by contrast, are least supportive of Bolsonaro, with racial identification blunting the conservatizing effect of education seen among white and brown identifiers. Black identifiers are less likely than their white and brown counterparts to support Bolsonaro. These differences grow with education, from 5 points among the least educated ($p = 0.134$) to 17 points among the high school ($p < 0.001$) and 13 points among the university-educated ($p < 0.001$). Overall, university-educated black voters exhibit the lowest levels of support for Bolsonaro when compared to other racial and educational strata.[9]

The racialized patterns of voter behavior in 2018 do not depart significantly from the pattern established after the 2005 *mensalão* scandal. In early electoral rounds, education appears to divide black voters between the mainstream PT candidate and more ideological leftist alternatives. But this division within the left masks the distinctive leftist preferences of black voters overall, as well as the positive relationship between education and leftist support. In the second round, black voters coalesce around the PT and are most likely to prefer the PT to conservative alternatives.

---

[9] See De Micheli (2023) for evidence that these findings are not driven solely by the northeast.

From this longer-term and behavioral perspective, the 2018 election may not have been as aberrational as initially thought. The emergence of an electorally competitive far-right candidate who explicitly featured race in his campaign was, no doubt, a novelty in Brazilian elections. But race was not salient in voter behavior in new ways, and nor did Bolsonaro "enchant" all nonwhite voters. Those most likely to perceive and reject Bolsonaro's racist and inflammatory rhetoric – those with high levels of education and who *choose* black identification, the racially conscious – in fact did so. In light of these findings, it's difficult to make sense of Bolsonaro's victory absent the broader political context of mass disillusionment in the aftermath of the corruption scandal, as well as absent the broader sociopolitical shifts in racial subjectivities.

CONCLUSION

In most accounts, highly educated black voters do not feature as central protagonists of Brazilian electoral politics in the three decades since redemocratization. To be sure, Brazil's electoral arena does not resemble that of the United States or South Africa, where the hyperpoliticization of racial differences structures the party system and voter behavior. Nor do black voters in Brazil always exhibit high degrees of electoral cohesion in their partisan attachments or candidate preferences. But as the analyses in this chapter have shown, it would be a mistake to disregard race altogether as a salient aspect of voters' electoral calculations. After 2002, racial identification has emerged as a significant predictor of voter behavior. The relevant question is not *if* race matters, but *how* and *for whom*.

Prior chapters in this book provided insight into the processes of racial identity formation and politicization, highlighting how educational access for the lower classes has led many to choose blackness as a function of a racialized political consciousness. The dependent variables of prior chapters – patterns of identification and the content of racial identities – became the independent variables in this chapter. In keeping with the objectives of the "identity-to-politics link," my analyses have revealed that the electoral arena is one venue to which educated black voters increasingly turn to articulate their politicized identities. Moreover, the analyses presented throughout this chapter operationalize more nuanced analysis of politicized racial identities in ways that can easily generalize to other cases in Latin America. While batteries of items probing aspects of group consciousness may not be readily available on the surveys we seek to analyze, ethnoracial identification and a proxy like education might provide an opportunity to better analyze ethnoracial electoral politics in Latin America.

Seeking to proxy for racial consciousness, my analyses revealed that increasingly over time racial identification and education interact to shape patterns of voter behavior. These patterns emerged after the 2005 *mensalão* scandal, which scholars have argued realigned the electoral arena around a partisan cleavage centered on the Workers' Party. This cleavage, however, has channeled other social identities and differences rooted in race, class, and region. While educated white voters moved to the right in the aftermath of the scandal, educated black voters remained committed leftists. But the leftist loyalties of black voters did not mean unconditional support for the PT among all black voters. Lesser-educated voters remained loyal, but highly educated black voters were divided in which leftist parties and candidates to support. Once accounting for this fragmentation, it becomes clear over time that highly educated black voters tend to exhibit the highest levels of electoral support for the left.

Though black identified voters constitute relatively small shares of the Brazilian electorate, this does not mean they are unable to exert considerable electoral influence. Indeed, African Americans have proven to be a formidable electoral constituency in the United States, despite comprising a small share of the total population. Patterns of reclassification in Brazil, moreover, have meant that black identifiers will continue to comprise increasingly large and decisive shares of the electorate. Educated black voters are more ideologically leftist, and despite their relatively small size have managed to realize some of their electoral desires. There is no denying the strong support for the PT among nonwhite voters in the northeastern states. But robust leftist support among highly educated black voters in all regions have also helped pad the PT's increasingly narrow margins of victory.

While black and leftist voters increasingly found success in the electoral arena, conservative and white voters likely reached the conclusion that competing in the electoral arena was unlikely to deliver the desired political result. This no doubt contributed to the anger and frustration during both rounds of protests that were overwhelmingly comprised of white university-educated voters – both the outcry of frustration in 2013 and the 2015/16 impeachment protests. Long considered a country with a relatively weak history of turning to the protest arena, educated white Brazilians clearly sought alternative political arenas in which to voice their demands and frustrations. When the *Lava Jato* scandal struck, educated white voters were already primed to depart from the electoral status quo, in which they hang their hopes on the center-right PSBD – a party that had failed to defeat the PT in the four general elections prior to 2018.

Whatever the true motivations of these voters, it's difficult not to see the election of Bolsonaro as the culmination of the political frustrations of white voters, who seemed unable to exert power or influence at the polls in the context of a socially and politically transformed Brazil. Though not as electorally cohesive or partisan as African Americans in the United States, black voters in Brazil have become important constituencies for leftist parties and candidates, and have largely gotten their way. By growing the black constituency and channeling them toward the left, the reclassification reversal has likely intensified the political and partisan polarization that emerged in the PT era and that helped fuel the rise of Bolsonaro. Situated in its full social and political context, then, the reclassification reversal is not only a product of the socially inclusive era of Brazilian politics (driven by educational expansion), but a force that feeds back into the same political struggles for power and inclusion in Brazil. It remains to be seen how or if the reclassification reversal and the social transformations that brought it about will survive the political backlash that culminated in the right's turn toward Bolsonaro.

8

Conclusion

"Census bureaus," writes Melissa Nobles (2000, 2), "are typically overlooked as participants in the creation and perpetuation of race." Black movement activists and their allies are wont to agree. From their perspective, the state's creation of an intermediate, mixed-race category was the institutionalization of the myth of racial democracy, an effort to undermine race-based solidarity and political mobilization among Afro-descendants. But as this book has demonstrated, race is not always uniformly perpetuated as it was initially created. Racial identifications and identities are not only subjective and often politically understood, but can also be reinterpreted and transformed over time. Despite continuity in the official practices of ethnoracial classification of the census bureau, Brazilians have come to demonstrate marked shifts in their racial identifications. These shifts remind us that the public does not always comply with the "political realities" or "ways of thinking and seeing" imposed by the state (Nobles 2002, 66). Indeed, if the reclassification reversal suggests anything about the census, it is that an individual's self-classification in an official census category can itself become an act of political resistance.

Findings from the Brazilian case also reaffirm that structural conditions alone are insufficient for explaining how or why identities become politicized. Brazil has long been cited among the world's most unequal and racially stratified societies, yet its racial identities and differences remained politically latent. Although social hierarchies and inequalities underpinned and helped legitimate the politicization of racial identities *once this had already occurred*, structure alone is no guarantee that individuals will claim membership in categories that coincide with the discrimination and disadvantage they inevitably face, let alone articulate identities in ways that make them available for political mobilization. This case demonstrates that institutions of social citizenship – the accessibility of social rights and benefits allocated by the state – can be critical to understanding the tendency and willingness of citizens to adopt and politicize identities laden with social stigma. Access to higher education, in particular, led individuals to adopt and politicize blackness as they became increasingly and personally exposed to racialized inequalities and discrimination.

These insights into the processes of identity politicization were derived from close examination of the unexpected phenomenon that I termed the reclassification reversal, the sudden shift in patterns of racial identification and reclassification in a context of racial fluidity and ambiguity. The reclassification reversal raised several questions: How could patterns of racial identification shift so suddenly? Who chooses to adopt nonwhite, and especially black, identities and why? And what consequences do shifting racial subjectivities carry for broader political developments in national politics? In this final chapter, I briefly revisit the answers I provided to these questions and reflect on the broader theoretical insights derived from this case, as well as the possibilities for generalization within and beyond Latin America.

SUMMARIZING THE ARGUMENT AND FINDINGS

In its broadest form, the argument I advance in this book centers social citizenship institutions as factors that shape citizens' subjective experiences, which in turn impact their self-understandings and political worldviews. How, when, and to whom the state grants access to certain rights and benefits can impact the tendency and willingness of citizens to center social structures in their political perspectives. In this case, the ostensibly sudden onset of the reclassification reversal can be explained both by the relative inaccessibility of social benefits in past decades, as well as the efforts to expand the scope of and access to social benefits following redemocratization – and to do so in practice, not just on paper. From the perspective of the state and political elites, the context of a newly expanded franchise increased competition for the votes of the poor masses, generating the political will and incentives to improve educational quality and expand educational access. New generations of Brazilians attended and completed higher education at unprecedented rates, and experienced unprecedented waves of upward mobility.

At the microlevel, this newfound access to secondary and university education, in particular, increased the exposure of newly mobile citizens to information, social networks, and the labor market. In turn, these heterogeneous pathways of personal exposure brought many face-to-face with racial hierarchies and inequalities in their pursuits of upward mobility, altering the personal experiences that inform their racial identifications and their political identities. That is, better-educated and darker-skinned Brazilians are increasingly coming to make sense of power relationships and their relative social positions in racial terms. The increasing adoption of nonwhite, and especially black, identities can thus be understood as an articulation of newfound and racialized political identities.

Both the actions and institutions of the state from above, as well as the actions of citizens from below, are critical to understanding the timing of the reclassification reversal and politicization of racial identities. Structural conditions long seemed ripe for the politicization of blackness and contestation of racial hierarchies and discrimination. But it was not until the era of social inclusion that citizens were granted the opportunities that would lead to reevaluation of the racial status quo. In broad strokes, the argument I develop in this book draws attention to the ways in which citizenship institutions (the accessibility of education) interact with social structures (social hierarchies and inequalities) to shape the subjective experiences of citizens and the processes of identity formation and politicization at the individual level.

After developing the puzzle and theory in Chapters 2 and 3, I proceeded to analysis in Chapters 4 through 7. Chapter 4 drew on in-depth interview and survey data to illustrate and test the causal pathways through which education impacts racial consciousness and identification. Interviews with reclassifiers revealed that, at the microlevel, education impacted racial subjectivities by increasing individuals' personal *exposure* to new information, social networks, and the labor market: by increasing the knowledge of Brazilian history and the extent of racial inequality, introducing them to more capacious understandings of race and blackness, and increasing their perceptions of racial discrimination in the workplace and other high-status locales. In these ways, education directly and indirectly impacts the personal experiences that inform individuals' self-understandings and the logics of racial identification. Analysis of survey data from the 1980s through the 2000s confirmed several of the insights of qualitative data: the *direction* of education's impact on black identification flipped from negative to positive between 1986 and 2008 (as education became more inclusive); and education and skin tone interact to shape racial consciousness and black identification. In sum, darker-skinned and better-educated Brazilians are most likely to exhibit racial consciousness and to choose black identification.

Chapter 5 sought to systematically test the longitudinal implications of this hypothesis with panel analysis of microlevel and municipal census data. Longitudinal analysis of birth cohorts showed that between the early 1990s and mid 2010s, highly educated Brazilians exhibited the greatest growth in nonwhite identification. Fixed-effects analysis of Brazilian municipalities also revealed that locales that experienced greater expansion of high school and university enrollments similarly saw the greatest increases in black identification. Moreover, increases in black identification were not unique to states with race-targeted affirmative action. Even in states without such laws, educational expansion correlated positively with reclassification. Chapter 6 further interrogated the impacts of affirmative action, the dominant alternative explanation for mass identity change of this sort. Survey experiments and difference-in-differences analyses of municipalities and federal university students provided mixed results. In the end, we could conclude only that, as a public policy designed to expand educational access, affirmative action provided an added boost to the effects of educational expansion. But the reclassification reversal could neither be reduced to new incentives generated by affirmative action, nor could we conclude that reclassification was contingent upon affirmative action laws.

Finally, Chapter 7 sought to identify the consequences of the reclassification reversal for broader political developments in the Brazilian case. Based on the notion that high levels of education and black identification proxy for racial consciousness, I argued that if this argument carried implications for political behavior, we ought to find that subjective racial identification and education interact to shape voter behavior in analysis of in national surveys. Indeed, my analyses of electoral behavior between 2002 and 2018 revealed that highly educated black voters have come to comprise a growing but overlooked leftist constituency in Brazilian electoral politics. More ideologically leftist than both lesser-educated black and highly educated white counterparts, these voters have exhibited an underappreciated loyalty to leftist candidates and parties. Most notably, these voters were loyal to the PT in the wake of the 2005 corruption scandal, which cost the party the support of educated white voters, and since have wrestled between supporting the center-left PT or more ideological alternatives. By identifying the consequences of these patterns for political behavior, this chapter highlighted the electoral arena as a venue in which the racially conscious seek to articulate their newfound and racialized political identities.

LESSONS FOR IDENTITY POLITICS

Centering Constructivism

The findings of this study carry implications most directly for debates on how, when, and why identities become politicized. In particular, the argument developed and tested in this book departs from rationalist theories that have come to dominate in the comparative ethnic politics literature. These theories have coalesced around institutional incentives as the primary determinants of the identities made salient and articulated in a variety of political domains (e.g., Huber 2017; Posner 2005; also see Laitin 1998). From this perspective, identity politicization is the product of means-ends calculations, often of political elites, who identify and mobilize from above the social cleavages and differences that they expect will maximize post-electoral payoffs – calculations made based on demographic structures largely presumed stable. Voters, whose identities are self-evident and readily available for mobilization, comply with these top-down strategies because elites control the distribution of state resources in contexts of scarcity (Bates 1974; Chandra 2004). In short, politicized social identities serve as reliable and exclusive channels through which voters and elites access material benefits.

The findings of the present study ought to give scholars pause before placing central theoretical weight on demography. While presumptions of stable group boundaries and demographic structures may be valid in some contexts, this case makes clear that the longitudinal dynamics of the reclassification reversal would fundamentally complicate strategic calculations based on easily observable and readily identifiable demographic groups. Such assumptions leave little room for bottom-up processes of identity change, the (nonmaterialist) reinterpretation of self-understandings, or the complicated role that social hierarchies can play in complicating the resonance of electoral strategies with mass subjectivities. To be sure, Brazil's is a rare context that allows for wide-scale racial reclassification of this sort, and not all contexts similarly resemble its racial fluidity and ambiguity. As a result, scholars might be tempted to dismiss or assume away the complications this case underscores in unreflectively imposing theoretical assumptions on social boundaries or identities – and some may do so even when studying this and similar cases of ethnoracial fluidity in Latin America. But these patterns ought to remind us that whether assumptions of boundary and demographic stability are deemed plausible in a given context should be based on empirical scrutiny rather than on lip service to fundamental tenets of constructivism.

The potential consequences of this go beyond "getting cases right," and raise questions about the extent to which constructivist insights have been integrated into theories of comparative ethnic politics. On one hand, the considerations earlier simply suggest that boundary stability and rigidity might be implicit scope conditions in extant theories, which tend to treat demographic groups as unproblematic units in their analyses.[1] But on the other hand, these considerations ought to raise questions about the compatibility of rationalist theories – many of which are also deemed constructivist – with the fundamental and widely accepted tenets of constructivism: that social boundaries and identities are subjective, mutable, and reconstructed over time (Barth 1969). In fact, that such identity change could unfold so suddenly and in terms of *race* – an all-too-often essentialized social category that is commonly believed to be immutable, even by scholars – ought to raise the question of whether analytical simplifications made in service of theoretical parsimony may in fact assume away the very empirical implications of constructivism itself. At the very least, the patterns of mass identity change and boundary crossing examined in this book ought to renew attention to constructivist due diligence in identity politics scholarship.

Elites and Institutions

In another respect, the findings and argument of this book – that educational access shapes citizens' identitarian subjectivities and political perspectives – departs from dominant theorizing by identifying alternative roles for the state and political elites in the processes of identity politicization. In dominant theories, political elites are often the central agents of identity politicization, responding to and reshaping state institutions to maximize their own material payoffs (Huber 2017; Laitin 1986; Posner 2005). By restricting citizenship rights in the past and more recently extending them, political elites were indeed central to the institutional reforms that catalyzed the reclassification reversal. And to be

---

[1] Madrid (2012) is an important exception.

sure, political elites behaved rationally and strategically in many ways, responding to the new incentives and imperatives of competing for the electoral support of the newly enfranchised poor. However, there is little evidence to suggest that elites engaged in the deliberate, top-down mobilization of identities or cleavages that influential theories have led us to expect. Instead, political elites played a far more indirect and unintentional role in these processes by unleashing unprecedented waves of upward mobility for lower-class citizens via social policy expansion. Thus, the reshaping and politicizing of racial identities in Brazil can be better understood not as a simple function of elites' electoral strategies, but rather as a policy feedback effect – a new and racialized politics of identity generated by new, and newly expanded, social policies. No doubt, political elites deserve credit and attention for the institutional reforms they oversaw, but the politicization of racial identities was ultimately shaped from the bottom up by citizens' personal and subjective experiences.

There is, however, an important an important caveat: one major difference between this and other studies in the comparative ethnic studies literature is the focus on blackness as a *stigmatized* category in this context. Thus, an added layer of complexity to understanding the politicization of stigmatized identities is that these identifications must be adopted before they can become politicized, or find expression in the political arena. Individuals themselves must overcome the hurdle of labelling themselves with categories they have often been socialized to devalue. Stigmatized or subordinate identities – which can easily extend beyond ethnoracial categories to include class, caste, gender or sexual identities, to name a few – might simply undergo different, or more complex or contested, politicization processes than other social or ethnic identities that do not carry this same burden. My findings cannot speak directly to this question, but it's entirely possible that the politicization of stigmatized identities has qualitatively different causes and mechanisms than unstratified social categories or differences. Thus, the structural variables we consider ought to extend beyond group size or intergroup inequality, and into the affective realm of social hierarchy and stigmatization.

The Identity-to-Politics Link and Policy Feedback

This study was able to uncover these alternative causes and mechanisms by leveraging the reclassification reversal to study the "identity-to-politics link" empirically and systematically. Doing so led us to discover the critical role of social citizenship in leading individuals to challenge social hierarchies and claim stigmatized identities. By shaping life pathways and opportunities, and expanding or limiting the degree of one's personal exposure, educational institutions altered individuals' racial subjectivities, which shaped their racial identifications, political identities, and electoral behavior.

The empirical puzzle lent itself to the theoretical agenda of the identity-to-politics link, which implores scholars not to take social groups and identities for granted, and instead to problematize identity formation and politicization, as well as its consequences. The reclassification reversal provided valuable variation that could be mined for insights. The dynamics and processes unfolding on the ground in this case highlight *identification* as one the most important aspects of the identity politicization processes, yet as something that is often overlooked in studies of identity politics (Clealand 2022). That is, identification with a social category or group in question is often assumed and taken for granted. This tendency is enabled, in part, by social identity theory (SIT) – which has become the dominant framework for understanding identity-motivated political behavior. While SIT is often regarded as compatible with constructivist frameworks by making no claims as to the nature or origins of social boundaries (Abdelal et al. 2006; Huddy 2013), this framework also assumes away the processes of identity formation by taking identification as its theoretical and analytical point of departure (Tajfel 1981). In short, SIT attributes identification to prior processes and treats it as a given. Taking the case of the reclassification reversal as an example, applying this framework here would lead us to miss entirely the causes that give rise to black identification in the first place, and that subsequently help make sense of variation *within* the black category in whether racial identification inspires political consciousness and for whom race is likely to motivate political behavior. Understanding the conditions under which racial identities became politically relevant here emanated precisely from identity formation processes and identification. While SIT is no doubt a useful framework for understanding mechanisms of identity-driven *once it has emerged*, these findings and implications of this case suggest there is additional insight to derived from more fulsome examinations of the identity-to-politics link that incorporate and problematize identification as it occurs in its full social and political context.

The broad-strokes finding of this book, that the politicization of stigmatized identities can be attributed to social citizenship institutions, also adds to the insights of earlier scholarship which attributed similar outcomes to the feedback effects of citizenship. The policy feedback literature has turned to consider specific public policies, and policy usage in particular, as the factors that impact political behavior and feed back into the democratic process (e.g., Campbell 2003). The pursuit of education of course entails a wide range of policies and experiences, both good and bad (e.g., Bruch and Soss 2018; Mettler 2007). But in a developing context like Brazil's, in which large swaths of the citizenry failed to complete even basic schooling just three decades ago, the recent era of educational expansion is an important example of the kinds of feedback effects one can expect even from social policy institutions that might be considered low-hanging fruit (also see Hern 2019; Hunter and Brill 2016).

Nonetheless, the dynamics between political identities and social policy in Brazil also draw attention to classic scholarship in the policy feedback literature which similarly identifies links between social policy and identity politics. Indeed, highly influential in this literature is Skocpol's analysis of twentieth century feminist movements in the United States, in which gender-based exclusion from the franchise motivated middle-class women to organize and demand equal rights. Similarly, Yashar's (2005) analysis of the sudden and uneven emergence of indigenous movements in Latin America identifies how the state's allocation of citizenship unwittingly politicized ethnic identities. Notably, in each of these cases social citizenship institutions played central roles in politicizing stigmatized or subordinate identities – ethnoracial identities in Brazil and Latin America, and gender identities in the United States – further highlighting the role of citizenship in the identity-to-politics link.

RACIAL POLITICS IN BRAZIL AND BEYOND

Rethinking the Brazilian Case

For scholars of racial politics in Brazil and elsewhere in Latin America, one major empirical finding of this book is not only that the direction of reclassification has reversed in recent decades, but indeed that upward mobility and education need not inevitably produce whitening. These findings contradict the traditional expectation in sociological and anthropological research. As I discuss and show in Chapter 4, it is not necessarily the case that prior scholarship was incorrect about these past dynamics. Instead, what we have begun to witness is a changing status quo that is the result of the recent era of social inclusion and social policy expansion in Latin America. As long as secondary and university education remained the near-exclusive domain the lighter-skinned, upward mobility appears to have produced whitening. But as higher education became more inclusive and incorporated Brazil's lower-class and darker-skinned sectors, the relationship between education and racial identification flipped. And ever since, national statistics on the country's racial composition indicate that self-darkening, rather than whitening, has become the dominant form of reclassification in the country.

This is an important finding for scholars who center the complexity of Latin American racial dynamics in their research. Take, for example, studies aiming to understand the extent of racial inequalities in Brazil, which relies upon a racially classified population. Scholars have argued that because of racial fluidity and the expectation that upwardly mobile (i.e., highly educated and wealthier) Brazilians self-lighten, statistics on racial inequality have been likely to overestimate racial inequalities since high earners exit darker categories for lighter ones (Bailey et al. 2013; Loveman et al. 2012; also see Muniz and Bastos 2017). This is an important critique and one that follows logically from the whitening thesis. But the reclassification reversal suggests this may not be so, and only further complicates our ability to assume what it is that racial categories are measuring. Recent studies have turned to other measurement techniques, such as the color palette included in Telles's (2014) PERLA survey, arguing that this is a more reliable and appropriate way to measure what is essentially color-based discrimination (Monk 2016). But the use of such measurement tools is far from widespread on survey instruments and are not included on census bureau questionnaires – by far the most reliable data for measuring systemic inequalities. As a result, these findings should only increase analytical attention to the noisiness of official racial categories, and remind scholars that, more than anything, these categories measure subjective identifications, which can indeed change over time.

Beyond practical issues of measurement, the resurgence in black identification and consciousness, and growing extent to which highly educated black identifiers are demonstrating a greater degree of electoral cohesion, also run counter to traditional expectations in the comparative politics literature, which characterized Brazil as devoid of racial politics. Indeed, in comparative studies of racial politics, Brazil has often served as the go-to example of weakly politicized racial cleavages despite structural and historical conditions that would suggest the opposite (e.g., Hanchard 1994; Lieberman 2003; Marx 1998). But in light of the growing salience of the black racial category, and the emergence of a leftist constituency among black voters, it would be a mistake to continue relying on past assessments of the state of racial politics when characterizing or analyzing contemporary national politics in this case. Instead, Brazil's racial politics are clearly in a state of flux: there is growing heterogeneity among the population in the subjective logics that determine racial identifications and the extent to which racial identities motivate political behavior.

Certainly, any movement in the direction of politicized racial differences would move the Brazilian case closer to the United States. But it would also be a mistake to suggest that Brazil now resembles, or will resemble, the hyper politicization of race we observe in cases like the United States or South Africa. Conversely, with growing mixed-race identification in the United States (Davenport 2018; Masuoka 2017; Waters 2002), it is tempting to suggest these countries are on "converging paths" (Daniel 2010). Such an assessment may be premature, but one thing is for certain: the Brazilian case is increasingly coming to occupy a middle ground in which race is increasingly politicized for some Brazilians, if not necessarily all.

One final parallel with the United States can be found in the impact of upward mobility and class-based experiences in impacting the political content of racial identities. Indeed, the processes of identity formation and politicization in Brazil mirror the identity processes that unfolded in the United States following the civil rights movement. As African Americans experienced unprecedented upward mobility in the 1970s and 1980s, scholars began speculating that class-based differentiation among black Americans would weaken racial consciousness (e.g., Frazier 1957). Yet the opposite occurred: middle-class black Americans exhibited deepened racial consciousness based on the perspective that their individual interests were inseparable from the interests of their racial group (Dawson 1995; Hochschild 1995). This is not unlike the ways in which upward mobility increased the exposure of Brazilians to racial hierarchies and inequalities, leading them to develop greater racial consciousness and to make sense of their social positions in racial terms. On one hand, such a parallel is a reminder that the politics of race and nation-making that may have, at one point in time, set these two countries apart (Marx 1998; also see Seigel 2009) can change and transform. But on the other, the parallel also indicates that the dynamics of race and class – and in particular the experiences of upward mobility for subordinate racial groups – are important components of racial politicization. For too long, scholars of racial politics in Brazil have pitted race and class against each other as master explanations for structural inequalities in this context (see Paschel 2016b). The dynamics behind the reclassification reversal – and the parallel with the United States – suggest that the question of whether race or class matters more is not only outdated, but also overlooks a more fundamental point. Our efforts should not be spent on adjudicating the relative importance of race or class; they should focus instead on understanding how race *and* class work together to shape the lives of the marginalized.

Ethnoracial Politics in Latin America

The findings of this case likely also carry implications for other Latin American contexts, which have also seen a growing salience of race and ethnicity in recent years. Of course, one can identify similar dynamics and parallels in other former colonies dependent on enslaved labor, especially in the Caribbean (Clealand 2017; Contreras 2016; Johnson 2020a, 2020b). Elsewhere, especially where the salient "other" is understood as culturally distinct indigenous groups, there are important differences, which might impact generalizability to some extent (see Seawright and Barrenechea 2021). Whereas in Brazil the single greatest indicators of increasing racial salience lie in the resurgence of black identification and the politics around affirmative action policies, countries in Spanish America – especially Ecuador, Peru, Bolivia, Mexico, and Guatemala – have seen patterns of indigenous mobilization, the formation of ethnopopulist parties, and the influence of ethnic constituencies in electing indigenous politicians and their allies to the presidency and congress.[2] Indigenous peoples face structural disadvantages similar to darker-skinned Brazilians (Telles 2014; Trejo and Altamirano 2016). And indigenous identities are similarly stigmatized in these contexts, which likely impacts the willingness of individuals to identify as such, and limiting the ability of political elites to mobilize electoral coalitions with ethnic appeals. Although politicians have successfully combined ethnic and class appeals to win significant vote shares (Madrid 2012), the question of identification even in other contexts is likely to be central to understanding who will articulate stigmatized identities and contest social hierarchies in the political arena (Clealand 2022).

While the exact form that these politics take in different contexts will no doubt vary, there is no a priori reason to expect that the mobility-related processes and mechanisms identified here will not travel to other

---

[2] On indigenous politics in Latin America, see Madrid (2012), Mattiace (2003), Rice (2012), Trejo (2009), Van Cott (2005), and Yashar (2005).

Latin American cases, including those in which indigenous groups comprise the significant subordinate group. Fundamentally, my argument pertains to the increased personal exposure to hierarchies and discrimination brought about through social mobility, which can lead individuals to identify with social categories they once avoided. Madrid (2012), for example, argues that politicians cannot assume that voters will identify as indigenous, let alone be mobilized by ethnic appeals. And in a recent article, Faguet (2019) argues that rural-to-urban migration in Bolivia increases exposure to ethnic discrimination, which in turn politicizes ethnic identities. Moreover, cursory analysis of recent demographic trends suggests that identification with stigmatized black and indigenous categories is on the rise in countries across the region. Indeed, as I note in the introductory chapter, census data reveals that the relative size of self-identified indigenous populations has been growing precipitously in Argentina, Chile, Colombia, Costa Rica, Guatemala, and Nicaragua. The number of black identifiers (not *mestizo* or *mulato*) has similarly grown in Puerto Rico, Mexico, Ecuador, and Uruguay.[3] Taken together, these dynamics suggest similar processes can play, and may in fact be playing, out in other Latin American contexts, where fluidity provides an exit strategy for the targets of discrimination. In our attempts to understand for whom ethnoracial identities are likely to shape political outlook, preferences, and behavior, we ought to more deeply probe and problematize the causes of identification with stigmatized categories before simply analyzing membership as a correlate of an outcome of interest.

No doubt, one major challenge for comparative analyses within the region will be data availability and consistency. A quick glance across the region reveals a number of developments that indicate a growing awareness and assertion of ethnoracial difference (e.g., Arteta 2017). In addition to mobilization and electoral politics, censuses are increasingly collecting racial data, and adding new categories to account for groups demanding visibility and recognition (Loveman 2014). These developments are viewed positively by many including activists, and enable progressive policies like affirmative action and empirical examination of racialized inequalities. But for analysts, such inconsistency also presents challenges to understanding the longitudinal dynamics of identification, and whether shifts in demographic composition are due to genuine identity change, or are functions of enumeration practices, for example. While indigenous and Afro-descendant populations appear

---

[3] See Table 1.1 and footnotes 15 and 16 in Chapter 1.

Conclusion 261

to be growing in countries across Latin America, not all contexts have continuously and consistently collected such data as has Brazil, creating challenges for analysts hoping to conduct similar longitudinal analyses. But at the same time, changes to census classification also presents important new opportunities for understanding ethnoracial identities and their consequences for politics, as recent analyses of the United States have shown us (Davenport 2018; Masuoka 2017). Thus, while analysts are likely to face practical challenges, there is good reason to expect ample opportunity for additional research into the causes and consequences of ethnoracial identity formation and its consequences for contemporary politics in Latin America.

BEYOND LATIN AMERICA

While the exact phenomenon in question – reclassification into stigmatized ethnoracial categories – might find its greatest parallel in Latin American cases, this does not mean that the broader phenomena in question will not translate to other social categories and other political contexts. To be sure, many contexts around the world do not subscribe to Latin American notions of ethnoracial fluidity and national unity through race mixture. But other kinds of social categories provide space for similar kinds of reclassification. An obvious example here is sexual and gender identities. Claiming an LGBT identity often entails a "coming out" process (Egan 2012, 2020). In fact, this is perhaps a much more common and widespread example of reclassification. Moreover, growing numbers of trans-identified individuals suggest a similar crossing (and blurring) of gender boundaries in Western societies (e.g., Brubaker 2016). These identities are stigmatized in ways similar to blackness, and adopting and politicizing such identities requires overcoming the hurdle of accepting and contesting the stigma one has been socialized to internalize. Sexual identities are especially likely to be widespread in contexts around the globe, but one could easily imagine that other kinds of lower-class or stigmatized caste identities might mirror the social and political dynamics identified with blackness in the Brazilian case. Thus, even where reclassification in terms of race is unlikely to occur, the structural conditions and institutional factors identified here could, in theory, travel to other contexts and other kinds of social categories.

Relatedly, even where the empirical phenomenon of reclassification, per se, does not occur, one can easily generalize the causal mechanism in this case and apply it to the politicization of identities without porous boundaries. Take, for example, identification as feminist, a politicized form of gender identity. Developing a political identity rooted in one's gender identity for many does not entail reclassification, but analogous questions would ask, as scholars have for decades, which women are likely to adopt feminist identities and which not, and what are the political consequences of holding such attitudes. In such cases, the educational exposure mechanism may indeed help us to make sense of microlevel identity politicization processes. Existing scholarship indicates there is evidence to suggest this is the case among women (Conover 1988; Cook and Wilcox 1991). But in any case, the point is that even in the absence of boundary crossing, the causal mechanism tested in this case may well help make sense of microlevel identity politicization among members of other stigmatized or subordinate social categories.

FROM RACIAL TO RACIALIZED DEMOCRACY

Readers already familiar with the history of Brazilian racial politics might find cause for optimism in the recent trajectory of racial politics in the country. Indeed, in the decades since redemocratization, the state has embraced progressive affirmative action policies, largely ceased to perpetuate racial democracy discourse, sought to create institutions for racial equity and recognition in the federal government, and has demonstrated a commitment to addressing the material and economic concerns for the country's darker-skinned masses. The reclassification reversal, moreover, signifies that increasing numbers of Brazilians are contesting the informal social hierarchies and forces that have reflected and reproduced racial inequalities for centuries. Nonwhite politicians remain woefully underrepresented among elected officeholders, but there are other marks of progress in terms of political representation. A 2020 quota law distributing public campaign funds to political parties rewards parties for racial and gender representation, combatting intraparty discrimination that distorts descriptive representation (Bueno and Dunning 2017; Janusz 2022). Consequently, the 2022 elections marked the first time that nonwhite candidates outnumbered white candidates in Brazil (Tribunal Superior Eleitoral 2022). And Lula's cabinet for his third presidential term set a historic record for the number of nonwhite appointees (eleven of thirty-seven appointees). This includes the appointment of Anielle Franco, sister of the Rio de Janeiro politician Marielle Franco assassinated in 2018, to head the Ministry of Racial Equality (Adorno and Marín 2023). That such developments in this former "racial democracy," once heralded for its colorblindness, can be tied to an unprecedented expansion of social welfare policies is without a doubt encouraging. Advances like these in one of the world's most unequal and racially stratified societies is testament to the transformations states in the developing world can deliver by working to realize the promises of citizenship for all.

But recent political developments in Brazil also serve as a harsh reminder that progress can be a bumpy road. The flip side of this optimism is a dose of pessimism regarding the future of social and racial inclusion in Brazil. Indeed, it is impossible to overlook the fact that the era of social inclusion also gave rise to fierce backlash, first in the form of major social mobilizations in 2013 and 2015–16, before ultimately fueling the election of far-right populist Jair Bolsonaro in 2018. Bolsonaro willingly deploy offensive rhetorical attacks on women, the poor, LGBT+ communities, and Afro-Brazilians to capitalize on white resentment (Layton et al. 2021; Porto 2023). And given Bolsonaro's mobilization of public backlash against progressive policies, it's no surprise that his administration targeted the federal education ministry, meddling in the administrative reforms of prior governments that sought to insulate the distribution of federal education funds from political and corrupt manipulation. During the four years of his presidency, Bolsonaro appointed five education ministers, all selected with the purpose of pushing an ideological agenda purported to combat leftist teachings in schools and to cut spending. Two of these ministers left their posts in disgrace, and one ultimately landed in prison on charges of corruption and for diverting education funds to Bolsonaro allies. Despite these scandals, these ministers nonetheless presided over historic cuts to the budgets of public universities and oversaw devastating policy responses to the COVID-19 pandemic. Many of the policies that made educational expansion possible remained intact by the end of Bolsonaro's presidency, and some of the reforms that transformed public education in Brazil were even codified via legislative amendments to the constitution under Bolsonaro's watch (e.g., Agência Senado 2020). But even despite this, Bolsonaro's actions and appointments made clear that the backlash rhetoric employed in his campaign was not an empty promise.

Bolsonaro, of course, did not create the social divisions he inflamed before and after his election. Yet he easily capitalized upon them to win strongest support from educated and upper-class white voters – those who had long abandoned the leftist Workers' Party and who have ceased to be dominant electoral players sizable enough to call the shots. As educated white voters have moved to the right, educated black voters have moved left, joining the poor in support of progressive social policies. With the significant institutional reforms and the channeling of emerging racial divisions into the partisan cleavage centered on the PT, it seems clear that the era of Brazilian racial democracy has decidedly come to a close. Talk of race mixture and racial fluidity will undoubtedly continue in public discourse, but it is difficult to maintain any claims that racial dynamics do not impact the country's democratic politics. Instead, what remains to be seen is not *whether* race will impact Brazilian politics, but how Brazilian democracy will contend with and manage what are growing racial and ideological divides within the population.

At the time of this writing, Bolsonaro has lost his bid for reelection and has been replaced in office by former president Lula of the Workers' Party. The return of the left to power will likely provide a measure of continuity with the era of social inclusion that preceded Bolsonaro's government. But given the degree of social and political polarization in the country, it is far from clear where or how Brazil's larger political crisis will end. For now, one can be optimistic that recent progress has not been fully reversed. But insofar as this study inspires optimism about the future of racial politics and the lived experiences of Brazil's racialized citizens, it must be a cautionary optimism, for the full picture of Brazilian politics is not so rosy. To the contrary, the highs and lows of Brazil's politics seem to indicate that the political dynamics that so transformed Brazilian society also contained the seeds of a political backlash that threatened the future and survival of that very progress. As Brazil's democratic institutions continue to be tested under growing polarization, one can only hope that the beneficiaries of this remarkable era of social inclusion will continue to mobilize in defense of the rights and benefits duly granted them in Brazil's new era of racialized democracy.

References

Abdelal, Rawi, Yoshiko M. Herrera, Alastair Iain Johnston, and Rose McDermott. 2006. "Identity as a Variable." *Perspectives on Politics* 4(4): 695–711.

Abrajano, Marisa, and Zoltan L. Hajnal. 2015. *White Backlash: Immigration, Race, and American Politics.* Princeton: Princeton University Press.

Acemoglu, Daron, Camilo García-Jimeno, and James A. Robinson. 2012. "Finding Eldorado: Slavery and Long-Run Development in Colombia." *Journal of Comparative Economics* 40(4): 534–64.

Acemoglu, Daron, and James A. Robinson. 2006. *Economic Origins of Dictatorship and Democracy.* New York: Cambridge University Press.

2013. *Why Nations Fail: The Origins of Power, Prosperity, and Poverty.* New York: Crown Publishers.

Achen, Christopher H., and Larry M. Bartels. 2016. *Democracy for Realists.* Princeton: Princeton University Press.

Adorno, Luís, and Liel Marín. 2023. "1/3 dos ministros de Lula se diz negro; no recorde veio de cobrança." UOL. https://noticias.uol.com.br/politica/ultimas-noticias/2023/01/12/13-dos-ministros-de-lula-se-diz-negro-apesar-de-recorde.htm (June 26, 2023).

Agence France-Presse. 2018. "¿Por qué gays y afrodescendientes votan por Jair Bolsonaro?" Clarín.com, October 23, 2018, sec. Mundo. www.clarin.com/mundo/gays-afrodescendientes-votan-jair-bolsonaro_0_DtfUl-4Py.html.

Agência Senado. 2020. "Senado aprova PEC do Fundeb, que será promulgada nesta quarta." *Senado Notícias.* www12.senado.leg.br/noticias/materias/2020/08/25/pec-do-fundeb-permanente-e-aprovada-no-senado-por-unanimidade (November 23, 2022).

Aguilar, Rosario, Saul Cunow, Scott Desposato, and Leonardo Sangali Barone. 2015. "Ballot Structure, Candidate Race, and Vote Choice in Brazil." *Latin American Research Review* 50(3): 175–202.

Alberto, Paulina L. 2011. *Terms of Inclusion: Black Intellectuals in Twentieth-Century Brazil.* Chapel Hill: University of North Carolina Press.

Albuquerque, Rosa Freitas, and Cristiane Pedron. 2017. "A trajetória histórica das ações afirmativas em uma universidade pública brasileira." *Mouseion* 28: 99–109.

Almeida, Marco Antonio Bettine de, and Livia Pizauro Sanchez. 2017. "Implementação da Lei 10.639/2003: competências, habilidades e pesquisas para a transformação social." *Pro-Posições* 28(1): 55–80.

Almond, Gabriel A., and Sidney Verba. 2015. *The Civic Culture: Political Attitudes and Democracy in Five Nations*. Princeton: Princeton University Press.

Alvarez, Sonia E. 1990. *Engendering Democracy in Brazil: Women's Movements in Transition Politics*. Princeton: Princeton University Press.

Alves, Jaime Amparo. 2018. *The Anti-Black City: Police Terror and Black Urban Life in Brazil*. University of Minnesota Press.

Anderson, Benedict. 1983. *Imagined Communities: Reflections on the Origin and Spread of Nationalism*. New York: Verso.

Andrews, George Reid. 1991. *Blacks and Whites in São Paulo, Brazil, 1888–1988*. Madison, Wis.: University of Wisconsin Press.

   1992. "Racial Inequality in Brazil and the United States: A Statistical Comparison." *Journal of Social History* 26(2): 229–63.

   2004. *Afro-Latin America, 1800–2000*. New York: Oxford University Press.

   2010. *Blackness in the White Nation: A History of Afro-Uruguay*. Chapel Hill: The University of North Carolina Press.

   2014. "Racial Inequality in Brazil and the United States, 1990–2010." *Journal of Social History* 47(4): 829–54.

Ansell, Ben W., and David J. Samuels. 2014. *Inequality and Democratization: An Elite-Competition Approach*. New York: Cambridge University Press.

Arkhangelsky, Dmitry, Susan Athey, David A. Hirshberg, Guido W. Imbens, and Stefan Wager. 2021. "Synthetic Difference-in-Differences." *American Economic Review* 111(12): 4088–4118.

Arretche, Marta. 2016. "Federalism, Social Policy, and Reductions in Territorial Inequality in Contemporary Brazil." In *New Order and Progress: Development and Democracy in Brazil*, ed. Ben Ross Schneider. New York: Oxford University Press, 162–84.

Artes, Amélia, and Arlene Martinez Ricoldi. 2015. "Acesso de negros no ensino superior: o que mudou entre 2000 e 2010." *Cadernos de Pesquisa* 45(158): 858–81.

Arteta, Itxaro. 2017. "'¿Es usted negro?', una pregunta mal planteada o ausente en los censos." *El País*. http://internacional.elpais.com/internacional/2017/01/24/actualidad/1485265647_183464.html (January 25, 2017).

Avendaño, Tom C., and Naiara Galarraga Gortázar. 2018. "Bolsonaro es el favorito de las muchas razas de Brasil, menos de los negros." El País, October 26, 2018, sec. America. https://elpais.com/internacional/2018/10/25/america/1540500511_296680.html

Bachrachand, Peter, and Morton S. Baratz. 1962. "Two Faces of Power." *American Political Science Review* 56(4): 947–52.

Bailey, Stanley R. 2002. "The Race Construct and Public Opinion: Understanding Brazilian Beliefs about Racial Inequality and Their Determinants." *American Journal of Sociology* 108(2): 406–39.
  2008. "Unmixing for Race Making in Brazil." *American Journal of Sociology* 114(3): 577–614.
  2009. *Legacies of Race: Identities, Attitudes, and Politics in Brazil*. Stanford, Calif.: Stanford University Press.
Bailey, Stanley R., and Edward E. Telles. 2006. "Multiracial versus Collective Black Categories: Examining Census Classification Debates in Brazil." *Ethnicities* 6(1): 74–101.
Bailey, Stanley R., and Fabrício M. Fialho. 2018. "Shifting Racial Subjectivities and Ideologies in Brazil." *Socius* 4: 1–12.
Bailey, Stanley R., Fabrício Fialho, and Mara Loveman. 2018. "How States Make Race: New Evidence from Brazil." *Sociological Science* 5: 722–51.
Bailey, Stanley R., Fabrício Fialho, and Michelle Peria. 2018. "Support for Race-Targeted Affirmative Action in Brazil." *Ethnicities* 18(6): 765–98.
Bailey, Stanley R., Mara Loveman, and Jeronimo O. Muniz. 2013. "Measures of 'Race' and the Analysis of Racial Inequality in Brazil." *Social Science Research* 42(1): 106–19.
Balán, Manuel. 2014. "Surviving Corruption in Brazil: Lula's and Dilma's Success Despite Corruption Allegations, and Its Consequences." *Journal of Politics in Latin America* 6(3): 67–93.
Bartels, Larry M. 2002. "Beyond the Running Tally: Partisan Bias in Political Perceptions." *Political Behavior* 24(2): 117–50.
Barth, Fredrik. 1969. *Ethnic Groups and Boundaries: The Social Organization of Culture Difference*. Long Grove: Waveland Press.
Bartolini, Stefano, and Peter Mair. 1990. *Identity, Competition, and Electoral Availability: The Stabilisation of European Electorates 1885–1985*. New York: Cambridge University Press.
Bates, Robert H. 1974. "Ethnic Competition and Modernization in Contemporary Africa." *Comparative Political Studies* 6(4): 457–84.
Benedito, Vera Lucia. 2015. "Equal Opportunity Policy in Brazil: Black Activism and the State." In *Race, Politics, and Education in Brazil: Affirmative Action in Higher Education*, eds. Ollie A. Johnson III and Rosana Heringer. New York: Palgrave Macmillan, 73–94.
Berquó, Elza, and Luiz Felipe de Alencastro. 1992. "A emergência do voto negro." *Novos Estudos* 33: 77–88.
Bertran, Maria Paula et al. 2022. "Neutralidade e viés judicial: Filiação partidária e os réus da Operação Lava Jato." https://preprints.scielo.org/index.php/scielo/preprint/view/4689 (November 15, 2022).
Birdsall, Nancy, and Richard H. Sabot, eds. 1996. *Opportunity Foregone: Education in Brazil*. Washington, D.C.: Inter-American Development Bank.
Blair, Graeme, and Kosuke Imai. 2012. "Statistical Analysis of List Experiments." *Political Analysis* 20(1): 47–77.
Bleck, Jaimie. 2015. *Education and Empowered Citizenship in Mali*. Baltimore: Johns Hopkins University Press.

Blumer, Herbert. 1958. "Race Prejudice as a Sense of Group Position." *The Pacific Sociological Review* 1(1): 3–7.
Bobo, Lawrence D. 1999. "Prejudice as Group Position: Microfoundations of a Sociological Approach to Racism and Race Relations." *Journal of Social Issues* 55(3): 445–72.
Boix, Carles. 2003. *Democracy and Redistribution.* New York: Cambridge University Press.
"Bolsonaro nega ser racista ao dizer que salvou colega negro do Exército." 2019. *Exame.* https://exame.com/brasil/na-tv-bolsonaro-nega-ser-racista-e-diz-que-salvou-colega-negro-do-exercito/ (October 13, 2022).
Bourdieu, Pierre. 1985. "The Social Space and the Genesis of Groups." *Theory and Society* 14(6): 723–44.
Bourdieu, Pierre, and Loïc Wacquant. 1999. "On the Cunning of Imperialist Reason." *Theory, Culture & Society* 16(1): 41–58.
Brubaker, Rogers. 2004. *Ethnicity Without Groups.* Cambridge: Harvard University Press.
  2016. *Trans: Gender and Race in an Age of Unsettled Identities.* Princeton: Princeton University Press.
Brubaker, Rogers, and Frederick Cooper. 2000. "Beyond 'Identity.'" *Theory and Society* 29: 1–47.
Brubaker, Rogers, Mara Loveman, and Peter Stamatov. 2004. "Ethnicity as Cognition." *Theory and Society* 33(1): 31–64.
Bruch, Sarah K., and Joe Soss. 2018. "Schooling as a Formative Political Experience: Authority Relations and the Education of Citizens." *Perspectives on Politics* 16(01): 36–57.
Bueno, Natália S., and Thad Dunning. 2017. "Race, Resources, and Representation: Evidence from Brazilian Politicians." *World Politics* 69(2): 327–65.
Bueno, Natália S., and Fabrício Mendes Fialho. 2009. "Race, Resources, and Political Participation in a Brazilian City." *Latin American Research Review* 44(2): 59–83.
Burdick, John. 1998a. *Blessed Anastacia: Women, Race and Popular Christianity in Brazil.* New York: Routledge.
  1998b. "The Lost Constituency of Brazil's Black Movements." *Latin American Perspectives* 25(1): 136–55.
Caldwell, Kia. 2007. *Negras in Brazil: Re-Envisioning Black Women, Citizenship, and the Politics of Identity.* New Brunswick: Rutgers University Press.
Caleiro, João Pedro. 2018. "Bolsonaro promete fim do 'coitadismo' de negro, gay, mulher e nordestino." Exame, October 23, 2018. https://exame.com/brasil/bolsonaro-promete-fim-do-coitadismo-de-negro-gay-mulher-e-nordestino/.
Calgaro, Fernanda. 2014. "Bolsonaro repete que não estupra deputada porque ela 'não merece.'" *Globo G1.* http://g1.globo.com/politica/noticia/2014/12/bolsonaro-repete-que-nao-estupra-deputada-porque-ela-nao-merece.html (October 13, 2022).
Calgaro, Fernanda, and Bernardo Caram. 2017. "Parlamentares de PT e PCdoB pedem para PGR apurar se Bolsonaro cometeu racismo." G1, April 6, 2017. https://g1.globo.com/politica/noticia/parlamentares-de-pt-e-pcdob-pedem-para-pgr-apurar-se-bolsonaro-cometeu-racismo.ghtml.

Campante, Filipe R., Anna R. V. Crespo, and Phillippe G. P. G. Leite. 2004. "Desigualdade salarial entre raças no mercado de trabalho urbano brasileiro: aspectos regionais." *Revista Brasileira de Economia* 58(2): 185–210.
Campbell, Andrea Louise. 2003. *How Policies Make Citizens: Senior Political Activism and the American Welfare State*. Princeton University Press.
2012. "Policy Makes Mass Politics." *Annual Review of Political Science* 15(1): 333–51.
Campbell, Angus, Philip E. Converse, Warren E. Miller, and Donald E. Stokes. 1960. *The American Voter*. Chicago: University of Chicago Press.
Cardoso, Fernando Henrique. 1995a. "Discurso de posse no Congresso Nacional." In *Presented at the Palacio do Planalto*. Brasilia: Distrito Federal, 23–33. www.biblioteca.presidencia.gov.br/presidencia/ex-presidentes/fernando-henrique-cardoso/discursos/1o-mandato/1995-1/01-discurso-de-posse-no-congresso-nacional-brasilia-distrito-federal-01-01-95/.
1995b. "Reunião de Trabalho Marcha contra o racismo, pela igualdade e a vida." In *Presented at the Palacio do Planalto*. Brasilia: Distrito Federal, 639–44. www.biblioteca.presidencia.gov.br/presidencia/ex-presidentes/fernando-henrique-cardoso/discursos/1o-mandato/1995-1/96%20-%20Reuniao%20de%20Trabalho%20Marcha%20contra%20o%20racism,%20pela%20igualdade%20e%20a%20vida%20-%20Palacio%20do%20Planalto%20-%20Brasilia%20-%20Distrito%20Federal%20-%2020-11-1995.pdf.
2001. "Discurso na cerimonia de entrega do Premio Nacional dos Direitos Humanos." In *Presented at the Palacio do Planalto*. Brasilia: Distrito Federal, 723–30. www.biblioteca.presidencia.gov.br/presidencia/ex-presidentes/fernando-henrique-cardoso/discursos/2o-mandato/2001/85.pdf/@@download/file/85.pdf.
Cardoso, Fernando Henrique, and Enzo Faletto. 1979. *Dependency and Development in Latin America*. University of California Press.
Cardoso, Fernando Henrique, and Octávio Ianni. 1960. *Côr e mobilidade social em Florianópolis*. São Paulo: Editora Nacional.
Carey, John M, and Matthew Soberg Shugart. 1995. "Incentives to Cultivate a Personal Vote: A Rank Ordering of Electoral Formulas." *Electoral Studies* 14(4): 417–39.
Carmines, Edward G., and James A. Stimson. 1990. *Issue Evolution: Race and the Transformation of American Politics*. Princeton: Princeton University Press.
Carneiro, Sueli. 2004. "Raça, gênero e ações afirmativas." In *Levando a raça a sério: ação afirmativa e universidade, Coleção Políticas da Cor*, eds. Joaze Bernardino and Daniela Galdino. Rio de Janeiro: DP&A Editora, 71–84.
Carvalho, José Alberto Magno de, Charles H. Wood, and Flávia Cristina Drumond Andrade. 2004. "Estimating the Stability of Census-Based Racial/Ethnic Classifications: The Case of Brazil." *Population Studies* 58(3): 331–43.
Castro, Cláudio de Moura. 1989. "What Is Happening in Brazilian Education." In *Social Change in Brazil, 1945–1985: The Incomplete Transition*, eds. Edmar Bacha and Herbert S. Klein. Albuquerque: University of New Mexico Press, 263–309.
Castro, Mônica Mata de. 1993. "Raça e comportamento político." *Dados* 36(3): 469–91.

Cederman, Lars-Erik, Kristian Skrede Gleditsch, and Halvard Buhaug. 2013. *Inequality, Grievances, and Civil War*. New York: Cambridge University Press.
Centeno, Miguel Angel. 2002. *Blood and Debt: War and the Nation-State in Latin America*. State College: Penn State Press.
Chandra, Kanchan. 2004. *Why Ethnic Parties Succeed*. New York: Cambridge University Press.
   2005. "Ethnic Parties and Democratic Stability." *Perspectives on Politics* 3(2): 235–52.
   2012. "Introduction." In *Constructivist Theories of Ethnic Politics*, ed. Kanchan Chandra. New York: Oxford University Press, 1–47.
Clealand, Danielle Pilar. 2017. *The Power of Race in Cuba: Racial Ideology and Black Consciousness During the Revolution*. New York: Oxford University Press.
   2022. "Las Vidas Negras Importan: Centering Blackness and Racial Politics in Latin American Research." *Annual Review of Political Science* 25(1): 341–56.
Collier, Ruth Berins, and David Collier. 2002. *Shaping the Political Arena: Critical Junctures, the Labor Movement, and Regime Dynamics in Latin America*. 2nd ed. South Bend: University of Notre Dame Press.
Congresso em Foco. 2017. "Bolsonaro: 'Quilombola não serve nem para procriar.'" *Congresso em Foco*. https://congressoemfoco.uol.com.br/especial/noticias/bolsonaro-quilombola-nao-serve-nem-para-procriar/ (October 6, 2021).
"Conheça o novo Fundeb, que amplia gradualmente os recursos da educação." 2020. *Agência Câmara Notícias*. www.camara.leg.br/noticias/687499-conheca-o-novo-fundeb-que-amplia-gradualmente-os-recursos-da-educacao/ (July 29, 2022).
Conniff, Michael L. 1981. *Urban Politics in Brazil: The Rise of Populism, 1925–1945*. Pittsburgh: University of Pittsburgh Press.
Conover, Pamela Johnston. 1988. "Feminists and the Gender Gap." *The Journal of Politics* 50(4): 985–1010.
Contreras, Danilo Antonio. 2016. "Exit over Voice in Dominican Ethnoracial Politics." *Latin American Research Review* 51(3): 202–26.
Cook, Elizabeth Adell, and Clyde Wilcox. 1991. "Feminism and the Gender Gap – A Second Look." *The Journal of Politics* 53(4): 1111–22.
Cornwell, Christopher, Jason Rivera, and Ian M. Schmutte. 2017. "Wage Discrimination When Identity Is Subjective: Evidence from Changes in Employer-Reported Race." *Journal of Human Resources* 52(3): 719–55.
Cramer, Katherine J. 2016. *The Politics of Resentment: Rural Consciousness in Wisconsin and the Rise of Scott Walker*. Chicago: University of Chicago Press.
Crenshaw, Kimberle. 1991. "Mapping the Margins: Intersectionality, Identity Politics, and Violence Against Women of Color." *Stanford Law Review* 43: 1241–99.
Cunha, José Marcos Pinto da. 2015. "A migração interna no Brasil nos últimos cinquenta anos: (des)continuidades e rupturas." In *Trajetórias das*

desigualdades: como o Brasil mudou nos últimos cinquenta anos, ed. Marta Arretche. São Paulo: Editora Unesp, 279–307.

Daflon, Verônica Toste, and João Feres Jr. 2012. "Ação afirmativa na revista Veja: estratégias editoriais e o enquadramento do debate público." *Revista Compolítica* 2(2): 66–91.

Dahl, Robert A. 1957. "The Concept of Power." *Behavioral Science* 2(3): 201–15.
  1961. *Who Governs? Democracy and Power in an American City.* New Haven: Yale University Press.

Daniel, G. Reginald. 2010. *Race and Multiraciality in Brazil and the United States: Converging Paths?* State College: Penn State Press.

Davenport, Lauren. 2018. *Politics Beyond Black and White: Biracial Identity and Attitudes in America.* New York: Cambridge University Press.
  2020. "The Fluidity of Racial Classifications." *Annual Review of Political Science* 23(1): 221–40.

Dávila, Jerry. 2003. *Diploma of Whiteness: Race and Social Policy in Brazil, 1917–1945.* Durham: Duke University Press.

Davis, F. James. 2001. *Who Is Black? One Nation's Definition.* 2nd ed. University Park: Penn State University Press.

Dawson, Michael C. 1995. *Behind the Mule: Race and Class in African-American Politics.* Princeton: Princeton University Press.

De Micheli, David. 2018. "The Racialized Effects of Social Programs in Brazil." *Latin American Politics and Society* 60(1): 52–75.
  2021. "Racial Reclassification and Political Identity Formation." *World Politics* 73(1): 1–51.
  2023. "Bolsonaro and the Black Vote: Racial Voting in Brazil's 2018 Election." *Latin American Politics and Society* 65(4): 1–25.

De Micheli, David, Jose T. Sanchez-Gomez, and Kenneth M. Roberts. 2022. "Tenuous Pacts and Multiparty Coalitions: The Politics of Presidential Impeachment in Latin America." *Journal of Latin American Studies* 54(2): 283–311.

Deaton, Angus. 1985. "Panel Data from Time Series of Cross-Sections." *Journal of Econometrics* 30(1–2): 109–26.

Degler, Carl N. 1971. *Neither Black nor White: Slavery and Race Relations in Brazil and the United States.* Madison: University of Wisconsin Press.

Dell, Melissa. 2010. "The Persistent Effects of Peru's Mining Mita." *Econometrica* 78(6): 1863–903.

Droitcour, Judith et al. 1991. "The Item-Count Technique as a Method of Indirect Questioning: A Review of Its Development and a Case Study Application." In *Measurement Errors in Surveys*, eds. Paul P. Biemer et al. New York: John Wiley & Sons, 185–210.

Dunning, Thad, and Lauren Harrison. 2010. "Cross-Cutting Cleavages and Ethnic Voting: An Experimental Study of Cousinage in Mali." *American Political Science Review* 104(1): 21.

Dzidzienyo, Anani. 1979. *The Position of Blacks in Brazilian Society.* London: Minority Rights Group.

Easton, David. 1953. *The Political System: An Inquiry into the State of Political Science.* New York: Knopf.

Egan, Patrick J. 2012. "Group Cohesion without Group Mobilization: The Case of Lesbians, Gays and Bisexuals." *British Journal of Political Science* 42(3): 597–616.

2020. "Identity as Dependent Variable: How Americans Shift Their Identities to Align with Their Politics." *American Journal of Political Science* 64(3): 699–716.

Escobar, Arturo, and Sonia E. Alvarez. 1992. *The Making of Social Movements in Latin America: Identity, Strategy, and Democracy*. New York: Westview Press.

Esping-Andersen, Gøsta. 1990. *The Three Worlds of Welfare Capitalism*. Princeton: Princeton University Press.

Faguet, Jean-Paul. 2019. "Revolution from Below: Cleavage Displacement and the Collapse of Elite Politics in Bolivia." *Politics & Society* 47(2): 205–50.

Faiola, Anthony, and Mariana Lopes. 2018. "How Jair Bolsonaro Entranced Brazil's Minorities – While Also Insulting Them." Washington Post, October 24, 2018. www.washingtonpost.com/world/the_americas/how-jair-bolsonaro-entranced-brazils-minorities--while-also-insulting-them/2018/10/23/a44485a4-d3b6-11e8-a4db-184311d27129_story.html.

Fanon, Frantz. 2008. *Black Skin, White Masks*. London: Pluto-Press.

Feres Jr., João, Verónica Toste, and Luiz Augusto Campos. 2015. "Affirmative Action in Brazil: Achievements and Challenges." In *Race, Politics, and Education in Brazil: Affirmative Action in Higher Education*, eds. Ollie A. Johnson III and Rosana Heringer. New York: Palgrave Macmillan, 179–98.

Fernandes, Florestan. 1965. *A Integração do negro na sociedade de classes*. Sao Paulo: Dominus editôra.

1969. *The Negro in Brazilian Society*. New York: Columbia University Press.

Ferree, Karen E. 2006. "Explaining South Africa's Racial Census." *Journal of Politics* 68(4): 803–15.

Fialho, Fabrício M. 2022. "Race and Non-Electoral Political Participation in Brazil, South Africa, and the United States." *The Journal of Race, Ethnicity, and Politics* 7(2): 262–93.

Filho, Irineu de Carvalho, and Renato P. Colistete. 2010. "Education Performance: Was It All Determined 100 Years Ago? Evidence From Sao Paulo, Brazil." In Evanston, IL. https://mpra.ub.uni-muenchen.de/24494/1/MPRA_paper_24494.pdf (March 6, 2018).

Fischer, Brodwyn, Keila Grinberg, and Hebe Mattos. 2018. "Law, Silence, and Racialized Inequalities in the History of Afro-Brazil." In *Afro-Latin American Studies: An Introduction*, eds. Alejandro de la Fuente and George Reid Andrews. New York: Cambridge University Press, 130–76.

Francis, Andrew M., and Maria Tannuri-Pianto. 2012. "Using Brazil's Racial Continuum to Examine the Short-Term Effects of Affirmative Action in Higher Education." *Journal of Human Resources* 47(3): 754–84.

2013. "Endogenous Race in Brazil: Affirmative Action and the Construction of Racial Identity among Young Adults." *Economic Development and Cultural Change* 61(4): 731–53.

Francis-Tan, Andrew, and Maria Tannuri-Pianto. 2015. "Inside the Black Box: Affirmative Action and the Social Construction of Race in Brazil." *Ethnic and Racial Studies* 38(15): 2771–90.

Frazier, E. Franklin. 1942. "Some Aspects of Race Relations in Brazil." *Phylon (1940–1956)* 3(3): 287–49.
  1957. *Black Bourgeoisie.* New York: Simon and Schuster.
Freire, Germán et al. 2018. *Afro-Descendants in Latin America: Toward a Framework of Inclusion.* Washington, D.C.: World Bank Group.
Freire, Germán, Steven Schwartz, and Flavia Carbonari. 2022. *Afro-Descendant Inclusion in Education: An Anti-Racist Agenda for Latin America.* Washington, D.C.: World Bank Group.
Freire, Paulo. 2005. *Education for Critical Consciousness.* 2nd ed. New York: Continuum.
  2014. *Pedagogy of the Oppressed.* New York: Bloomsbury Publishing.
French, John D. 2000. "The Missteps Of Anti-Imperialist Reason: Bourdieu, Wacquant and Hanchard's Orpheus and Power." *Theory, culture & society* 17(1): 107–28.
Freyre, Gilberto. 1986. *The Masters and the Slaves.* 2nd ed. Berkeley: University of California Press.
Friedman, Debra, and Doug McAdam. 1992. "Collective Identity and Activism: Networks, Choices, and the Life of a Social Movement." In *Frontiers in Social Movement Theory,* eds. Aldon D. Morris and Carol McClurg Mueller. New Haven: Yale University Press, 156–73.
Fry, Peter, ed. 2007. *Divisões perigosas: políticas raciais no Brasil contemporâneo.* Rio de Janeiro: Civilização Brasileira.
Fry, Peter, and Yvonne Maggie. 2004. "Cotas raciais – Construindo um país dividido?" *Econômica* 6(1): 153–161.
G1. 2019. "Protestos e paralisações contra cortes na educação ocorrem em todos os estados e no DF." *Globo.* https://g1.globo.com/educacao/noticia/2019/05/15/cidades-brasileiras-tem-atos-contra-bloqueios-na-educacao.ghtml (June 24, 2022).
G1 Rio. 2017. "MPF processa Bolsonaro por ofensas à população negra em evento no Rio." G1, October 4, 2017, sec. Rio de Janeiro. https://g1.globo.com/rio-de-janeiro/noticia/mpf-processa-bolsonaro-por-ofensas-a-populacao-negra-em-evento-no-rio.ghtml.
Garay, Candelaria. 2016. *Social Policy Expansion in Latin America.* New York: Cambridge University Press.
Gaventa, John. 1982. *Power and Powerlessness: Quiescence and Rebellion in an Appalachian Valley.* Urbana: University of Illinois Press.
Gilliam, Angela, and Onik'a Gilliam. 1999. "Odyssey: Negotiating the Subjectivity of Mulata Identity in Brazil." *Latin American Perspectives* 26(3): 60–84.
Glynn, Adam N. 2013. "What Can We Learn with Statistical Truth Serum?" *Public Opinion Quarterly* 77(S1): 159–72.
Gomes, Alfredo Macedo, and Karine Numes de Moraes. 2012. "Educação superior no Brasil contemporâneo: transição para um sistema de massa." *Educação & Sociedade* 33(118): 171–90.
Gonzalez, Lélia. 1982. "O Movimento Negro Na Ultima Decada." In *Lugar de Negro,* eds. Lélia Gonzalez and Carlos Hasenbalg. Rio de Janeiro: Editora Marco Zero.
  1985. "The Unified Black Movement: A New Stage in Black Political Mobilization." In *Race, Class and Power in Brazil,* ed. Pierre-Michel

Fontaine. Los Angeles: Center for Afro-American Studies University of California, Los Angeles, 120–34.

Gramsci, Antonio. 1971. *Selections from the Prison Notebooks of Antonio Gramsci*. International Publishers.

Guillerm, Marine. 2017. "Les méthodes de pseudo-panel: une application aux données de patrimoine." *Economie et Statistique / Economics and Statistics* (491–492): 119–40.

Guimarães, Antonio Sérgio Alfredo. 1999. *Racismo e Antirracismo no Brasil*. São Paulo: Editora 34.

  2005. "Entre o medo de fraudes e o fantasma das raças." *Horizontes Antropológicos* 11(23): 215–17.

Gurin, Patricia, Arthur H. Miller, and Gerald Gurin. 1980. "Stratum Identification and Consciousness." *Social Psychology Quarterly* 43(1): 30–47.

Hagopian, Frances. 1996. *Traditional Politics and Regime Change in Brazil*. New York: Cambridge University Press.

  2018. "The Political Economy of Inequality." In *Routledge Handbook of Brazilian Politics*, ed. Barry Ames. New York: Routledge, 375–90.

Hanchard, Michael George. 1994. *Orpheus and Power: The Movimento Negro of Rio de Janeiro and São Paulo, Brazil, 1945–1988*. Princeton: Princeton University Press.

Handlin, Samuel. 2013. "Social Protection and the Politicization of Class Cleavages During Latin America's Left Turn." *Comparative Political Studies* 46(12): 1582–609.

Harris, Marvin. 1952. "Race Relations in Minas Velhas, a Community in the Mountain Region of Central Brazil." In *Race and Class in Rural Brazil*, ed. Charles Wagley. Paris: UNESCO, 47–81.

  1964a. *Patterns of Race in the Americas*. New York: W. W. Nortion and Company.

Harris, Marvin. 1964b. "Racial Identity in Brazil." *Luso-Brazilian Review* 1(2): 21–28.

  1970. "Referential Ambiguity in the Calculus of Brazilian Racial Identity." *Southwestern Journal of Anthropology* 26(1): 1–14.

Harris, Marvin, Josildeth Gomes Consorte, Joseph Lang, and Bryan Byrne. 1993. "Who Are the Whites?: Imposed Census Categories and the Racial Demography of Brazil." *Social Forces* 72(2): 451–62.

Hasenbalg, Carlos A. 1979. *Discriminação e desigualdades raciais no Brasil*. Rio de Janeiro: Graal.

  1985. "Race and Socioeconomic Inequalities in Brazil." In *Race, Class and Power in Brazil*, ed. Pierre-Michel Fontaine. Los Angeles: Center for Afro-American Studies University of California, Los Angeles, 25–41.

Heringer, Rosana. 2015. "Affirmative Action and the Expansion of Higher Education in Brazil." In *Race, Politics, and Education in Brazil: Affirmative Action in Higher Education*, eds. Ollie A. Johnson III and Rosana Heringer. New York: Palgrave Macmillan, 111–31.

Heringer, Rosana, and Renato Ferreira. 2009. "Análise das principais políticas de inclusão de estudantes negro no ensino superior no Brasil no período 2001–2008." In *Caminhos convergentes: estado e sociedade na superação das desigualdades raciais no Brasil*, eds. Marilene de Paula, Rosana Heringer, and José Maurício A. Arruti. Rio de Janeiro: Heinrich Böll Stiftung and Actionaid Brasil, 137–94.

Hern, Erin. 2019. *Developing States, Shaping Citizenship: Service Delivery and Political Participation in Zambia*. University of Michigan Press.

Hirschman, Albert O. 1970. *Exit, Voice, and Loyalty: Responses to Decline in Firms, Organizations, and States*. Cambridge: Harvard University Press.

Hochschild, Arlie Russell. 2016. *Strangers in Their Own Land: Anger and Mourning on the American Right*. New York: The New Press.

Hochschild, Jennifer L. 1995. *Facing up to the American Dream: Race, Class, and the Soul of the Nation*. Princeton: Princeton University Press.

Hochschild, Jennifer L., and Brenna Marea Powell. 2008. "Racial Reorganization and the United States Census 1850–1930: Mulattoes, Half-Breeds, Mixed Parentage, Hindoos, and the Mexican Race." *Studies in American Political Development* 22(01): 59–96.

Hoddie, Matthew. 2006. *Ethnic Realignments: A Comparative Study of Government Influences on Identity*. Lanham: Lexington Books.

Hordge-Freeman, Elizabeth. 2015. *The Color of Love: Racial Features, Stigma, and Socialization in Black Brazilian Families*. Austin: University of Texas Press.

Hordge-Freeman, Elizabeth, and Edlin Veras. 2020. "Out of the Shadows, into the Dark: Ethnoracial Dissonance and Identity Formation among Afro-Latinxs." *Sociology of Race and Ethnicity* 6(2): 146–60.

Horowitz, Donald L. 1985. *Ethnic Groups in Conflict*. Berkeley: University of California Press.

Htun, Mala. 2004. "From 'Racial Democracy' to Affirmative Action: Changing State Policy on Race in Brazil." *Latin American Research Review* 39(1): 60–89.

Huber, John D. 2017. *Exclusion by Elections: Inequality, Ethnic Identity, and Democracy*. New York: Cambridge University Press.

Huddy, Leonie. 2001. "From Social to Political Identity: A Critical Examination of Social Identity Theory." *Political Psychology* 22(1): 127–56.

  2013. "From Group Identity to Political Cohesion and Commitment." In *The Oxford Handbook of Political Psychology*, eds. Leonie Huddy, David O. Sears, and Jack S. Levy. New York: Oxford University Press.

Hunter, Wendy. 2010. *The Transformation of the Workers' Party in Brazil, 1989–2009*. New York: Cambridge University Press.

Hunter, Wendy, and Natasha Borges Sugiyama. 2014. "Transforming Subjects into Citizens: Insights from Brazil's Bolsa Família." *Perspectives on Politics* 12(4): 829–45.

Hunter, Wendy, and Robert Brill. 2016. "'Documents, Please': Advances in Social Protection and Birth Certification in the Developing World." *World Politics* 68(2): 191–228.

Hunter, Wendy, and Timothy J. Power. 2007. "Rewarding Lula: Executive Power, Social Policy, and the Brazilian Elections of 2006." *Latin American Politics and Society* 49(1): 1–10.

IBGE. 2003. *Metodologia do Censo Demográfico 2000*. Rio de Janeiro: Instituto Brasileiro de Geografia e Estatística – IBGE.

2011. *Características Étnico-Raciais da População: um estudo das categorias de classificação de cor ou raça*. Rio de Janeiro, Brazil: Instituto Brasileiro de Geografia e Estatística.

2016. *Metodologia do Censo Demográfico 2010*. Rio de Janeiro: Instituto Brasileiro de Geografia e Estatística – IBGE.

Imai, Kosuke. 2011. "Multivariate Regression Analysis for the Item Count Technique." *Journal of the American Statistical Association* 106(494): 407–16.

INEP. 2016a. *Relatorio Do 10 Ciclo de Monitoramento Das Metas Do PNE: Bieneio 2014–2016*. Brasília: Ministério da Educação.

2016b. *Resumo Técnico: Resultados do Índice de Desenvolvimento da Educação Básica, 2005–2015*. Brasília, Brazil: Instituto Nacional de Estudos e Pesquisas Educacionais Anísio Teixeira, Ministério da Educação.

IPEA. 2016. "Indicadores." *O Retrato das desigualdades de gênero e raça*. www.ipea.gov.br/retrato/indicadores.html.

Irizarry, Yasmiyn, Ellis P. Monk, and Ryon J. Cobb. 2023. "Race-Shifting in the United States: Latinxs, Skin Tone, and Ethnoracial Alignments." *Sociology of Race and Ethnicity* 9(1): 37–55.

Janusz, Andrew. 2018. "Candidate Race and Electoral Outcomes: Evidence from Brazil." *Politics, Groups, and Identities* 6(4): 702–24.

2021. "Electoral Incentives and Elite Racial Identification: Why Brazilian Politicians Change Their Race." *Electoral Studies* 72: 1–11.

2022. "Race and Resources in Brazilian Mayoral Elections." *Political Research Quarterly* 75(3): 846–59.

2023. "The Electoral Consequences of Racial Fluidity." *Electoral Studies* 82: 1–10.

Jesus, Josimar Gonçalves de, and Rodolfo Hoffmann. 2020. "De norte a sul, de leste a oeste: mudança na identificação racial no Brasil." *Revista Brasileira de Estudos de População* 37: 1–25.

Johnson III, Ollie. 2006. "Locating Blacks in Brazilian Politics: Afro-Brazilian Activism, New Political Parties, and pro-Black Public Policies." *International Journal of Africana Studies* 12(2): 170–93.

Johnson III, Ollie A. 1998. "Racial Representation and Brazilian Politics: Black Members of the National Congress, 1983–1999." *Journal of Interamerican Studies and World Affairs* 40(4): 97–118.

2015. "Blacks in National Politics." In *Race, Politics, and Education in Brazil: Affirmative Action in Higher Education*, eds. Rosana Heringer and Ollie A. Johnson III. New York: Palgrave Macmillan, 17–58.

Johnson, Marcus. 2020a. "Electoral Discrimination: The Relationship between Skin Color and Vote Buying in Latin America." *World Politics* 72(1): 80–120.

2020b. "Fluidity, Phenotype and Afro-Latin Group Consciousness." *Journal of Race, Ethnicity and Politics* 5(2): 356–83.

Junge, Benjamin, Sean T. Mitchell, Charles H. Klein, and Matthew Spearly. 2023. "Mobility Interrupted: A New Framework for Understanding Anti-Left Sentiment Among Brazil's 'Once-Rising Poor.'" *Latin American Politics and Society* 65(2): 1–30.

Junn, Jane, and Natalie Masuoka. 2008. "Asian American Identity: Shared Racial Status and Political Context." *Perspectives on Politics* 6(4): 729–40.

Kalyvas, Stathis N. 1996. *The Rise of Christian Democracy in Europe*. Ithaca: Cornell University Press.

2003. "The Ontology of 'Political Violence': Action and Identity in Civil Wars." *Perspectives on Politics* 1(3): 475–94.

Kapiszewski, Diana, Steven Levitsky, and Deborah J. Yashar, eds. 2021. *The Inclusionary Turn in Latin American Democracies*. New York: Cambridge University Press.

Kay, Kristine, Gladys Mitchell-Walthour, and Ismail K. White. 2015. "Framing Race and Class in Brazil: Afro-Brazilian Support for Racial versus Class Policy." *Politics, Groups, and Identities* 3(2): 222–38.

Keck, Margaret E. 1992. *The Workers' Party and Democratization in Brazil*. New Haven, Conn.: Yale University Press.

Kertzer, David I., and Dominique Arel. 2002. "Censuses, Identity Formation, and the Struggle for Political Power." In *Census and Identity: The Politics of Race, Ethnicity, and Language in National Censuses*, eds. David I. Kertzer and Dominique Arel. New York: Cambridge University Press, 1–42.

Kinder, Donald R., and David O. Sears. 1981. "Prejudice and Politics: Symbolic Racism versus Racial Threats to the Good Life." *Journal of personality and social psychology* 40(3): 414.

Klandermans, Bert. 1992. "The Social Construction of Protest and Multiorganizational Fields." In *Frontiers in Social Movement Theory*, eds. Aldon D. Morris and Carol McClurg Mueller. New Haven: Yale University Press, 77–103.

2002. "How Group Identification Helps to Overcome the Dilemma of Collective Action." *American Behavioral Scientist* 45(5): 887–900.

Klein, Charles H., Sean T. Mitchell, and Benjamin Junge. 2018. "Naming Brazil's Previously Poor: 'New Middle Class' as an Economic, Political, and Experiential Category." *Economic Anthropology* 5(1): 83–95.

Kruks-Wisner, Gabrielle. 2018. *Claiming the State: Active Citizenship and Social Welfare in Rural India*. New York: Cambridge University Press.

Kumlin, Staffan, and Bo Rothstein. 2005. "Making and Breaking Social Capital: The Impact of Welfare-State Institutions." *Comparative Political Studies* 38(4): 339–65.

Kuo, Alexander, Neil Malhotra, and Cecilia Hyunjung Mo. 2017. "Social Exclusion and Political Identity: The Case of Asian American Partisanship." *Journal of Politics* 79(1): 17–32.

Laitin, David D. 1986. *Hegemony and Culture: Politics and Religious Change among the Yoruba*. Chicago: University of Chicago Press.

1998. *Identity in Formation: The Russian-Speaking Populations in the Near Abroad*. Ithaca: Cornell University Press.

Lamont, Michèle et al. 2016. *Getting Respect: Responding to Stigma and Discrimination in the United States, Brazil, and Israel*. Princeton: Princeton University Press.

Larsen, Christian Albrekt. 2007. "How Welfare Regimes Generate and Erode Social Capital: The Impact of Underclass Phenomena." *Comparative Politics* 40(1): 83–101.

Layton, Matthew L., and Amy Erica Smith. 2017. "Is It Race, Class, or Gender? The Sources of Perceived Discrimination in Brazil." *Latin American Politics and Society* 59(1): 52–73.

Layton, Matthew L., Amy Erica Smith, Mason W. Moseley, and Mollie J. Cohen. 2021. "Demographic Polarization and the Rise of the Far Right: Brazil's 2018 Presidential Election." *Research & Politics* 8(1): 1–7.

Lee, Taeku. 2008. "Race, Immigration, and the Identity-to-Politics Link." *Annual Review of Political Science* 11: 457–78.

   2009. "Between Social Theory and Social Science Practice: Toward a New Approach to the Survey Measurement of 'Race.'" In *Measuring Identity: A Guide for Social Science Research*, eds. Rawi Abdelal, Yoshiko M. Herrera, Alastair Iain Johnston, and Rose McDermott. New York: Cambridge University Press, 33–71.

Lerman, Amy E., and Vesla M. Weaver. 2014. *Arresting Citizenship: The Democratic Consequences of American Crime Control*. University of Chicago Press.

Lesser, Jeff. 1999. *Negotiating National Identity: Immigrants, Minorities, and the Struggle for Ethnicity in Brazil*. Durham: Duke University Press.

Levy, Maria Stella Ferreira. 1974. "O papel da migração internacional na evolução da população brasileira (1872 a 1972)." *Revista de Saúde Pública* 8(supl.): 49–90.

Lieberman, Evan S. 2003. *Race and Regionalism in the Politics of Taxation in Brazil and South Africa*. New York: Cambridge University Press.

   2009. *Boundaries of Contagion: How Ethnic Politics Have Shaped Government Responses to AIDS*. Princeton: Princeton University Press.

Lieberman, Evan S., and Prerna Singh. 2017. "Census Enumeration and Group Conflict: A Global Analysis of the Consequences of Counting." *World Politics* 69(1): 1–53.

Lima, Márcia. 2010. "Desigualdades raciais e políticas públicas: ações afirmativas no governo Lula." *Novos estudos CEBRAP* 87: 77–95.

Lipset, Seymour Martin, and Stein Rokkan. 1967. "Cleavage Structure, Party Systems, and Voter Alignments: An Introduction." In *Party Systems and Voter Alignments: Cross-National Perspectives*, edited by Seymour Martin Lipset and Stein Rokkan, 1–64. New York: Free Press.

López-Calva, Luis Felipe, and Nora Lustig. 2010. Declining Inequality in Latin America: A Decade of Progress? United Nations Development Programme.

Love, Joseph L. 1970. "Political Participation in Brazil, 1881–1969." *Luso-Brazilian Review* 7(2): 3–24.

Lovell, Peggy A. 1999. "Development and the Persistence of Racial Inequality in Brazil: 1950–1991." *The Journal of Developing Areas* 33(3): 395–418.

   2006. "Race, Gender, and Work in São Paulo, Brazil, 1960–2000." *Latin American Research Review* 41(3): 63–87.

Lovell, Peggy A., and Charles H. Wood. 1998. "Skin Color, Racial Identity, and Life Chances in Brazil." *Latin American Perspectives* 25(3): 90–109.

Loveman, Mara. 1999. "Is 'Race' Essential? A Comment on Bonilla-Silva." *American Sociological Review* 64(6): 891–98.
  2014. *National Colors: Racial Classification and the State in Latin America*. New York: Oxford University Press.
Loveman, Mara, and Jeronimo O. Muniz. 2007. "How Puerto Rico Became White: Boundary Dynamics and Intercensus Racial Reclassification." *American Sociological Review* 72(6): 915–39.
Loveman, Mara, Jeronimo O. Muniz, and Stanley R. Bailey. 2012. "Brazil in Black and White? Race Categories, the Census, and the Study of Inequality." *Ethnic and Racial Studies* 35(8): 1466–83.
Lowi, Theodore J. 1964. "American Business, Public Policy, Case-Studies, and Political Theory." *World Politics* 16(4): 677–715.
Lukes, Steven. 2005. *Power: A Radical View*. 2nd ed. New York: Palgrave Macmillan.
Lustig, Nora. 2015. "Most Unequal on Earth." *Finance and Development* September: 14–16.
Lynch, Julia. 2006. *Age in the Welfare State: The Origins of Social Spending on Pensioners, Workers, and Children*. Illustrated edition. New York: Cambridge University Press.
Lynch, Julia, and Mikko Myrskylä. 2009. "Always the Third Rail?: Pension Income and Policy Preferences in European Democracies." *Comparative Political Studies* 42(8): 1068–97.
Macedo, Fausto, Ricardo Brandt, and Julia Affonso. 2015. "Rombo na Petrobrás pode chegar a R$ 42 bilhões, aponta laudo da PF." *Estadão*. https://politica.estadao.com.br/blogs/fausto-macedo/o-presidente-eleito-queimou-a-largada/ (November 15, 2022).
MacLean, Lauren M. 2011. "State Retrenchment and the Exercise of Citizenship in Africa." *Comparative Political Studies* 44(9): 1238–66.
Madrid, Raúl L. 2012. *The Rise of Ethnic Politics in Latin America*. New York: Cambridge University Press.
Maggie, Yvonne. 1994. "Cor, hierarquia e sistema de classificação: a diferença fora do lugar." *Estudos Históricos* 7(14): 149–60.
  2001. "Os Novos bacharéis: a experiência do pré-vestibular para negros e carentes." *Novos Estudos CEBRAP* 59: 193–202.
Mainwaring, Scott. 1999. *Rethinking Party Systems in the Third Wave of Democratization: The Case of Brazil*. Stanford: Stanford University Press.
Mainwaring, Scott, Rachel Meneguello, and Timothy Power. 2000. "Conservative Parties, Democracy, and Economic Reform in Contemporary Brazil." In *Conservative Parties, the Right, and Democracy in Latin America*, ed. Kevin J. Middlebrook. Baltimore: Johns Hopkins University Press, 164–222.
Maio, Marcos Chor, and Ricardo Ventura Santos. 2005. "Política de cotas raciais, os 'olhos da sociedade' e os usos da antropologia: o caso do vestibular da Universidade de Brasília (UnB)." *Horizontes Antropológicos* 11(23): 181–214.
"Mapa das manifestações pelo Brasil." *Globo*. http://especiais.g1.globo.com/politica/mapa-manifestacoes-no-brasil/todos/ (May 26, 2017).

Marshall, T.H. 1950. *Citizenship and Social Class*. Cambridge, UK: Cambridge University Press.
Marteleto, Leticia J. 2012. "Educational Inequality by Race in Brazil, 1982–2007: Structural Changes and Shifts in Racial Classification." *Demography* 49(1): 337–58.
Martin, Cathie Jo. 2013. "Crafting Interviews to Capture Cause and Effect." In *Interview Research in Political Science*, ed. Layna Mosley. Ithaca: Cornell University Press, 109–24.
Martins, Leonardo. 2018. "Unesp expulsa 27 estudantes por fraude no sistema de cotas." *UOL*. https://educacao.uol.com.br/noticias/2018/12/13/unesp-expulsa-27-estudantes-por-fraude-no-sistema-de-cotas.htm (December 14, 2018).
Marx, Anthony W. 1998. *Making Race and Nation: A Comparison of South Africa, the United States, and Brazil*. New York: Cambridge University Press.
Masuoka, Natalie. 2017. *Multiracial Identity and Racial Politics in the United States*. New York: Oxford University Press.
Mattiace, Shannan L. 2003. *To See with Two Eyes: Peasant Activism & Indian Autonomy in Chiapas, Mexico*. UNM Press.
McAdam, Doug. 1982. *Political Process and the Development of Black Insurgency, 1930–1970*. Chicago: University of Chicago Press.
McClain, Paula D., Jessica D. Johnson Carew, Eugene Walton Jr., and Candis S. Watts. 2009. "Group Membership, Group Identity, and Group Consciousness: Measures of Racial Identity in American Politics?" *Annual Review of Political Science* 12(1): 471–85.
McNamee, Lachlan. 2020. "Colonial Legacies and Comparative Racial Identification in the Americas." *American Journal of Sociology* 126(2): 318–53.
McNamee, Lachlan, and Anna Zhang. 2019. "Demographic Engineering and International Conflict: Evidence from China and the Former USSR." *International Organization* 73(2): 291–327.
Means, Sheryl Felecia. 2020. "Bikuda: Hair, Aesthetic, and Bodily Perspectives from Women in Salvador, Bahia, Brazil." *African and Black Diaspora: An International Journal* 13(3): 269–82.
de Mello, Luiz, and Mombert Hoppe. 2005. *Education Attainment in Brazil: The Experience of FUNDEF*. Paris: OECD Publishing. OECD Economics Department Working Papers.
Melo, Marcus André. 2017. "Checking the Power of Mayors: Explaining Improvements in Brazilian Educational Outcomes." In *Democratic Brazil Divided*, eds. Peter R. Kingstone and Timothy J. Power. Pittsburgh: University of Pittsburgh Press, 113–30.
Mettler, Suzanne. 2007. *Soldiers to Citizens: The G.I. Bill and the Making of the Greatest Generation*. Oxford University Press.
  2011. *The Submerged State*. Chicago: University of Chicago Press.
Mettler, Suzanne, and Joe Soss. 2004. "The Consequences of Public Policy for Democratic Citizenship: Bridging Policy Studies and Mass Politics." *Perspectives on Politics* 2(1): 55–73.
Miller, Arthur H., Patricia Gurin, Gerald Gurin, and Oksana Malanchuk. 1981. "Group Consciousness and Political Participation." *American Journal of Political Science* 25(3): 494–511.

Minnesota Population Center. 2018. "Integrated Public Use Microdata Series, International: Version 7.1." http://international.ipums.org (April 23, 2019).

Miranda, Vitor. 2015. "A Resurgence of Black Identity in Brazil? Evidence from an Analysis of Recent Censuses." *Demographic Research* 32(59): 1603–30.

Miranda-Ribeiro, Paula, and André Junqueira Caetano. 2005. *Como Eu Me Vejo e Como Ela Me vê: Um Estudo Exploratório Sobre a Consistência Das Declarações de Raça/Cor Entre as Mulheres de 15 a 59 Anos No Recife, 2002*. Cedeplar, Universidade Federal de Minas Gerais.

Mische, Ann. 2008. *Partisan Publics: Communication and Contention across Brazilian Youth Activist Networks*. Princeton: Princeton University Press.

Mitchell, Gladys. 2009. "Campaign Strategies of Afro-Brazilian Politicians: A Preliminary Analysis." *Latin American Politics and Society* 51(3): 111–42.

Mitchell, Michael James. 1977. "Racial Consciousness and the Political Attitudes and Behavior of Blacks in Sao Paulo, Brazil." Ph.D. Diss. Indiana University.

Mitchell-Walthour, Gladys. 2015. "Afro-Brazilian Support for Affirmative Action." In *Race, Politics, and Education in Brazil: Affirmative Action in Higher Education*, eds. Ollie A. Johnson III and Rosana Heringer. New York: Palgrave Macmillan, 133–53.

 2018. *The Politics of Blackness: Racial Identity and Political Behavior in Contemporary Brazil*. New York: Cambridge University Press.

 2020. "Afro-Brazilian Women YouTubers' Use of African-American Media Representations to Promote Social Justice in Brazil." *Journal of African American Studies* 24(1): 149–63.

Moehlecke, Sabrina. 2002. "Ação afirmativa: História e debates no Brasil." *Cadernos de Pesquisa* 117: 197–217.

Moffitt, Robert. 1993. "Identification and Estimation of Dynamic Models with a Time Series of Repeated Cross-Sections." *Journal of Econometrics* 59(1–2): 99–123.

Monk, Ellis P. 2013. "Color, Bodily Capital, and Ethnoracial Division in the U.S. and Brazil." Ph.D. University of California, Berkeley.

 2016. "The Consequences of 'Race and Color' in Brazil." *Social Problems* 63(3): 413–30.

Morales, Daniel E. Moreno. 2019. "The Mysterious Case of the Disappearing Indians: Changes in Self-Identification as Indigenous in the Latest Inter-Census Period in Bolivia." *Latin American and Caribbean Ethnic Studies* 14(2): 151–70.

Morse, Janice M. 1998. "What's Wrong with Random Selection?" *Qualitative Health Research* 8(6): 733–35.

 1999. "Qualitative Generalizability." *Qualitative Health Research* 9(1): 5–6.

Mouffe, Chantal. 1992. "Citizenship and Political Identity." *October* 61: 28–32.

Moura, Clóvis. 1994. *Dialética radical do Brasil negro*. Brazil: Editora Anita.

Muniz, Jerônimo Oliveira, and João Luiz Bastos. 2017. "Classificatory Volatility and (in)Consistency of Racial Inequality." *Cadernos de Saúde Pública* 33(1): 1–12.

Munson, Ziad W. 2010. *The Making of Pro-Life Activists: How Social Movement Mobilization Works*. Chicago: University of Chicago Press.

Musacchio, Aldo, André Martínez Fritscher, and Martina Viarengo. 2014. "Colonial Institutions, Trade Shocks, and the Diffusion of Elementary

Education in Brazil, 1889–1930." *The Journal of Economic History* 74(3): 730–66.

Nagel, Joane. 1996. *American Indian Ethnic Renewal: Red Power and the Resurgence of Identity and Culture.* Oxford University Press.

Naritomi, Joana, Rodrigo R. Soares, and Juliano J. Assunção. 2012. "Institutional Development and Colonial Heritage within Brazil." *The Journal of Economic History* 72(2): 393–422.

Nascimento, Abdias. 2016. *O Genocídio do negro brasileiro: processo de um racismo mascarado.* São Paulo: Editora Perspectiva S.A.

Nascimento, Abdias do. 1989. *Brazil, Mixture Or Massacre? Essays in the Genocide of a Black People.* 2nd ed. Dover: Majority Press.

Nascimento, Beatriz. 2021. *Uma história feita por mãos negras.* Rio de Janeiro: Zahar.

Negreiros, Dalila Fernandes de. 2017. *Educação das relações étnico-raciais: avaliação da formação de docentes.* São Bernardo do Campo: Editora UFABC.

Neri, Marcelo Cortes. 2011. *A nova classe média: o lado brilhante da base da pirâmide.* São Paulo, Brazil: Editora Saraiva.

Nobles, Melissa. 2000. *Shades of Citizenship: Race and the Census in Modern Politics.* Stanford: Stanford University Press.

2002. "Racial Categorization and Censuses." In *Census and Identity: The Politics of Race, Ethnicity, and Language in National Censuses,* edited by David I. Kertzer and Dominique Arel, 43–70. New York: Cambridge University Press.

Nogueira, Oracy. 1998. *Preconceito de marca: as relações raciais em Itapetininga.* São Paulo, Brazil: EdUSP.

Nolen, Stephanie. 2016. "The Photo That's Become the Emblem of Brazil's Political Turmoil." *The Globe and Mail.* www.theglobeandmail.com/news/world/the-photograph-thats-become-the-emblem-of-brazils-political-turmoil/article29230399/ (March 16, 2016).

Norris, Pippa, and Ronald Inglehart. 2003. *Rising Tide: Gender Equality and Cultural Change around the World.* New York: Cambridge University Press.

OECD. 2011. *Strong Performers and Successful Reformers in Education: Lessons from PISA for the United States.* OECD Publishing.

2018. *Education at a Glance 2018: OECD Indicators.* Paris: OECD Publishing.

Okamura, Jonathan Y. 1981. "Situational Ethnicity." *Ethnic & Racial Studies* 4(4): 452.

Oliveira, Cloves Luiz Pereira. 2007. "A Inevitável visibilidade da cor: Estudo comparativo das campanhas de Benedita da Silva e Celso Pitta às prefeituras do Rio de Janeiro e São Paulo, nas eleições de 1992 e 1996." Ph.D. Diss. Instituto Universitário de Pesquisas do Rio de Janeiro.

Oliveira, Tory. 2016. "Como evitar fraudes nas cotas raciais?" *CartaCapital.* www.cartacapital.com.br/sociedade/como-evitar-fraudes-nas-cotas-raciais (June 2, 2018).

Olson, Mancur. 1965. *The Logic of Collective Action: Public Goods and the Theory of Groups.* Cambridge: Harvard University Press.

Omi, Michael, and Howard Winant. 1994. *Racial Formation in the United States: From the 1960s to the 1990s.* New York: Routledge.

Osorio, Rafael Guerreiro. 2004. "O sistema classificatório de 'cor ou raça' do IBGE." In *Levando a raça a sério: ação afirmativa e universidade, Coleção Políticas da Cor*, eds. Joaze Bernardino and Daniela Galdino. Rio de Janeiro: DP&A Editora, 85–135.

Paixão, Marcelo. 2009. "La variable color o raza en los censos demográficos brasileños: historia y estimación reciente de las asimetrías." In *Notas de población*. Santiago de Chile: UN Cepal, 187–224.

Paixão, Marcelo, and Luiz M. Carvano, eds. 2008. *Relatório Anual Das Desigualdades Raciais No Brasil; 2007–2008*. Rio de Janeiro: Editora Garamond Ltda.

Paixão, Marcelo, Irene Rossetto, Fabiana Montovanele, and Luiz M. Carvano, eds. 2010. *Relatório Anual Das Desigualdades Raciais No Brasil; 2009–2010*. Rio de Janeiro: Editora Garamond Ltda.

Papadia, Andrea. 2017. "Slavery, Fiscal Capacity, and Public Goods Provision in Brazil: Evidence from Rio de Janeiro and Sao Paulo, 1836–1912." London. http://personal.lse.ac.uk/papadia/Paper%203-draft4.pdf (March 6, 2018).

Pardue, Derek. 2008. *Ideologies of Marginality in Brazilian Hip Hop*. New York: Palgrave Macmillan.

Paschel, Tianna S. 2016a. *Becoming Black Political Subjects: Movements and Ethno-Racial Rights in Colombia and Brazil*. Princeton: Princeton University Press.

  2016b. "Beyond Race or Class: Entangled Inequalities in Latin America." In *The Double Bind: The Politics of Racial and Class Inequalities in the Americas*, eds. Juliet Hooker and Alvin B. Tillery. Washington, D.C.: American Political Science Association, 57–71.

Penha-Lopes, Vânia. 2017. *Confronting Affirmative Action in Brazil: University Quota Students and the Quest for Racial Justice*. Lanham: Lexington Books.

Pepinsky, Thomas B. 2017. "Regions of Exception." *Perspectives on Politics* 15(4): 1034–52.

  2019. "The Return of the Single-Country Study." *Annual Review of Political Science* 22(1): 187–203.

Peria, Michelle, and Stanley R. Bailey. 2014. "Remaking Racial Inclusion: Combining Race and Class in Brazil's New Affirmative Action." *Latin American and Caribbean Ethnic Studies* 9(2): 156–76.

Perlman, Janice. 2010. *Favela: Four Decades of Living on the Edge in Rio de Janeiro*. New York: Oxford University Press.

Perry, Keisha-Khan Y. 2012. "The Black Movement's Foot Soldier's: Black Women and Neighborhood Struggles for Land Rights in Brazil." In *Comparative Perspectives on Afro-Latin America*, eds. Kwame Dixon and John Burdick. Gainesville: University Press of Florida, 219–40.

  2013. *Black Women against the Land Grab: The Fight for Racial Justice in Brazil*. Minneapolis: University of Minnesota Press.

Petruccelli, José Luis. 2002. *A declaração de cor/raça no Censo 2000: um estudo comparativo*. Instituto Brasileiro de Geografia e Estatística – IBGE.

Phillips, Tom. 2018. "Brazil's Fearful LGBT Community Prepares for a 'Proud Homophobe.'" *The Guardian*. www.theguardian.com/world/2018/oct/27/

dispatch-sao-paulo-jair-bolsonaro-victory-lgbt-community-fear (October 13, 2022).

Pierson, Donald. 1942. *Negroes in Brazil: A Study of Race Contact at Bahia*. Chicago: University of Chicago Press.

Pierson, Paul. 1993. "When Effect Becomes Cause: Policy Feedback and Political Change." *World Politics* 45(4): 595–628.

Pinheiro-Machado, Rosana, and Lucia Mury Scalco. 2020. "From Hope to Hate: The Rise of Conservative Subjectivity in Brazil." *HAU: Journal of Ethnographic Theory* 10(1): 21–31.

Plank, David N., José Amaral Sobrinho, and Antonio Carlos da Ressurreição Xavier. 1996. "Why Brazil Lags Behind in Educational Development." In *Opportunity Foregone: Education in Brazil*, eds. Nancy Birdsall and Richard H. Sabot. Washington, D.C.: Johns Hopkins University Press, 117–45.

Porto, Mauro. 2023. *Mirrors of Whiteness: Media, Middle-Class Resentment, and the Rise of the Far Right in Brazil*. Pittsburgh: University of Pittsburgh Press.

Posner, Daniel N. 2005. *Institutions and Ethnic Politics in Africa*. New York: Cambridge University Press.

Pragmatismo. 2013. "Jair Bolsonaro Agride Militantes Do Movimento Negro: 'Voltem Para o Zoológico.'" *Redação Pragmatismo*. www.pragmatismopolitico.com.br/2013/03/jair-bolsonaro-agride-militantes-do-movimento-negro-voltem-para-o-zoologico.html (May 3, 2016).

Rangel, Marcos A. 2015. "Is Parental Love Colorblind? Human Capital Accumulation within Mixed Families." *The Review of Black Political Economy* 42(1–2): 57–86.

Rice, Roberta. 2012. *The New Politics of Protest: Indigenous Mobilization in Latin America's Neoliberal Era*. Tucson: University of Arizona Press.

Roberts, Kenneth M. 1998. *Deepening Democracy? The Modern Left and Social Movements in Chile and Peru*. Stanford: Stanford University Press.

2002. "Social Inequalities without Class Cleavages in Latin America's Neoliberal Era." *Studies in Comparative International Development* 36(4): 3–33.

2014. *Changing Course in Latin America: Party Systems in the Neoliberal Era*. New York: Cambridge University Press.

Rogowski, Ronald. 1990. *Commerce and Coalitions: How Trade Affects Domestic Political Alignments*. Princeton: Princeton University Press.

Rose, Deondra. 2018. *Citizens by Degree: Higher Education Policy and the Changing Gender Dynamics of American Citizenship*. New York: Oxford University Press.

Rueschemeyer, Dietrich, Evelyne Huber Stephens, and John D. Stephens. 1992. *Capitalist Development and Democracy*. Chicago: University of Chicago Press.

Samuels, David. 2006. "Sources of Mass Partisanship in Brazil." *Latin American Politics and Society* 48(2): 1–27.

Samuels, David J., and Cesar Zucco. 2018. *Partisans, Antipartisans, and Nonpartisans: Voting Behavior in Brazil*. New York: Cambridge University Press.

Sanchez Talanquer, Mariano. 2017. "States Divided: History, Conflict, and State Formation in Mexico and Colombia." Ph.D. Diss. Cornell University.

Sansone, Livio. 1993. "Pai Preto, Filho Negro: Trabalho, Cor e Diferencas de Geracao." *Estudos Afro-Asiáticos* 25: 73–98.
2003. *Blackness Without Ethnicity: Constructing Race in Brazil*. New York: Palgrave Macmillan.
Santos, Jaqueline Lima. 2016. "Hip-Hop and the Reconfiguration of Blackness in Sao Paulo: The Influence of African American Political and Musical Movements in the Twentieth Century." *Social Identities* 22(2): 160–77.
Santos, Renato E. dos. 2003. "Racialidade e novas formas de ação social: o pré-vestibular para negros e carentes." In *Ações afirmativas: políticas públicas contra as desigualdades raciais*, eds. Renato Emerson dos Santos and Fátima Lobato. Rio de Janeiro: DP&A, 127–53.
Santos, Sales Augusto dos. 2002. "Historical Roots of the 'Whitening' of Brazil." *Latin American Perspectives* 29(1): 61–82.
Santos, Sales Augusto dos, and Obianuju C. Anya. 2006. "Who Is Black in Brazil? A Timely or a False Question in Brazilian Race Relations in the Era of Affirmative Action?" *Latin American Perspectives* 33(4): 30–48.
Saperstein, Aliya, and Andrew M. Penner. 2012. "Racial Fluidity and Inequality in the United States." *American Journal of Sociology* 118(3): 676–727.
Schattschneider, E.E. 1935. *Politics, Pressures, and the Tariff*. New York: Prentice-Hall.
Schwarcz, Lilia Moritz. 2011. "Previsões são sempre traiçoeiras: João Baptista de Lacerda e seu Brasil branco." *História, Ciências, Saúde-Manguinhos* 18(1): 225–42.
Schwartzman, Luisa Farah. 2007. "Does Money Whiten? Intergenerational Changes in Racial Classification in Brazil." *American Sociological Review* 72(6): 940–63.
2008. "Who Are the Blacks? The Question of Racial Classification in Brazilian Affirmative Action Policies in Higher Education." *Cahiers de la Recherche sur l'Education et les Savoirs* 7: 27–47.
Schwartzman, Luisa Farah, and Graziella Moraes Dias da Silva. 2012. "Unexpected Narratives from Multicultural Policies: Translations of Affirmative Action in Brazil." *Latin American and Caribbean Ethnic Studies* 7(1): 31–48.
Schwartzman, Simon. 2016. *Educação média profissional no Brasil: situação e caminhos*. São Paulo: Fundação Santillana.
Schwartzman, Simon, Rómulo Pinheiro, and Pundy Pillay, eds. 2015. *Higher Education in the BRICS Countries*. Dordrecht: Springer.
Scott, James C. 1985. *Weapons of the Weak: Everyday Forms of Peasant Resistance*. New Haven: Yale University Press.
1998. *Seeing Like a State: How Certain Schemes to Improve the Human Condition Have Failed*. New Haven: Yale University Press.
Seawright, Jason, and Rodrigo Barrenechea. 2021. "Shaping the People: Populism and the Politics of Identity Formation in South America." In *The Inclusionary Turn in Latin American Democracies*, eds. Diana Kapiszewski, Steven Levitsky, and Deborah J. Yashar. New York: Cambridge University Press, 491–517.
Seawright, Jason, and John Gerring. 2008. "Case Selection Techniques in Case Study Research: A Menu of Qualitative and Quantitative Options." *Political Research Quarterly* 61(2): 294–308.

Seigel, Micol. 2005. "Beyond Compare: Comparative Method after the Transnational Turn." *Radical History Review* 91(1): 62–90.

2009. *Uneven Encounters: Making Race and Nation in Brazil and the United States*. Duke University Press.

Senado, Agência. 2020. "Senado aprova PEC do Fundeb, que será promulgada nesta quarta." *Senado Notícias*. www12.senado.leg.br/noticias/materias/2020/08/25/pec-do-fundeb-permanente-e-aprovada-no-senado-por-unanimidade (November 23, 2022).

Senkevics, Adriano Souza. 2021. "A Expansão recente do ensino superior: cinco tendências de 1991 a 2020." *Cadernos de Estudos e Pesquisas em Políticas Educacionais* 3(4): 199–246.

2022. "De Brancos para Negros? Uma Análise Longitudinal da Reclassificação Racial no Enem 2010–2016." *Dados* 65(3): 1–40.

Senkevics, Adriano Souza, and Ursula Mattioli Mello. 2019. "O Perfil discente das universidades federais mudou pós-lei de cotas?" *Cadernos de Pesquisa* 49(172): 184–208.

2022. "Balanço dos dez anos da política federal de cotas na educação superior (Lei No 12.711/2012)." Cadernos de Estudos e Pesquisas em Políticas Educacionais 6. Brasília: INEP.

"Serviço de Acesso a Dados Protegidos – INEP." 2018. *Instituto Nacional de Estudos e Pesquisas Educacionais Anísio Teixeira, Ministério da Educação*. http://inep.gov.br/web/guest/cibec/servico-de-acesso-a-dados-protegidos (April 22, 2019).

Sheriff, Robin E. 2001. *Dreaming Equality: Color, Race, and Racism in Urban Brazil*. New Brunswick: Rutgers University Press.

Silva, Antonio José Bacelar da, and Erika Robb Larkins. 2019. "The Bolsonaro Election, Antiblackness, and Changing Race Relations in Brazil." *The Journal of Latin American and Caribbean Anthropology* 24(4): 893–913.

Silva, Graziella Moraes, and Luciana T. de Souza Leão. 2012. "O paradoxo da mistura: identidades, desigualdades e percepção de discriminação entre brasileiros pardos." *Revista Brasileira de Ciências Sociais* 27(80): 117–33.

Silva, Graziella Moraes, Luciana Souza Leão, and Barbara Grillo. 2020. "Seeing Whites: Views of Black Brazilians in Rio de Janeiro." *Ethnic and Racial Studies* 43(4): 632–51.

Silva, Graziella Moraes da, and Elisa P. Reis. 2011. "Perceptions of Racial Discrimination among Black Professionals in Rio de Janeiro." *Latin American Research Review* 46(2): 55–78.

Silva, Graziella Moraes Dias da. 2006. "Ações afirmativas no Brasil e na África do Sul." *Tempo Social* 18(2): 131–65.

Silva, Marinete dos Santos. 1980. *A educação brasileira no estado novo (1937–1945)*. São Paulo: Livraria Panorama.

Silva, Maristela Rosa da. 2020. "'O que é ser mulher negra no Brasil?': o Youtube a serviço de uma nova representação." Master's Thesis. Universidade Federal de Juiz de Fora.

Silva, Nelson do Valle. 1978. "Black-White Income Differentials: Brazil, 1960." Ph.D. Diss. University of Michigan.

1985. "Updating the Cost of Not Being White in Brazil." In *Race, Class and Power in Brazil*, ed. Pierre-Michel Fontaine. Los Angeles: Center for Afro-American Studies, University of California, 42–55.

1994. "Uma nota sobre 'raça social' no Brasil." *Estudos Afro-Asiáticos* 26: 67–80.

1996. "Morenidade: Modo de Usar." *Estudos Afro-Asiáticos* 30: 79–95.

2000. "A Research Note on the Cost of Not Being White in Brazil." *Studies in Comparative International Development* 35(2): 18–27.

Silveira, Leonardo Souza. 2019. "Reclassificação racial e desigualdade: Análise Longitudinal de Variações Socioeconômicas e Regionais no Brasil entre 2008 e 2015." Ph.D. Universidade Federal de Minas Gerais.

Skidmore, Thomas E. 1993. *Black into White: Race and Nationality in Brazilian Thought.* Durham: Duke University Press.

Skocpol, Theda. 1992. *Protecting Soldiers and Mothers: The Political Origins of Social Policy in the United States.* Cambridge: Harvard University Press.

Smith, Christen A. 2016. *Afro-Paradise: Blackness, Violence, and Performance in Brazil.* Urbana: University of Illinois Press.

Smith, Rogers M. 2004. "Identities, Interests, and the Future of Political Science." *Perspectives on Politics* 2(2): 301–12.

Sniderman, Paul M., and Edward G. Carmines. 1997. *Reaching Beyond Race.* Cambridge: Harvard University Press.

Snow, David A., E. Burke Rochford, Steven K. Worden, and Robert D. Benford. 1986. "Frame Alignment Processes, Micromobilization, and Movement Participation." *American Sociological Review* 51(4): 464–81.

Soares, Glaucio Ary Dillon, and Nelson do Valle Silva. 1987. "Urbanization, Race, and Class in Brazilian Politics." *Latin American Research Review* 22(2): 155–76.

Soares, Laura Tavares. 2013. "O papel da rede federal na expansão e na reestruturação da educação superior pública no Brasil." 3. Cadernos do GEA. FLACSO Brasil.

Soares, Sergei. 2008. "A Demografia da cor: a composição da população brasileira de 1890 a 2007." In *As Políticas públicas e a desigualdade racial no Brasil 120 anos após a abolição*, eds. Mário Theodoro, Luciana Jaccoud, Rafael Guerreiro Osorio, and Sergei Soares. Brasília, Brazil: Instituto de Pesquisa Econômica Aplicada, 97–117.

Soares, Sergei Suarez Dillon. 2000. *O perfil da discriminação no mercado de trabalho: homens negros, mulheres brancas e mulheres negras.* Brasília, Brazil: Instituto de Pesquisa Econômica Aplicada.

Sokoloff, Kenneth L., and Stanley L. Engerman. 2000. "History Lessons: Institutions, Factors Endowments, and Paths of Development in the New World." *The Journal of Economic Perspectives* 14(3): 217–32.

Soss, Joe. 2002. *Unwanted Claims: The Politics of Participation in the U.S. Welfare System.* University of Michigan Press.

Soss, Joe, and Sanford F. Schram. 2007. "A Public Transformed? Welfare Reform as Policy Feedback." *American Political Science Review* 101(1): 111–27.

Sousa, Marcelo Silva de. 2018. "Un negro, un gay, una mujer y un ex simpatizante de Lula explican por qué votaron por Jair Bolsonaro." infobae (blog).

October 14, 2018. www.infobae.com/america/america-latina/2018/10/14/un-negro-un-gay-una-mujer-y-un-ex-simpatizante-de-lula-explican-por-que-votaron-por-jair-bolsonaro/.
Souza, Amaury de. 1971. "Raça e política no Brasil urbano." *RAE-Revista de Administração de Empresas* 11(4): 61–70.
  2011. "The Politics of Personality in Brazil." *Journal of Democracy* 22(2): 75–88.
Souza, Neusa Santos. 1983. *Tornar-se negro*. Rio de Janeiro, Brazil: Graal.
Spektor, Matias. 2018. "It's Not Just the Right That's Voting for Bolsonaro. It's Everyone." Foreign Policy (blog). October 26, 2018. https://foreignpolicy.com/2018/10/26/its-not-just-the-right-thats-voting-for-bolsonaro-its-everyone-far-right-brazil-corruption-center-left-anger-pt-black-gay-racism-homophobia/.
Sperb, Paula. 2017. "Defesa de acusados de fraudar cotas vê 'tribunal racial' na UFRGS." *Veja*. https://veja.abril.com.br/blog/rio-grande-do-sul/defesa-de-acusados-de-fraudar-cotas-ve-tribunal-racial-na-ufrgs/ (June 2, 2018).
Stepan, Nancy Leys. 1991. *"The Hour of Eugenics": Race, Gender, and Nation in Latin America*. Ithaca: Cornell University Press.
Stokes, Susan C. 1995. *Cultures in Conflict: Social Movements and the State in Peru*. Berkeley: University of California Press.
Summerhill, William. 2010. "Colonial Institutions, Slavery, Inequality, and Development: Evidence from Sao Paulo, Brazil." UCLA. https://mpra.ub.uni-muenchen.de/22162/1/MPRA_paper_22162.pdf (March 6, 2018).
Tajfel, Henri. 1974. "Social Identity and Intergroup Behaviour." *Social Science Information* 13(2): 65–93.
  1981. *Human Groups and Social Categories: Studies in Social Psychology*. New York: Cambridge University Press.
Tannenbaum, Frank. 1992. *Slave and Citizen: The Classic Comparative Study of Race Relations in the Americas*. Boston: Beacon Press.
Tate, Katherine. 1994. *From Protest to Politics: The New Black Voters in American Elections*. Cambridge: Harvard University Press.
Teixeira, Moema de Poli. 2003. *Negros na universidade: identidade e trajetórias de ascensão social no Rio de Janeiro*. Rio de Janeiro: Pallas.
Telles, Edward E. 1993. "Racial Distance and Region in Brazil: Intermarriage in Brazilian Urban Areas." *Latin American Research Review* 28(2): 141–62.
  2004. *Race in Another America: The Significance of Skin Color in Brazil*. Princeton: Princeton University Press.
  2014. *Pigmentocracies: Ethnicity, Race, and Color in Latin America*. Chapel Hill: University of North Carolina Press.
Telles, Edward E., and Nelson Lim. 1998. "Does It Matter Who Answers the Race Question? Racial Classification and Income Inequality in Brazil." *Demography* 35(4): 465–74.
Telles, Edward E., and Stanley Bailey. 2013. "Understanding Latin American Beliefs about Racial Inequality." *American Journal of Sociology* 118(6): 1559–95.
Telles, Edward E., and Tianna Paschel. 2014. "Who Is Black, White, or Mixed Race? How Skin Color, Status, and Nation Shape Racial Classification in Latin America." *American Journal of Sociology* 120(3): 864–907.

Theiss-Morse, Elizabeth. 2009. *Who Counts as an American?: The Boundaries of National Identity*. New York: Cambridge University Press.

Thompson, E. P. 1963. *The Making of the English Working Class*. New York: Vintage Books.

Touchton, Michael, and Brian Wampler. 2013. "Improving Social Well-Being through New Democratic Institutions." *Comparative Political Studies* 20(10): 1–28.

Trejo, Guillermo. 2009. "Religious Competition and Ethnic Mobilization in Latin America: Why the Catholic Church Promotes Indigenous Movements in Mexico." *American Political Science Review* 103(03): 323.

Trejo, Guillermo, and Melina Altamirano. 2016. "The Mexican Color Hierarchy." In *The Double Bind: The Politics of Racial and Class Inequalities in the Americas*, eds. Juliet Hooker and Alvin B. Tillery. Washington, D.C.: American Political Science Association, 3–16.

Tribunal Superior Eleitoral. 2022. "Mais da metade dos candidatos aos cargos das Eleições 2022 se autodeclarou negra." *Justiça Eleitoral*. www.tse.jus.br/comunicacao/noticias/2022/Novembro/mais-da-metade-dos-candidatos-aos-cargos-das-eleicoes-2022-se-autodeclarou-negra (June 27, 2023).

Turgeon, Mathieu, Bruno Sant'Anna Chaves, and Willian Washington Wives. 2014. "Políticas de Ação Afirmativa e o Experimento de Listas: O Caso Das Cotas Raciais Na Universidade Brasileira." *Opinião Pública* 20(3): 363–76.

Turgeon, Mathieu, and Philip Habel. 2022. "Prejudice, Political Ideology, and Interest: Understanding Attitudes Toward Affirmative Action in Brazil." *Political Psychology* 43(3): 489–510.

Turner, John C. et al. 1987. *Rediscovering the Social Group: A Self-Categorization Theory*. New York: Basil Blackwell.

Twine, France Winddance. 1998. *Racism in a Racial Democracy: The Maintenance of White Supremacy in Brazil*. New Brunswick: Rutgers University Press.

  1996. "O hiato de gênero nas percepções de racismo: o caso dos afro-brasileiros socialmente ascendentes." *Estudos Afro-Asiáticos* 29: 37–54.

"Unesp vai adotar comissão para evitar fraudes em cotas raciais." 2017. *Globo*. https://oglobo.globo.com/sociedade/unesp-vai-adotar-comissao-para-evitar-fraudes-em-cotas-raciais-21572736 (June 2, 2018).

Valente, Ana Lúcia E. F. 1986. *Política e relações raciais: os negros e as eleições paulistas de 1982*. São Paulo: FFLCH-USP.

Van Cott, Donna Lee. 2005. *From Movements to Parties in Latin America: The Evolution of Ethnic Politics*. New York: Cambridge University Press.

Vargas, João H. Costa. 2004. "Hyperconsciousness of Race and Its Negation: The Dialectic of White Supremacy in Brazil." *Identities* 11(4): 443–70.

Verbeek, Marno, and Theo Nijman. 1992. "Can Cohort Data Be Treated as Genuine Panel Data?" *Empirical Economics* 17(1): 9–23.

Vieira, Renato Schwambach, Adriano Souza Senkevics, and Mary Arends-Kuenning. 2019. "Ações afirmativas na década de 2000 e suas consequências para o perfil discente das Universidades Federais." *Cadernos de Estudos e Pesquisas em Políticas Educacionais* 3: 137–64.

Wagley, Charles, ed. 1952. *Race and Class in Rural Brazil*. New York: UNESCO.

Wagley, Charles. 1965. "On the Concept of Social Race in the Americas." In *Contemporary Cultures and Societies of Latin America*, ed. Dwight B. Heath. New York: Random House, 531–46.

Waters, Mary C. 1990. *Ethnic Options: Choosing Identities in America*. Berkeley: University of California Press.

1999. *Black Identities: West Indian Immigrant Dreams and American Realities*. Cambridge: Harvard University Press.

2002. "The Social Construction of Race and Ethnicity: Some Examples from Demography." In *American Diversity: A Demographic Challenge for the Twenty-First Century*, eds. Nancy A. Denton and Stewart E. Tolnay. Albany: SUNY Press, 25–49.

Weber, Max. 1978. *Economy and Society: An Outline of Interpretive Sociology*. Berkeley: University of California Press.

Weinstein, Barbara. 2015. *The Color of Modernity: São Paulo and the Making of Race and Nation in Brazil*. Durham: Duke University Press.

Weisbrot, Mark, Jake Johnston, and Stephan Lefebvre. 2014. *The Brazilian Economy in Transition: Macroeconomic Policy, Labor and Inequality*. Center for Economic and Policy Research (CEPR).

Weitz-Shapiro, Rebecca, and Matthew S. Winters. 2017. "Can Citizens Discern? Information Credibility, Political Sophistication, and the Punishment of Corruption in Brazil." *The Journal of Politics* 79(1): 60–74.

Wilfahrt, Martha. 2018. "Precolonial Legacies and Institutional Congruence in Public Goods Delivery." *World Politics* 70(2): 239–74.

Winters, Matthew S., and Rebecca Weitz-Shapiro. 2014. "Partisan Protesters and Nonpartisan Protests in Brazil." *Journal of Politics in Latin America* 6(1): 137–50.

Wong, Janelle, S. Karthick Ramakrishnan, Taeku Lee, and Jane Junn. 2011. *Asian American Political Participation: Emerging Constituents and Their Political Identities*. New York: Sage.

Wood, Charles H., and José Alberto Magno de Carvalho. 1994. "Categorias do censo e classificação subjetiva de cor no Brasil." *Revista Brasileira de Estudos de Populacão* 11(1): 3–17.

World Bank. 2002. Brazil Municipal Education: Resources, Incentives, and Results. World Bank. Policy Report.

Yanow, Dvora. 2002. *Constructing "Race" and "Ethnicity" in America: Category-Making in Public Policy and Administration*. Armonk: M.E. Sharpe.

Yashar, Deborah J. 2005. *Contesting Citizenship in Latin America: The Rise of Indigenous Movements and the Postliberal Challenge*. New York: Cambridge University Press.

Zucco, Cesar. 2008. "The President's 'New' Constituency: Lula and the Pragmatic Vote in Brazil's 2006 Presidential Elections." *Journal of Latin American Studies* 40(1): 29–49.

Zucco, Cesar, and Timothy J. Power. 2013. "Bolsa Família and the Shift in Lula's Electoral Base, 2002–2006: A Reply to Bohn." *Latin American Research Review* 48(2): 3–24.

Zumbi, Marcha. 1996. *Por uma política nacional de combate ao racismo e à desigualdade racial: Marcha Zumbi contra o racismo, pela cidadania e a vida*. Brasília: Cultura Gráfica e Ed. Ltda.

Index

abolition, of slavery, 38
affirmative action policies
  in Brazilian municipalities, 158–63
  under Cardoso, 133, 174–75, 181–82
  contaminating effects of, 133, 135–36
  critiques of, 175–76
  evolution of policies, 159
  under Federal Affirmative Action Law, 92–93
  fraud, 178, 187, 191
  historical development of, 173–76
  as incentive, 176–79
  inclusionary effects of, 135
  list experiments and, 191–95
    affirmative responses in, 194
    design for, 191–92
    means of item count comparisons, 193
  for Native Americans, 177
  politicization of identity and, 10–12
  racial identification influenced by, 183–91
    difference-in-difference analysis of, 205
    predictable probabilities of, 189
    priming experiment I, 183–87
    priming experiment II, 187–91
    skin tones and, 185–87
  racial quotas, 119–20
  real world applications of, 195–207
    difference-in-difference analysis of, 196, 198–200, 205
    at federal level, 201–7
    at state level, 196–200
  reclassification of race and, 45–48
  SES quota, 204–6
  as state policy, 11–12, 45–48
  as state-centered racemaking, 179–83
  theoretical approach to, 171–73
  in university system, 175
Afro-Brazilians, 180–81
  reclassification of race by, 50–51
agenda-setting, power through, 212–16
Alberto, Luiz, 174
Alckmin, Geraldo, 227–28, 241–42
amarela, as census category, 31
Annual Household Sample Survey (PNAD), 137–38
ascription, racial, 53–54, 206
  education as exposure and, 127, 130
Australia
  ethnic identities in, 10–11
  ethnic reclassification in, 95

Barbosa, Joaquim, 231
"Black bourgeoisie," 78
Black Consciousness Day, in Brazil, 47–48, 180–81
"black do not vote for blacks" concept. *See negro não vota em negro* ("blacks do not vote for blacks")
Black identity, 80, 89, 108–9, 117, 119
Black intellectuals, 173. *See also* "Black bourgeoisie"
  embrace of racial democracy thesis, 43
Black movements, in Brazil. *See also* Civil Rights Movement
  Blackness and, 9

Black movements, in Brazil (cont.)
  colorist logic in, 9
  negro não vota em negro and, 13
  political influence of, 15–16
  Unified Black Movement, 80–81
Black Skin, White Masks (Fanon), 110
Blackness
  Black movements in Brazil and, 9
  in Brazil, 11
  reclassification toward, 74
  as stigmatized category, 254
Boas, Franz, 183–91
Bolivia, indigenous populations in, 20
Bolsa Família program, 72, 92–93, 219, 223–24
Bolsonaro, Jair, 233, 237–45, 263
  electoral support for
    by education level, 240, 242, 244
    as first round vote choice, 241
    racial identification as influence on, 240, 244
    as second-round vote choice, 244
  political polarization and, 9
  racial rhetoric by, 238
boundary construction, in reclassification of race, 34
branco/branca, 90
  whiteness and, 26, 184
Brazil. *See also* Recife, Brazil; reclassification of race; São Paulo, Brazil; *specific topics*
  affirmative action in, 10–11
  Afro-descendant population in, 87
  Black Consciousness Day, 47–48, 180–81
  Black racial identity in, 1
  eugenics movement in, 37–38
  Federal Affirmative Action Law, 92–93
  federal education reforms in, 92–93
  income distribution in, 17
  indigenous populations in, 87
  mensalão corruption scandal and, 9
  racial composition of, 117
  racial consciousness in, 79–83
  as racial democracy, 123, 212
  racial fluidity and, 123
  racial politics in, 256–59
  self-classification as Black in, 1
Brazilian Eugenics Conference, 42
Brazilian Social Survey (PESB), 184

Calheiros, Renan, 233–34
Cardoso, Fernando Henrique, 70–71, 198
  affirmative action policies under, 133, 174–75, 181–82
  on racism, 180–81
  Workers' Party and, 70, 210, 230, 232–33, 237–38, 242
Casa-Grande e Senzala (Freyre), 123
Catholic political identity, 58
Census Bureau. *See also specific categories*
  enumeration practices, 30–37
    demographic trends, 107
    inter-census differences, 35
    for social identification, 30
    subjectivity in, 30
    subnational variations, 108
  public opinion surveys, 90
China
  ethnic identities in, 10–11
  ethnic reclassification in, 95
citizenship, 112–13. *See also* social citizenship
civil citizenship, 112–13
Civil Rights Act, U.S. (1964), 173
Civil Rights Movement, in U.S., 8
classification. *See also* reclassification of race; self-classification
  toward Blackness, 74
  hetero, 123
  by others, 108, 130, 206
  racial, 139
  toward whiteness, 2
cleavage structures, politicization of identity and, 16–17
Collor de Mello, Fernando, 231
colonialism, slavery and, 17, 156–57
color nondeclaration, rates of, 203
colorism, 109–10
  reclassification of race and, 48–54
  whitening and, 48–50
common political identity, 58
consciousness. *See* racial consciousness
constructivism
  abuses of, 92–93
  identity politics and, 252–53
  reclassification of race and, 65
contaminating effects, of affirmative action, 133, 135–36
Crenshaw, Kimberlé, 149
Cunha, Eduardo, 233–34

Index

"darkening" effect, 79, 91
Deaton, Angus, 135–37
decision-making, power through, 212–16
Degler, Carl, 50–51
democracy. See racial democracy
discrimination. See also racism
  personal exposure to, 89, 117, 259–60

education, reclassification and
  birth cohort pseudo-analysis, 136–48
    age and, 144–48
    controls in, 139
    dependent variables, 138–39
    by education, 145–47
    estimation fixed-effects models, 139–40
    independent variables, 139
    models in, 139–40
    period effects and, 144–48
    PNAD surveys, 137–38
  in Brazilian municipalities, 154–68
    affirmative action policies, 158–63
    fixed effects models for, 166–68
    high-school level attendance rates, 157, 162–63
    histograms of change for, 164
    Inter-Census differences, 155
    panel analysis of, 163–66
    partial effects models for, 169
    subnational variations for, 156–58
    university level attendance rates, 158
  gender and, 148–53
    intersectionality and, 149
    rates of reclassification, 150–51
    as region-specific, 151–53
  implications of, 133–35
  inferential challenges for, 135–36
  longitudinal analysis
    multinomial logit models of racial identification, 142–44
    of nonwhite identification, 140–42
  political identity hypothesis and, 133–35, 154, 169–70
education as exposure
  under Federal Law 10.369, 92–93, 105
  information and
    interpretive frames, 108–9
    as mechanism of exposure, 103–11
    in Recife, 103–11
    in reclassification of race, 84–85
  mechanisms of, 102–31
    information, 103–11
    labor markets, 117–22
    social networks, 111–17
    survey analysis of, 122–31
  methodological approaches to, 95–102
    interviews, 96–102
    positionality in, 99–102
    research sites, 96–97
    sampling, 96–102
  qualitative analysis of, 96
  racial ascriptions and, 127, 130
  racial consciousness and, 126–28, 130
    estimated effects on, 129
    group, 129
    predicted probabilities of, 127
    racial identification and, 128
  racial identification and
    average partial effects on, 125
    racial consciousness and, 128
  in Recife, 98
    information through exposure, 103–11
  in reclassification of race, 77–90
    for information, 84–85
    in labor markets, 88–90
    racial consciousness and, 79–83
    social networks and, 86–88
    in university settings, 86–88
  in São Paulo, 96–98
  social movements and, 114–17
Education for Critical Consciousness (Freire), 227–28
educational expansion
  completion rates for Brazilians by race, 70
  federal funding for, 73–74
  FUNDEF/FUNDEB, 70–73
  high school completion rates, 76
  INEP, 68–69
  LDB, 69, 71–72
  under Lula, 72–73
  primary school completion rates, 72
  reclassification of race and, 67–90, 221
    social citizenship and, 65–66
    state-led, 67–77
  REUNI, 75
  SISU, 75
  social citizenship and, 65–66
  university education by income level, 76
  under Vargas, 68–69

educational levels
  Bolsonaro support by, 240, 242, 244
  completion rates for Brazilians by race, 70
  high school completion rates, 76
  primary school completion rates, 72
  reclassification of race and, 4
  Rousseff by, 232
  university education by income level, 76
ENEM (*Exame nacional do ensino médio*), 92–93, 201
ethnoracial identity, 46, 57, 182, 245–46, 248, 256
ethnoracial politics
  Indigenous people and, 259
  in Latin America, 259–61
eugenics movement, 37–38
  Brazilian Eugenics Conference, 42
Exame nacional do ensino médio. See ENEM
exposure. *See* education as exposure

Fanon, Frantz, 110
fate. *See* linked fate
Federal Affirmative Action Law, Brazil (2012), 92–93
Federal Law 10.369, 92–93, 105
feedback. *See* policy feedback
Fernandes, Florestan, 47, 117
FIES (Fundo de financiamento ao estudante ao ensinso superior), 47–48, 92–93
Francis-Tan, Andrew, 178
Franco, Anielle, 262–63
Franco, Marielle, 262–63
fraud, in affirmative action policies, 178, 187, 191
Freire, Paulo, 227–28
Freyre, Gilberto, 123
  on racial democracy, 183–91
FUNDEF/FUNDEB, 70–73, 92–93
Fundo de financiamento ao estudante ao ensinso superior. *See* FIES

gender, reclassification of race and, 148–53
  intersectionality and, 149
  rates of, 150–51
  as region-specific, 151–53
Gomes, Ciro, 241–43
Great Depression, 112–13
group consciousness theory, 62–63
group position theory and, 64
group racial consciousness, 129

Haddad, Fernando, 237, 242–43
Hanchard, Michael, 80–81
Harris, Marvin, 50, 52
Hasenbalg, Carlos, 45–46
hetero-classification, 123
hyper-consciousness, 80
hyper-politicization, of race, 8

identity. *See also* Black identity; ethnoracial identity; politicization of identity; racial identity
  formation of, 7, 92–93
  political, 196
    racial consciousness and, 9
  social
    reclassification of race and, 30
    social identity theory, 59, 133, 255
  stigmatized, 129
identity politics. *See also* political identity; politicization of identity
  constructivism, 252–53
  for elites, 253–54
  institutions and, 253–54
  policy feedback effects and, 254
identity-to-politics link, 56
  analysis of, 7
  cleavages in, 7
  identity formation as element of, 7, 92–93
  policy feedback and, 254–56
  social citizenship and, 254–55
income distribution, in Brazil, 17
India, ethnic reclassification in, 95
indigena, as census category, 31
Indigenous peoples. *See also specific people*
  in Bolivia, 20
  in Brazil, 87
  ethnoracial politics and, 259
  indigena census category, 31
  in Latin America, 21
  maroon communities, 87, 107
INEP (Institute of Educational Study and Research), 68–69
informal racism
  institutional, 177–78
  reclassification of race and, 48–54
  whitening and, 48–50
information
  education as exposure and interpretive frames, 108–9
  as mechanism, 103–11

in Recife, 103–11
in reclassification of race, 84–85
personal exposure to, 131, 250
Institute of Educational Study and Research. *See* INEP
institutional informal racism, 177–78
instrumentality, instrumentalism and, 142–43, 159–62, 178, 182
The Integration of the Negro in Brazilian Society (Fernandes), 117
intersectionality, 149

Jefferson, Roberto, 218–19

Katendê, Moa do, 239
Kruks-Wisner, Gabrielle, 78

labor markets
  education as exposure and, 117–22
  reclassification of race and, 88–90
Latin America. *See also specific countries*
  Black populations in, 21
  ethnoracial politics in, 259–61
  indigenous populations in, 21
  racial fluidity in, 20
Lava Jato corruption scandal, 231–37, 246
LDB (Lei de Diretrizes Básicas), 69, 71–72, 92–93
Lee, Taeku, 56
left parties, in Brazil. *See also* Workers' Party; *specific political parties*
  Black constituency in, 218–45
Lei de Diretrizes Básicas. *See* LDB
LGBT+ populations, 261–62
linked fate, 78, 80
"Lula." *See* Silva, Luiz Inácio da

manipulation, power through, 212–16
maroon communities (*quilombos*), 87, 107
Marshall, T. H., 65, 112–13
The Masters and Slaves (Freyre), 183–91
mensalão corruption scandal, 9, 211, 246
mestiço/mestiçagem, 38–39
mestizo/a, 21, 260
military regimes, racial democracy and, 43–44, 46
miscegenation, 259–60
Mische, Ann, 88
mixed-race, 26
  as census category, 31
  as path to whiteness, 37–38
mixture, racial. *See* mixed-race

moreno/morena, 26, 90, 109, 112–13
Moura, Clóvis, 16
Movement for Democratic Brazil Party (*Partido do Movimento Democrático Brasileiro*) (PMDB), 233–34, 236–37
Movimento Negro Unificado. *See* Unified Black Movement
Movimento Passe Livre (MPL), 227–28
mulatto/mulato/mulata, 21, 260
Munson, Ziad, 88
myth of racial unity. *See* racial unity

Nascimento, Abdias do, 173–74
national politics, in Brazil. *See also* Workers' Party; *specific people*
  Lava Jato corruption scandal, 231–37, 246
  left parties
    Black constituency in, 218–45
    first round support for, 243
  Movement for Democratic Brazil Party, 233–34, 236–37
  race in
    data availability for, 216–18
    electoral support by, 215
    irrelevance of, 212–16
    negro não vota em negro, 13
    relevance of, 210–11
  Social Democracy Party, 70–73, 230, 232–33, 237–38, 242
  Social Liberal Party, 237, 239
Native Americans
  affirmative actions policies for, 177
  racial identification for, 10–11
Negão, Hélio, 239
negro, 26, 109, 113, 118–19
negro não vota em negro ("blacks do not vote for blacks"), 13
networks. *See* social networks
Nobles, Melissa, 248
Nogueira, Oracy, 52
nonwhite populations. *See also specific populations*
  longitudinal analysis of, 140–42
  reclassification of race for, 103
  self-classification for, 32–33

Orpheus and Power (Hanchard), 80

Paim, Paulo, 174
Palmares, Zumbi dos, 174

pardo/parda, 26, 110–11, 179–80
Partido da Social Democracia Brasileira.
    See Social Democracy Party
*Partido do Movimento Democrático
    Brasileiro. See* Movement for
    Democratic Brazil Party
Partido dos Trabalhadores. See Workers'
    Party
Partido Social Liberal. See Social Liberal
    Party
partisanship, political identity and, 58, 59
Pedagogy of the Oppressed (Freire),
    227–28
personal exposure, 77, 103. *See also*
    education as exposure
  to discrimination, 89, 117, 259–60
  to hierarchies, 259–60
  to new information, 131, 250
PESB. *See* Brazilian Social Survey
phenotypes
  racial consciousness and, 128–30
  racial identification and, 133
Pierson, Donald, 52
PMDB. *See* Movement for Democratic
    Brazil Party
PNAD. *See* Annual Household Sample
    Survey
PNAES (Programa nacional de assistência
    estudantil), 92–93
polarization, political, Bolsonaro election
    and, 9
policy feedback
  for identity politicization, 90–91, 93–94
  identity politics and, 254
  identity-to-politics link and, 254–56
  social citizenship and, 254–55
political citizenship, 112–13
political demography, 95
political identity, 196. *See also* identity-to-
    politics link
  Catholic, 58
  common, 58
  definitions of, 57–64
    affirmed identification, 62–63
    for individual in groups, 61–62
    maximalist, 132–33
    perceptions of power, 63–64
    power-centered, 61–64
  group consciousness theory, 62–63
  group position theory and, 64
  ideology and, 58, 59
  partisanship and, 58, 59
  prevailing usages of, 58–60
  racial consciousness and, 9
  for Russian-speaking populations, 58
  scope of, 61
  self-categorization theory and, 59
  social identity theory and, 59–60, 133
political identity hypothesis, 133–35, 154,
    169–70
politicization of identity, 92–93
  alternative theories for, 10–17
    affirmative action, 10–12
    cleavage structure and, 16–17
    through mobilization from above,
      12–13, 87
    through mobilization from below,
      14–16
  class identity formation and, 14
  group-based inequality and, 17, 67–90
  minimum-winning coalitions, 5
  policy feedback for, 90–91, 93–94
  social citizenship and, 143
  institutions for, 10
  through vote buying, 13
positionality, 99–102
power
  through agenda-setting, 212–16
  through decision-making, 212–16
  through manipulation, 212–16
  political identity and, 63–64
preto/preta, 26, 108, 110–11, 118–22,
    179–80
Program for the Restructuring and
    Expansion of Federal Universities.
    See REUNI
Programa nacional de assistência
    estudantil. *See* PNAES
ProUni (*Programa universidade para
    todos*), 92–93, 181, 196
PSDB. *See* Social Democracy Party
PSL. *See* Social Liberal Party
PT. *See* Workers' Party
Puerto Rico, 20

quilombos. See maroon communities
quotas. *See* racial quotas; SES quotas

race. *See also* reclassification of race;
    specific topics
  hyper-politicization of, 8
  social, 49, 93–94
race-mixing. *See also* mixed-race
  scientific racism and, 189

Index

racial consciousness
　"Black bourgeoisie" and, 78
　in Brazil, 79–83
　education as exposure and, 79–83, 126–28, 130
　　estimated effects on, 129
　　group consciousness, 129
　　predicted probabilities of, 127
　　racial identification and, 128
　linked fate and, 78, 80
　methodological approach to, 83
　phenotypes and, 128–30
　political identity and, 9
　Unified Black Movement and, 80–81
racial democracy
　Black intellectuals' embrace of, 43
　Brazil as, 123, 212
　critiques of, 45–46
　Freyre on, 183–91
　military regimes and, 43–44, 46
　myth of racial unity, 43, 85, 248
　racial silence and, 194
　racialized democracy from, 262–64
　reclassification of race and, 41–46
　resilience of, 45–46
　scientific racism and, 112–13
　as state policy, 41–45
　Vargas and, 44–45
racial fluidity
　in Brazil, 123
　in Latin America, 20
　reclassification of race and, 48–54
　　scholarship approach to, 52
　　self-classification and, 53–54
　　whitening and, 48–54
　upward mobility and, 8
racial identity. *See also* Blackness; mixed-race; white-identifying populations
　affirmative action policies as influence on, 183–91
　difference-in-difference analysis of, 205
　predictable probabilities of, 189
　priming experiment I, 183–87
　priming experiment II, 187–91
　skin tones and, 185–87
　as Black, 1
　Bolsonaro support influenced by, 240, 244
　branco/branca, 90
　　whiteness and, 26, 184

　"darkening" effect and, 79, 91
　education as exposure and
　　average partial effects on, 125
　　racial consciousness and, 128
　mestiço/mestiçagem, 38–39
　mestizo/a, 21, 260
　methodological approach to, 67–90, 254–56
　　comparative studies, 18–19
　　data collection in, 19–20
　　positionality in, 22–24
　　race terminology, 25–26
　moreno/morena, 26, 90, 109, 112–13
　negro, 26, 109, 113, 118–19
　pardo/parda, 26, 110–11, 179–80
　phenotypes and, 133
　preto/preta, 26, 108, 110–11, 118–19, 120–22, 179–80
　Rousseff support and, 232
racial politics, racial policies and, 8–9
　in Brazil, 256–59
　reclassification of race, 37–48
　　affirmative action, 45–48
　　conceptual approach to, 37–38
　　racial democracy strategies, 41–48
　　scientific racism, 38–41
　　upward mobility and, 8
racial quotas, 119, 120
racial reclassification. *See* reclassification of race
racial silence, 194
racial unity, myth of, 43, 85, 248
racialization, 83, 206
racialized democracy, 262–64
racism. *See also* informal racism; scientific racism
　Bolsonaro and, 238
　Cardoso on, 180–81
　World Conference on Race and Racism, in Durban, 174
Recife, Brazil, education as exposure in, 98
　information through, 103–11
reclassification of race, in Brazil, 139
　analysis of, 54–55
　boundary construction in, 34
　census enumeration practices, 30–37
　　demographic trends, 107
　　inter-census differences, 35
　　for social identification, 30
　　subjectivity in, 30
　　subnational variations, 108

reclassification of race, in Brazil (cont.)
  colorism as factor in, 48–54
    whitening and, 48–50
  conceptual approach to, 3–5, 27–28
  constructivism and, 65
  education as exposure and, 77–90
    for information, 84–85
    in labor markets, 88–90
    racial consciousness and, 79–83
    social networks and, 86–88
    in university settings, 86–88
  education levels and, 4
  educational expansion and, 67–90, 221
    social citizenship and, 65–66
    state-led, 67–77
  implications of, 90–91, 93–94
  informal racism as influence on, 48–54
    whitening and, 48–50
  through institutional mechanisms, 4
  measurement errors in, 123–24
  methodological approach to, 27–28
  miscegenation and, 259–60
  for nonwhite populations, 103
    self-classification for, 32–33
  patterns in, 48–49, 259–60
  policy feedback on, 67, 221
  political identity, formation of, 56–57
  political salience for, 34
  racial composition (1992–2019), 29, 30
  as racial democracy, 259–60
  racial fluidity and, 48–54
    scholarship approach to, 52
    self-classification and, 53–54
    whitening and, 48–54
  racial state policies, 37–48
    affirmative action, 45–48
    conceptual approach to, 37–38
    racial democracy strategies, 41–48
    scientific racism, 38–41
  racial subjectivity and, 221
  reversal of, 28–30
  self-classification, 28–29
    ascription and, 53–54, 206
    identification and, 206
    for nonwhite populations, 32–33
    percent change by racial category, 32–33, 105
    racial fluidity and, 53–54
    for white populations, 32–33
  as stigma-minimizing strategy, 50–51
    by Afro-Brazilians, 50–51
  for white populations, 103

self-classification for, 32–33
REUNI (Program for the Restructuring and Expansion of Federal Universities), 75, 92–93
reversal, of reclassification of race, 28–30
Rousseff, Dilma, 224–37
  electoral support for
    by education level, 232
    by racial identification, 232
  impeachment of, 231–37
    socioeconomic profiles of protesters, 235, 236
  reelection of, 231–37

São Paulo, Brazil, 96–98
scientific racism
  Boas critique of, 183–91
  eugenics movement, 37–38
  by political elites, 38–39
  race-mixing and, 189
  racial democracy and, 112–13
  reclassification of race and, 38–41
  whitening, 189
self-categorization theory, 59
self-classification
  as Black, 1
  as *branco/branca*, 90
    whiteness and, 26, 184
  as *mestiço/mestiçagem*, 38–39
  as *mestizo/a*, 21, 260
  as *moreno/morena*, 26, 90, 109, 112–13
  as *negro*, 26, 109, 113, 118–19
  as *pardo/parda*, 26, 110–11, 179–80
  as *preto/preta*, 26, 108, 110–11, 118–22, 179–80
  reclassification of race through, 28–29
    ascription and, 53–54, 206
    identification and, 206
    for nonwhite populations, 32–33
    percent change by racial category, 32–33, 105
    racial fluidity and, 53–54
    for white populations, 32–33
SES quotas, 204–6
Sheriff, Robin, 52
Silva, Benedita da, 174
Silva, Luiz Inácio da ("Lula"). *See also* Workers' Party
  Bolsa Família program, 72, 92–93, 219, 223–24
  education expansion under, 72–73
  FUNDEF/FUNDEB, 70–73, 92–93

mensalão corruption scandal, 9, 211, 246
  reelection of, 264
REUNI, 75, 92–93
Silva, Marina, 226–27, 231, 241–42
SINAES (Sistema nacional de avaliação da Educação Superior), 92–93
Sistema de seleção unificada. *See* SISU
Sistema nacional de avaliação da Educação Superior. *See* SINAES
SISU (Sistema de seleção unificada), 75, 92–93, 181
SIT. *See* social identity theory
skin tones, racial identification and, 185–87
slavery, 104–7
  abolition of, 38
  benign forms of, 183–91
  colonialism and, 17, 156–57
  historical legacy of, 18–19, 45–46, 107–8
social citizenship, 77, 129
  benefits of, 64–65
  educational expansion and, 65–66
  identity-to-politics link and, 254–55
  institutions of, 66–67, 249
  policy feedback and, 254–55
  politicization of identity and, 143
  scope of, 65–66
social construction. *See* constructivism
Social Democracy Party (*Partido da Social Democracia Brasileira*) (PSDB), 70–73, 230, 232–33, 237–38, 242
social identity, reclassification of race and, 30
social identity theory (SIT), 59–60, 133, 255
Social Liberal Party (*Partido Social Liberal*) (PSL), 237, 239
social networks, education as exposure and, 86–88, 111–17
social race, 49, 93–94
South Africa
  apartheid in, 173
  hyper-politicization of race in, 8
  racial census in, 213
Souza, Neusa Santos, 89, 95
state-centered racemaking, 179–83
stigmatized identities, 129

Tannuri-Pianto, Maria, 178
Temer, Michel, 236–37
Tornar-se negro (Souza), 89, 95

UN. *See* United Nations
UNESCO. *See* United Nations
Unified Black Movement (*Movimento Negro Unificado*), 80–81
United Nations (UN)
  Conference on Race and Racism, 47
  Educational, Scientific, and Cultural Organization, 42
United States (U.S.)
  affirmative action in, 10–11
  "Black bourgeoisie" in, 78
  Civil Rights Act of 1964, 173
  Civil Rights Movement in, 8
  hyper-politicization of race in, 8
  Native Americans
    affirmative actions policies for, 177
    racial identification for, 10–11
universities and colleges
  affirmative action policies in, 175
  cursinho pré-vestibular, 87, 97–98, 106–7
  vestibular, 98
university entrance exam (*vestibular*), 98
university exam preparatory course (*cursinho pré-vestibular*), 87, 97–98, 106–7
upward mobility
  Black stigmatization and, 8
  racial fluidity and, 8
U.S. *See* United States

Valle Silva, Nelson do, 45–46, 49, 206
Vargas, Getúlio, 42–43, 112–13
  educational agenda under, 68–69
  racial democracy and, 44–45
vestibular. *See* university entrance exam
voting rights, citizenship and, 112–13

white-identifying populations
  in Puerto Rico, 20
  reclassification of race for, 103
  self-classification, 32–33
whiteness
  branco/branca and, 26, 184
  mixed-race as path to, 37–38
  reclassification toward, 2
  scientific racism and, 189
whitening, 123–24, 151–52, 256–57
  colorism and, 48–50
  of Puerto Rico, 20
  racial fluidity and, 48–54
  reclassification of race and, 48–50
  scientific racism and, 189

Wood, Charles, 123
Workers' Party (*Partido dos Trabalhadores*) (PT), 70, 210, 214, 230, 232–33, 237–38, 242
    Black support for, 218–39
        breaks in, 224–31
        education level as influence on, 219, 220–21
            first-round support and, 225–27
            for protesters, 229
        university-level, 222, 226–27
        left self-placement by, 223–24
        preferred presidential candidates, 230
        racial identification as influence on, 219, 221
            first-round support and, 225
            for protesters, 229
        Rousseff and, 224–37
World Conference on Race and Racism, in Durban, 174

For EU product safety concerns, contact us at Calle de José Abascal, 56–1°,
28003 Madrid, Spain or eugpsr@cambridge.org.

www.ingramcontent.com/pod-product-compliance
Lightning Source LLC
LaVergne TN
LVHW011800060526
838200LV00053B/3643